THE
HOLY
ORTHODOX
BIBLE

THE HOLY ORTHODOX BIBLE
© 2004 BY Mr. Peter A. Papoutsis

All rights reserved. No part of this book may be reproduced or transmitted in any form or by any means, electronic or mechanical, including photocopying, recording, or by any information or storage retrieval system, without permission in writing from Mr. Peter A. Papoutsis

Mr. Peter A. Papoutsis can be contacted at:

> The Law Offices of Nicholas C. Syregelas & Associates
> 19 North Green Street, 1st Floor
> Chicago, Illinois 60607
> E-Mail: info@peterpapoutsis.com
> www.peterpapoutsis.com

To The Reader
Of The Old Testament of
The Holy Orthodox Bible

What you hold in your hands dear Christian reader is one of the first English translations of the Greek Old Testament, traditionally called the *Septuagint*, which has been rendered in the last 150 years. Further, this present English translation of the *Septuagint* is based on Greek Old Testament texts as they are found and used in the scriptural and liturgical life of The Holy Orthodox Church. Many may ask, "What is the *Septuagint*?" This is a legitimate question and one that is very easy to answer. The *Septuagint* is the Old Testament of the Christian Church as founded by Our Lord and Savior Jesus Christ and established and protected by the Holy Apostles and by the grace of the Most Holy and Life Giving Spirit. The *Septuagint* was read and used by Our Most Blessed Savior and His Holy Apostles and by His beloved Church. It was the Old Testament that was used by the Holy Fathers of the Church when they studied God's Holy Word and defended the faith against the heresies of Arianism, Nestorianism and Monophysitism. It was the sacred words of the *Septuagint* that uplifted men's souls, especially through the Psalms, which helped them experience the love of Almighty God, and it was these same words that the Holy Martyrs recited as they met their death at the hands of the pagans and heathens of old. It was the *Septuagint* that the Holy Writers of the New Testament almost exclusively quoted from and referenced as the Holy Spirit gave them utterance to proclaim the Holy Gospel of Our Most Blessed Lord and Savior Jesus Christ. It was the *Septuagint* that laid the ground work for the spreading of the Holy Gospel, as it was through this version of the Old Testament that the faith and knowledge of Almighty God, that was the exclusive property of the Hebrew people, was given to the entire world at large that, during the time of Christ, spoke Greek and thought in Greek concepts. It was the *Septuagint* that became the foundation of the Church and the vehicle through which the one true faith penetrated the hearts of men and became the flame that has never been quenched. That dear Christian reader is the *Septuagint*.

The history of the *Septuagint*, according to tradition, is first mentioned in The Letter of Aristeas in which the following origins of the *Septuagint* are found. Ptolemy II Philadelphos, King of Egypt and head of the Greek Macedonian

To The Reader

House of Ptolemy (287-247 B.C.) had recently established the famous Library of Alexandria. Demetrios of Phalaros, the chief librarian persuaded the king to enrich the famous library with a copy of the sacred books of the Hebrew people. To win favor with the Hebrew people, whom he needed to translate the sacred books from Hebrew into Greek, King Ptolemy freed 100,000 Hebrew slaves in different parts of his kingdom. He then sent delegates, including Aristeas, who was an officer in the Royal Guard, an Egyptian by birth and a pagan by religion, to Jerusalem, to ask Eleazar, the Jewish High Priest, to provide him with a copy of the Torah, and Jewish scholars capable of translating it into Greek. Eleazar agreed to the King's request and sent seventy-two scholars (six from each tribe) to the King so that they could translate the Law into Greek. The letter further states that the Jewish scholars were successful in translating the Hebrew Torah into Greek and presented a richly ornamented copy to King Ptolemy. Tradition also holds that the Hebrew Torah was translated in seventy-two days. Finally, the Letter of Aristeas also states that the first reading of the translation was in the presence of the Jewish priests, rulers and people assembled in Alexandria, Egypt, who all recognized and praised its perfect conformity with the Hebrew original. King Ptolemy was greatly pleased with the translation and had it placed in the great Library of Alexandria. The name *Septuagint* is latin for seventy, in reference to the seventy-two scholars who translated the Hebrew scriptures into Greek, and is also referenced with the Roman numerals LXX for seventy.

Many Jewish and Christian scholars regarded the Letter of Aristeas, and its account of the origin of the *Septuagint*, as authentic in late antiquity. Aristoboulos, in an account preserved by the Church Father and Historian Eusebios, says "through the efforts of Demetrios of Phaleros a complete translation of the Jewish Law was executed in the days of Ptolemy". Aristeas' story is repeated, almost word for word, by the Jewish Historian Flavius Josephus, and substantially the same by Philo of Alexandria. Many Church Fathers and ecclesiastical writers up to the beginning of the sixteenth century accepted the Letter and the story as genuine. However, the authenticity of the Letter and its story about the origins of the *Septuagint* were later questioned. Today the authenticity of the Letter of Aristeas is almost universally denied. Nevertheless, many continue to hold to the authenticity of the Letter and the account of the *Septuagint's* origins therein. In fact, many scholars do believe that there is much historical fact that underlies the account of the *Septuagint's* origin.

In any event, at some point in the history of their stay in Alexandria, Egypt, the Jewish people forgot the Hebrew Language and they needed to have the Torah, and the later writings of the Old Testament, rendered into their new language of Greek for public readings and for use in their liturgy. It was only natural that such a translation should take place. However, many go a step more

To The Reader

and believe that the creation of the *Septuagint* was intended by Almighty God and was, therefore, inspired. St. Irenaeos, St. John Chrysostomos, Blessed Augustine, Clement of Alexandria, Tertullian, Origen and others believed that God inspired the seventy-two Jewish scholars that translated the *Septuagint*. Further, the Greek Orthodox Church so deeply believes that Almighty God ordained the origin of the *Septuagint*, and thus inspired it, that Almighty God ordained Alexander the Great to bring the Greek Language and Greek Culture to the Middle East. This action created the environment that was necessary to produce the *Septuagint*, as well as the New Testament, which greatly aided in the spread of the Holy Gospel of Our Most Blessed Lord and Savior Jesus Christ. The remainder of The Holy Orthodox Church also believes in the full inspiration of the *Septuagint* and continues to use it to this day in all its liturgical services and doctrinal formulations. Therefore, the very history and sacredness of the *Septuagint* and its connection with the Church demands our attention, as well as a new rendering in the English Language for English-Speaking Christians.

The *Septuagint* texts that have been used for this edition are approved ecclesiastical texts from The Holy Orthodox Church. The Holy Orthodox Church uses these texts because of their time-honored use and approval within the Church, as well as the high degree of scholarship that has gone in to their formation. The first text that is used is the *Septuagint* text as published by the Apostoliki Diakonia. This text is simply a modified version of Alfred Rahlfs' critical edition of the *Septuagint*. It's modified in the sense that it takes into consideration some, but not all, of the Church's liturgical readings from the *Septuagint* and then uses Rahlfs' critical edition for the remainder of the text. The second text that was used is the *Septuagint* text as it is published by the Zoe Brotherhood. This text is also Alfred Rahlfs' modified critical edition of the *Septuagint*, but with very slight textual differences and with slightly more critical annotations. The third text that was used was the excellent critical *Septuagint* text that was compiled by the eminent *Septuagint* scholar Alfred Rahlfs. Although Rahlfs' pure critical text was extensively used in the present edition, it was primarily used as a reference work to provide some clarity as to the origin of certain textual variants contrary to the Apostoliki Diakonia and Zoe Brotherhood texts, as well as, any textual variants that could be identified in the Church's liturgical readings of the *Septuagint*. Further, extensive reference was made to the *Phos* editions of very popular Orthodox liturgical compilations that include all of the Orthodox Church's *Septuagint* liturgical readings and renderings that are found in the *Triodion*, the *Greek Menaion*, the *Prophetologion*, which is found in the vesper readings of the *Greek Menaion*, the vesper services for the Holy and Great Week of *Pascha*, and various other liturgical services. Finally, as it concerns

To The Reader

the Psalms and the Odes, the English translation of the *Psalter According to the Seventy*, Together With the Nine Odes, as published by Holy Transfiguration Monastery, has been wholly adopted with the permission of the monks of Holy Transfiguration Monastery, with the proviso that its traditional English would be slightly modernized to fit the overall format of the present edition, as well as extensive annotations added to their text. The Psalms and Odes as published by Holy Transfiguration Monastery are based on the famous Moscow Edition of the *Septuagint* as published in Moscow, Russia in 1821, and used extensively by the monks of Mount Athos. The Moscow Edition of the *Septuagint* is actually a reprint of Grabe's 1720 version based almost entirely on Codex Alexandrinus. The monks of Mount Athos have long borne witness to the accuracy of this particular edition, and continue to use it to this day. Therefore, it is these ecclesiastically approved and sanctioned *Septuagint* texts, with the exception of Rahlfs' *Septuaginta* text which is only greatly honored, but not sanctioned by the Church, that underlie the present edition.

    The English style that is used throughout this translation is what many would call "Biblical" or "Traditional" English, but in a slightly modernized form. The philosophy behind this current work is that the reader, and hearer, might be instilled with reverence and awe as he approaches the Word of God, and that one might realize the sacredness of scripture and that this is truly God's revelation of Himself to man. Therefore, by presenting God's Word in "Biblical" English the sacred and holy nature of Almighty God is clearly and succinctly conveyed and the soul of the partaker of Holy Scripture is uplifted to the very heights of God's love and mercy that He has for all mankind. Contemporary English fails to do this. We cannot feel the sense or depth of God's sacredness when we approach God with the same language we use in business and everyday conversation. In other words, since there is nothing special about Contemporary English, there is nothing special about God. Thus, the style of English in this present translation is intended to uplift men's souls and bring them to a sense of fear and trembling people must have of the Lord.

    Finally, this work was a labor of love. It not only took years to translate, but years of study of *Septuagint* Greek. There have been countless hours of Internet research, hundreds of E-Mails with *Septuagint* scholars and Greek Orthodox Monastics in checking and reviewing this present translation, and many sleepless nights translating and revising the text until it was ready for publishing.

    Septuagint Greek is very difficult to translate because it is hard to convey in English exactly what the Greek means. In fact, *Septuagint* Greek, or all Greek for that matter, is so difficult to convey in English that this present translation can be properly termed an "approximation". In any event, whether this present work is a translation or an approximation I will leave to the reader to decide. My

To The Reader

most earnest prayer is that Almighty God, by Our Most Blessed Lord and Savior Jesus Christ, through the Power of the Most Holy Spirit, sanctify the present translation and use it for the glory of his Holy Church and for the edification of all Mankind.

May the Grace and Mercy of Our Lord and Savior Jesus Christ be upon all who abide in Christ's love and sincerely seek to apply the message of Our Lord's Gospel everyday in their lives and, in general, in our world at large.

Glory be to God in the Highest, and in Our Lord and Savior Jesus Christ.

Translator,

PETER A. PAPOUTSIS

The Pentateuch

The Books of the Pentateuch

Genesis

Exodus

Leviticus

Numbers

Deuteronomy

THE BOOK OF
Genesis

Chapter 1

In the beginning God made the heaven and the earth. 2 And the earth was invisible and without form and darkness was over the abyss and the Spirit of God moved over the water. 3 And God said, Let light be created, and light was created. 4 And God saw the light that it was good, and God divided between the light and between the darkness. 5 And God called the light Day, and the darkness He called Night, and there was evening and there was morning, the first day.

6 And God said, Let a firmament be created in the midst of the water, and let it be a division between water and water, and it was so. 7 And God made the firmament, and God divided between the water, which was under the firmament, and the water, which was above the firmament. 8 And God called the firmament Sky, and God saw that it was good, and there was evening and there was morning, the second day.

9 And God said, Let the water, which is under the sky be collected into one place, and let the dry land appear, and it was so. And the water, which was under the sky, was collected into its places, and the dry land appeared. 10 And God called the dry land Earth, and the gatherings of the waters He called Seas, and God saw that it was good. 11 And God said, Let the earth bring forth the herb of grass bearing seed according to its kind and according to its likeness, and the fruit tree bearing fruit whose seed is in it, according to its kind on the earth, and it was so. 12 And the earth brought forth the herb of grass bearing seed according to its kind and according to its likeness, and the fruit tree bearing fruit whose seed is in it, according to its kind on the earth, and God saw that it was good. 13 And there was evening and there was morning, the third day.

14 And, God said Let luminaries be created in the firmament of the sky to give light upon the earth, to divide between day and night, and let them be for signs and for seasons and for days and for years. 15 And let them be for light in the firmament of the sky, so as to shine upon the earth, and it was so. 16 And God made the two great luminaries, the greater luminary for regulating the day and the lesser luminary for regulating the night, and the stars. 17 And God placed them in the firmament of the sky, so as to shine upon the earth, 18 and to regulate day and night, and to divide between the light and between the darkness. And God saw that it was good. 19 And there was evening and there was morning, the fourth day.

Genesis 2

20 And God said, Let the waters bring forth reptiles having life and winged creatures flying above the earth in the firmament of the sky, and it was so. 21 And God made great sea creatures, and every living reptile, which the waters brought forth according to their kinds, and every creature that flies with wings according to its kind, and God saw that they were good. 22 And God blessed them, saying, Increase and multiply and fill the waters in the seas, and let the creatures that fly be multiplied on the earth. 23 And there was evening and there was morning, the fifth day.

24 And God said, Let the earth bring forth the living creature according to its kind, quadrupeds and reptiles and wild beasts of the earth according to their kind, and it was so. 25 And God made the wild beasts of the earth according to their kind, and cattle according to their kind, and all the reptiles of the earth according to their kind, and God saw that they were good. 26 And God said, Let us make man according to our image and likeness, and let them have dominion over the fish of the sea, and over the flying creatures of the sky, and over the cattle and all the earth, and over all the reptiles that creep on the earth. 27 And God made man, according to the image of God He made him, male and female He made them. 28 And God blessed them, saying, Increase and multiply and fill the earth and subdue it, and have dominion over the fish of the seas and the flying creatures of the sky, and all the cattle and the earth, and all the reptiles that creep on the earth. 29 And God said, Behold I have given to you every seed bearing herb sowing seed which is upon all the earth, and every tree which has in itself the fruit of seed that is sown, to you it shall be for food. 30 And to all the wild beasts of the earth and to all the flying creatures of the sky and to every reptile creeping on the earth, which has in itself the breath of life, even every green plant for food; and it was so. 31 And God saw all the things that he had made, and behold they were very good. And there was evening and there was morning, the sixth day.

Chapter 2

And the heavens and the earth were finished, and the whole world of them. 2 And God finished on the sixth day His works, which He made, and He ceased on the seventh day from all His works, which He made. 3 And God blessed the seventh day and sanctified it, because in it He ceased from all His works, which God began to do.

4 This *is* the book of the generation of heaven and earth, when they were created, in the day in which the Lord God made the heaven and the earth, 5 and every herb of the field before it was on the earth, and all the grass of the field before it sprang up, for God had not rained on the earth, and there was not a

man to cultivate it.

6 But there raised a fountain out of the earth, and watered the whole face of the earth. 7 And God formed the man of dust of the earth and breathed upon his face the breath of life, and the man became a living soul.

8 And God planted a garden to the east in Edem, and placed there the man whom He formed. 9 And God made to spring up also out of the earth every tree beautiful to the eye and good for food, and the tree of life in the midst of the garden, and the tree of learning the knowledge of good and evil. 10 And a river proceeds out of Edem to water the garden; thence it divides itself into four heads. 11 The name of the one, Phisom, this it is which encircles the whole land of Evilat, where there is gold. 12 And the gold of that land is good; there also is carbuncle and emerald. 13 And the name of the second river is Geon; this it is which encircles the whole land of Ethiopia. 14 And the third river is Tigris; this is that which flows forth over against the Assyrians. And the fourth river is *the* Euphrates. 15 And the Lord God took the man whom He had formed, and placed him in the garden of delight, to cultivate and keep it. 16 And the Lord God gave a charge to Adam, saying, Of every tree that is in the garden thou may freely eat, 17 but of the tree of the knowledge of good and evil; of it ye shall not eat, but in whatever day ye eat of it, ye shall surely die by death.

18 And the Lord God said, *It is* not good that the man is alone, let us make for him a helper. 19 And God formed yet farther out of the earth all the wild beasts of the field, and all the birds of the sky, and he brought them to Adam, to see what he would call them, and whatever Adam called any living creature, that was the name of it. 20 And Adam gave names to all the cattle and to all the birds of the sky and to all the wild beasts of the field, but for Adam there was not found a helper like himself? 21 And God brought a trance upon Adam, and he slept, and He took one of his ribs, and filled up the flesh instead thereof. 22 And God formed the rib, which He took from Adam into a woman, and brought her to Adam. 23 And Adam said, This now is bone of my bones, and flesh of my flesh; she shall be called woman, because she was taken out of her man. 24 Therefore shall a man leave his father and his mother and shall cleave to his wife, and they two shall be one flesh. 25 And the two were naked both Adam and his wife, and were not ashamed.

Chapter 3

Now the serpent was the most cunning of all the beasts on the earth, which the Lord God made, and the serpent said to the woman, Wherefore has God said, Eat not of every tree of the garden? 2 And the woman said to the serpent, We may eat of the fruit of the trees of the garden,

Genesis 3

3 but of the fruit of the tree which is in the middle of the garden, God said Ye shall not eat of it, neither shall ye touch it, lest ye die. 4 And the serpent said to the woman, Ye should not surely die by death. 5 For God knew that in whatever day ye should eat of it your eyes would be opened and ye would be as gods, knowing good and evil. 6 And the woman saw that the tree was good for food, and that it was pleasant to the eyes to look upon and beautiful to contemplate and having taken of its fruit she ate, and she gave to her man also with her, and they ate. 7 And the eyes of both were opened, and they perceived that they were naked, and they sowed fig leaves together and made for themselves aprons.

8 And they heard the voice of the Lord God walking in the garden in the afternoon; and both Adam and his woman hid themselves from the face of the Lord God in the midst of the trees of the garden. 9 And the Lord God called Adam and said to him, Adam, where art thou? 10 And he said to Him, I heard thy voice as thou walked in the garden, and I feared because I was naked and I hid myself. 11 And God said to him, Who told thee that thou was naked, unless thou has eaten of the tree concerning which I charged thee of it alone not to eat? 12 And Adam said, The woman whom thou gave to be with me, she gave me of the tree and I ate. 13 And the Lord God said to the woman, Why has thou done this? And the woman said, The serpent deceived me and I ate. 14 And the Lord God said to the serpent, Because thou has done this thou art cursed above all cattle and all the beasts of the earth on thy breast and belly thou shall go, and thou shall eat earth all the days of thy life. 15 And I will put enmity between thee and the woman and between thy seed and her seed, He shall watch for thy head, and thou shall watch for His heel. 16 And to the woman He said, I will greatly multiply thy pain and thy groaning; in pain thou shall bring forth children, and thy submission shall be to thy man, and he shall rule over thee. 17 And to Adam He said, Because thou has hearkened to the voice of thy woman, and eaten of the tree concerning which I charged thee of it only not to eat, of that thou has eaten, cursed is the ground in thy labors, in pain shall thou eat of it all the days of thy life. 18 Thorns and thistles shall it bring forth to thee, and thou shall eat the herb of the field. 19 In the sweat of thy face shall thou eat thy bread until thou return to the earth out of which thou were taken, for earth thou art and to earth thou shall return. 20 And Adam called the name of his wife Life, because she was the mother of all living.

21 And the Lord God made for Adam and his wife garments of skin, and clothed them. 22 And God said, Behold, Adam is become as one of us, to know good and evil and now lest at any time he stretch forth his hand, and take of the tree of life and eat, and so he shall live forever. 23 So the Lord God sent him forth out of the garden of delight to cultivate the ground out of which he was taken.

Genesis 4

24 And He cast out Adam and caused him to live over against the garden of delight, and stationed the cherubs and the fiery sword that turns about to guard the way of the tree of life.

Chapter 4

And Adam knew Eve his wife, and she conceived and brought forth Kain and said I have gained a man through God. 2 And she again bore his brother Abel. And Abel was a keeper of sheep, but Kain was a tiller of the ground. 3 And it was so after some time that Kain brought of the fruits of the earth *as* a sacrifice to the Lord. 4 And Abel also brought of the firstborn of his sheep and of his fatlings and God looked upon Abel and his gifts, 5 but Kain and his sacrifices he regarded not, and Kain was exceedingly sorrowful and his countenance fell. 6 And the Lord God said to Kain, Why art thou become very sorrowful and why is thy countenance fallen? 7 Has thou not sinned if thou have brought it rightly, but not rightly divided it? Be still, to thee shall be his submission, and thou shall rule over him. 8 And Kain said to Abel his brother, Let us go out into the plain; and it came to pass that when they were in the plain Kain raised up against Abel his brother and killed him. 9 And the Lord God said to Kain, Where is Abel thy brother? And he said, I know not, am I my brother's keeper? 10 And the Lord said, What have thou done? The voice of thy brother's blood cries out to me from the ground. 11 And now thou art cursed from the earth, which has opened her mouth to receive thy brother's blood from thy hand. 12 When thou tillest the earth, then it shall not continue to give its strength to thee: thou shall be groaning and trembling on the earth. 13 And Kain said to the Lord God, My crime is too great for me to be forgiven. 14 If thou *will* cast me out this day from the face of the earth, and I shall be hidden from thy presence, and I shall be groaning and trembling upon the earth, then it will be that any one that finds me shall kill me. 15 And the Lord God said to him, Not so, any one that kills Kain shall suffer seven fold vengeance; and the Lord God set a mark upon Kain that no one that found him might kill him. 16 So Kain went forth from the presence of God and lived in the land of Nod over against Edem.

17 And Kain knew his wife, and having conceived she bore Enoch; and he built a city; and he named the city after the name of his son, Enoch. 18 And to Enoch was born Gaidad; and Gaidad begot Maleleel; and Maleleel begot Mathusala; and Mathusala begot Lamech. 19 And Lameh took to himself two wives; the name of the one was Ada, and the name of the second Sella. 20 And Ada bore Jobel; he was the father of those that live in tents, feeding cattle. 21 And the name of his brother was Jubal; it was he who invented the psaltery and harp.

22 And Sella also bore Thobel; he was a smith, a manufacturer both of brass and iron: and the sister of Thobel was Noëma. 23 And Lameh said to his wives, Ada and Sella, Hear my voice, ye wives of Lameh, consider my words, because I have killed a man to my sorrow and a youth to my grief. 24 Because vengeance has been exacted seven times on Kain's behalf, on Lameh's it shall be seventy times seven. 25 And Adam knew Eve his wife, and she conceived and bore a son, and called his name Seth, saying, For God has raised up to me another seed instead of Abel, whom Kain killed. 26 And Seth had a son, and he called his name Enos: he hoped to call on the name of the Lord God.

Chapter 5

This *is* the book of the generation of men in the day in which God made Adam; in the image of God He made him: 2 male and female He made them, and blessed them; and He called his name Adam, in the day in which He made them. 3 And Adam lived two hundred and thirty years, and begot a son after his own form and after his own image, and he called his name Seth. 4 And the days of Adam, which he lived after his begetting Seth, were seven hundred years; and he begot sons and daughters. 5 And all the days of Adam, which he lived were nine hundred and thirty years, and he died.

6 Now Seth lived two hundred and five years, and begot Enos. 7 And Seth lived after his begetting Enos, seven hundred and seven years, and he begot sons and daughters. 8 And all the days of Seth were nine hundred and twelve years, and he died.

9 And Enos lived an hundred and ninety years, and begot Kainan. 10 And Enos lived after his begetting Kainan, seven hundred and fifteen and he begot sons and daughters. 11 And all the days of Enos were nine hundred and five years, and he died.

12 And Kainan lived an hundred and seventy years, and he begot Maleleel. 13 And Kainan lived after his begetting Maleleel, seven hundred and forty years, and he begot son and daughters. 14 And all the days of Kainan were nine hundred and ten years, and he died.

15 And Maleleel lived an hundred and sixty and five years, and he begot Jared. 16 And Maleleel lived after his begetting Jared, seven hundred and thirty years, and he begot sons and daughters. 17 And all the days of Maleleel were eight hundred and ninety and five years, and he died.

18 And Jared lived an hundred and two years, and begot Enoch: 19 and Jared lived after his begetting Enoch, eight hundred years, and he begot sons and daughters. 20 And all the days of Jared were nine hundred and sixty and two years, and he died.

Genesis 6

21 And Enoch lived an hundred and sixty and five years, and begat Mathusala. 22 And Enoch was well pleasing to God after his begetting Mathusala, two hundred years, and he begot sons and daughters. 23 And all the days of Enoch were three hundred and sixty and five years. 24 And Enoch was well pleasing to God, and was not found, because God translated him.

25 And Mathusala lived an hundred and sixty and seven years and begot Lameh. 26 And Mathusala lived after his begetting Lameh eight hundred and two years, and begot sons and daughters. 27 And all the days of Mathusala which he lived, were nine hundred and sixty and nine years, and he died.

28 And Lameh lived an hundred and eighty and eight years, and begot a son. 29 And he called his name Noe, saying, This one will cause us to cease from our works, and from the toils of our hands, and from the earth, which the Lord God has cursed. 30 And Lameh lived after his begetting Noe, five hundred and sixty and five years, and begot sons and daughters. 31 And all the days of Lamech were seven hundred and fifty-three years, and he died.

32 And Noe was five hundred years old, and he begot three sons, Sem, Ham, and Japheth.

Chapter 6

And it came to pass when men began to be numerous upon the earth, and daughters were born to them, 2 that the * sons of God having seen the daughters of men that they were beautiful, took to themselves wives of all whom they chose. 3 And the Lord God said, My Spirit shall certainly not remain among these men forever, because they are flesh, but their days shall be an hundred and twenty years. 4 Now the giants were upon the earth in those days; and after that when the * sons of God were used to go in to the daughters of men, they bore children to them, those were the giants of old, the men of renown.

5 And the Lord God having seen that the wicked actions of men were multiplied upon the earth, and that every one in his heart was purposefully brooding over evil continually, 6 then God laid it to heart that he had made man upon the earth, and he pondered it deeply. 7 And God said, I will blot out man whom I have made from the face of the earth, even man with cattle, and reptiles with flying creatures of the sky, for * I am grieved that I have made them. 8 But Noe found grace before the Lord God.

9 And these are the generations of Noe. Noe was a just man; being perfect in his generation, Noe was well pleasing to God. 10 And Noe begot three sons, Sem, Ham, and Japheth. 11 But the earth was corrupted before God, and the earth was filled with iniquity.

12 And the Lord God saw the earth, and it was corrupted because all flesh had corrupted its way upon the earth. 13 And the Lord God said to Noe, The period for all mankind is come before me; because they have filled the earth with iniquity, and, behold, I am completely destroying them and the earth. 14 So make therefore for thyself an ark of square timber. Thou shall make the ark with compartments, and thou shall pitch it within and without with pitch. 15 And thus shall thou make the ark: three hundred cubits the length of the ark, and fifty cubits the breadth, and thirty cubits the height of it. 16 Thou shall narrow the ark in making it, and in a cubit above thou shall finish it, and the door of the ark thou shall make on the side; with lower, second, and third stories thou shall make it. 17 And behold I bring a flood of water upon the earth, to destroy all flesh in which is the breath of life under heaven, and whatsoever things are upon the earth shall die. 18 And I will establish my covenant with thee, and thou shall enter into the ark, and thy sons and thy wife, and thy sons' wives with thee. 19 And of all cattle and of all reptiles and of all wild beasts, even of all flesh, thou shall bring into the ark two by two, that thou may feed them with thyself; male and female they shall be.

20 Of all winged birds after their kind and of all cattle after their kind and of all reptiles creeping upon the earth after their kind, two by two of all shall come in to thee, male and female to be fed with thee. 21 And thou shall take to thyself of all kinds of food, which ye eat, and thou shall gather them to thyself, and it shall be for thee and them to eat. 22 And Noe did all things whatever the Lord God commanded him, he so did.

* *Codex Alexandrinus* reads: "angels of God". * The Zoe Brotherhood text cites to an alternative reading for Chapter Six verse seven in *Codex Alexandrinus* which reads: "I am angered."

Chapter 7

And the Lord God said to Noe, Enter thou and all thy family into the ark, for thee have I seen righteous before me in this generation. 2 And of the clean cattle take in to thee seven by seven, male and female, and of the unclean cattle two by two, male and female. 3 And of clean flying creatures of the sky seven by seven, male and female, and of all unclean flying creatures two by two, male and female, to maintain *their* seed on all the earth. 4 For yet seven days having passed I bring rain upon the earth forty days and forty nights, and I will blot out every offspring, which I have made from the face of all the earth. 5 And Noe did all things whatever the Lord God commanded him.

6 And Noe was six hundred years old when the flood of water was upon the earth. 7 And then went in Noe and his sons and his wife, and his sons' wives with him into the ark, because of the water of the flood.

Genesis 8

8 And of clean flying creatures and of unclean flying creatures, and of clean cattle and of unclean cattle, and of all things that creep upon the earth, 9 Two by twos went in to Noe into the ark, male and female, as God commanded Noe. 10 And it came to pass after the seven days that the water of the flood came upon the earth. 11 In the six hundredth year of the life of Noe, in the second month, on the twenty-seventh of the month, on this day all the fountains of the abyss were broken up, and the floodgates of heaven were opened. 12 And the rain was upon the earth forty days and forty nights. 13 On that very day entered Noe, Sem, Ham, and Japheth the sons of Noe, and the wife of Noe, and the three wives of his sons with him into the ark. 14 And all the wild beasts after their kind, and all cattle after their kind, and every reptile moving itself on the earth after its kind, and every flying bird after its kind, 15 went in to Noe into the ark, two by two, male and female of all flesh in which is the breath of life. 16 And they that entered went in male and female of all flesh, as God commanded Noe and the Lord God closed the ark outside of him.

17 And the flood was upon the earth forty days and forty nights, and the water abounded greatly and bore up the ark, and it was lifted on high from off the earth. 18 And the water prevailed and abounded exceedingly upon the earth, and the ark was borne upon the water. 19 And the water prevailed exceedingly upon the earth, and covered all the high mountains, which were under heaven. 20 Fifteen cubits upwards was the water raised, and it covered all the high mountains. 21 And there died all flesh that moved upon the earth, of flying creatures and cattle, and of wild beasts, and every reptile moving upon the earth, and every man. 22 And all things, which have the breath of life, and whatever was on the dry land, died. 23 And he blotted out every offspring which was upon the face of the earth, both man and beast, and reptiles, and birds of the sky, and they were blotted out from the earth, and Noe was left alone, and those with him in the ark. 24 And the water was raised over the earth an hundred and fifty days.

Chapter 8

And God remembered Noe, and all the wild beasts, and all the cattle, and all the birds, and all the reptiles that creep, as many as were with him in the ark and God brought a wind upon the earth and the water stayed. 2 And the fountains of the abyss were closed up, and the floodgates of heaven and the rain from heaven were withheld. 3 And the water subsided, and went off the earth, and after an hundred and fifty days the water was diminished, and the ark rested in the seventh month, on the twenty-seventh day of the month, on the mountains of Ararat.

4 And the water continued to decrease until the tenth month. 5 And in the tenth month, on the first day of the month, the heads of the mountains were seen. 6 And it came to pass after forty days Noe opened the window of the ark, which he had made, and he sent forth a raven to see if the water had ceased 7 And it went forth and returned not until the water was dried off from the earth. 8 And he sent a dove after it to see if the water had ceased off from the earth. 9 And the dove not having found rest for her feet, returned to him into the ark, because the water was on all the face of the earth and he stretched out his hand and took her, and brought her to himself into the ark. 10 And having waited yet seven other days, he again sent forth the dove from the ark. 11 And the dove returned to him in the evening and had a leaf of olive, a sprig in her mouth; and Noe knew that the water had ceased from off the earth. 12 And having waited yet seven other days, he again sent forth the dove, and she did not return to him again any more. 13 And it came to pass in the six hundred and first year of the life of Noe, in the first month, on the first day of the month, the water subsided from off the earth and Noe opened the covering of the ark which he had made, and he saw that the water had subsided from the face of the earth. 14 And in the second month the earth was dried, on the twenty-seventh of the month.

15 And the Lord God spoke to Noe, saying, 16 Come out from the ark, thou and thy wife and thy sons, and thy sons' wives with thee. 17 And all the wild beasts as many as are with thee and all flesh both of birds and beasts and every reptile moving upon the earth, bring forth with thee: and increase ye and multiply upon the earth. 18 And Noe came forth, and his wife and his sons, and his sons' wives with him. 19 And all the wild beasts and all the cattle and every bird, and every reptile creeping upon the earth after their kind, came forth out of the ark. 20 And Noe built an altar to the Lord, and took of all clean beasts, and of all clean birds, and offered a whole burnt offering upon the altar. 21 And the Lord God smelled a smell of sweetness, and the Lord God, having considered, said, I will not any more curse the earth, because of the works of men, because the imagination of man is purposefully bent upon evil things from his youth, I will not therefore any more smite all living flesh as I have done. 22 All the days of the earth, seed and harvest, cold and heat, summer and spring, shall not cease by day or night.

Chapter 9

And God blessed Noe and his sons, and said to them, Increase and multiply, and fill the earth and have dominion over it. 2 And the dread and the fear of you shall be upon all the wild beasts of the earth, on all the birds of the sky, and on all things moving upon the earth, and upon all the fishes of the sea, I

Genesis 9

have placed them under your power. 3 And every reptile, which is living, shall be to you for meat, I have given all things to you as the green herbs.

4 But flesh with blood of life ye shall not eat. 5 For your blood of your lives will I require at the hand of all wild beasts, and I will require the life of man at the hand of his brother. 6 He that sheds man's blood in return for this blood shall his own be shed, for in the image of God I made man. 7 But do ye increase and multiply, and fill the earth, and have dominion over it.

8 And God spoke to Noe and to his sons with him, saying, 9 And behold I will establish my covenant with you, and with your seed after you, 10 and with every living creature with you of birds and of beasts, and with all the wild beasts of the earth, as many as are with you, of all that came out of the ark. 11 And I will establish my covenant with you and all flesh shall not any more die by the water of the flood, and there shall no more be a flood of water to destroy all the earth. 12 And the Lord God said to Noe, This is the sign of the covenant, which I set between you and Me and between every living creature, which is with you for perpetual generations. 13 I set My bow in the cloud, and it shall be for a sign of covenant between the earth and me. 14 And it shall be when I gather clouds upon the earth, that My bow shall be seen in the cloud. 15 And I will remember My covenant, which is between you and Me and between every living soul in all flesh, and there shall no longer be water for a deluge, so as to blot out all flesh. 16 And my bow shall be in the cloud, and I will look to remember the everlasting covenant between the earth, and Me and between *every* living soul in all flesh, which is upon the earth. 17 And God said to Noe, This *is* the sign of the covenant, which I have made between all flesh, and Me, which is upon the earth.

18 Now the sons of Noe which came out of the ark were Sem, Ham, and Japheth. And Ham was father of Canaan. 19 These three are the sons of Noe, of these were men scattered over all the earth.

20 And Noe began to be a husbandman, and he planted a vineyard. 21 And he drank of the wine, and was drunk, and was naked in his house. 22 And Ham the father of Canaan saw the nakedness of his father, and he went out and told his two brothers outside. 23 And Sem and Japheth having taken a garment, put it on both their backs and went backwards, and covered the nakedness of their father; and their faces were backwards and they saw not the nakedness of their father. 24 And Noe recovered from the wine, and knew all that his younger son had done to him. 25 And he said, Cursed be the slave Canaan, a slave shall he be to his brothers. 26 And he said, Blessed be the Lord God of Sem, and Canaan shall be his slave. 27 May God make room for Japheth, and let him live in the habitations of Sem, and let Canaan be his slave.

28 And Noe lived after the flood three hundred and fifty years. 29 And all the days of Noe were nine hundred and fifty years, and he died.

Chapter 10

Now these are the generations of the sons of Noe, Sem, Ham, Japheth; and sons were born to them after the flood. 2 The sons of Japheth, Gamer, and Magog, and Madoi, and Jovan, and Elisa, and Thobel, and Mosoch, and Thiras. 3 And the sons of Gamer, Aschanaz, and Riphath, and Thorgama. 4 And the sons of Jovan, Elisa, and Tharseis, Cetians, Rhodians. 5 From these were the islands of the Gentiles divided in their land, each according to his tongue, in their tribes and in their nations.

6 And the sons of Ham, Hus, and Mesrain, Phud, and Canaan. 7 And the sons of Hus, Saba, and Evila, and Sabatha, and Rhegma, and Sabathaka. And the sons of Rhegma, Saba, and Dadan. 8 And Hus begot Nimrod; he began to be a giant upon the earth. 9 He was a great hunter before the Lord God; therefore they say, As Nimrod the great hunter before the Lord. 10 And the beginning of his kingdom was Babylon, and Orech, and Arhad, and Halanne, in the land of Sennaar. 11 Out of that land came Assur, and built Ninevi, and the city Rhooboth, and Halach, 12 and Dase between Ninevi and Halach; this is the great city. 13 And Mesrain begot the Ludiim and the Nephthalim, and the Enemetiim, and the Labiim, and the Patrosoniim 14 and the Hasmoniim (whence came forth Phylistiim) and the Gaphthoriim. 15 And Canaan begot Sidon his firstborn 16 and the Hettite, and the Jebusite, and the Amorite, and the Girgashite, and the Evite, and the Arukite, 17 and the Asennite, and the Aradian, and the Samarean, and the Amathite; 18 and after this the tribes of the Canaanites were dispersed. 19 And the boundaries of the Canaanites were from Sidon till one comes to Gerara and Gaza, till one comes to Sodom and Gomorrah, Adama and Seboim, as far as Dasa. 20 These were the sons of Ham in their tribes according to their tongues, in their countries, and in their nations.

21 And to Sem himself also were children born, the father of all the sons of Heber, the brother of Japheth the elder. 22 Sons of Sem, Elam, and Assur, and Arphaxad, and Lud, and Aram, and Cainan. 23 And sons of Aram, Uz, and Ul, and Gater, and Mosoch. 24 And Arphaxad begot Cainan and Cainan begot Sala. And Sala begot Heber. 25 And to Heber were born two sons, the name of the one, Phaleg, because in his days the earth was divided, and the name of his brother Jektan. 26 And Jektan begot Elmodad, and Saleth, and Sarmoth, and Jarah, and Odorrha, and Aibel, and Dekla, 27 and Eval, and Abimael, and Saba, 28 and Uphir, and Evila, and Jobab, 29 all these were the sons of Jektan. 30 And their dwelling was from Masse, till one comes to Saphera, a mountain of the east. 31 These were the sons of Sem in their tribes, according to their tongues, in their countries, and in their nations.

Genesis 11

32 These are the tribes of the sons of Noe, according to their generations, according to their nations; of them were the islands of the Gentiles scattered over the earth after the flood.

Chapter 11

And all the earth was one lip, and there was one speech to all. 2 And it came to pass as they moved from the east, they found a plain in the land of Sennaar, and they lived there. 3 And a man said to his neighbor, Come, let us make bricks and bake them with fire. And the brick was to them for stone, and their mortar was bitumen. 4 And they said, Come, let us build to ourselves a city and tower, whose top shall be to heaven, and let us make to us a name, before we are scattered abroad upon the face of all the earth. 5 And the Lord came down to see the city and the tower, which the sons of men built. 6 And the Lord said, Behold, one race, and one lip of all, and they have begun to do this and now nothing shall fail from them of all that they may have undertaken to do. 7 Come, and let us go down there *and* confound their tongue, that they may not understand each the voice of his neighbor. 8 And the Lord scattered them thence over the face of all the earth and they left off building the city and the tower. 9 On this account its name was called Confusion, because there the Lord confounded the lips of all the earth, and thence the Lord scattered them upon the face of all the earth.

10 And these are the generations of Sem; and Sem was a hundred years old when he begot Arphaxad, the second year after the flood. 11 And Sem lived, after he had begotten Arphaxad, five hundred years, and begot sons and daughters, and died.

12 And Arphaxad lived a hundred and thirty-five years, and begot Canaan. 13 And Arphaxad lived after he had begotten Canaan, four hundred years, and begot sons and daughters, and died. And Canaan lived a hundred and thirty years and begot Sala; and Canaan lived after he had begotten Sala, three hundred and thirty years, and begot sons and daughters, and died.

14 And Sala lived an hundred and thirty years, and begot Heber. 15 And Sala lived after he had begotten Heber, three hundred and thirty years, and begot sons and daughters, and died.

16 And Heber lived an hundred and thirty-four years, and begot Phaleg. 17 And Heber lived after he had begotten Phaleg two hundred and seventy years, and begot sons and daughters, and died.

18 And Phaleg lived an hundred and thirty years, and begot Ragau. 19 And Phaleg lived after he had begotten Ragau, nine and two hundred years, and begot sons and daughters, and died.

20 And Ragau lived an hundred thirty and two years, and begot Seruh. 21 And Ragau lived after he had begotten Seruh, two hundred and seven years, and begot sons and daughters, and died. 22 And Seruh lived hundred and thirty years, and begot Nachor.

23 And Seruh lived after he had begotten Nahor, two hundred years, and begot sons and daughters, and died.

24 And Nahor lived a hundred and seventy-nine years, and begot Tharrha. 25 And Nahor lived after he had begotten Tharrha, an hundred and twenty-five years, and begot sons and daughters, and he died.

26 And Pharrha lived seventy years, and begot Abram, and Nahor, and Arrhan.

27 And these are the generations of Tharrha. Tharrha begot Abram and Nahor, and Arrhan; and Arrhan begot Lot. 28 And Arrhan died in the presence of Tharrha his father, in the land in which he was born, in the country of the Chaldees. 29 And Abram and Nahor took to themselves wives, the name of the wife of Abram was Sara and the name of the wife of Nahor, Malha, daughter of Arrhan, and he was the father of Malha, the father of Jesha. 30 And Sara was barren, and did not bear children. 31 And Tharrha took Abram his son, and Lot the son of Arrhan, the son of his son, and Sara his daughter-in-law, the wife of Abram his son, and led them forth out of the land of the Chaldees, to go into the land of Canaan, and they came as far as Harrhan, and he lived there. 32 And all the days of Tharrha in the land of Harrhan were two hundred and five years, and Tharrha died in Harrhan.

Chapter 12

And the Lord said to Abram, Go forth out of thy land and out of thy kind, and out of the house of thy father, and come into the land, which I shall show thee. 2 And I will make thee a great nation, and I will bless thee and magnify thy name, and thou shall be blessed. 3 And I will bless those that bless thee, and curse those that curse thee, and in thee shall all the tribes of the earth be blessed. 4 And Abram went as the Lord spoke to him, and Lot departed with him. And Abram was seventy-five years old, when he went out of Harrhan. 5 And Abram took Sara his wife, and Lot the son of his brother, and all their possessions, as many as they had got, and every soul which they had got in Harrhan, and * they went forth to go into the land of Canaan. 6 And Abram traversed the length of the land as far as the place Sychem, to the high oak, and the Canaanites then inhabited the land. 7 And the Lord appeared to Abram, and said to him, I will give this land to thy seed. And Abram built an altar there to the Lord who appeared to him.

Genesis 13

8 And he departed thence to the mountain eastward of Bethel and there he pitched his tent, in Bethel near the sea, and Aggai toward the east, and there he built an altar to the Lord, and called on the name of the Lord. 9 And Abram departed and went and lived in the wilderness.

10 And there was a famine in the land, and Abram went down to Egypt to travel there, because the famine prevailed in the land. 11 And it came to pass when Abram drew near to enter into Egypt, Abram said to Sara his wife, I know that thou art a beautiful woman. 12 It shall come to pass then that when the Egyptians shall see thee, they shall say, This is his wife, and they shall kill me, but they shall keep thee alive. 13 Say, therefore, I am his sister, that it may be well with me on account of thee, and my soul shall live because of thee. 14 And it came to pass when Abram entered into Egypt - the Egyptians having seen his wife that she was very beautiful - 15 that the princes of Pharaoh saw her, and praised her to Pharaoh and brought her into the house of Pharaoh. 16 And they treated Abram well on her account, and he had sheep, and calves, and mules, and male slaves, and female slaves, and donkeys, and camels. 17 And God afflicted Pharaoh with great and severe afflictions, and his house, because of Sara, Abram's wife. 18 And Pharaoh having called Abram, said, What is this thou has done to me, that thou did not tell me that she was thy wife? 19 Why did thou say she is my sister? And I took her for a wife to myself; and now, behold, thy wife is before thee, take her and leave quickly. 20 And Pharaoh gave charge to men concerning Abram to join in sending him forward, and his wife, and all that he had, * and Lot with him.

*Codex Alexandrinus for verse five reads: "and arrived into the land of Canaan". *Codex Alexandrinus also includes the additional phrase: "...and Lot with him" at the end of Chapter Twelve.

Chapter 13

And Abram went up out of Egypt, he and his wife, and all that he had, and Lot with him, into the wilderness. 2 And Abram was very rich in cattle and silver, and gold. 3 And he went whence he came, into the wilderness as far as Bethel, as far as the place where his tent was before, between Bethel and Aggai, 4 to the place of the altar, * which he built there at first, and Abram there called on the name of the Lord. 5 And Lot, who went out with Abram, had sheep, and oxen, and * tents. 6 And the land was not large enough for them to live together, because their possessions were great; and the land was not large enough for them to live together. 7 And there was strife between the herdsmen of Abram's cattle, and the herdsmen of Lot's cattle, and the Canaanites and the Pherezites then lived in the land.

Genesis 14

8 And Abram said to Lot, Let there not be strife between thee, and me and between my herdsmen and thy herdsmen for we are brothers. 9 Behold, is not the whole land before thee? Separate thyself from me if thou will go to the left, I will go to the right, and if thou will go to the right I will go to the left. 10 And Lot having lifted up his eyes, observed all the country around Jordan, that it was all watered, before God overthrew Sodom and Gomorrah, as the garden of the Lord, and as the land of Egypt, until thou come to Zogora. 11 And Lot chose for himself all the country around Jordan, and Lot went from the east, and they were separated each from his brother. 12 And Abram lived in the land of Canaan; And Lot lived in a city of the neighboring people, and pitched his tent in Sodom. 13 But the men of Sodom were evil, and exceedingly sinful before God.

14 And God said to Abram after Lot was separated from him, Look up with thine eyes, and behold from the place where thou now art to the north and to the south and to the east and towards the sea; 15 for all the land which thou sees, I will give it to thee and to thy seed forever. 16 And I will make thy seed like the sand of the earth; if any one is able to number the sand of the earth, then shall thy seed be numbered. 17 Arise and traverse the land, both in the length of it and in the breadth; for to thee will I give it, and to thy seed forever. 18 And Abram having removed his tent came and lived by the Oak of Mambre, which was in Hebron, and there he built an altar to the Lord.

Codex Alexandrinus reads: "where he established his tent." *Codex Alexandrinus* reads "cattle" instead of "tents."

Chapter 14

And it came to pass in the reign of Amarphal king of Sennaar, and Arioch king of Ellahsar, that Hodollogomor king of Elam, and Thargal king of nations, 2 made war with Balla king of Sodom, and with Barsa king of Gomorrah, and with Sennaar king of Adama, and with Symobor king of Seboim and the king of Balak, (this is Segor). 3 All these met with one consent at the valley of salt, (this is the sea of salt). 4 Twelve years they served Hodollogomor, and the thirteenth year they revolted. 5 And in the fourteenth year came Hodollogomor, and the kings with him, and cut to pieces the giants in Astaroth, and Karnain, and strong nations with them, and the Ommaeans in the city Savve. 6 And the Horrhaeans in the mountains of Seir, to the turpentine tree of Pharan, which is in the wilderness. 7 And having turned back they came to the Well of Judgment, (this is Kades) and they cut to pieces all the rulers of Amalek, and the Amorites living in Asasonthamar.

Genesis 15

8 And the king of Sodom went out, and the king of Gomorrah, and king of Adama, and king of Seboim, and king of Balak, (this is Segor) and they set themselves in array against them for war in the Valley of Salt, 9 against Hodollogomor king of Elaan, and Thargal king of nations and Amarphal king of Sennaar, and Arioch king of Ellasar, the four kings against the five. 10 Now the valley of salt *consists of* slime-pits. And the king of Sodom and the king of Gomorrah fled, and they fell in there, and they that were left fled to the mountains. 11 And they took all the cavalry of Sodom and Gomorrah, and all their provisions, and departed. 12 And they took also Lot the son of Abram's brother, and his baggage, and departed, for he lived in Sodom.

13 And one of them that had been rescued came and told Abram the emigrant, and he lived by the Oak of Mambre the Amorite the brother of Eschol, and the brother of Aunan, who were confederates with Abram. 14 And Abram having heard that Lot his nephew had been taken captive numbered his own home born slaves three hundred and eighteen, and pursued after * them to Dan. 15 And he came up on them by night, he and his slaves, and he smote them and pursued them as far as Hoba, which is on the left of Damascus. 16 And he recovered all the cavalry of Sodom, and he recovered Lot his nephew, and all his possessions, and the women and the people.

17 And the king of Sodom went out to meet him, after he returned from the slaughter of Hodollogomor, and the kings with him, to the valley of Saby (this was the plain of the kings). 18 And Melchisedek king of Salem brought forth loaves and wine, and he was the priest of the Most-High God. 19 And he blessed Abram, and said, Blessed be Abram of the Most-High God, who made heaven and earth, 20 and blessed be the Most-High God who delivered thine enemies into thy * power. And Abram gave him a tenth of all. 21 And the king of Sodom said to Abram, Give me the men and take the cavalry to you. 22 And Abram said to the king of Sodom, I will stretch out my hand to the Lord the Most-High God, who made the heaven and the earth, 23 *and* I will not take from all thy goods from a string to a shoe-latchet, lest thou should say, I have made Abram rich. 24 Except what things the young men have eaten, and the portion of the men that went with me, Eshol, Aunan, Mambre, these shall *I* take a portion.

* The July vesper reading from the *Greek Menaion* and *Prohetologion* for Genesis Chapter Fourteen, verse fourteen reads: "*his* enemies", and verse twenty reads: "hand".

Chapter 15

And after these things the word of the Lord came to Abram in a vision, saying, Fear not, Abram, I shield thee, thy reward shall be very great.

2 And Abram said, Master *and* Lord, what will thou give me? Whereas I am departing without a child, but for the son of Masek my home-born female slave, this Eliezer of Damascus. 3 And Abram said, since thou have given me no seed, my home born slave should be my heir. 4 And immediately there was a voice of the Lord to him, saying, This shall not be thine heir but he that shall come out of thee shall be thine heir. 5 And He brought him out and said to him; Look up now to the sky and count the stars, if thou shall be able to number them fully, and He said, Thus shall thy seed be. 6 And Abram believed God, and it was reckoned to him for righteousness. 7 And He said to him, I am *the* God that brought thee out of the land of the Chaldeans, so as to give thee this land as an inheritance. 8 And he said, Master *and* Lord, how should I know that I should inherit it? 9 And he said to him, Take for me a heifer in her third year, and a she-goat in her third year, and a ram in his third year, and a dove and a pigeon. 10 So he took to him all these, and divided them in the midst, and set them opposite to each other, but the birds he did not divide. 11 And birds came down upon the bodies, *even* upon the divided parts of them, and Abram sat down by them. 12 And about sunset a trance fell upon Abram, and, behold a great dark terror fell upon him.

13 And it was said to Abram, Thou shall surely know that thy seed shall be a wanderer in a land not their own, and they shall enslave them, and afflict them, and humble them *for* four hundred years. 14 And the nation, whomever they shall serve, I will judge; and after this, they shall come forth hither with much property. 15 But thou shall depart to thy fathers in peace, nourished in a good old age. 16 And in the fourth generation they shall return hither, for the sins of the Amorites are not yet filled up, even until now. 17 And when the sun was about to set, there was a flame, and behold a smoking furnace and lamps of fire, which passed between these divided pieces. 18 In that day the Lord made a covenant with Abram, saying, To thy seed I will give this land, from the river of Egypt to the great river Euphrates. 19 The Kenites, and the Kenezites, and the Kedmoneans, 20 and the Hettites, and the Pherezites, and the Raphaim, and the Amorites, and the Canaanites, and the Evites, and the Gergesites and the Jebusites.

Chapter 16

Now Sara the wife of Abram bore him no children; and she had an Egyptian slave, whose name was Agar. 2 And Sara said to Abram, Behold, the Lord has restrained me from bearing; go therefore in to my slave that I may get children for myself through her. And Abram hearkened to the voice of Sara.

Genesis 17

3 So Sara the wife of Abram having taken Agar the Egyptian her slave, after Abram had lived ten years in the land of Canaan, gave her to Abram her husband as a wife to him. 4 And he went in to Agar, and she conceived, and saw that she was with child, and her mistress was dishonored before her.

5 And Sara said to Abram, I am injured by thee; I gave my slave into thy bosom, and when I saw that she was with child, I was dishonored before her. The Lord judge between thee and me. 6 And Abram said to Sara, Behold thy slave is in thy hands, use her, as it may seem good to thee. And Sara afflicted her, and she fled from her face. 7 And an angel of the Lord found her by the fountain of water in the wilderness, by the fountain in the way to Sur. 8 And the angel of the Lord said to her, Agar, Sara's slave, whence comes thou, and whither go thou? And she said, I am fleeing from the face of my mistress Sara. 9 And the angel of the Lord said to her, Return to thy mistress, and submit thyself under her hands. 10 And the angel of the Lord said to her, I will surely multiply thy seed, and it shall not be numbered for multitude. 11 And the angel of the Lord said to her, Behold, thou art with child, and shall bear a son, and shall call his name Ishmael, for the Lord hath hearkened to thy humiliation. 12 He shall be a wild man, his hands against all, and the hands of all against him, and he shall live in the presence of all his brothers. 13 And she called the name of the Lord God who spoke to her, Thou art God who sees me; for she said, For I have openly seen him that appeared to me. 14 Therefore she called the well, The well of him whom I have openly seen; behold it is between Kades and Barad.

15 And Agar bore a son to Abram; and Abram called the name of his son, which Agar bore to him, Ishmael. 16 And Abram was eighty-six years old, when Agar bore Ishmael to Abram.

Chapter 17

And Abram was ninety-nine years old and the Lord appeared to Abram and said to him, I am thy God, be well pleasing before Me, and be blameless. 2 And I will establish my covenant between Me, and between thee and I will multiply thee exceedingly. * 3 And Abram fell upon his face, and God spoke to him, saying, 4 And I, behold, My covenant *is* with thee, and thou shall be a father of a multitude of nations. 5 And thy name shall no more be called Abram, but thy name shall be Abraham, for I have made thee a father of many nations. 6 And I will increase thee very exceedingly, and I will make nations of thee, and kings shall come out of thee. * 7 And I will establish My covenant between thee and thy seed after thee, to their generations, for an everlasting covenant, to be thy God, and of thy seed after thee.

Genesis 17

8 And I will give to thee and to thy seed after thee the land wherein thou wandered, even all the land of Canaan for an everlasting possession, and I will be to them a God. 9 And God said to Abraham, Thou also should fully keep My covenant, thou and thy seed after thee for their generations. 10 And this covenant which thou shall fully keep between you and me and between thy seed after thee for their generations, every male of you shall be circumcised. 11 And ye shall be circumcised in the flesh of your foreskin, and it shall be for a sign of a covenant between Me and you. 12 And the *newborn* child of eight days shall be circumcised by you, every male throughout your generations, and born in the house and he that is bought with money, of every son of a stranger, who is not of thy seed. 13 He that is born in thy house, and he that is bought with money shall be surely circumcised, and My covenant shall be on your flesh for an everlasting covenant. 14 And the uncircumcised male, who shall not be circumcised in the flesh of his foreskin on the eighth day, that soul shall be destroyed from its family, for he has broken My covenant.

15 And * God said to Abraham, Sara thy wife--her name shall not be called Sara, *but* Sarah shall be her name. 16 And I will bless her, and give thee a son of her, and I will bless him and he shall become nations, and kings of nations shall be of him. 17 And Abraham fell upon his face, and laughed; and spoke in his heart, saying, Shall there be a son to one who is a hundred years old, and shall Sarah who is ninety years old, bear? 18 Abraham said to God Let this Ishmael live before thee. 19 God said to Abraham, Yea behold, Sarah thy wife shall bear thee a son, and thou shall call his name Isaac; and I will establish my covenant with him, for an everlasting covenant, to be a God to him and to his seed after him. 20 And concerning Ishmael, behold, I have heard thee and, behold, I have blessed him, and will increase him and multiply him exceedingly; twelve nations shall he beget, and I will make him a great nation. 21 But I will establish My covenant with Isaac, whom Sarah shall bear to thee at this time, in the next year. 22 And be left off speaking with him, and God went up from Abraham.

23 And Abraham took Ishmael his son, and all his home born *slaves*, and all those bought with money, and every male of the men in the house of Abraham, and he circumcised their foreskins in the time of that day according as God spoke to him. 24 And Abraham was ninety-nine years old, when he was circumcised in the flesh of his foreskin. 25 Ishmael his son was thirteen years old when he was circumcised in the flesh of his foreskin.

---

* The scripture reading in the *Greek Menaion* and *Prophetologion* for the reading of vespers for January is somewhat complex than what is present in the biblical text as published by the Apostoliki Diakonia and the Zoe Brotherhood. In particular, verse 3 is made to follow verse 7, and verse 3 reads: "And Abraham fell upon his face, and he worshipped the Lord."

Genesis 18

26 And at the period of that day, Abraham was circumcised, and Ishmael his son, 27 and all the men of his house, both those born in the house, and those bought with money of foreign nations, he circumcised them.

* The June vesper reading from the *Greek Menaion* and *Prohetologion* for Genesis Chapter Seventeen, verse fifteen reads: "The Lord God".

Chapter 18

Now God appeared to him by the Oak of Mambre, as he sat by the door of his tent at noon. 2 And he lifted up his eyes and beheld and lo! Three men stood before him; and having seen them he ran to meet them from the door of his tent, and did obeisance to the ground. 3 And he said, Lord, if indeed I have found grace in thy sight, pass not by thy servant. 4 Let water now be brought, and let them wash your feet, and do ye refresh under the tree.

5 And I will bring bread, and ye shall eat, and after this ye shall depart on your journey, on account of which ye have turned aside to your servant. And they said, So do, as thou hast said. 6 And Abraham hasted to the tent to Sarah, and said to her, Hasten, and knead three measures of fine flour, and make *bread* loaves baked in ashes. 7 And Abraham ran to the herd, and took a young calf, tender and good, and gave it to his slave, and he hasted to dress it. 8 And he took butter and milk, and the calf, which he had dressed and he set it before them, and they did eat, and he stood by them under the tree.

9 And he said to him, Where is Sarah thy wife? And he answered and said, Behold, in the tent. 10 And he said, I will return and come to thee according to this period seasonably, and Sarah thy wife shall have a son; and Sarah heard at the door of the tent, being behind him. 11 And Abraham and Sarah were old, advanced in days, and the custom of women ceased with Sarah. 12 And Sarah laughed in herself, saying, This thing has not as yet happened to me, even until now, and my lord is old. 13 And the * Lord said to Abraham, Why is it that Sarah has laughed in herself, saying, Shall I then truly bear? I am grown old. 14 Shall anything be impossible with God? At this time I will return to thee seasonably, and Sarah shall have a son. 15 But Sarah denied, saying, I did not laugh, for she was afraid. And he said to her, Nay, but thou did laugh.

16 And the men having risen up from thence looked towards Sodom and Gomorrah. And Abraham went with them, attending them on their journey. 17 And the Lord said Should I hide from Abraham My servant what things I intend to do? 18 Abraham shall become a great and populous nation, and in him shall all the nations of the earth be blessed. 19 For I know that he will order his sons, and his house after him, and they will keep the ways of the Lord, to do justice

Genesis 19

* The June vesper reading from the *Greek Menaion* and *Prohetologion* for Genesis Chapter Eighteen, verse thirteen reads: "the Lord God".

and judgment, that the Lord may bring upon Abraham all things whatever he has spoken to him. 20 And the Lord said, The cry of Sodom and Gomorrah has been increased towards me, and their sins are very great. 21 I will therefore go down and see, if they completely correspond with the cry, which comes to me, and if not, that I may know. 22 And the men having departed thence came to Sodom. Abraham was still standing before the Lord. 23 And Abraham drew near and said, Would thou destroy the righteous with the wicked and shall the righteous be as the wicked? 24 If there be fifty righteous in the city, will, thou destroy them? Will thou not spare the whole place for the sake of the fifty righteous, if they be in it? 25 By no means shall thou do as this thing so as to destroy the righteous with the wicked, so the righteous shall be as the wicked: by no means. Thou that judges the whole earth, shall thou not do right? 26 And the Lord said, If there should be in Sodom fifty righteous in the city, I would spare the whole city and the whole place for their sakes. 27 And Abraham answered and said; Now I have begun to speak to my Lord, and I am earth and ashes.

28 But if the fifty righteous should be diminished to forty-five, will thou destroy the whole city because of the five? And he said, I will not destroy it, if I should find there forty-five. 29 And he continued to speak to him still, and said, But if there should be found there forty? And he said, I will not destroy it for the forty's sake. 30 And he said, will there be anything Lord, if I speak? If there be found there thirty? And he said, I will not destroy it for the thirty's sake. 31 And he said, Since I am able to speak to the Lord, what if there should be found there twenty? And he said, I will not destroy it, if I should find there twenty. 32 And he said, Will there be anything, Lord, if I speak yet once *more*? If there should be found there ten? And he said, I will not destroy it for the ten's sake. 33 And the Lord departed when he left off speaking to Abraham, and Abraham returned to his place.

Chapter 19

Now the two angels came to Sodom at evening. And Lot sat by the gate of Sodom, and Lot having seen them, rose up to meet them, and he worshipped with his face to the ground, and said, 2 Behold, lords, turn aside to the house of your servant, and rest from your journey, and wash your feet, and having risen early in the morning ye shall depart on your journey. And they said, Nay, but we will lodge in the street. 3 And he constrained them, and they turned aside to him, and they entered into his house, and he made a feast for them, and baked unleavened loaves for them, and they did eat.

Genesis 19

4 However, before they went to sleep, the men of the city, the Sodomites, encircled the house, both young and old, all the people together. 5 And they called out Lot, and said to him, Where are the men that went in to thee this night? Bring them out to us that we may have relations with them. 6 And Lot went out to them to the doorway, and he shut the door behind him. 7 And said to them, By no means, brothers, do not act wickedly. 8 I have two daughters, who have not known a man. I will bring them out to you, and do ye use them as it may please you, only do no injury to these men, to avoid *this*, which they came under the shelter of my roof. 9 And they said to him, Stand back there, thou came to live as a foreigner, was it also to judge? Now then we would harm thee more than them. And they pressed hard on the man, even Lot, and they drew near to break the door.

10 And the men stretched forth their hands and drew Lot in to them into the house, and shut the door of the house. 11 And they struck the men that were at the door of the house with blindness, both small and great, and they were wearied with seeking the door. 12 And the men said to Lot, Has thou here sons-in-law or sons or daughters, or if thou has any one else in the city, bring them out of this place. 13 For we are going to destroy this place; for their cry has been raised up before the Lord, and the Lord has sent us to destroy it.

14 And Lot went out, and spoke to his sons-in-law who had married his daughters, and said, Rise up, and depart out of this place, for the Lord is about to destroy the city; but he seemed to be speaking absurdly before his sons-in-law. 15 But when it was morning, the angels hastened Lot, saying, Arise and take thy wife, and thy two daughters whom thou have, and go forth; lest thou also be destroyed with the iniquities of the city. 16 And they were troubled, and the angels laid hold on his hand, and the hand of his wife, and the hands of his two daughters, in that the Lord spared him. 17 And it came to pass in the morning when they brought them out, that they said, Save thine own soul by all means; look not around to that which is behind, nor stay in all the country around, escape to the mountain, lest perhaps thou be overtaken. 18 And Lot said to them, I pray, Lord, 19 since thy servant has found mercy before thee, and thou has magnified thy righteousness, in what thou does towards me that my soul may live, but I shall not be able to escape to the mountain, lest perhaps the calamity overtake me and I die. 20 Behold, this city is near for me to escape thither, which is a small one, and there shall I be preserved, is it not little? And my soul shall live because of thee. 21 And he said to him, Behold, I have had respect to thee also about this thing that I should not overthrow the city about which thou hast spoken. 22 Hasten therefore to escape thither, for I shall not be able to do anything until thou art come thither; therefore he called the name of that city, Segor. 23 The sun was raised upon the earth, when Lot entered into Segor.

24 And the Lord rained on Sodom and Gomorrah brimstone and fire from the Lord out of heaven. 25 And He destroyed these cities, and all the country around, and all that lived in the cities, and the plants of the ground. 26 And his wife looked back, and she became a pillar of salt. 27 And Abraham rose up early to go to the place, where he had stood before the Lord. 28 And he looked towards Sodom and Gomorrah, and towards the surrounding country, and saw, and behold a flame went up from the earth, as the smoke of a furnace. 29 And it came to pass that when God raised all the cities of the region around, God remembered Abraham, and sent Lot out of the midst of the destruction, when the Lord destroyed these cities in which Lot lived.

30 And Lot went up out of Segor, and lived in the mountain, he and his two daughters with him, for he feared to live in Segor; and he lived in a cave, he and his two daughters with him.31 And the elder said to the younger, Our father is old, and there is no one on the earth who shall come in to us, as it is fit in all the earth. 32 Come and let us make our father drink *wine*, and let us sleep with him, and let us raise up seed from our father. 33 So they made their father drink *wine* that night, and the older daughter went in and lay with her father that night, and he knew nothing when he slept and when he rose up. 34 And it came to pass on the next day that the older daughter said to the younger daughter, Behold I slept last night with our father, let us make him drink *wine* in this night also and do thou go in and sleep with him and let us raise up seed of our father.

35 So they made their father drink *wine* in that night also, and the younger daughter went in and slept with her father, and he knew nothing when he slept, nor when he arose. 36 And the two daughters of Lot conceived by their father. 37 And the older daughter bore a son, and called his name Moab, saying, From my father. This is the father of the Moabites to this present day. 38 And the younger daughter also bore a son, and called his name Amman, saying, The son of my family. This is the father of the Ammanites to this present day.

Chapter 20

And Abraham traveled towards to the southern country, and lived between Kades and between Sur, and traveled in Gerara. 2 And Abraham said concerning Sarah his wife, She is my sister for he feared to say, She is my wife, lest at any time the men of the city should kill him for her sake. So Abimelek king of Gerara sent and took Sarah. 3 And God came to Abimelek by night in sleep, and said, Behold, thou will die for the woman, whom thou has taken, whereas she is married to a man. 4 But Abimelek had not touched her, and he said, Lord will thou destroy an ignorant and just nation?

Genesis 21

5 Said he not to me, She is my sister, and said she not to me, He is my brother? With a pure heart and in the righteousness of my hands I did this. 6 And God said to him in sleep, Yea, I knew that thou did this with a pure heart, and I spared thee, so that thou should not sin against me, therefore I suffered thee not to touch her.

7 But now return the man his wife; for he is a prophet, and shall pray for thee, and thou shall live; but if thou restore her not, know that thou shall die and all thine. 8 And Abimelek rose in the morning, and called all his slaves, and he spoke all these things in their ears, and all the men feared exceedingly. 9 And Abimelek called Abraham and said to him, What is this that thou have done to us? Have we sinned against thee, that thou has brought upon me and upon my kingdom a great sin? Thou have done to me a deed, which no one ought to do. 10 And Abimelek said to Abraham, What have thou seen in that thou has done this? 11 And Abraham said, Why I said, Surely there is not the worship of God in this place, and they will slay me because of my wife. 12 For truly she is my sister by my father, but not by my mother, and she became my wife. 13 And it came to pass when God brought me forth out of the house of my father, that I said to her, This righteousness thou shall perform to me, in every place into which we may enter, say of me, He is my brother.

14 And Abimelek took a thousand pieces of silver, and sheep, and calves and male slaves, and female servants, and gave them to Abraham, and he returned him Sarah his wife. 15 And Abimelek said to Abraham, Behold, my land is before thee, dwell wherever it may please thee. 16 And to Sarah he said, Behold, I have given thy brother a thousand pieces of silver, those shall be to thee for the price of thy countenance, and to all the women with thee, and speak the truth in all things. 17 And Abraham prayed to God, and God healed Abimelek, and his wife, and his female slaves, and they bore children. 18 Because the Lord had quickly closed from without every womb in the house of Abimelek, because of Sarah, Abraham's wife.

Chapter 21

And the Lord visited Sarah, as He said, and the Lord did to Sarah, as he spoke. 2 And she conceived and bore to Abraham a son in old age, at the set time according as the Lord spoke to him. 3 And Abraham called the name of his son that was born to him whom Sarah bore to him, Isaac. 4 And Abraham circumcised Isaac on the eighth day, as * God commanded him. 5 And Abraham was a hundred years old when Isaac his son was born to him. 6 Sarah said, The Lord has made laughter for me, for whoever shall hear shall rejoice with me. 7 And she said, Who shall say to Abraham that Sarah suckles a child? For I have born a child in my old age.

Genesis 21

* The June vesper reading from the *Greek Menaion* and *Prohetologion* for Genesis Chapter Twenty-One, verse four reads: "the Lord God".

8 And the child grew and was weaned, and Abraham made a great feast the day that his son Isaac was weaned. 9 And Sarah, having seen the son of Agar the Egyptian who was born to Abraham, playing with Isaac her son, 10 she said to Abraham, Cast out this female slave and her son, for the son of this female slave shall not inherit together with my son Isaac. 11 But the matter appeared very hard in the sight of Abraham concerning his son. 12 God said to Abraham, Let it not be hard in thy sight concerning the child, and concerning the female slave; in all things whatever Sarah shall say to thee hear her voice for in Isaac shall thy seed be named for thee. 13 And moreover I will make the son of this female slave a great nation, because he is thy seed. 14 And Abraham rose up in the morning and took *bread* loaves and a skin of water, and gave *them* to Agar, and he put the child on her shoulder, and sent her away, and she having departed wandered in the wilderness near the Well of the Oath. 15 And the water fell out of the skin, and she cast the child under a fir tree. 16 And after departing she sat down opposite him at a distance, as it were a bow-shot, for she said, Surely I cannot see the death of my child: and she sat opposite him, and the child cried aloud and wept.

17 And God heard the voice of the child from the place where he was, and an angel of God called *to* Agar out of heaven, and said to her, What is it, Agar? Fear not, for God has heard the voice of the child from the place where he is. 18 Rise up, and take the child, and hold him in thine hand, for I will make him a great nation. 19 And God opened her eyes, and she saw a well of springing water; and she went and filled the skin with water, and gave the child drink. 20 And God was with the child. And he grew and lived in the wilderness, and became an archer. 21 And he lived in the wilderness of Pharan, and his mother took him a wife out of the land of Egypt.

22 And it came to pass at that time that Abimelek spoke, and Ochozath his groomsman, and Phihol the commander-in-chief of his army, to Abraham, saying, God is with thee in all things, whatever thou may do. 23 Now therefore swear to me by God that thou will not injure me, or my seed, or my name, but according to the righteousness, which have performed with thee thou shall deal with me, and with the land in which thou has traveled. 24 And Abraham said, I will swear. 25 And Abraham reproved Abimelek because of the wells of water, which the slaves of Abimelek took away. 26 And Abimelek said to him, I know not who has done this thing to thee neither did thou tell it to me, neither heard I it but only today. 27 And Abraham took sheep and calves, and gave them to Abimelek, and both made a covenant. 28 And Abraham set seven ewe-lambs by themselves.

Genesis 22

29 And Abimelek said to Abraham, Why are these seven ewe-lambs, of the sheepfold, that thou have set to stand alone? 30 And Abraham said, Thou shall receive the seven ewe-lambs of me, that they may be for me as a witness, that I dug this well. 31 Therefore he named the name of that place, The Well of the Oath, for there they both swore an oath. 32 And they made a covenant at the well of the oath. And there rose up Abimelek, Ochozath his groomsman, and Phihol the commander-in-chief of his army, and they returned to the land of the Philistines. 33 And Abraham planted a ploughed field at the Well of the Oath, and called there on the name of the Lord, the everlasting God. 34 *And* Abraham traveled in the land of the Philistines many days.

Chapter 22

And it came to pass after these things that God tempted Abraham, and said to him, Abraham, Abraham; and he said, Behold! I am. 2 And he said, Take thy son, thy beloved whom thou have loved -- Isaac, and go into the high land, and offer him there for a whole burnt offering on one of the mountains which I will tell thee of.

3 And Abraham rose up in the morning and saddled his mule, and he took with him two slaves, and Isaac his son, and having split wood for a whole burnt offering, he arose and departed, and came to the place of which God spoke to him, on the third day. 4 and Abraham having looked up with his eyes, he saw the place afar off. 5 And Abraham said to his slaves, Sit ye here with the mule, and the child and I will proceed thus far, and having worshipped we will return to you. 6 And Abraham took the wood of the whole burnt offering, and laid it on Isaac his son, and he took into his hands both the fire and the knife, and the two went together. 7 And Isaac said to Abraham his father, Father. He said, What is it, son? And he said, Behold the fire and the wood, where is the sheep for a whole burnt offering? 8 Abraham said, God will provide himself a sheep for a whole burnt offering, *my* child. And both having walked on together, 9 came to the place which God spoke of to him and there Abraham built the altar and laid the wood on it, and having bound the feet of Isaac his son together, he laid him on the altar upon the wood. 10 And Abraham stretched forth his hand to take the knife to kill his son. 11 And an angel of the Lord called *to* him out of heaven, and said Abraham, Abraham. And he said, Behold, I am. 12 And he said, Lay not thine hand upon the child, neither do anything to him, for now I know that thou fears God, and for My sake thou has not spared thy beloved son. 13 And Abraham looked up with his eyes and beheld, and lo! A ram caught by his horns in a plant of Sabek; and Abraham went and took the ram, and offered him up for a whole burnt offering in the place of Isaac his son.

14 And Abraham called the name of that place, The Lord Hath Seen; that they might say today; on the mountain the Lord was seen. 15 And an angel of the Lord called to Abraham a second time out of heaven, saying, 16 I have sworn by myself, says the Lord, because thou has done this thing, and on my account has not spared thy beloved son, 17 surely blessings I will bless thee, and multiplying I will multiply thy seed as the stars of heaven, and as the sand which is by the shore of the sea, and thy seed shall inherit the cities of their enemies. 18 And in thy seed shall all the nations of the earth be blessed, because thou have hearkened to my voice. 19 Abraham returned to his slaves, and when they arose they went together to the Well of the Oath. And Abraham lived at the Well of the Oath.

20 And it came to pass after these things, that it was reported to Abraham, saying, Behold, Melha herself too has born sons to Nahor thy brother, 21 Uz the firstborn, and Baux his brother, and Kamuel the father of the Syrians, 22 and Hazad, and Azav and Phaldes, and Jeldaph, and Bathuel, 23 Bathuel begot Rebecca; these are eight sons, which Melha bore to Nahor the brother of Abraham. 24 And his concubine whose name was Rheuma, she also bore Tabek and Taam, and Tohos, and Moha.

Chapter 23

And the life of Sarah was an hundred and twenty-seven years. 2 And Sarah died in the city of Arbok, which is in the valley, (this is Hebron) in the land of Canaan. Abraham came to lament for Sarah and to mourn. 3 And Abraham stood up from before his dead; and Abraham spoke to the sons of Het, saying, 4 I am a traveler and a stranger among you, give me therefore possession of a burial place among you, and I will bury my dead away from me. 5 And the sons of Het answered to Abraham, saying, Not so, lord, 6 but hear us; thou art in the midst of us a king from God; bury thy dead in our choice sepulchers, for not one of us will by any means withhold his sepulcher from thee, so that thou should not bury thy dead there. 7 And Abraham rose up and did obeisance to the people of the land, to the sons of Het. 8 And Abraham spoke to them, saying, If ye have it in your soul that I should bury my dead far from my presence, hearken to me, and speak for me to Ephron the son of Saar. 9 And let him give me the double cave which he has, which is in a part of his field, let him give it *to* me for the money it is worth for possession of a burial place among you. 10 Now Ephron was sitting in the midst of the sons of Het, and Ephron the Hittite answered Abraham and spoke in the hearing of the sons of Het, and of all who entered the city, saying, 11 Attend to me, my lord, and hear me, I give to thee the field and the cave which is in it; I have given it *to* thee before all my countrymen; bury thy dead.

Genesis 24

12 And Abraham did obeisance before the people of the land. 13 And he said to Ephron in the hearing of the people of the land, Since thou art in my presence, hear me, take the price of the field from me, and I will bury my dead there.

14 But Ephron answered Abraham, saying, 15 Nay, my lord, I have heard indeed, the land *is worth* four hundred silver didrachms, but what can this be between me and thee? Nay, do thou bury thy dead. 16 And Abraham hearkened to Ephron, and Abraham rendered to Ephron the money, which he mentioned in the ears of the sons of Het, four hundred didrachms of silver approved with merchants.

17 And the field of Ephron, which was at the Double Cave, which is opposite Mambre, the field and the cave, which was in it, and every tree which was in the field, and whatever is in its borders around, were made sure 18 to Abraham for a possession, before the sons of Het, and all that entered into the city. 19 After this Abraham buried Sarah his wife in the Double Cave of the field, which is opposite Mambre, (this is Hebron) in the land of Canaan. 20 So the field and the cave, which was in it, were made sure to Abraham for possession of a burial place, by the sons of Het.

Chapter 24

And Abraham was old, advanced in days; and the Lord blessed Abraham in all things. 2 And Abraham said to his slave, the elder of his house, who had rule over all his possessions, Put thy hand under my thigh, 3 and I will adjure thee by the Lord the God of heaven, and the God of the earth, that thou take not a wife for my son Isaac from the daughters of the Canaanites, with whom I live, in the midst of them. 4 But thou shall go to my country where I was born, and to my tribe, and thou shall take from thence a wife for my son Isaac. 5 And the slave said to him, Should I carry back thy son to the land whence thou came forth, if happily the woman should not be willing to return with me to this land? 6 Abraham said to him, Take heed to thyself that thou carry not my son back thither. 7 The Lord God of heaven, and the God of the earth, who took me out of my father's house, and out of the land whence I was born, who spoke to me, and who swore to me, saying, I will give this land to thee and to thy seed, he shall send his angel before thee, and thou shall take a wife to my son from thence. 8 And if the woman should not be willing to come with thee into this land, thou shall be cleared from my oath, only carry not my son thither again. 9 And the slave put his hand under the thigh of his master Abraham, and swore to him concerning this matter.

Genesis 24

10 And the servant took ten camels of his lord's camels, and of all the goods of his lord with him, and he arose and went into Mesopotamia to the city of Nahor. 11 And he allowed the camels to sleep outside the city by the well of water towards evening, when the maidens who draw water go out. 12 And he said, O Lord God of my lord Abraham, prosper my way before me today, and deal mercifully with my lord Abraham. 13 Behold, I stand by the well of water, and the daughters of them that inhabit the city come out to draw water. 14 And it shall be, the virgin to whomever I shall say, Incline thy water-pot, that I may drink, and she shall say, Drink thou, and I will give thy camels drink, until they shall have done drinking -- even this one thou has prepared for thy servant Isaac, and hereby shall I know that thou has dealt mercifully with my lord Abraham.

15 And it came to pass before he had done speaking in his mind, that behold, Rebecca the daughter of Bathuel, the son of Melha, the wife of Nahor, and the brother of Abraham came out, having a water-pot on her shoulders. 16 And the virgin was very beautiful in appearance, she was a virgin, a man had not known her; and she went down to the well, and filled her water-pot, and came up. 17 And the slave ran up to meet her, and said, Give me a little water to drink out of thy pitcher. 18 and she said, Drink, lord; and she hasted, and let down the pitcher upon her arm, and gave him to drink, till he ceased drinking. 19 And she said, I will also draw water for thy camels, till they shall all have drunk. 20 And she hasted, and emptied the water-pot into the trough, and ran to the well to draw again, and drew water for all the camels. 21 And the man took great notice of her, and remained silent to know whether the Lord had made his way prosperous or not. 22 And it came to pass when all the camels ceased drinking, that the man took golden earrings, each of a drachma weight, and he *put* two bracelets on her hands, their weight was ten pieces of gold. 23 And he asked her, and said, Whose daughter art thou? Tell me if there is room for us to lodge with thy father. 24 And she said to him I am the daughter of Bathuel the son of Melha, whom she bore to Nahor. 25 And she said to him, We have both straw and much provender, and a place for resting. 26 And the man being well pleased, worshipped the Lord, and said 27 Blessed be the Lord God of my lord Abraham, who has not suffered his righteousness to fail, nor his truth from my lord and the Lord has brought me prosperous to the house of the brother of my lord.

28 And the maiden ran and reported to the house of her mother according to these words. 29 And Rebecca had a brother whose name was Laban; and Laban ran out to meet the man, at the well. 30 And it came to pass when he saw the ear-rings and the bracelets on the hands of his sister, and when he heard the words of Rebecca his sister, saying, Thus the man spoke to me, that he went to the man, as he stood by the camels at the well.

Genesis 24

31 And he said to him, Come in hither, thou blessed of the Lord, why stand thou outside, whereas I have prepared the house and a place for the camels? 32 And the man entered into the house, and unloaded the camels, and gave the camels straw and provender, and water to wash his feet, and the feet of the men that were with him. 33 And he set before them bread to eat; but be said, I will not eat, until I have spoken my words. And he said, Speak.

34 And he said, I am a slave of Abraham. 35 and the Lord has blessed my lord greatly, and he is exalted, and he has given him sheep, and calves, and silver, and gold, servants and male slaves and female slaves, camels, and asses. 36 And Sarah my lord's wife bore one son to my lord after he had grown old; and be gave him whatever he had.

37 And my lord caused me to swear, saying, Thou shall not take a wife to my son of the daughters of the Canaanites, among whom I travel in their land. 38 But thou shall go to the house of my father, and to my tribe, and thou shall take thence a wife for my son. 39 And I said to my lord, Happily the woman will not go with me. 40 And he said to me, The Lord God, to whom I have been acceptable in his presence, he shall send out his angel with thee, and shall prosper thy journey, and thou shall take a wife for my son of my tribe, and of the house of my father. 41 Then shall thou be cleared from my curse, for whenever thou shall have come to my tribe, and they shall not give her to thee, then shall thou be cleared from my oath. 42 And having come this day to the well, I said, Lord God of my lord Abraham, if thou prosper my journey on which I am now going, 43 behold, I stand by the well of water, and the daughters of the men of the city come forth to draw water, and it shall be the maiden to whom I shall say, Give me a little water to drink out of thy pitcher, 44 and she shall say to me, Both drink thou, and I will draw water for thy camels, this *shall be* the wife whom the Lord has prepared for his own servant Isaac; and hereby shall I know that thou has wrought mercy with my lord Abraham. 45 And it came to pass before I had done speaking in my mind, straightway Rebecca came forth having her pitcher on her shoulders; and she went down to the well, and drew water and I said to her, Give me to drink. 46 And she hasted and let down the pitcher from herself, and said, Drink thou and I will give thy camels drink; and I drank, and she gave the camels drink. 47 And I asked her, and said, Whose daughter art thou? Tell me; and she said, I am daughter of Bathuel the son of Nahor, whom Melha bore to him; and I put on her the earrings, and the bracelets on her hands. 48 And being well pleased I worshipped the Lord, and I blessed the Lord God of my lord Abraham, who has prospered me in a true way, so that I should take the daughter of my lord's brother for his son. 49 If then ye deal mercifully and justly with my lord, and if not, tell me, that I may turn to the right or to the left.

50 Laban and Bathuel answered and said, This matter has come forth from the Lord; we shall not be able to answer thee bad or good. 51 Behold, Rebecca is before thee, take her and run away, and let her be *a* wife to the son of thy lord, as the Lord has said. 52 And it came to pass when the slave of Abraham heard these words; he bowed himself to the Lord down to the earth. 53 And the slave having brought forth jewels of silver and gold and raiment, gave them to Rebecca, and gave gifts to her brother, and to her mother. 54 And both he and the men with him ate and drank and went to sleep. And he arose in the morning and said, Send me away, that I may go to my lord. 55 And her brethren and her mother said, Let the virgin remain with us about ten days, and after that she shall depart. 56 But he said to them, Hinder me not, for the Lord has prospered my journey for me; send me away, that I may depart to my lord. 57 And they said, Let us call the lady, and enquire what she says.

58 And they called Rebecca, and said to her, Will thou go with this man? And she said, I will go. 59 So they sent forth Rebecca their sister, and her goods, and the slave of Abraham and his attendants. 60 And they blessed Rebecca, and said to her, thou art our sister; become thou thousands of myriads, and let thy seed possess the cities of their enemies. 61 And Rebecca rose up and her maidens, and they mounted the camels and went with the man; and the slave having taken up Rebecca, departed. 62 And Isaac went through the wilderness to the well of the vision, and he lived in the land toward the south. 63 And Isaac went forth into the plain toward evening to contemplate and having lifted up his eyes he saw camels coming. 64 And Rebecca lifted up her eyes, and saw Isaac; and she alighted briskly from the camel. 65 and said to the slave, Who is that man that walks in the plain to meet us? And the slave said, This is my lord; and she took her veil and covered herself. 66 And the slave told Isaac all the things he had done. 67 And Isaac went into the house of his mother, and took Rebecca, and she became his wife, and he loved her; and Isaac was comforted for Sarah his mother.

Chapter 25

And Abraham again took a wife, whose name was Hettura. 2 And she bore to him Zombran, and Jezan, and Madal, and Madiam, and Jesboc, and Soke. 3 And Jezan begot Saba and Dedan. And the sons of Dedan were the Assurians and the Latusians, and Laomim. 4 And the sons of Madiam *were* Gephar and Aphir, and Enoch, and Abeida, and Eldaga; all these were sons of Hettura.

5 But Abraham gave all his possessions to Isaac his son. 6 But to the sons of his concubines Abraham gave gifts, and he sent them away from his son Isaac, while he was yet living to the east into the country of the east.

Genesis 25

7 And these were the years of the days of the life of Abraham as many as he lived a hundred and seventy-five years. 8 And a failing Abraham died in a good old age, an old man and full of days, and was added to his people. 9 And Isaac and Ishmael his sons buried him in the double cave, in the field of Ephron the son of Saar the Hittite, which is over against Mambre. 10 The field and the cave which Abraham bought from the sons of Chet; there they buried Abraham and Sarah his wife. 11 And it came to pass after Abraham was dead that God blessed Isaac his son, and Isaac dwelt by the well of the vision. 12 And these are the generations of Ishmael the son of Abraham, whom Agar the Egyptian the slave of Sarah bore to Abraham. 13 And these *are* the names of the sons of Ishmael, according to the names of their generations. The firstborn of Ishmael *are*, Nabaioth, and Kedar, and Nabdeel and Massam, 14 and Masma, and Duma, and Masse, 15 and Hoddan, and Thaeman, and Jetur and Naphes, and Kedma.

16 These are the sons of Ishmael, and these are their names in their tents and in their dwellings, twelve rulers according to their nations. 17 And these are the years of the life of Ishmael a hundred and thirty-seven years; and he failed and died, and was added to his kindred. 18 And he lived from Evilat to Sur, which is opposite Egypt, until one comes to the Assyrians; he lived in the presence of all his brothers.

19 And these are the generations of Isaac the son of Abraham. 20 Abraham begot Isaac. And Isaac was forty years old when he took Rebecca, daughter of Bathuel the Syrian, out of Mesopotamia Syria, sister of Laban the Syrian, as his wife. 21 And Isaac prayed the Lord concerning Rebecca his wife, because she was barren; and the Lord heard him, and his wife Rebecca conceived in her womb. 22 And the babies leaped within her; and she said, If it will be so with me, why is this to me? And she went to enquire of the Lord. 23 And the Lord said to her, There are two nations in thy womb and two peoples shall be separated from thy belly, and one people shall excel the other, and the greater shall serve the lesser. 24 And the days were fulfilled that she should be delivering, and she had twins in her womb. 25 And the first came out red, hairy all over like a skin; and she called his name Esau. 26 And after this came forth his brother, and his hand took hold of the heel of Esau; and she called his name Jacob. And Isaac was sixty years old when Rebecca bore them.

27 And the lads grew, and Esau was a man skilled in hunting, living in the country, and Jacob a simple man, living in a house. 28 And Isaac loved Esau, because his venison was his food, but Rebecca loved Jacob. 29 And Jacob cooked pottage, and Esau came from the plain, fainting. 30 And Esau said to Jacob, Let me taste of that red pottage because I am fainting; therefore his name was called Edom. 31 And Jacob said to Esau, Sell me this day thy birthright. 32 And Esau said, Behold, I am going to die, and for what good does this birthright to me?

33 And Jacob said to him, Swear to me this day and he swore to him; and Esau sold his birthright to Jacob. 34 And Jacob gave bread to Esau, and pottage of lentils; and he ate and drank, and he arose and departed; so Esau slighted his birthright.

Chapter 26

And there was a famine in the land, besides the former famine, which was in the time of Abraham; and Isaac went to Abimelek the king of the Philistines to Gerara. 2 And the Lord appeared to him and said, Go not down to Egypt but live in the land, which I shall tell thee of. 3 And travel in this land; and I will be with thee, and bless thee, for I will give to thee and to thy seed all this land; and I will establish my oath, which I swore to thy father Abraham.

4 And I will multiply thy seed as the stars of heaven and I will give to thy seed all this land, and all the nations of the earth shall be blessed in thy seed. 5 Because Abraham thy father hearkened to my voice, and kept my injunctions, and my commandments, and my ordinances, and my statutes. 6 And Isaac lived in Gerara. 7 And the men of the place questioned him concerning Rebecca his wife, and he said, She is my sister, for he feared to say, She is my wife, lest at any time the men of the place should kill him because of Rebecca, because she was fair in appearance. 8 And he remained there a long time, and Abimelek the king of Gerara leaned to look through the window, and saw Isaac sporting with Rebecca his wife. 9 And Abimelek called Isaac, and said to him, Is she then thy wife? Why has thou said, she is my sister? And Isaac said to him, for I said, Lest at any time I die on her account. 10 And Abimelek said to him, Why has thou done this to us? One of my kindred very nearly lain with thy wife, and thou would have brought ignorance upon us. 11 And Abimelek charged all his people, saying; Every man that touches this man and his wife shall be liable to death. 12 And Isaac sowed in that land, and he found in that year barley a hundred-fold, and the Lord blessed him. 13 And the man was exalted, and advancing he increased, till he became very great.

14 And he had cattle of sheep, and cattle of oxen, and many tilled lands, and the Philistines envied him. 15 And all the wells, which the slaves of his father had dug in the time of his father, the Philistines stopped them, and filled them with earth. 16 Abimelek said to Isaac, Depart from us, for thou art become much mightier than we. 17 And Isaac departed thence, and rested in the valley of Gerara, and lived there. 18 And Isaac dug again the wells of water, which the slaves of his father Abraham had dug, and the Philistines had stopped them, after the death of his father Abraham; and he gave them names according to the names by which his father named them.

Genesis 27

19 And the slaves of Isaac dug in the valley of Gerara, and they found there a well of living water. 20 And the shepherds of Gerara strove with the shepherds of Isaac saying that the water was theirs; and they called the name of the well, Injury, for they injured him. 21 And having departed thence Isaac dug another well, and they strove also for that; and he named the name of it, Enmity. 22 And he departed thence and dug another well; and they did not strive about that; and he named the name of it, Room, saying, Because now the Lord has made room for us, and has increased us upon the earth.

23 And he went up thence to the Well of the Oath. 24 And the Lord appeared to him in that night, and said, I am the God of Abraham thy father; fear not, for I am with thee, and I will bless thee, and multiply thy seed for the sake of Abraham thy father. 25 And he built there an altar, and called on the name of the Lord, and there he pitched his tent, and there the slaves of Isaac dug a well in the valley of Gerara.

26 And Abimelek came to him from Gerara, and so did Ochozath his groomsman and Phihol the commander-in-chief of his army. 27 And Isaac said to them, Wherefore have ye come to me? Whereas ye hated me, and sent me away from you. 28 And they said, We have surely seen that the Lord was with thee, and we said, Let there be an oath between us and thee, and we will make a covenant with thee, 29 that thou shall do no wrong by us, as we have not abhorred thee, and according as we have treated thee well and have sent thee forth peaceably; and now thou art blessed of the Lord. 30 And he made a feast for them, and they ate and drank. 31 And they arose in the morning, and swore each to his neighbor; and Isaac sent them forth, and they departed from him in safety. 32 And it came to pass in that day that the slaves of Isaac came and told him of the well which they had dug; and they said, We have not found water. 33 And he called it, Oath; therefore he called the name of that city, the Well of Oath, until this day. 34 And Esau was forty years old; and he took to wife Judith the daughter of Beoh the Hittite, and Basemath, daughter of Helon the * Hittite. 35 And they were provoking to Isaac and Rebecca.

* *Codex Alexandrinus* reads: "Hivite."

Chapter 27

And it came to pass after Isaac was old, that his eyes were dimmed so that he could not see; and he called Esau, his elder son, and said to him, My son; and he said, Behold, I am. 2 And he said, Behold, I am grown old, and know not my last day. 3 Now then take thy weapons, both thy quiver and thy bow, and go into the plain, and get me venison,

4 and make me meats, as I like them, and bring them to me that I may eat, that my soul may bless thee, before I die. 5 And Rebecca heard Isaac speaking to Esau his son; and Esau went to the plain to procure venison for his father. 6 And Rebecca said to Jacob her younger son, Behold, I heard thy father speaking to Esau thy brother, saying, 7 Bring me venison, and prepare me meats, that I may eat and bless thee before the Lord before I die. 8 Now then my son, hearken to me, as I command thee. 9 And go to the cattle and take for me thence two kids, tender and good, and I will make them meats for thy father, as he likes. 10 And thou shall bring them in to thy father, and he shall eat, that thy father may bless thee before he dies. 11 And Jacob said to his mother Rebecca, Esau my brother is a hairy man, and I a smooth man. 12 Peradventure my father may feel me, and I shall be before him as one ill intentioned, and I shall bring upon me a curse, and not a blessing. 13 And his mother said to him, on me be thy curse, son, only hearken to my voice, and go and bring me.

14 So he went and took and brought them to his mother; and his mother made meats, as his father liked. 15 And Rebecca having taken the fine raiment of her elder son Esau, which was with her in the house, put it on Jacob her younger son. 16 And she put on his arms the skins of the kids, and on the bare parts of his neck. 17 And she gave the meats, and the loaves, which she had prepared, into the hands of Jacob her son. 18 And he brought to his father, and said, Father; and he said, Behold I am here; who art thou, son? 19 And Jacob said to his father, I, Esau thy firstborn, have done as thou told me; rise, sit, and eat of my venison, that thy soul may bless me. 20 Isaac said to his son, what is this, which thou have quickly found? And he said, That which the Lord thy God presented before me. 21 And Isaac said to Jacob, Draw close to me, and I will feel thee, son, if thou art my son Esau or not. 22 And Jacob drew close to his father Isaac, and he felt him, and said, The voice *is* Jacob's voice, but the hands *are* the hands of Esau. 23 And he knew him not, for his hands were as the hands of his brother Esau, hairy; and he blessed him, 24 and he said, Art thou my son Esau? And he said, I *am*. 25 And he said, Bring hither, and I will eat of thy venison, son, that my soul may bless thee; and he brought *it* near to him, and he ate, and he brought him wine, and he drank. 26 And Isaac his father said to him, Draw close to me, and kiss me, son. 27 And he drew close and kissed him, and smelled the smell of his garments, and blessed him, and said, Behold, the smell of my son is as the smell of an abundant field, which the Lord has blessed. 28 And may God give thee of the dew of heaven, and of the fatness of the earth and abundance of corn and wine. 29 And let nations serve thee, and princes bow down to thee, and be thou lord of thy brother, and the sons of thy father shall do thee reverence; accursed is he that curses thee, and blessed is he that blesses thee.

Genesis 27

30 And it came to pass after Isaac had ceased blessing his son Jacob, it even came to pass, just when Jacob had gone out from the presence of Isaac his father, that Esau his brother came in from his hunting. 31 And he also had made meats and brought them to his father; and he said to his father, Let my father arise and eat of his son's venison, that thy soul may bless me. 32 And Isaac his father said to him, Who art thou? And he said, I am thy first-born son Esau. 33 And Isaac was amazed with very great amazement, and said, Who then is it that has procured venison for me and brought it to me? And I have eaten of all before thou came, and I have blessed him, and he shall be blessed. 34 And it came to pass when Esau heard the words of his father Isaac, he cried out with a great and very bitter cry, and said, Bless, I pray thee, me also, father. 35 And he said to him, Thy brother has come with subtlety, and taken thy blessing. 36 And he said, Rightly was his name called Jacob, for behold, this second time has he supplanted me; he has both taken my birthright and now he has taken my blessing; and Esau said to his father, Have thou not left a blessing for me, father?

37 And Isaac answered and said to Esau, If I have made him thy lord, and have made all his brothers his servants, and have strengthened him with corn and wine, what then shall I do for thee, son? 38 And Esau said to his father, Has thou one blessing father? Bless, I pray thee, me also, father. And Isaac cut to the quick, Esau cried aloud and wept. 39 And Isaac his father answered and said to him, Behold, thy dwelling shall be of the fatness of the earth, and of the dew of heaven from above. 40 And thou shall live by thy sword, and shall serve thy brother; and there shall be when thou shall break and loosen his yoke from off thy neck.

41 And Esau was angry with Jacob because of the blessing, with which his father blessed him; and Esau said in his mind, Let the days of my father's mourning draw near, that I may slay my brother Jacob. 42 And the words of Esau her elder son were reported to Rebecca, and she sent and called Jacob her younger son, and said to him, Behold, Esau thy brother threatens thee to kill thee. 43 Now then, my son, hear my voice, and rise and depart quickly into Mesopotamia to Laban my brother into Harran. 44 And live with him certain days 45 until thy brother's anger and rage depart from thee, and he forget what thou has done to him; and I will send and fetch thee thence, lest at any time I should be bereaved of you both in one day.

46 And Rebecca said to Isaac, I am weary of my life, because of the daughters of the sons of Het; if Jacob shall take a wife of the daughters of this land, wherefore should I live?

Chapter 28

And Isaac having called for Jacob, blessed him, and charged him, saying, Thou shall not take a wife of the daughters of the Canaanites. 2 Rise and depart quickly into Mesopotamia, to the house of Bathuel, the father of thy mother, and take to thyself thence a wife of the daughters of Laban thy mother's brother. 3 And may my God bless thee, and increase thee, and multiply thee and thou shall become a gathering of nations; 4 And may he give thee the blessing of my father Abraham, even to thee and to thy seed after thee, to inherit the land of thy traveling, which God gave to Abraham. 5 So Isaac sent Jacob away, and he went into Mesopotamia to Laban the son of Bethuel the Syrian, the brother of Rebecca the mother of Jacob and Esau. 6 And Esau saw that Isaac blessed Jacob, and sent him away to Mesopotamia of Syria as he blessed him, to take to himself a wife thence, and he charged him, saying, Thou shall not take a wife of the daughters of the Canaanites; 7 and Jacob hearkened to his father and his mother, and went to Mesopotamia of Syria. 8 And Esau also having seen that the daughters of Canaan were evil before his father Isaac,

9 Esau went to Ishmael, and took Maeleth the daughter of Ishmael, the son of Abraham, the sister of Nabeoth, a wife in addition to his wives. 10 And Jacob went forth from the Well of the Oath, and departed into Harrhan. 11 And came to a certain place and slept there, for the sun had gone down; and he took of the stones of the place, and put it at his head, and lay down to sleep in that place. 12 And dreamed, and behold a ladder fixed on the earth, whose top reached to heaven, and the angels of God ascended and descended on it. 13 And the Lord was established upon it, and said, I am the God of Abraham thy father, and the God of Isaac; fear not, the land on which thou * sits, to thee will I give it, and to thy seed.

14 And thy seed shall be as the sand of the earth; and it shall spread abroad to the sea, and the south, and the north, and to the east; and in thee and in thy seed shall all the tribes of the earth be blessed. 15 And behold, I am with thee to preserve thee continually in all the way wherein thou shall go; and I will bring thee back to this land for I will not desert thee, until I have done all that I have said to thee. 16 And Jacob awaked out of his sleep, and said, The Lord is in this place, and I knew it not. 17 And he was afraid, and said, How fearful is this place! This is none other than the house of God, and this is the gate of heaven. 18 And Jacob rose up in the morning, and took the stone he placed beneath his head, and he set it up as a pillar, and poured oil on the top of it. 19 And he called the name of that place, the House of God; and the name of the city before was Ulamluz.

Genesis 29

20 And Jacob vowed a vow, saying, If the Lord God will be with me, and guard me throughout on this journey, on which I am going, and give me bread to eat, and raiment to put on, 21 and bring me back in safety to the house of my father, then shall the Lord be for a God to me. 22 And this stone, which I have set up for a pillar, shall be to me a house of God; and of all whatsoever thou shall give me, I will tithe a tenth for thee.

* The March vesper reading from the *Greek Menaion* and *Prohetologion* for Genesis Chapter Twenty-Eight, verse thirteen reads: "sleeps".

Chapter 29

And Jacob having raised his feet, went to the land of the east to Laban, the son of Bathuel the Syrian, and the brother of Rebecca, mother of Jacob and Esau. 2 And he looks, and behold! A well in the plain; and there were there three flocks of sheep resting at it, for out of that well they watered the flocks, but there was a great stone at the mouth of the well. 3 And there were all the flocks gathered, and they used to roll away the stone from the mouth of the well, and water the flocks, and set the stone again in its place on the mouth of the well. 4 And Jacob said to them, Brothers, whence are ye? And they said, We are of Harrhan.

5 And he said to them, Know ye Laban, the son of Nachor? And they said, We do know. 6 And he said to them, Is he well? And they said, He is well. And behold Rachel his daughter came with the sheep. 7 And Jacob said it is yet high day, it is not yet time that the flocks be gathered together; water ye the sheep, and depart and feed them. 8 And they said, We should not be able, until all the shepherds are gathered together, and they shall roll away the stone from the mouth of the well, then we will water the sheep. 9 While he was yet speaking to them, behold, Rachel the daughter of Laban came with her father's sheep, for she fed the sheep of her father.

10 And it came to pass when Jacob saw Rachel the daughter of Laban, his mother's brother, and the sheep of Laban, his mother's brother, that Jacob came and rolled away the stone from the mouth of the well, and watered the sheep of Laban, his mother's brother. 11 And Jacob kissed Rachel, and cried with a loud voice and wept. 12 And he told Rachel that he was the near relative of her father, and the son of Rebecca; and she ran and reported to her father according to these words. 13 And it came to pass when Laban heard the name of Jacob, his sister's son, he ran to meet him, and embraced and kissed him, and brought him into his house; and he told Laban all these sayings. 14 And Laban said to him, Thou art of my bones and of my flesh; and he was with him a month of days.

15 And Laban said to Jacob, Surely thou shall not serve me for nothing, because thou art my brother; tell me what thy reward is to be. 16 Now Laban had two daughters, the name of the elder was Lea, and the name of the younger, Rachel. 17 And the eyes of Lea were weak. But Rachel was beautiful in appearance, and exceedingly fair in countenance. 18 And Jacob loved Rachel, and said I will serve thee seven years for thy younger daughter Rachel. 19 And Laban said to him, better that I should give her to thee, than that I should give her to another man; live with me. 20 And Jacob worked for Rachel seven years, and they were before him as a few days, by reason of his loving her. 21 And Jacob said to Laban, Give me my wife, for my days are fulfilled, that I may go in to her. 22 And Laban gathered together all the men of the place, and made a marriage feast. 23 And it was evening, and he took his daughter Lea, and brought her in to Jacob, and Jacob went in to her. 24 And Laban gave to his daughter Lea, Zelpha his slave, as a slave for her.

25 And it was morning, and behold it was Lea; and Jacob said to Laban, What is this that thou has done to me? Did I not serve thee for Rachel? And wherefore has thou deceived me? 26 And Laban answered, It is not done thus in our country, to give the younger before the elder. 27 Fulfill then her sevens, and I will give to thee her also in return for thy labor, which thou *will* labor with me, yet seven other years. 28 And Jacob did so, and fulfilled her sevens; and Laban gave him his daughter Rachel to wife. 29 And Laban gave to his daughter his slave Balla, for a slave to her.

30 And he went in to Rachel; and he loved Rachel more than Lea; and he worked *for* him seven other years. 31 And when the Lord God saw that Lea was hated, he opened her womb; but Rachel was barren. 32 And Lea conceived and bore a son to Jacob; and she called his name, Ruben; saying, Because the Lord has looked on my humiliation, and has given me a son, now then my husband will love me. 33 And she conceived again, and bore a second son to Jacob; and she said, Because the Lord has heard that I am hated, he has given to me this one also; and she called his name, Simeon. 34 And she conceived yet again, and bore a son, and said, In the present time my husband will be with me, for I have born him three sons; therefore she called his name, Levi. 35 And having conceived yet again, she bore a son, and said, Now yet again this time will I give thanks to the Lord; therefore she called his name, Judah; and ceased bearing.

Chapter 30

And Rachel having perceived that she bore Jacob no children, was jealous of her sister; and said to Jacob, Give me children; and if not, I shall die.

Genesis 30

2 And Jacob was angry with Rachel, and said to her, Am I in the place of God, who has deprived thee of the fruit of the womb? 3 And Rachel said to Jacob, Behold my slave Balla, go in to her, and she shall bear upon my knees, and I also shall have children by her. 4 And she gave him Balla her slave, for a wife to him; and Jacob went in to her. 5 And Balla, Rachel's slave, conceived, and bore Jacob a son. 6 And Rachel said, God has given judgment for me, and hearkened to my voice, and has given me a son; therefore she called his name, Dan. 7 And Balla, Rachel's slave, conceived yet again, and bore a second son to Jacob. 8 And Rachel said, God has helped me, and I contended with my sister and prevailed; and she called his name, Nephthalim.

9 And Lea saw that she ceased from bearing, and she took Zelpha her slave, and gave her to Jacob for a wife; and he went in to her. 10 And Zelpha the slave of Lea conceived, and bore Jacob a son. 11 And Lea said, happily; and she called his name, Gad. 12 And Zelpha the maid of Lea conceived yet again, and bore Jacob a second son. 13 And Lea said, I am blessed, for the women will pronounce me blessed; and she called his name, Aser.

14 And Ruben went in the day of barley-harvest, and found apples of mandrakes in the field, and brought them to his mother Lea; and Rachel said to Lea her sister, Give me of thy son's mandrakes. 15 And Lea said, Not enough for thee that thou hast taken my husband, will thou also take my son's mandrakes? And Rachel said, Not so; let him lie with thee tonight for thy son's mandrakes. 16 And Jacob came in out of the field at evening; and Lea went forth to meet him, and said, Thou shall come in to me this day, for I have hired thee for my son's mandrakes; and he lay with her that night. 17 And God hearkened to Lea, and she conceived, and bore Jacob a fifth son. 18 And Lea said, God has given me my reward, because I gave my slave to my husband; and she called his name Issahar, which is, Reward. 19 And Lea conceived again, and bore Jacob a sixth son. 20 And Lea said, God has given me a good gift in this time; my husband will choose me, for I have born him six sons: and she called his name, Zebulon. 21 And after this she bore a daughter; and she called her name, Dina. 22 And God remembered Rachel, and God hearkened to her, and he opened her womb. 23 And she conceived, and bore Jacob a son; and Rachel said, God has taken away my reproach. 24 And she called his name Joseph, saying, Let God add to me another son.

25 And it came to pass when Rachel had born Joseph, Jacob said to Laban; Send me away, that I may go to my place and to my land. 26 Restore my wives and my children, for whom I have worked *for* thee, that I may depart, for thou knows the work wherewith I have worked *for* thee. 27 And Laban said to him, If I have found grace in thy sight, I would have discerned it by augury, for the Lord has blessed me at thy coming in. 28 Appoint thy wages to me, and I will give them.

29 And Jacob said, Thou know in what things I have worked *for* thee, and how many cattle of thine are with me. 30 For it was little thou had before my time, and it is increased to a multitude, and the Lord God has blessed thee at my foot; now then, when shall I set up also my own house? 31 And Laban said to him, What shall I give thee? And Jacob said to him, Thou should not give me anything; if thou will do this thing for me, I will again tend thy flocks and keep them. 32 Let all thy sheep pass by today, and separate thence every gray sheep among the rams, and every one that is speckled and spotted among the goats -- shall be my reward. 33 And my righteousness shall hear me tomorrow, for it is my reward before thee; whatever shall not be spotted and speckled among the goats, and gray among the rams, shall be taken with me. 34 And Laban said to him, Let it be according to thy word. 35 And he separated in that day the spotted and speckled he-goats, and all the spotted and speckled she-goats, and all that was gray among the rams, and every one that was white among them, and he gave them into the hand of his sons. 36 And he set a distance of a three days' journey between them and between Jacob. And Jacob tended the cattle of Laban that were left behind.

37 And Jacob took to himself green rods of storax tree and walnut and plane-tree; and Jacob peeled in them white stripes; and drawing off the green, the white stripe which he had made appeared alternate on the rods. 38 And he lay the rods, which he had peeled, in the hollows of the watering-troughs, that whenever the cattle should come to drink, as they should have come to drink before the rods, the cattle might conceive at the rods. 39 So the cattle conceived at the rods, and the cattle brought forth speckled, and streaked and spotted with ash-colors. 40 And Jacob separated the lambs, and set before the sheep a speckled ram, and every variegated one among the lambs, and he separated flocks for himself alone, and did not mingle them with the sheep of Laban. 41 And it came to pass in the time wherein the cattle came into yearning, as they were conceiving; Jacob put the rods before the cattle in the troughs that they might come into yearning by the rods. 42 But he did not put them in whenever the cattle happened to bring forth, but the unmarked ones were Laban's, and the marked ones were Jacob's. 43 And the man became very rich, and he had many cattle, and oxen, and male slaves, and female slaves, and camels, and mules.

Chapter 31

And Jacob heard the words of the sons of Laban, saying, Jacob has taken all that was our father's, and of our father's property has he gotten all this glory. 2 And Jacob saw the countenance of Laban, and behold it was not toward him as yesterday and three days *ago*.

Genesis 31

3 And the Lord said to Jacob, Return to the land of thy father, and to thy family, and I will be with thee. 4 And Jacob sent and called Lea and Rachel to the plain where the flocks were. 5 And he said to them, I see the face of your father, which is not toward me as yesterday and three days *ago*, but the God of my father was with me. 6 And ye too know that with all my might I have worked for thy father. 7 But your father deceived me, and changed my wages for the ten lambs, yet God gave him not the authority to hurt me. 8 If he should say thus, The speckled shall be thy reward, then all the cattle would bear speckled; and if he should say, The white shall be thy reward, then would all the cattle bear white. 9 So God has taken away all the cattle of your father, and given them to me. 10 And it came to pass when the cattle conceived and were with young, that I beheld with mine eyes in sleep, and behold the he-goats and the rams leaping on the sheep and the she-goats, speckled and variegated and spotted with ash-colored spots. 11 And the angel of God said to me in *my* sleep, Jacob; and I said, What is it? 12 And he said, Look up with thine eyes, and behold the he-goats and the rams leaping on the sheep and the she-goats, speckled and variegated and spotted with ash-colored spots; for I have seen all things that Laban does to thee. 13 I am God that appeared to thee in the place of God, where thou anointed a pillar to me, and vowed to me there a vow, now then arise and depart out of this land, depart into the land of thy birth, and I will be with thee. 14 And Rachel and Lea answered and said to him, Have we yet a part or inheritance in the house of our father? 15 Are we not considered strangers by him? For he has sold us, and quite devoured our money.

16 All the wealth and the glory which God has taken from our father, it shall be ours and our children's; now then do whatever God has said to thee. 17 And Jacob arose and took his wives and his children up on the camels; 18 and he took away all his possessions and all his store, which he had gotten in Mesopotamia, and all that belonged to him, to depart to Isaac his father in the land of Canaan. 19 And Laban went to shear his sheep; and Rachel stole her father's idols. 20 And Jacob hid *this from* Laban the Syrian, so as not to tell him that he ran away. 21 And he departed himself and all that belonged to him, and passed over the river, and went into the mountain Galaad.

22 But it was told to Laban the Syrian on the third day, that Jacob was fled. 23 And having taken his brethren with him, he pursued after him *for a* seven days' journey, and overtook him on Mount Galaad. 24 And God came to Laban the Syrian in sleep by night, and said to him, Take heed to thyself that thou speak not at any time to Jacob evil things. 25 And Laban overtook Jacob; and Jacob pitched his tent on the mountain; and Laban stationed his brothers on the mountain Galaad. 26 And Laban said to Jacob, What hast thou done? Wherefore did thou run away secretly, and pillage me, and lead away my daughters as captives taken with the sword?

27 Whereas if thou had told me, I would have sent thee away with mirth, and with songs, and cymbals, and harp. 28 And I was not counted worthy to embrace my children and my daughters; now then thou has wrought foolishly. 29 And now my hand has power to hurt thee; but the God of thy father spoke to me yesterday, saying, Take heed to thyself that thou speak not evil words to Jacob. 30 Now then go on thy way, for thou have earnestly desired to depart to the house of thy father; wherefore have thou stolen my gods? 31 And Jacob answered and said to Laban, Because I was afraid for I said, Lest at any time thou should take away thy daughters from me, and all my possessions. 32 And Jacob said, With whomever thou shall find thy gods, he shall not live in the presence of our brethren; take notice of what I have of thy property, and take it; and he observed nothing with him, but Jacob knew not that his wife Rachel had stolen them.

33 And Laban went in and searched in the house of Lea, and found *them* not; and he went out of the house of Lea, and searched in the house of Jacob, and in the house of the two female slaves, and found them not; and he went also into the house of Rachel. 34 And Rachel took the idols, and cast them among the camel's packs, and sat upon them. 35 And she said to her father, Be not indignant, lord; I cannot rise up before thee, for it is with me according to the manner of women. Laban searched in the entire house, and found not the idols.

36 And Jacob was angry, and strove with Laban; and Jacob answered and said to Laban, What is my injustice, and what is my sin, which thou have pursued after me, 37 and that thou has searched all the furniture of my house? What has thou found of all the furniture of thine house? Set it here between thy relations and my relations, and let them decide between us two. 38 These twenty years have I been with thee; thy sheep, and thy she-goats have not failed in bearing; I devoured not the rams of thy cattle. 39 That which was taken of beasts I brought not to thee; I made good of myself the thefts of the day, and the thefts of the night. 40 I was parched with heat by day, and *chilled* with frost by night, and my sleep departed from my eyes. 41 These twenty years have I been in thy house; I worked for thee fourteen years for thy two daughters, and six years among thy sheep, and thou did falsely rate my wages for ten lambs. 42 Unless I had the God of my father Abraham, and the fear of Isaac, now thou would have sent me away empty; God saw my humiliation, and the labor of my hands, and rebuked thee yesterday.

43 And Laban answered and said to Jacob, The daughters are my daughters, and the sons my sons, and the cattle are my cattle, and all things which thou see are mine, and of my daughters; what shall I do to them today, or their children which they bore? 44 Now then come, let me make a covenant, both I and thou, and it shall be for a witness between me and thee; and he said to him, Behold, there is no one with us; behold, God is witness between me and thee.

Genesis 32

45 And Jacob having taken a stone set it up for a pillar. 46 And Jacob said to his brothers, Gather stones; and they gathered stones and made a heap, and ate there upon the heap. 47 And Laban said to him, This heap witnesses between thee and me today. 48 And Laban called it, the Heap of Testimony; and Jacob called it, the Witness Heap. Laban said to Jacob, Behold this heap, and the pillar, which I have set between thee and me; this heap witnesses, and this pillar witnesses; therefore its name was called, the Heap witnesses. 49 And the vision of which he said -- Let God look to it between me and thee, because we are about to depart from each other, -50 If thou shall humble my daughters, if thou should take wives in addition to my daughters, see, there is no one with us looking on. God witnesses between thee and me.

51 And Laban said to Jacob, Behold, this heap, and this pillar are a witness. 52 For if I should not cross over unto thee, neither should thou cross over to me, for mischief beyond this heap and this pillar. 53 The God of Abraham and the God of Nahor judge between us, and Jacob swore by the Fear of his father Isaac. 54 And he offered a sacrifice on the mountain, and called his brothers, and they ate and drank, and slept on the mountain.

55 And Laban arose in the morning, and kissed his sons and his daughters, and blessed them; and Laban having turned back, departed to his place.

Chapter 32

And Jacob departed for his journey; and having looked up, he saw the camp of God encamped; and the angels of God met him. 2 And Jacob said, when he saw them, This is the Camp of God; and he called the name of that place, Encampments.

3 And Jacob sent messengers before him to Esau his brother to the land of Seir, to the country of Edom. 4 And he charged them, saying, Thus shall ye say to my lord Esau: Thus saith thy servant Jacob; I have traveled with Laban and tarried until now. 5 And there were born to me oxen, and mules, and sheep, and male slaves and female slaves; and I sent to tell my lord Esau, that thy servant might find grace in thy sight.

6 And the messengers returned to Jacob, saying, We came to thy brother Esau, and behold! He comes to meet thee, and four hundred men with him. 7 And Jacob was greatly terrified, and was perplexed; and he divided the people that were with him, and the cows, and the camels, and the sheep, into two camps. 8 And Jacob said, If Esau should come to one camp, and destroy it, the other camp shall be in safety.

Genesis 32

9 And Jacob said, God of my father Abraham, and God of my father Isaac, O Lord, thou *art* he that said to me, Depart quickly to the land of thy birth, and I will do thee good. 10 Let there be to me a sufficiency of all the justice and all the truth which thou have wrought with thy servant; for with this my staff I passed over this Jordan, and now I am become two camps. 11 Deliver me from the hand of my brother, from the hand of Esau, for I am afraid of him, unless he gladly should come and kill me, and the mother upon the children. 12 But thou said, I will do thee good, and will make thy seed as the sand of the sea, which shall not be numbered for multitude.

13 And he slept there that night, and took of the gifts which he carried, and sent out to Esau his brother, 14 two hundred she-goats, twenty he-goats, two hundred sheep, twenty rams, 15 milch camels, and their foals, thirty, forty kine, ten bulls, twenty asses, and ten colts. 16 And he gave them to his slaves, *and each* drove apart; and he said to his slaves, Go on before me, and put a space between drove and drove. 17 And he charged the first, saying, If Esau my brother meet thee, and he ask thee, saying, Whose art thou? And whither would thou go, and whose are these possessions advancing before thee? 18 Thou shall say, Thy servant Jacob's; he has sent gifts to my lord Esau, and Behold! He is behind us. 19 And he charged the first and the second and the third, and all that went before him after these flocks, saying, These words shall ye speak to Esau when ye find him; 20 and ye shall say, Behold thy servant Jacob comes after us. For he said, I will propitiate his countenance with the gifts going before his presence, and afterwards I will behold his face, for peradventure he will my face. 21 So the presents went on before him, but he himself lodged that night in the camp.

22 And he arose in that night, and took his two wives and his two female slaves, and his eleven children, and crossed over the ford of Jabok. 23 And he took them, and passed over the torrent, and brought over all his possessions. 24 And Jacob was left alone; and a man wrestled with him till the morning. 25 And he saw that he prevailed not against him; and he touched the broad part of his thigh, and the broad part of Jacob's thigh was benumbed in his wrestling with him. 26 And he said to him, Let me go, for the day has dawned; but he said, I will not let thee go, except thou bless me. 27 And he said to him, What is thy name? And he answered, Jacob. 28 And he said to him, Thy name shall no longer be called Jacob, but Israel shall be thy name, for thou has prevailed with God, and shall be mighty with men. 29 And Jacob asked and said, Tell me thy name; and he said, Wherefore does thou ask after my name? And he blessed him there. 30 And Jacob called the name of that place, the Face of God; for, *he said*, I have seen God face to face, and my soul was preserved. 31 And the sun rose upon him, when he passed the Face of God; and he halted upon his thigh.

Genesis 33

32 Therefore the sons of Israel will by no means eat of the sinew which was benumbed, which is on the broad part of the thigh, until this day, because the broad part of the thigh of Jacob was touched *even* the sinew, which was benumbed.

Chapter 33

And Jacob looked up with his eyes, and saw, and Behold! Esau his brother coming, and four hundred men with him and Jacob divided the children to Lea and to Rachel, and the two female slaves. 2 And he put the two female slaves and their children with the first, and Lea and her children behind, and Rachel and Joseph last. 3 But he advanced himself before them, and did reverence to the ground seven times, until he drew near to his brother. 4 And Esau ran on to meet him, and embraced him, and fell on his neck, and kissed him; and they both wept. 5 And Esau looked up and saw the women and the children, and said, What are these to thee? And he said, The children with which God has mercifully blessed thy servant. 6 And the female slaves and their children drew near and did reverence. 7 And Lea and her children drew near and did reverence; and after this Rachel and Joseph drew near, and did reverence. 8 And he said, What are these things to thee, all these companies that I have met? And he said, That thy servant might find grace in thy sight, my lord. 9 Esau said, I have much, my brother; keep thine own.

10 Jacob said, If I have found grace in thy sight, receive the gifts through my hands; therefore have I seen thy face, as if any one should see the face of God, and thou shall be well pleased with me. 11 Receive my blessings, which I have brought thee, because God has had mercy on me, and I have all things; and he embraced him, and he took. 12 And he said, Let us depart, and proceed right onward. 13 And he said to him, My lord knows, that the children are very tender, and the flocks and the herds with me are with young; if then I shall drive them hard one day, all the cattle will die. 14 Let my lord go on before his servant, and I shall have strength on the road according to the ease of the journey before me, and according to the feet of the children, until I come to my lord to Seir.

15 Esau said I would leave with thee some of the people who are with me. And he said, Why so? It is enough that I have found favor before thee lord. 16 And Esau returned on that day on his journey to Seir. 17 And Jacob departs to his tents; and he made for himself there habitations, and for his cattle he made tents; therefore he called the name of that place, Tents. 18 And Jacob came to Salem, a city of Sekima, which is in the land of Canaan, when he departed out of Mesopotamian Syria, and encamped in front of the city.

19 And he bought the portion of the field, where he pitched his tent, of Emmor the father of Sychem, for a hundred lambs. 20 And he built there an alter, and called on the God of Israel.

Chapter 34

And Dina, the daughter of Lea, whom she bore to Jacob, went forth to observe the daughters of the inhabitants. 2 And Sychem the son of Emmor the * Evite, the ruler of the land, saw her, and took her and lay with her, and humbled her. 3 And he was attached to the soul of Dina the daughter of Jacob, and he loved the virgin, and he spoke to her according to the virgin's heart. 4 Sychem spoke to Emmor his father, saying, Take for me this maiden to wife. 5 And Jacob heard that the son of Emmor had defiled Dina his daughter; now his sons were with his cattle in the plain. Jacob was silent until they came. 6 And Emmor the father of Sychem went forth to Jacob, to speak to him. 7 And the sons of Jacob came from the plain; and when they heard, the men were cut to the quick, and it was very grievous to them, because folly was wrought to Israel, having lain with the daughter of Jacob, and it shall not be so.

8 And Emmor spoke to them, saying, Sychem my son has chosen in his soul your daughter; give her therefore to him for a wife, 09 and intermarry with us. Give us your daughters, and take our daughters for your sons. 10 And dwell in the midst of us; and, behold, the land is spacious before you, dwell in it, and trade, and get possessions in it.

11 And Sychem said to her father and to her brothers, I would find grace before you, and we will give whatever ye shall name. 12 Increase *your demand of* dowry very much, and I will give accordingly as ye shall say to me, only ye shall give me this maiden for a wife.

13 And the sons of Jacob answered to Sychem and Emmor his father craftily, and spoke to them, because they had defiled Dina their sister. 14 And Symeon and Levi, the brothers of Dina, said to them, We shall not be able to do this thing, to give our sister to a man who is uncircumcised, for it is a reproach to us. 15 Only on these terms will we conform to you, and live among you, if ye also will be as we are, in that every male of you be circumcised. 16 And we will give our daughters to you, and we will take of your daughters for wives to us, and we will dwell with you, and we will be as one race. 17 But if ye will not hearken to us to be circumcised, we will take our daughter and depart. 18 And the words pleased Emmor, and Sychem the son of Emmor. 19 And the young man did not delayed in doing this thing, for he was much attached to Jacob's daughter, and he was the most honorable of all in his father's house.

Genesis 35

20 And Emmor and Sychem his son came to the gate of their city, and spoke to the men of their city, saying, 21 These men are peaceable, let them dwell with us upon the land, and let them trade in it, and behold the land is extensive before them; we will take their daughters to us for wives, and we will give them our daughters. 22 Only on these terms will the men conform to us to live with us so as to be one people, if every male of us were circumcised, as they also are circumcised. 23 And shall not their cattle and their quadrupeds, and their possessions, be ours? Only in this let us conform to them, and they will live with us. 24 And all that went in at the gate of their city hearkened to Emmor and Sychem his son, and they were circumcised in the flesh of their foreskin every male.

25 And it came to pass on the third day, when they were in pain, the two sons of Jacob, Simon and Levi, Dina's brothers, took each man his sword, and came upon the city securely, and killed every male. 26 And they killed Emmor and Sychem his son with the edge of the sword, and took Dina out of the house of Sychem, and went forth. 27 But the sons of Jacob came upon the traumatized, and ravaged the city wherein they had defiled Dina their sister. 28 And their sheep, and their oxen, and their mules they took, and all things whatever were in the city, and whatever was in the plain. 29 And they took captive all the persons of them, and their entire store, and their wives, and plundered both whatever things there were in the city, and whatever things there were in the houses.

30 And Jacob said to Simon and Levi, Ye have made me hateful so that I should be evil to all the inhabitants of the land, both among the Canaanites and the Pherezites, and I am few in number; they will gather themselves against me and cut me in pieces, and I shall be utterly destroyed, and my house.

31 And they said, Nay, but shall they treat our sister as a harlot?

* *Codex Alexandrinus* reads: "Horrean".

Chapter 35

And God said to Jacob, Arise, go up to the place, Bethel, and live there; and make there an altar to the God that appeared to thee, when thou fled from the face of Esau thy brother. 2 And Jacob said to his house, and to all that were with him, Remove the strange gods that are with you from the midst of you, and purify yourselves, and change your clothes. 3 And let us rise and go up to Bethel, and let us there make an alter to God who hearkened to me in the day of calamity, who was with me, and preserved me throughout in the journey, by which I went.

Genesis 35

4 And they gave to Jacob the strange gods, which were in their hands, and the earrings, which were in their ears, and Jacob hid them under the turpentine tree, which is in Sekima, and let them go to this day.

5 So Israel departed from Sekima, and the fear of God was upon the cities round about them, and they did not pursue after the sons of Israel. 6 And Jacob came to Luza, which is in the land of Canaan, which is Bethel, he and all the people that were with him. 7 And he built an altar there, and called the name of the place Bethel; for there God appeared to him, when he fled from the face of his brother Esau. 8 And Deborah, Rebecca's nurse, died, and was buried below Bethel under the oak; and Jacob called its name, The Oak of Mourning.

9 And God appeared to Jacob once more in Luza, when he came out of Mesopotamia of Syria, and God blessed him. 10 And God said to him, Thy name shall not be called Jacob, but Israel shall be thy name; and he called his name Israel. 11 And God said to him, I am thy God; increase and multiply, for nations and gatherings of nations shall be of thee, and kings shall come out of thy loins. 12 And the land, which I gave to Abraham and Isaac, I have given it to thee; and it shall come to pass that I will give this land also to thy seed after thee. 13 And God went up from him from the place where he spoke with him. 14 And Jacob set up a pillar in the place where God spoke with him, a pillar of stone; and offered a libation upon it, and poured oil upon it. 15 And Jacob called the name of the place in which God spoke with him, Bethel.

16 And Jacob removed from Bethel, and pitched his tent beyond the tower of Gader. And it came to pass when he drew near to Habratha, to enter into Ephratha, Rachel travailed; and in her travail she was in hard labor. 17 And it came to pass in her hard labor that the midwife said to her, Be of good courage, for thou shall also have this son.

18 And it came to pass in her giving up her soul for she was dying, that she called his name, The son of my pain, but his father called his name Benjamin. 19 So Rachel died, and was buried in the way of the course of Ephratha, (this is Bethlehem). 20 And Jacob set up a pillar on her tomb; this is the pillar on the tomb of Rachel, until this day. 21 And it came to pass when Israel lived in that land, that Ruben went and lay with Balla, the concubine of his father Jacob; and Israel heard, and the thing appeared evil before him.

22 And the sons of Jacob were twelve. 23 The sons of Lea, the firstborn of Jacob; Ruben, Simon, Levi, Judas, Issahar, Zabulon. 24 And the sons of Rachel; Joseph and Benjamin. 25 And the sons of Balla, the female slave of Rachel; Dan and Nephthalim. 26 And the sons of Zelpha, the female slave of Lea; Gad and Aser. These sons of Jacob were born to him in Mesopotamia of Syria.

27 And Jacob came to Isaac his father to Mambre, to a city of the plain (this is Hebron) in the land of Canaan, where Abraham and Isaac traveled. 28 And the days of Isaac, which he lived, were an hundred and eighty years.

Genesis 36

29 And Isaac faded and died, and was laid to his family, old and full of days; and Esau and Jacob his sons buried him.

Chapter 36

And these *are* the generations of Esau (this is Edom). 2 And Esau took to himself wives of the daughters of the Canaanites; Ada, the daughter of Elom the Hittite; and Olibema, daughter of Ana the son of Sebegon, the Evite; 3 and Basemath, daughter of Ishmael, sister of Nabaioth. 4 And Ada bore to him Eliphas; and Basemath bore Raguel. 5 And Olibema bore Jeus, and Jeglom, and Kore; these *are* the sons of Esau, which were born to him in the land of Canaan.

6 And Esau took his wives, and his sons, and his daughters, and all the persons of his house, and all his possessions, and all his cattle, and all that he had got, and all things whatever he had acquired in the land of Canaan; and Esau went forth from the land of Canaan, from the face of his brother Jacob. 7 For their substance was too great for them to live together, and the land of their traveling could not bear them, because of the abundance of their possessions. 8 And Esau lived on mount Seir (Esau, he is Edom).

9 And these *are* the generations of Esau, the father of Edom on the mountain Seir. 10 And these *are* the names of the sons of Esau; Eliphas, the son of Ada, the wife of Esau; and Raguel, the son of Basemath, wife of Esau. 11 And the sons of Eliphas were Thaeman, Omar, Sophar, Gothom, and Kenez. 12 And Thamna was a concubine of Eliphaz, the son of Esau; and she bore Amalek to Eliphas. These *are* the sons of Ada, the wife of Esau.

13 And these *are* the sons of Raguel; Nahoth, Zare, Some, and Moze. These were the sons of Basemath, wife of Esau. 14 And these *are* the sons of Olibema, the daughter of Ana, the son of Sebegon, the wife of Esau; and she bore to Esau, Jeus, and Jeglom, and Kore.

15 These *are* the rulers of the son of Esau, *even* the sons of Eliphas, the firstborn of Esau, ruler Thaeman, ruler Omar, ruler Sophar, ruler Kenez, 16 ruler Kore, ruler Gothom, ruler Amalec. These *are* the rulers of Eliphas, in the land of Edom; these are the sons of Ada. 17 And these *are* the sons of Raquel, the son of Esau, ruler Nahoth, ruler Zare, ruler Some, ruler Moze. These are the rulers of Raquel, in the land of Edom; these are the sons of Basemath, wife of Esau. 18 And these *are* the sons of Olibema, wife of Esau, ruler Jeus, ruler Jeglom, ruler Kore. These *are* the rulers of Olibema, daughter of Ana, wife of Esau. 19 These *are* the sons of Esau, and these are the rulers. These are the sons of Edom.

20 And these *are* the sons of Seir, the Horrhite, who inhabited the land; Lotan, Sobal, Sebegon, Ana, 21 and Deson, and Asar, and Rison. These *are* the rulers of the Horrhite, the son of Seir, in the land of Edom.

22 And the sons of Lotan *were* Horrhi and Haeman; and the sister of Lotan, Thamna. 23 And these *are* the sons of Sobal, Golam, and Manahath, and Gaebel, and Sophar, and Omar. 024 And these *are* the sons of Sebegon; Aei, and Ana; this is the Ana who found Jamin in the wilderness, when he tended the beasts of his father Sebegon. 25 And these *are* the sons of Ana, Deson and Olibema daughter of Ana. 26 And these *are* the sons of Deson, Amada, and Asban, and Ithran, and Harrhan. 27 And these *are* the sons of Asar, Balaam, and Zucam, and Jucam. 28 And these *are* the sons of Rison, Hos, and Aaron. 29 And these *are* the rulers of Horri; ruler Lotan, ruler Sobal, ruler Sebegon, ruler Ana, 30 ruler Deson, ruler Asar, ruler Rison. These *are* the rulers of Horri, in their principalities in the land of Edom.

31 And these *are* the kings, which reigned in Edom, before a king reigned in Israel. 32 And Balac, son of Beor, reigned in Edom; and the name of his city *was* Dennaba. 33 And Balac died; and Jobab, son of Zara, reigned in his stead from Bosorrha. 34 And Jobab died; and Asom reigned in his stead from the land of the Thaemanites. 35 And Asom died; and Adad son of Barad, who cut off Madiam in the plain of Moab, ruled in his stead; and the name of his city was Getthaim. 36 And Adad died; and Samada of Massekka reigned in his stead. 37 And Samada died; and Saul of Rhovouth both reigned in his stead by the river. 38 And Saul died; and Ballenon the son of Ahobor reigned in his stead. 39 And Ballenon the son of Achobor died; and Arad the son of Barad reigned in his stead; and the name of his city was Phogor; and the name of his wife was Metebeel, daughter of Matraith, son of Maizof.

40 These *are* the names of the rulers of Esau, in their tribes, according to their place, in their countries, and in their nations; ruler Thamna, ruler Gola, ruler Jether, 41 ruler Olibema, ruler Helas, ruler Phinon, 42 ruler Kenez, ruler Thaeman, ruler Mazar, 43 ruler Magediel, ruler Zaphoin. These are the rulers of Edom in their dwelling-places in the land of their possession; this is Esau, the father of Edom.

Chapter 37

And Jacob lived in the land where his father traveled, in the land of Canaan. 2 These are the generations of Jacob. Joseph was seventeen years old, feeding the sheep of his father with his brothers, being young; with the sons of Balla, and with the sons of Zelpha, the wives of his father; and Joseph brought back an evil reproach to Israel their father. 3 And Jacob loved Joseph more than all his sons, because he was to him the son of old age; and he made for him a coat of many colors. 4 And his brothers, having seen that his father loved him more than all his sons, hated him, and could not speak anything peaceable to him.

Genesis 37

5 And Joseph dreamed a dream, and reported it to his brothers. 6 And he said to them, Hear this dream, which I have dreamt. 7 I thought ye were binding sheaves in the middle of the field, and my sheaf stood up and was erected, and your sheaves turned round, and did obeisance to my sheaf. 8 And his brothers said to him, Shall thou indeed reign over us, or shall thou indeed be lord over us? And they hated him still more for his dreams and for his words. 9 And he saw another dream, and related it to his father, and to his brothers, and said, Behold, I have dreamed another dream; as it was the sun, and the moon, and the eleven stars did me reverence. 10 And his father rebuked him, and said to him, What is this dream, which thou have dreamed? Shall indeed both thy mother and I and thy brothers come and bow before thee to the Earth? 11 And his brothers were jealous of him; but his father observed the saying.

12 And his brothers went to feed the sheep of their father to Sychem. 13 And Israel said to Joseph, Do not thy brethren feed their flock in Sychem? Come, I will send thee to them; and he said to him, Behold, I am *here*. 14 And Israel said to him, Go and see if thy brothers and the sheep are well, and bring me word; and he sent him out of the valley of Hebron, and he came to Sychem. 15 And a man found him wandering in the field; and the man asked him, saying, What does thou seek? 16 And he said, I am seeking my brothers; tell me where they feed *their flocks*. 17 And the man said to him, They have departed hence, for I heard them saying, Let us go to Dothaim; and Joseph went after his brothers, and found them in Dothaim. 18 And they spied him from a distance before he drew close to them, and they wickedly took counsel to kill him. 19 And each said to his brother, Behold, that dreamer comes. 20 Now then come, let us kill him, and throw him into one of the pits; and we will say, an evil wild beast has devoured him; and we shall see what his dreams will be.

21 And Ruben having heard it, rescued him out of their hands, and said; Let us not strike his soul. 22 And Ruben said to them, Shed not blood; throw him into one of these pits in the wilderness, but do not lay *your* hands upon him, that he might rescue him out of their hands, and restore him to his father. 23 And it came to pass, when Joseph came to his brothers, that they stripped Joseph of his many-colored coat that was upon him. 24 And they took him and threw him into the pit; and the pit was empty, it had no water.

25 And they sat down to eat bread; and having lifted up their eyes they saw, and behold, Ishmaelite travelers came from Galaad, and their camels were heavily loaded with spices, and resin, and myrrh; and they went to bring them to Egypt. 26 And Judas said to his brothers, What profit is it if we kill our brother, and conceal his blood? 27 Come, let us sell him to these Ishmaelites, but let not our hands be upon him, because he is our brother and our flesh; and his brothers hearkened.

28 And the merchants, the men of Madian, went by, and they drew and lifted Joseph out of the pit, and sold Joseph to the Ishmaelites for twenty pieces of gold; and they brought Joseph down into Egypt. 29 And Ruben returned to the pit, and did not see Joseph in the pit; and he rent his garments. 30 And he returned to his brothers and said, Where is the boy, and where am I yet to go? 31 And having taken the coat of Joseph, they butchered a kid of the goats, and stained the coat with the blood. 32 And they sent the coat of many colors; and they brought it to their father, and said, This have we found; know if it be thy son's coat or no. 33 And he recognized it, and said, It is my son's coat, an evil wild beast has devoured him; a wild beast has caught Joseph. 34 And Jacob rent his clothes, and put sackcloth on his loins, and mourned for his son many days. 35 And all his sons and his daughters gathered themselves together, and came to comfort him; but he would not be comforted, saying, I will go down to my son mourning to Hades; and his father wept for him.

36 And the Madianites sold Joseph into Egypt to Petephres, the eunuch of Pharaoh, the chief cook.

Chapter 38

It came to pass at that time that Judas went down from his brothers, and came as far as to a certain man of Odollam, whose name was Iras. 2 And Judas saw there the daughter of a Canaanite man, whose name was Sava; and he took her, and went in to her. 3 And she conceived and bore a son, and called his name, Er. 4 And she conceived and bore a son again; and called his name, Aunan. 5 And she again bore a son; and called his name, Selom: and she was in Hasbi when she bore them.

6 And Judas took a wife for Er his firstborn, whose name was Thamar. 7 And Er, the firstborn of Judas, was evil before the Lord; and God killed him. 8 And Judas said to Aunan, Go in to thy brother's wife, and marry her as her brother-in-law, and rise up seed to thy brother. 9 And Aunan, knowing that the seed should not be his, it came to pass when he went in to his brother's wife, that he spilled it upon the ground, so that he should not give seed to his brother's wife. 10 And his doing this appeared evil before God; and he killed him also. 11 And Judas said to Thamar, his daughter-in-law, Sit thou a widow in the house of thy father-in-law, until Selom my son be grown; for he said, lest he also die as his brothers; and Thamar departed, and sat in the house of her father.

12 And the days were fulfilled, and Sava the wife of Judas died; and Judas, being comforted, went to them that sheared his sheep, himself and Iras his Shepherd the Odollamite, to Thamna.

Genesis 39

13 And it was told Thamar his daughter-in-law, saying, Behold, thy father-in-law goes up to Thamna, to shear his sheep. 14 And having taken off the garments of her widowhood from her, she put on a veil, and ornamented her face, and sat by the gates of Aenan, which is in the way to Thamna, for she saw that Selom was grown; but he gave her not to him for a wife. 15 And when Judas saw her, he thought her to be a harlot, for she covered her face, and he knew her not. 16 And he turned his way to her, and said to her, Let me come in to thee; for he knew not that she was his daughter-in-law; and she said, What will thou give me if thou should come in to me? 17 And he said, I will send thee a kid of the goats from my flock; and she said, Well, if thou will give me a Pledge, until thou send it. 18 And he said, What is the Pledge that I shall give thee? And she said, Thy ring, and thy necklace, and the staff in thy hand; and he gave them to her, and went in to her, and she conceived by him. 19 And she arose and departed, and took her veil from off her, and put on the garments of her widowhood.

20 And Judas sent the kid of the goats by the hand of his shepherd the Odollamite, to receive the pledge from the woman; and he found her not. 21 And he asked the men of the place, Where is the harlot who was in Aenan by the roadway? And they said, There was no harlot here. 22 And he returned to Judas, and said, I have not found her; and the men of the place say, There is no harlot here. 23 And Judas said, Let her have them, but let us not be ridiculed; I sent this kid, but thou has not found her.

24 And it came to pass after three months that it was told Judas, saying, Thamar thy daughter-in-law has grievously played the harlot, and behold she is with child by whoredom; and Judas said, Bring her out, and let her be burnt. 25 And as they were bringing her, she sent to her father-in-law, saying, I am with child by the man whose these things are; and she said, See whose ring this is, and bracelet and staff. 26 And Judas knew them, and said, Thamar is cleared rather than I, forasmuch as I gave her not to Selom my son: and he knew her not again.

27 And it came to pass when she was in labor, that she also had twins in her womb. 28 And it came to pass as she was bringing forth, one thrust forth his hand, and the midwife having taken hold of it, bound upon his hand a red thread, saying, This one shall come out first. 29 And when he drew back his hand, then immediately came forth his brother; and she said Why has the barrier been cut through because of thee? And she called his name, Phares. 30 And after this came forth his brother, on whose hand was the red thread; and she called his name, Zara.

Chapter 39

Joseph was brought down to Egypt; and Petephres the eunuch of

Genesis 39

Pharaoh, the chief cook, an Egyptian, bought him of the hands of the Ishmaelites, who brought him down thither. 2 And the Lord was with Joseph, and he was a prosperous man; and he was in the house with his lord the Egyptian. 3 And his lord knew that the Lord was with him, and the Lord prospers in his hands whatever he happens to do. 4 And Joseph found grace in the presence of his lord, and was well pleasing to him; and he set him over his house, and all that he had he gave into the hand of Joseph. 5 And it came to pass after that he was set over his house, and over all that he had, that the Lord blessed the house of the Egyptian for Joseph's sake; and the blessing of the Lord was on all his possessions in the house, and in his field. 6 And he committed all that he had into the hands of Joseph; and he knew not of anything that belonged to him, save the bread, which he himself ate. And Joseph was handsome in form, and exceedingly beautiful in appearance.

7 And it came to pass after these things, that his lord's wife cast her eyes upon Joseph, and said, Sleep with me. 8 But he would not; but said to his lord's wife, Because of me my lord knows nothing in his house, and has given into my hands all things that belong to him, 9 and in this house there is nothing above me, nor has anything been kept back from me, but thou, because thou art his wife, how then shall I do this evil thing, and sin against God? 10 And when she talked with Joseph day by day, and he hearkened not to her to sleep with her, so as to be with her.

11 It came to pass on a specific day that Joseph went into the house to do his business and there was no one of the household within. 12 And she caught hold of him by his clothes, and said, Sleep with me; and having left his clothes in her hands, he fled, and went forth. 13 And it came to pass, when she saw that he had left his clothes in her hands, and fled, and gone forth; 14 that she called those that were in the house, and spoke to them, saying, See, he has brought in to us a Hebrew slave to mock us, he came in to me, saying, Sleep with me, and I cried with a loud voice. 15 And when he heard that I lifted up my voice and cried, having left his clothes with me, he fled, and went out forth. 16 So she leaves the clothes by her, until the lord came to his house. 17 And she spoke to him according to these words, saying, The Hebrew slave, whom thou brought in to us, came in to me to mock me, and said to me, I will sleep with thee. 18 And when he heard that I lifted up my voice and cried, having left his clothes with me, he fled and departed forth.

19 And it came to pass, when his lord heard all the words of his wife, that she spoke to him, saying, Thus did thy slave to me, that he was very angry. 20 And his lord took Joseph, and cast him into the prison, into the place where the king's prisoners are kept, there in the prison. 21 And the Lord was with Joseph, and poured down mercy upon him; and he gave him favor in the sight of the chief prison-keeper.

Genesis 40

22 And the chief prison keeper gave the prison into the hand of Joseph, and all the men led away who were in prison; and all things whatever they were doing there. 23 Because of him the chief prison keeper knew nothing, for all things were in the hand of Joseph, because the Lord was with him; and whatever things he did, the Lord made them to prosper in his hands.

Chapter 40

And it came to pass after these things that the chief cupbearer of the king of Egypt and the chief baker trespassed against their lord the king of Egypt. 2 And Pharaoh was wroth with his two eunuchs, with his chief cupbearer, and with his chief baker. 3 And he put them in ward, into the prison, into the place where into Joseph had been led. 4 And the chief prison-keeper committed them to Joseph, and he stood by them; and they were days in the prison. 5 And they both saw a dream in one night; and the vision of the dream of the chief cupbearer and chief baker, who belonged to the king of Egypt, who were in the prison, was this. 6 Joseph went in to them in the morning, and saw them, and they had been troubled. 7 And he asked the eunuchs of Pharaoh who were with him in the prison with his lord, saying, Why is it that your appearances are sad today? 8 And they said to him, We have seen a dream, and there is no interpreter of it. And Joseph said to them, Is not the interpretation of them through God? Tell then to me.

9 And the chief cupbearer related his dream to Joseph, and said; In my sleep a vine was before me. 10 And in the vine three stems; and its budding shot forth blossoms; the clusters of grapes were ripe. 11 And the cup of Pharaoh was in my hand; and I took the bunch of grapes, and squeezed it into the cup, and gave the cup into Pharaoh's hand. 12 And Joseph said to him, This is the interpretation of it. The three stems are three days.

13 Yet three days and Pharaoh shall remember thy office, and he shall restore thee to thy place of chief cupbearer, and thou shall give the cup of Pharaoh into his hand, according to thy former high place, as thou was wont to be cupbearer. 14 But remember me of thyself, when it shall be well with thee, and thou shall deal mercifully with me, and thou shall make mention of me to Pharaoh, and thou shall bring me forth out of this dungeon. 15 For surely I was stolen away out of the land of the Hebrews, and here I have done nothing, but they have cast me into this pit.

16 And the chief baker saw that he interpreted aright; and he said to Joseph, I also saw a dream, and I thought I took up on my head three baskets of mealy food.

17 And in the upper basket there was the work of the baker of every kind, which Pharaoh eats; and the fowls of the air ate them out of the basket that was on my head. 18 And Joseph answered and said to him, This is the interpretation of it; The three baskets are three days. 19 Yet three days, and Pharaoh shall take away thy head from off thee, and shall hang thee on a tree, and the birds of the sky shall eat thy flesh from off thee.

20 And it came to pass on the third day that it was Pharaoh's birthday, and he made a banquet for all his servants, and he remembered the office of the cupbearer and the office of the baker in the midst of his servants. 21 And he restored the chief cupbearer to his office, and he gave the cup into Pharaoh's hand. 22 And he hanged the chief baker, as Joseph, interpreted to them. 23 Yet did not the chief cupbearer remember Joseph, but forgot him.

Chapter 41

And it came to pass after two years of days that Pharaoh had a dream. He thought he stood upon the river. 2 And behold, there came up as it were out of the river seven cows, fair in appearance, and choice of flesh, and they fed on the marshy grass. 3 And other seven cows came up after these out of the river, ill favored and lean-fleshed, and fed by the cows on the bank of the river. 4 And the seven ill favored and lean cows devoured the seven well-favored and choice-fleshed cows, and Pharaoh awoke. 5 And he dreamed a second time. And, behold, seven ears came up on one stalk, choice and good. 6 And, behold, seven ears thin and blasted with the wind, grew up after them. 7 And the seven thin ears and blasted with the wind devoured the seven choice and full ears; and Pharaoh awoke, and it was a dream. 8 And it was morning, and his soul was troubled, and he sent and called all the interpreters of Egypt, and all her wise men; and Pharaoh related to them his dream, and there was no one to tell it to Pharaoh.

9 And the chief cupbearer spoke to Pharaoh, saying, My sin I remember this day. 10 Pharaoh was angry with his slaves, and put us in prison in the house of the captain of the guard, both the chief baker and me. 11 And we both saw a dream one night, he and I; we saw, each according to his dream. 12 And there was there with us a young man, a Hebrew slave of the captain of the guard, and we shared with him, and he interpreted for us. 13 And it came to pass, as he interpreted them to us, so also it happened, both that I was restored to my office, and that he was hanged.

14 And Pharaoh having sent, called Joseph; and they brought him out from the prison, and shaved him, and changed his dress, and he came to Pharaoh.

Genesis 41

15 Pharaoh said to Joseph, I have seen a vision, and there is no one to interpret it; but I have heard them saying concerning thee that thou do hear dreams and interpret them. 16 Joseph answered Pharaoh and said, Without God an answer safely shall not be given to Pharaoh. 17 Pharaoh spoke to Joseph, saying, In my dream I thought I stood by the bank of the river, 18 and there came up as it were out of the river, seven cows well favored and choice-fleshed, and they fed on the marshy grass. 19 And behold seven other cows came up after them out of the river, evil and ill favored and lean-fleshed, such that I never saw worse in the entire land of Egypt. 20 And the seven ill-favored and thin cows devoured the seven first good and choice cows. 21 And they went into their bellies; and they did not become perceptible considering they had gone into their bellies, and their appearance was ill favored, as was from the beginning; and after I awoke I slept, 22 and saw again in my sleep, and as it were seven ears came up on one stem, full and good. 23 Other seven ears, thin and blasted with the wind, sprang up close to them. 24 And the seven thin and blasted ears devoured the seven fine and full ears; so I spoke to the interpreters, and there was no one to explain it to me.

25 And Joseph said to Pharaoh, The dream of Pharaoh is this; whatever God does, he has shown to Pharaoh. 26 The seven good cows are seven years, and the seven good ears are seven years; the dream of Pharaoh is this. 27 And the seven thin kind that came up after them are seven years, and the seven thin and blasted ears are seven years; there shall be seven years of famine. 28 And as for the word, which I have told Pharaoh, whatever God intends to do, he has shown to Pharaoh, 29 behold, for seven years there is coming great plenty in all the land of Egypt. 30 But there shall come seven years of famine after these, and they shall forget the plenty that shall be in all Egypt, and the famine shall cover the land. 31 And the plenty shall not be known in the land by reason of the famine that shall be after this, for it shall be very grievous. 32 And concerning the repetition of the dream to Pharaoh twice, *it is* because the saying, which is from God shall be true, and God will hasten to accomplish it. 33 Now then, look out a wise and prudent man, and set him over the land of Egypt.

34 And let Pharaoh make and appoint local governors over the land; and let them take up a fifth part of all the produce of the land of Egypt for the seven years of the plenty. 35 And let them gather all the food of these seven good years that are coming, and let the corn be gathered under the hand of Pharaoh, let food be kept in the cities. 36 And the stored food shall be for the land against the seven years of famine, which shall be in the land of Egypt; and the land shall not be utterly destroyed by the famine.

37 And the word was pleasing in the sight of Pharaoh, and in the sight of all his slaves. 38 And Pharaoh said to all his slaves, Should we find such a man as this, who has the Spirit of God in him?

39 Pharaoh said to Joseph, Since God has showed thee all these things; there is not a wiser or more prudent man than thou. 40 Thou shall be over my house, and all my people shall be obedient to thy mouth; only in the throne will I be above thee. 41 Pharaoh said to Joseph, Behold, I set thee this day over all the land of Egypt. 42 And Pharaoh took his ring off his hand, and put it on the hand of Joseph, and put on him a robe of fine linen, and put a necklace of gold about his neck. 43 And he mounted him on the second of his chariots, and a herald made proclamation before him; and he set him over all the land of Egypt. 44 And Pharaoh said to Joseph, I am Pharaoh; without thee no one shall lift up his hand on all the land of Egypt. 45 And Pharaoh called the name of Joseph, Psonthomphanek, and he gave him Aseneth, the daughter of Petephres, priest of Heliopolis, to wife. 46 And Joseph was thirty years old when he stood before Pharaoh, king of Egypt. And Joseph went out from the face of Pharaoh, and went through all the land of Egypt. 47 And the land produced, in the seven years of plenty, handfuls. 48 And he gathered all the food of the seven years, in which was the plenty in the land of Egypt, and he laid up the food in the cities; the food of the fields of a city round about it he laid up in it. 49 And Joseph gathered very much corn as the sand of the sea, until it could not be numbered, for there was no number.

50 *And* to Joseph were born two sons, before the seven years of famine came, which Aseneth, the daughter of Petephres, priest of Heliopolis, bore to him. 51 And Joseph called the name of the firstborn, Manasse, for God has made me forget all my pain, and all things belonging to my father. 52 *And* he called the name of the second, Ephraim, for God has increased me in the land of my humiliation.

53 And the seven years of plenty passed away, which were in the land of Egypt. 54 And the seven years of famine started, as Joseph said, and there was a famine in all the land; but in all the land of Egypt there was bread. 55 And all the land of Egypt was hungry, and the people cried to Pharaoh for bread. And Pharaoh said to all the Egyptians, Go to Joseph, and do whatever he shall tell you. 56 And the famine was on the face of the entire earth; and Joseph opened all the granaries, and sold to all the Egyptians. 57 And all countries came to Egypt to buy of Joseph, for the famine prevailed on the entire earth.

Chapter 42

And Jacob having seen that there was a sale in Egypt, said to his sons, Why are ye indolent? 2 Behold, I have heard that there is corn in Egypt; go down there, and buy for us a little food that we may live, and not die. 3 And the ten brothers of Joseph went down to buy corn out of Egypt.

Genesis 42

4 But sent not Benjamin, the brother of Joseph, with his brothers saying, so that no disease befalls him. 5 The sons of Israel came to buy with those that came, for the famine was in the land of Canaan.

6 *And* Joseph was the ruler of the land; he sold to all the people of the land. And the brothers of Joseph, having come, did reverence to him, with face to the ground. 7 When Joseph saw his brothers, he knew them, and estranged himself from them, and spoke hard words to them; and said to them, From where have ye come? They said, Out of the land of Canaan, to buy food. 8 Joseph knew his brothers, but they knew not him. 9 And Joseph remembered his dream, which he saw; and he said to them, Ye are spies; to observe the marks of the land are ye come. 10 But they said, No, lord, we thy subjects are come to buy food; 11 We are all sons of one man; we are peaceful, thy subjects are not spies. 12 And he said to them, No, but ye are come to observe the marks of the land. 13 And they said, We thy subjects are twelve brothers, in the land of Canaan; and, behold, the youngest is with our father today, but the other one is not. 14 And Joseph said to them, This is it that I spoke to you, saying, ye are spies; 15 herein shall ye be manifested; by the health of Pharaoh, ye shall not depart hence, unless your younger brother come here. 16 Send one of you, and get your brother; and go ye to prison, till your words be clear, whether ye speak the truth or not, but, if not, by the health of Pharaoh, truly ye are spies. 17 And he put them in prison three days.

18 And he said to them on the third day, This do, and ye shall live, for I fear God. 19 If ye be peaceable, let one of your brothers be held in prison; but go ye, and carry back the purchase of your gift of corn. 20 And bring your younger brother to me, and your words shall be believed; but, if not, ye shall die. And they did so. 21 And each said to his brother, Yes, indeed, for we are in fault concerning our brother, when we disregarded the anguish of his soul, when he besought us, and we did not hearkened to him; and therefore has this affliction come upon us. 22 And Ruben answered them, saying, Did I not speak to you, saying, Hurt not the boy, and ye heard me not? And, behold, his blood is required.

23 But they knew not that Joseph heard them for there was an interpreter between them. 24 And Joseph turned away from them, and wept; and again he came to them, and spoke to them; and he took Simon from them, and bound him before them. 25 And Joseph gave orders to fill their vessels with corn, and to return their money to each into his sack, and to give them provision for the way; and it was so done to them.

26 And having put the corn on the donkeys, they departed thence. 27 And one having opened his sack to give his donkeys fodder, at the place where they rested, also saw his bundle of money, for it was on the mouth of his sack.

28 And he said to his brothers, My money has been restored to me, and behold this is in my sack. And their heart was ecstatic, and they were troubled, saying one to another, What is this that God has done to us? 29 And they came to their father, Jacob, into the land of Canaan, and reported to him all that had happened to them, saying, 30 The man, the lord of the land, spoke harsh words to us, and put us in prison as spies of the land. 31 We said to him, We are men of peace, we are not spies. 32 We are twelve brothers, sons of our father; one is not, and the youngest is with his father today in the land of Canaan. 33 And the man, the lord of the land, said to us, Herein shall I know that ye are peaceable; leave one brother here with me, and having taken the corn ye have purchased for your family, leave. 34 And bring to me your younger brother; then I shall know that ye are not spies, but that ye are men of peace: and I will restore *to* you your brother, and ye shall trade in the land.

35 And it came to pass as they were emptying their sacks, there was each man's bundle of money in his sack; and they and their father saw their bundles of money, and they were afraid. 36 Their father Jacob said to them, Ye have grieved me, Joseph is not, Simon is not, and will ye have Benjamin? All these things have occurred to me. 37 Ruben spoke to his father, saying, Kill my two sons, if I bring him not to thee, give him into my hand, and I will bring him back to thee. 38 But he said, My son shall not go down with you, because his brother is dead, and he only has been left; and suppose it shall come to pass that he is afflicted on the way by which ye go, then ye shall bring down my old age with sorrow unto Hades. 39 But the famine prevailed in the land.

Chapter 43

And it came to pass, when they had finished eating the corn which they had brought out of Egypt, that their father said to them, Go again; buy us *a* little food. 2 Judas spoke to him, saying, The man, the lord of the country, positively testified to us, saying, Ye shall not see my face, unless your younger brother be with you.

3 If, then, thou send our brother with us, we will go down, and buy thee food. 4 However, if thou send not our brother with us, we will not go, for the man spoke to us, saying, Ye shall not see my face, unless your younger brother be with you. 5 Israel said Why did ye harm me, inasmuch as ye told the man that ye had a brother? 6 And they said, The man closely questioned us about our family also, saying, Does your father still live, and have ye a brother? And we answered him according to this question: did we know that he would say to us, Bring your brother?

Genesis 43

7 Judas said to his father Israel, Send the boy with me, and we will arise and go, that we may live and not die, both we and thou, and our store. 8 I engage for him; at my hand do thou require him if I bring him not to thee, and place him before thee, I shall be guilty toward thee forever. 9 For if we had not delayed, we should now have returned twice. 10 Israel, their father, said to them, If it be so, do this; take of the fruits of the earth in your vessels, and carry down to the man presents of gum and honey, and frankincense, and stacte, and turpentine, and almonds.

11 And take double money in your hands, and the money that was returned in your sacks; carry back with you, lest by chance it is a mistake. 12 And take your brother; and arise, go down to the man. 13 My God give you favor in the sight of the man, and send away your one brother, and Benjamin, for as accordingly as I have been bereaved of children, *I* am bereaved of children. 14 *And* the men having taken these presents, and the double money, took in their hands also Benjamin; and they rose up and went down to Egypt, and stood before Joseph. 15 Joseph saw them and his brother Benjamin, born of the same mother; and he said to the steward of his household, Bring the men into the house, and slaughter beasts and make ready, for the men are to eat bread with me at noon.

16 The man did as Joseph said; and he brought the men into the house of Joseph. 17 The men, when they saw that they were brought into the house of Joseph, said, We are brought in because of the money that was returned in our sacks at the beginning; even in order to inform against us, and lay it to our charge; to take us for slaves, and our donkeys. 18 *And* having approached the man, who was over the house of Joseph, they spoke to him in the porch of the house, 19 saying, We pray, lord; we came down in the beginning to buy food. 20 And it came to pass, when we came to unload, and opened our sacks, *there was* also this money of each in his sack; we have now brought back our money by weight in our hands. 21 And we have brought other money with us to buy food; we know not who put the money into our sacks. 22 He said to them, mercy be with you, be not afraid; your God, and the God of your fathers, has given you riches in your sacks, and I have your good money in full. And he brought Simon out to them. 23 And he brought water to wash their feet; and gave fodder to their donkeys.

24 They prepared their presents, until Joseph came at noon, for they heard that he was going to dine there. 25 Joseph entered into the house, and they brought him the presents, which they had in their hands, into the house; and they gave him reverence with their face to the ground. 26 And he asked them, How are ye? And he said to them, Is your father, the old man of whom ye spoke, well? Does he yet live?

27 They said, Thy servant, our father, is well; he is yet alive. And he said, Blessed be that man by God; and they bowed, and did him reverence. 28 *then* Joseph looked up with his eyes, and saw his brother Benjamin, born of the same mother; and he said, Is this your younger brother, whom ye spoke of bringing to me? And he said, God have mercy on thee, my son. 29 Joseph was distraught, for his bowels yearned over his brother, and he sought to weep; and he went into his chamber, and wept there.

30 And he washed his face and came out, and constrained himself and said, Take bread. 31 And they took for him alone, and for them by themselves, and for the Egyptians feasting with him by themselves, for the Egyptians could not eat bread with the Hebrews, for it is an abomination to the Egyptians. 32 they sat before him, the firstborn according to his seniority, and the younger according to his youth; and the men were amazed every one at his brother. 33 They took their portions from him to themselves; but Benjamin's portion was magnified beyond the portions of all five times in comparison to their *portion*. And they drank and became inebriated with him.

Chapter 44

And Joseph charged the steward of his house, saying, Fill the men's sacks with food, as much as they can carry, and put the money of each in the mouth of his sack. 2 And put my silver cup into the sack of the youngest, and the price of his corn. And it was done according to the word of Joseph, as he said. 3 The morning dawned, and the men were sent away, they and their donkeys. 4 And when they had left the city, *and* were not far outside, then Joseph said to his steward, Arise, and pursue after the men; and thou shall overtake them, and say to them, Why have ye returned evil for good? Why have ye stolen my silver cup? 5 Is it not this in which my lord drinks? He divines augury with it; ye have accomplished evil in that which ye have done.

6 He found them, and spoke to them according to these words. 7 They said to him, Why does our lord speak according to these words? Far be it from thy subjects to do according to this word. 8 If we brought back to thee out of the land of Canaan the money, which we found in our sacks, how should we steal silver or gold out of the house of thy lord? 9 With whomever of thy subjects thou shall find the cup, let him die; and, moreover, we will be slaves to our lord.

10 And he said, Now then it shall be as ye say; with whomever the cup shall be found, he shall be my slave, and ye shall be clear. 11 And they hurried, and took down every man his sack on the ground, and they opened every man his sack. 12 He searched, beginning with the eldest, until he came to the youngest; and he found the cup in Benjamin's sack.

Genesis 44

13 And they rent their garments, and laid each man his sack on his donkey, and returned to the city.

14 Judas and his brothers came in to Joseph, while he was yet there, and fell on the ground before him. 15 Joseph said to them, What is this thing that ye have done? Know ye not that a man such as I can surely divine? 16 Judas said, What shall we answer to our lord, or what shall we say, or wherein should we be justified? But God has discovered the unrighteousness of thy subjects, behold, we are slaves to our lord, both he and we with whom the cup has been found. 17 Joseph said, Far be it for me to do this thing; the man with whom the cup has been found, he shall be my slave; but do ye go up with safety to your father.

18 Judas drew near him, and said, I pray, lord, let thy subject speak a word before thee, and be not angry with thy subject, for thou art next to Pharaoh. 19 Lord, thou asked thy subjects, saying, Have ye a father or a brother? 20 And we said to our lord, We have a father, an old man, and he has a son in his old age, a young one, and his brother is dead, and he alone has been left behind to his mother, and his father loves him. 21 Thou said to thy servants, Bring him down to me, and I will take care of him. 22 We said to our lord, The child will not be able to leave his father; but if he should leave his father, he will die. 23 But thou said to thy subjects, Except your younger brother come down with you, ye should not see my face again. 24 And it came to pass, when we went up to thy subject our father, we reported to him the words of our lord.

25 Our father said, Go again, and buy us a little food. 26 And we said, We shall not be able to go down; but if our younger brother goes down with us, we will go down; for we shall not be able to see the man's face, *when* our younger brother is not with us. 27 Thy subject our father said to us, Ye know that my wife bore me two; 28 and one is departed from me; and ye said that he was devoured of wild beasts, and I have not seen him since. 29 If then ye take this one also from my presence, and an affliction happen to him by the way, then shall ye bring down my old age with sorrow to Hades.

30 Now then, if I should go in to thy subject, our father, and the boy should not be with us, and his life depends on this life, 31 and it shall come to pass, when he sees the boy is not with us, that he will die, and thy subjects will bring down the old age of thy subject, our father, with sorrow to Hades. 32 For thy subject has received the boy from his father, saying, If I bring him not to thee, and place him before thee, I shall be guilty towards my father forever. 33 Now then I will remain a slave with thee instead of the boy, a house servant of my lord; but let the boy go up with his brothers.

34 For how shall I go up to my father, the boy not being with us? Lest I behold the evils which will befall my father.

Chapter 45

And Joseph could not refrain himself when all were standing by him, but said, Dismiss all from me; and no one stood near Joseph, when he made himself known to his brothers. 2 And he let loose his voice with weeping; and all the Egyptians heard, and it was reported to the house of Pharaoh. 3 And Joseph said to his brothers, I am Joseph, does my father still live? And his brothers could not answer him, for they were troubled. 4 Joseph said to his brothers, Draw near to me; and they drew near; and he said, I am your brother Joseph, whom ye sold into Egypt. 5 Now then be not grieved, and let it not seem hard to you that ye sold me here, for God sent me before you for life. 6 For this second year there is famine on the earth, and there are yet five years remaining, in which there is to be neither ploughing, nor mowing. 7 For God sent me before you, that there might be left to you a remnant upon the earth, even to nourish a great remnant of you. 8 Now then ye did not send me here, but God; and he has made me as a father of Pharaoh, and lord of his entire house, and ruler of all the land of Egypt. 9 Go quickly, therefore, and go up to my father, and say to him, These things said thy son Joseph; God has made me lord of all the land of Egypt; come down therefore to me, and do not delay. 10 And thou shall live in the land of Gesem of Arabia; and thou shall be near me, you and thy sons, and thy sons' sons, thy sheep and thine oxen, and whatever things are thine. 11 And I will nourish thee there; for the famine is still for five years, lest thou be consumed, and thy sons, and all thy possessions. 12 Behold, your eyes see, and the eyes of my brother Benjamin that it is my mouth that speaks to you. 13 Report, therefore, to my father all my glory in Egypt, and all things that ye have seen, and be quick and bring down my father here. 14 And he fell on his brother Benjamin's neck, and wept on him; and Benjamin wept on his neck. 15 And he kissed all his brothers, and wept on them; and after these things his brothers spoke to him.

16 And the report was carried into the house of Pharaoh, saying, Joseph's brothers are come; and Pharaoh was glad, and his household. 17 Pharaoh said to Joseph, Say to thy brothers, Do this; fill your wagons, and depart into the land of Canaan. 18 And take up your father, and your possessions, and come to me; and I will give you of all the goods of Egypt, and ye shall eat the marrow of the land. 19 Thou do charge them thus; that they should take for them wagons out of the land of Egypt, for your little ones, and for your wives; and take up your father, and come. 20 And be not sparing in regard to your property, for all the good of Egypt shall be yours.

21 The sons of Israel did so; and Joseph gave to them wagons, according to the words spoken by Pharaoh the king; and he gave them provision for the journey. 22 And he gave to them all two sets of raiment apiece; but to Benjamin he gave three hundred pieces of gold, and five changes of raiment.

Genesis 46

23 And to his father he sent at the same rate, and ten donkeys, bearing some of all the good things of Egypt, and ten mules, bearing bread for his father for thy journey. 24 He sent away his brothers, and they went; and he said to them, Be not angry by the way. 25 And they went up out of Egypt, and came into the land of Canaan, to Jacob their father. 26 And they reported to him, saying, Thy son Joseph is living, and he is ruler over all the land of Egypt; and Jacob was astonished in *his* mind, for he did not believe them. 27 But they spoke to him all the words spoken by Joseph, whatever he said to them; and having seen the wagons, which Joseph sent to take him up, the spirit of Jacob their father revived. 28 Israel said It is a great thing for me if Joseph my son is still alive. I will go and see him before I die.

Chapter 46

Israel departed, he and everything that he had, and came to the well of the oath; and he offered sacrifice to the God of his father Isaac. 2 God spoke to Israel in a night vision, saying, Jacob, Jacob; and he said, What is it? 3 And he says to him, I am the God of thy fathers; fear not to go down into Egypt, for I will make thee there a great nation. 4 And I will go down with thee into Egypt, and I will bring thee up at the end; and Joseph shall put his hands on thine eyes. 5 And Jacob arose from the well of the oath; and the sons of Israel took up their father, and the baggage, and their wives on the wagons, which Joseph sent to take them. 6 And they took up their goods, and all their property, which they had gotten in the land of Canaan; they came into the land of Egypt, Jacob, and all his seed with him. 7 The sons, and the sons of his sons with him, daughters, and the daughters of his daughters, and he brought his entire seed into Egypt.

8 And these are the names of the sons of Israel that went into Egypt with their father Jacob--Jacob and his sons. Jacob's firstborn *was* Ruben. 9 The sons of Ruben; Enoch, and Phallus, Asron, and Harmi. 10 The sons of Simon; Jemuel, and Jamin, and Aod, and Achin, and Saar, and Saul, the son of a Canaanite woman. 11 The sons of Levi; Gerson, Kath, and Merari. 12 The sons of Judas, Er, and Aunan, and Selom, and Phares, and Zara: and Er and Aunan died in the land of Canaan. *And* sons were born to Phares, Esron, and Jemuel. 13 The sons of Issahar; Thola, and Phua, and Asum, and Sambran. 14 The sons of Zabulun, Sered, and Allon, and Achoel.

15 These *are* the sons of Lea, which she bore to Jacob in Mesopotamia of Syria, and Dina his daughter, all the souls, sons and daughters, thirty-three. 16 The sons of Gad; Saphon, and Angis, and Sannis, and Thasoban, and Aedis, and Aroedis, and Areelis. 17 The sons of Aser; Jemna, Jessua, and Jeul, and Baria, and Sara their sister. The sons of Baria; Hobor, and Melhiil.

18 These *are* the sons of Zelpha, which Laban gave to his daughter Lea, who bore these to Jacob, sixteen souls. 19 The sons of Rachel, the wife of Jacob; Joseph, and Benjamin. 20 There were sons born to Joseph in the land of Egypt, whom Aseneth, the daughter of Petephres, priest of Heliopolis, bore to him, *such as* Manassas and Ephraim. And there were sons born to Manasse, which the Syrian concubine bore to him, *such as* Mahir. And Machir begot Galaad. The sons of Ephraim, the brother of Manasse; Sutalaam, and Taam. The sons of Sutalaam; Edom. 21 The sons of Benjamin; Bala, and Bochor, and Asbel. And the sons of Bala were Gera, and Noeman, and Anchis, and Ros, and Mamphim. And Gera begot Arad. 22 These *are* the sons of Rachel, whom she bore to Jacob; all the souls were eighteen. 23 The sons of Dan; Asom. 24 The sons of Nephthalim; Asiel, and Goni, and Issaar, and Sollem. 25 These *are* the sons of Balla, whom Laban gave to his daughter Rachel, who bore these to Jacob; all the souls were seven. 26 All the souls that came with Jacob into Egypt, who came out of his thighs, besides the wives of the sons of Jacob, all the souls were sixty-six. 27 And the sons of Joseph, who were born to him in the land of Egypt, were nine souls; all the souls of the house of Jacob who came with Joseph into Egypt, were seventy-five souls.

28 He sent Judas before him to Joseph, to meet him at the city of Heroes, into the land of Ramesses. 29 *And* Joseph having hitched his chariots went up to meet Israel his father, at the city of Heroes; and having appeared to him, fell on his neck, and wept with abundant weeping. 30 And Israel said to Joseph, After this I will die, since I have seen thy face, for thou art yet living. 31 Joseph said to his brothers, I will go up and tell Pharaoh, and will say to him, My brothers, and my father's house, who were in the land of Canaan, are come to me. 32 The men are shepherds, for they have been feeders of cattle, and they have brought with them their cattle, and their herd, and all their property. 33 If then Pharaoh calls you, and says to you, What is you occupation? 34 Ye shall say, We thy subjects are herdsmen from our youth until now, both we and our fathers: that ye may live in the land of Gesem of Arabia, for every shepherd is an abomination to the Egyptians.

Chapter 47

And Joseph came and told Pharaoh, saying, My father, and my brothers, and their cattle, and their herd, and all their possessions, are come out of the land of Canaan, and behold, they are in the land of Gesem. 2 *And* he took from his brothers' five men, and set them before Pharaoh. 3 And Pharaoh said to the brothers of Joseph, What is your occupation? And they said to Pharaoh, Thy subjects are shepherds, both our father and we.

Genesis 47

4 They said to Pharaoh, We are come to travel in the land, for there is no pasture for the flocks of thy subjects, for the famine has prevailed in the land of Canaan; now then, let us live in the land of Gesem. 5 Pharaoh said to Joseph, Let them live in the land of Gesem; and if thou know that there are among them able men, make them rules of my herds. So Jacob and his sons came into Egypt, to Joseph; and Pharaoh, king of Egypt, heard. 6 And Pharaoh spoke to Joseph, saying, Thy father, and thy brothers, are come to thee. Behold, the land of Egypt is before thee; settle thy father and thy brothers in the best land.

7 Joseph brought in Jacob his father, and set him before Pharaoh; and Jacob blessed Pharaoh. 8 Pharaoh said to Jacob, How many are the years of the days of thy life? 9 And Jacob said to Pharaoh, The days of the years of my life, wherein I traveled, are a hundred and thirty years; few and evil have been the days of the years of my life, they have not attained to the days of the life of my fathers, in which days they traveled. 10 And Jacob blessed Pharaoh, and departed from him. 11 And Joseph settled his father and his brothers, and gave them a possession in the land of Egypt, in the best land, in the land of Ramesses, as Pharaoh commanded. 12 And Joseph gave provision to his father, and his brothers, and to all the house of his father, corn to each person.

13 *Now*, there was no corn in all the land, for the famine prevailed greatly; and the land of Egypt, and the land of Canaan, fainted from the famine. 14 Joseph gathered all the money that was found in the land of Egypt, and the land of Canaan, *for* the corn that they bought, and he distributed corn to them; and Joseph brought all the money into the house of Pharaoh. 15 And all the money disappeared out of the land of Egypt, and out of the land of Canaan; *and* all the Egyptians came to Joseph, saying, Give us bread, and why do we die in thy presence? For our money is spent. 16 Joseph said to them, Bring your herds and I will give you bread for your herds, if your money is spent. 17 They brought their herd to Joseph; and Joseph gave them bread in return for their horses, and for their sheep, and for their chattel, and for their donkeys; and Joseph maintained them with bread for all their herds in that year. 18 The year passed, and they came to him in the second year, and said to him, Must we then be consumed from before our lord? For if our money has disappeared, and our possessions, and our herd, *given* to thee our lord, and there has not been left to us before our lord more than our own bodies and our land. 19 In order, then, that we die not before thee, and the land is made desolate, buy us and our land for bread, and we and our land will be slaves to Pharaoh: give seed that we may sow, and live and not die, so our land shall not be made desolate.

20 And Joseph bought all the land of the Egyptians, for Pharaoh; for the Egyptians sold their land to Pharaoh, for the famine prevailed against them, and the land became Pharaoh's. 21 And he brought the people into bondage to him, as slaves, from one end of Egypt to the other end,

22 except only the land of the priests; Joseph bought not this, for Pharaoh gave a portion in the way of gift to the priests; and they ate their portion which Pharaoh gave them; therefore they sold not their land. 23 Joseph said to all the Egyptians, Behold, I have bought you and your land this day for Pharaoh; take seed for you, and sow the land. 24 And there shall be the fruits of it; and ye shall give the fifth part to Pharaoh, and the four parts shall be for yourselves, for seed for the earth, and for food for you, and all that are in your houses. 25 And they said, Thou have saved us, we have found favor before our lord, and we will be slaves to Pharaoh. 26 And Joseph appointed it to them for an ordinance until this day; to reserve a fifth part for Pharaoh, on the land of Egypt, except only the land of the priests, that was not Pharaoh's.

27 Israel lived in Egypt, in the land of Gesem, and they gained an inheritance upon it; and they increased and multiplied very greatly. 28 Jacob survived seventeen years in the land of Egypt; and Jacob's days of the years of his life were a hundred and forty-seven years.

29 The days of Israel drew near for him to die: and he called his son Joseph, and said to him, If I have found favor before thee, put thy hand under my thigh, and thou shall execute mercy and truth toward me, so as not to bury me in Egypt. 30 For I will sleep with my fathers, and thou shall carry me up out of Egypt, and bury me in their tome. And he said, I will do according to thy word. 31 He said, Swear to me; and he swore to him. And Israel did reverence, leaning on the top of his staff.

Chapter 48

And it came to pass after these things, that it was reported to Joseph, Behold, thy father is ill; and, having taken his two sons, Manasse and Ephraim, he came to Jacob. 2 It was reported to Jacob, saying, Behold, thy son Joseph comes to thee; and Israel having strengthened himself, sat upon the bed. 3 And Jacob said to Joseph, My God appeared to me in Luza, in the land of Canaan, and blessed me, 4 and said to me, Behold, I will increase thee, and multiply thee, and will make of thee multitudes of nations; and I will give this land to thee, and to thy seed after thee, for an everlasting possession. 5 Now then thy two sons, who were born to thee in the land of Egypt, before I came to thee into Egypt, are mine; Ephraim and Manasse, as Ruben and Simeon they shall be mine. 6 And the children, whom thou shall beget hereafter, shall be in the name of their brothers; they shall be named after their inheritances. 7 As for me, when I came out of Mesopotamia of Syria, Rachel, thy mother, died in the land of Canaan, as I drew near to the hippodrome of Habratha of the land, so as to come to Ephratha; and I buried her in the road of the course (this is Bethlehem).

Genesis 49

8 When Israel saw the sons of Joseph, he said, Who are these to thee? 9 Joseph said to his father, They are my sons, whom God gave me here; and Jacob said, Bring me them, that I may bless them. 10 Now the eyes of Israel were dim through age, and he could not see; and he brought them near to him, and he kissed them, and embraced them. 11 And Israel said to Joseph, Behold, I have not been deprived of thy face, and behold! God has also showed me thy seed. 12 And Joseph brought them out from his knees, and they did reverence to him, with their face to the ground. 13 And Joseph took his two sons, Ephraim in his right hand, but on the left of Israel, and Manasse on his left hand, but on the right of Israel, and brought them near to him. 14 But Israel having stretched out his right hand, laid it on the head of Ephraim, for he was the younger; and his left hand on the head of Manasse, he *then* crossed his hands. 15 And he blessed them and said, The God in whose sight my fathers were well pleasing, Abraham and Isaac, the God who continues to feed me from my youth until this day. 16 The angel who delivers me from all evils, bless these children, and my name shall be called upon them, and the name of my fathers, Abraham and Isaac; and let them be increased to a great multitude on the earth.

17 And Joseph having seen that his father put his right hand on the head of Ephraim, it seemed grievous to him; and Joseph took hold of the hand of his father, to remove it from the head of Ephraim to the head of Manasse. 18 Joseph said to his father, Not so, father; for this is the firstborn; lay thy right hand upon his head. 19 And he did not want, but said, I know it, son, I know it; he also shall be a people, and he shall be exalted, but his younger brother shall be greater than he, and his seed shall become a multitude of nations. 20 And he blessed them in that day, saying, In you shall Israel be blessed, saying, God make thee as Ephraim and Manasse; and he set Ephraim before Manasse. 21 Israel said to Joseph, Behold, I die; and God shall be with you, and restore you to the land of your fathers. 22 I give to thee Sicima, a select portion above thy brothers, which I took out of the hand of the Amorites with my sword and bow.

Chapter 49

Jacob called his sons, and said to them; assemble yourselves, that I may tell you what shall happen to you in the last days. 2 Gather yourselves together, and hear me, sons of Jacob; hear Israel, hear your father. 3 Ruben, thou *are* my firstborn, thou *are* my strength, and the first of my children, hard to be endured, *and* self-willed. 4 Thou were insolent like water, burst not forth with violence, for thou went up to the bed of thy father; then thou defiled the couch, whereupon thou went up. 5 Simon and Levi, brothers, accomplished the injustice of their cutting off.

6 Let not my soul come into their counsel, and let not mine inward parts contend in their conspiracy, for in their wrath they killed men, and in their passion they houghed a bull. 7 Cursed be their wrath, for it was willful, and their anger, for it was hardened: I will divide them in Jacob, and scatter them in Israel.

8 Judah, thy brothers have praised thee, and thy hands shall be on the back of thine enemies; thy father's sons shall do thee reverence. 9 Judah is a lion's whelp: from the tender plant, my son, thou art gone up, having couched thou sleep as a lion, and as a whelp; who shall stir him up? 10 A ruler shall not fail from Judah, nor a leader from his thighs, until there come the things stored up for him; and he is the expectation of nations. 11 Tying his foal to the vine, and the foal of his donkey to the branch, he shall wash his robe in wine and his garment in the blood of the grape * in his garden. 12 His eyes shall be more cheering than wine, and his teeth whiter than milk.

13 Zabulon shall dwell on the coast, and he *shall be* by a haven of ships, and shall extend to Sidon.

14 Issahar has desired that which is good, resting between the inheritances. 15 And having seen the resting place that it was good, and the land that it was fertile, he subjected his shoulder to labor, and became a farmer.

16 Dan shall judge his people as one of the tribes in Israel. 17 And let Dan be a serpent in the way, besetting the path, biting the heel of the horse and the horse rider shall fall backward, 18 waiting for the salvation of the Lord.

19 Gad, a plundering troop shall plunder him; but he shall plunder him, closely.

20 Aser, his bread shall be fat; and he shall yield dainties to rulers.

21 Nephthalim is a spreading stem, bestowing goodness on its fruit.

22 Joseph is a son increased; my dearly loved son is increased; my youngest son, turn to me. 23 Against whom men taking evil counsel reproached and the archers pressed hard upon him. 24 But their bow and arrows were mightily consumed, and the sinews of their arms were slackened by the hand of the mighty one of Jacob; thence is he that strengthened Israel from the God of thy father; 25 and my God helped thee, and he blessed thee with the blessing of heaven from above, and the blessing of the earth possessing all things, because of the blessing of the breasts and of the womb, 26 the blessings of thy father and thy mother, it has prevailed above the blessing of the lasting mountains, and beyond the blessings of the everlasting hills; they shall be upon the head of Joseph, and upon the head of the brothers of whom he took the lead.

27 Benjamin, as a ravaging wolf, shall eat still in the morning, and at evening he gives food.

---

* The phrase: "in his garden" is omitted from the Great Vesper reading from the Book of Genesis Chapter Forty-Nine verse eleven for Saturday evening on Palm Sunday.

Genesis 50

28 All these *are* the twelve sons of Jacob; and their father spoke these words to them, and he blessed them; he blessed each of them according to his blessing. 29 And he said to them, I am added to my people; ye shall bury me with my fathers in the cave, which is in the field of Ephron the Hittite, 30 in the double cave, which is opposite Mambre, in the land of Canaan, the cave which Abraham bought from Ephron the Hittite, for a possession of a sepulcher. 31 There they buried Abraham and Sarah his wife; there they buried Isaac, and Rebecca his wife; there they buried Lea; 32 in the portion of the field, and of the cave that was in it, of the sons of Het.

33 And Jacob ceased giving charges to his sons; and having lifted up his feet on the bed, he died, and was gathered to his people.

Chapter 50

And Joseph fell upon his father's face, and wept on him, and kissed him. 2 And Joseph commanded his slaves the embalmers to embalm his father; and the embalmers embalmed Israel. 3 And they fulfilled forty days for him, for so are the days of embalming numbered; and Egypt mourned for him seventy days.

4 And when the days of mourning were past, Joseph spoke to the princes of Pharaoh, saying, If I have found favor in your sight, speak concerning me in the ears of Pharaoh, saying, 5 My father made me swear, saying, In the sepulcher, which I dug for myself in the land of Canaan, there thou shall bury me; now then I will go up and bury my father, and return again. 6 And Pharaoh said to Joseph, Go up; bury thy father, as he made thee to swear.

7 So Joseph went up to bury his father; and all the slaves of Pharaoh went up with him, and the elders of his house, and all the elders of the land of Egypt. 8 And all the household of Joseph, and his brothers, and all the house of his father, and his kindred; and they left behind the sheep and the oxen in the land of Gesem. 9 And there went up with him also chariots and horsemen; and there was a very great company.

10 And they came to the threshing-floor of Atad, which is beyond Jordan; and they bewailed him with a great and very sore lamentation; and he made mourning for his father seven days. 11 And the inhabitants of the land of Canaan saw the mourning at the floor of Atad, and said, This is a great mourning to the Egyptians; therefore he called its name, The mourning of Egypt, which is beyond Jordan. 12 And thus his sons did to him. 13 So his sons carried him up into the land of Canaan, and buried him in the double cave, which cave Abraham bought for possession of a burying place, of Ephrom the Hittite, before Mambre. 14 And Joseph returned to Egypt, he and his brothers, and those that had gone up with him to bury his father.

Genesis 50

15 When the brothers of Joseph saw that their father was dead, they said, May Joseph never remember evil against us, and recompense to us all the evils, which we have done against him. 16 And they came to Joseph, and said, Thy father made us swear before his death, saying, 17 Thus say ye to Joseph, Forgive them their injustice and their sin, forasmuch as they have done thee evil; and now accept the injustice of the servants of the God of thy father. And Joseph wept while they spoke to him. 18 And they came to him and said, We, these, are thy servants. 19 And Joseph said to them, Fear not, for I am God's. 20 Ye took counsel against me for evil, but God took counsel for me for good that might be as today and many people might be fed. 21 And he said to them, Fear not, I will maintain you, and your families: and he comforted them, and spoke kindly to them.

22 And Joseph lived in Egypt, he and his brothers, and all the family of his father; and Joseph lived a hundred and ten years. 23 And Joseph saw the children of Ephraim to the third generation; and the sons of Mahir the son of Manasse were borne on the thighs of Joseph. 24 And Joseph spoke to his brethren, saying, I die, and God will surely visit you, and will bring you out of this land to the land concerning which God promised to our fathers, Abraham, Isaac, and Jacob. 25 And Joseph swore the sons of Israel, saying, At the visitation with which God shall visit you, then ye shall carry up my bones hence with you. 26 And Joseph died, aged an hundred and ten years; and they buried him, and placed him in the coffin in Egypt.

The Book of
Exodus

Chapter 1

These are the names of the sons of Israel that came into Egypt together with Jacob their father; they came in each with their whole family. 2 Ruben, Simeon, Levi, Judas, 3 Issahar, Zabulon, Benjamin, 4 Dan and Nephthalim, Gad and Aser. 5 Joseph was in Egypt. All the souls born of Jacob were seventy-five. 6 And Joseph died, and all his brothers, and all that generation. 7 The sons of Israel increased and multiplied, and became numerous and grew very strong, and the land multiplied with them. 8 And there arose another king over Egypt, who did not know Joseph. 9 And he said to his nation, Behold, the race of the sons of Israel is a great multitude, and is stronger than we; 10 come then, let us deal craftily with them, lest at any time they be increased, and whenever war shall happen to us, these also shall be added to our enemies, and having prevailed against us in war, they will depart out of the land. 11 And he set over them taskmasters, who did afflict them in their works; and they built fortified cities, Pitho, and Ramesse, and On, which is Heliopolis, for Pharaoh. 12 But as they humbled them, by so much they multiplied, and grew very strong; and the Egyptians greatly abhorred the sons of Israel. 13 And the Egyptians tyrannized over the sons of Israel by force. 14 And they embittered their life by hard labors, in the mortar and in brick making, and all the works in the plains, according to all the works, wherein they reduced them to slavery with force.

15 And the king of the Egyptians spoke to the midwives of the Hebrews; the name of the one was Sepphora; and the name of the second, Phua. 16 And he said, When ye act as midwives to the Hebrew women, and they are about to be delivered, if it be a male, kill it; but if a female, save it. 17 But the midwives feared God, and did not as the King of Egypt commanded them; and they saved the males alive. 18 The King of Egypt *then* called the midwives, and said to them, Why is it that ye have done this thing, and saved the males alive? 19 And the midwives said to Pharaoh, The Hebrew women are not as the women of Egypt, for they deliver before the midwives go in to them. So they bore children. 20 And God did well to the midwives, and the people multiplied, and grew very strong. 21 And as the midwives feared God, they established for themselves families. 22 And Pharaoh charged all his people, saying, Whatever male child shall be born to the Hebrews, throw it into the river; and every female, save it alive.

Exodus 2

Chapter 2

There was a certain man from the tribe of Levi, who took to wife one of the daughters of Levi. 2 And she conceived, and bore a male child; and having seen that he was fair, they hid him three months. 3 And when they could no longer hide him, his mother took for him a basket, and besmeared it with tar, and cast the child into it, and put it in the marsh by the river. 4 And his sister was watching from a distance, to learn what would happen to him.

5 And the daughter of Pharaoh came down to the river to bathe; and her maids walked by the river's side, and having seen the basket in the marsh, she sent her maid, and took it up. 6 And having opened it, she sees the babe weeping in the basket: and the daughter of Pharaoh had compassion on him, and said, From the male children of the Hebrews this *one* is. 7 And his sister said to the daughter of Pharaoh, Will thou that I call to thee a nurse of the Hebrews, and shall she suckle the child for thee? 8 And the daughter of Pharaoh said, Go, and the young woman went, and called the mother of the child. 9 And the daughter of Pharaoh said to her, Take care of this child, and suckled it for me, and I will give thee your wages; and the woman took the child, and suckled it. 10 And when the boy was grown, she brought him to the daughter of Pharaoh, and he became her son; and she named his name, Moses, saying, I drew him out of the water.

11 And it came to pass in that length of days, that Moses having grown up, went out to his brothers the sons of Israel; and having pondered their pain, he saw an Egyptian striking a certain Hebrew of his brothers of the sons of Israel. 12 And having looked around this way and that way, he saw no one; and he struck the Egyptian, and hid him in the sand. 13 And having gone out the second day he saw two Hebrew men fighting; and he said to the one was in the wrong, Wherefore strikes thou thy neighbor? 14 And he said, Who made thee a ruler and a judge over us? Do you want to kill me in the same manner you yesterday killed the Egyptian? Then Moses was afraid, and said, If *it is* thus, this matter has become known. 15 When Pharaoh heard this matter he sought to kill Moses; and Moses departed from the face of Pharaoh, and lived in the land of Madiam; and having come into the land of Madiam, he sat by a well.

16 And the priest of Madiam had seven daughters, tending the sheep of their father Jethro; and they came and drew water until they filled their pitchers, to water the sheep of their father Jethro. 17 And the shepherds came, and were driving them away; and Moses arose and rescued them, and drew water for them, and watered their sheep. 18 And they came to * Ragouel their father; and he said to them, Why have ye come so quickly today? 19 And they said, An Egyptian delivered us from the shepherds, and drew water for us and watered our sheep. 20 And he said to his daughters, And where is he? And why have ye left the man? Call him therefore, that he may eat bread.

21 And Moses stayed with the man, and he gave Sepphora his daughter to Moses for a wife. 22 And the woman conceived and bore a son, and Moses called his name Gersam, saying, I am a traveler in a foreign land. * 23 And in those days after a length of time, the king of Egypt died; and the sons of Israel groaned because of their tasks, and cried, and their cry because of their tasks went up to God. 24 And God heard their groaning, and God remembered his covenant made with Abraham and Isaac and Jacob. 25 And God looked upon the sons of Israel, and was made known to them.

* *Codex Alexandrinus* reads: "Jethro".

* The vesper reading for Holy and Great Wednesday for the Holy Week of *Pascha* reads Chapter Two, verse twenty-three much differently than what is present in the Apostoliki Diakonia and Zoe Brotherhood texts. This variant or additional reading may also be a continuation of verse twenty-two. The reading is translated as follows:

"And she conceived again, and bore a second son, and called his name Eliezer, saying, For the God of my father is my helper, and has rescued me from the hand of Pharaoh."

Chapter 3

And Moses was feeding the sheep of Jethro his father-in-law, the priest of Madiam; and he brought the sheep near to the wilderness, and came to the mountain of Horeb. 2 And an angel of the Lord appeared to him in a fire of flame out of the bush, and he saw that the bush was burning with fire, but the bush was not consumed. 3 And Moses said, When I go by, I will see this great sight, why the bush is not consumed. 4 And when the Lord saw that he drew near to see, the Lord called to him out of the bush, saying, Moses, Moses, and he said, What is it? 5 And He said, Draw not near here; loose thy sandals from off thy feet, for the place whereon thou stand is holy ground. 6 And He said, I am the God of thy father, the God of Abraham, and the God of Isaac, and the God of Jacob; and Moses turned away his face, for he was afraid to look at God.

7 And the Lord said to Moses, I have surely seen the affliction of My people that are in Egypt, and I have heard their cry caused by their taskmasters for I know their affliction. 8 And I have come down to deliver them out of the hand of the Egyptians, and to bring them out of that land, and to bring them into a good and wide land, into a land flowing with milk and honey, into the place of the Canaanites, and the Hittites, and Amorites, and Pherezites, and Gergesites, and Evites, and Jebusites. 9 And now, behold, the cry of the sons of Israel is come to Me, and I have seen the affliction with which the Egyptians afflict them.

Exodus 4

10 And now come, I will send thee to Pharaoh King of Egypt, and thou shall bring out My people the sons of Israel from the land of Egypt. 11 And Moses said to God, Who am I, that I should go to Pharaoh King of Egypt, and that I should bring out the sons of Israel from the land of Egypt? 12 And God spoke to Moses, saying, I will be with thee, and this shall be the sign to thee that I shall send thee forth, when thou bring out My people out of Egypt, then ye shall serve God in this mountain. 13 And Moses said to God, Behold, I shall go forth to the sons of Israel, and shall say to them, The God of our fathers has sent me to you; and they will ask me, What is His name? What shall I say to them? 14 And God spoke to Moses, saying, I am THE ONE WHO IS; and He said, Thus shall ye say to the sons of Israel, THE ONE WHO IS has sent me to you.

15 And God said again to Moses, Thus shall thou say to the sons of Israel, The Lord God of our fathers, the God of Abraham, and God of Isaac, and God of Jacob, has sent me to you; this is My name forever, and My memorial to generations of generations. 16 Go then and gather the elders of the sons of Israel, and thou shall say to them, The Lord God of our fathers has appeared to me, the God of Abraham, and God of Isaac, and God of Jacob, saying, I have surely looked upon you, and upon all the things which have happened to you in Egypt. 17 And he said, I would bring you up out of the affliction of the Egyptians to the land of the Canaanites and the Hittites, and Amorites and Pherezites, and Gergesites, and Evites, and Jebusites, to a land flowing with milk and honey. 18 And they shall hearken to thy voice, and thou and the rulers of Israel shall go in to Pharaoh King of Egypt, and thou shall say to him, The God of the Hebrews has called us; we will go then a journey of three days into the wilderness that we may sacrifice to our God.

19 I know that Pharaoh King of Egypt will not let you go, save with a mighty hand; 20 and I will stretch out my hand, and strike the Egyptians with all my wonders, which I shall work among them, and after that he will send you forth. 21 And I will give this people favor in the sight of the Egyptians, and whenever ye shall escape, ye shall not depart empty. 22 But every woman shall ask of her neighbor and fellow lodger, articles of gold and silver, and apparel; and ye shall put them upon your sons and upon your daughters, and spoil ye the Egyptians.

Chapter 4

And Moses answered and said, If they believe me not, and do not hearken to my voice, for they will say, God has not appeared to thee, what shall I say to them? 2 And the Lord said to him, What is this thing that is in thine hand? And he said, a rod. 3 And He said, Cast it on the ground; and he cast it on the ground, and it became a serpent, and Moses fled from it.

Exodus 4

4 And the Lord said to Moses, Stretch forth thine hand, and take hold of its tail. So he stretched forth his hand and took hold of the tail, 5 and it became a rod in his hand that they may believe thee that the God of thy fathers has appeared to thee, the God of Abraham, and God of Isaac, and God of Jacob. 6 And the Lord said again to him, Put thine hand into thy bosom; and he put his hand into his bosom, and brought his hand out of his bosom, and his hand became as snow.

7 And he said again, Put thy hand into thy bosom; and he put his hand into his bosom, and brought his hand out of his bosom, and it was again restored to the complexion of his other flesh. 8 And if they will not believe thee, nor hearken to the voice of the first sign, they will believe thee because of the voice of the second sign.

9 And it shall come to pass if they will not believe thee for these two signs, and will not hearken to thy voice, that thou shall take of the water of the river and pour it upon the dry land, and the water, which thou shall take from the river, shall be blood upon the dry land. 10 And Moses said to the Lord, I pray, Lord, I have not been sufficient before yesterday, neither before the third day or since thou has begun to speak to thy servant: I am weak in speech, and slow-tongued. 11 And the Lord said to Moses, Who has given a mouth to man, and who has made the very hard of hearing, and the deaf, the seeing and the blind? Have not I, God? 12 And now go and I will open thy mouth, and will instruct thee in what thou shall say. 13 And Moses said, I pray thee, Lord, appoint another able person whom thou shall send.

14 And the Lord was greatly angered against Moses, and said, Behold! Is not Aaron the Levite thy brother? I know that he will surely speak to thee; and, behold, he will come forth to meet thee, and beholding thee he will rejoice within himself. 15 And thou shall speak to him; and thou shall put my words into his mouth, and I will open thy mouth and his mouth, and I will instruct you in what ye shall do. 16 And he shall speak for thee to the people, and he shall be thy mouth, and thou shall be for him in things pertaining to God. 17 And this rod that was turned into a serpent thou shall take in thine hand, wherewith thou shall work miracles. 18 And Moses went and returned to Jethro his father-in-law, and says, I will go and return to my brethren in Egypt, and will see if they are yet living. And Jethro said to Moses, Go in health. And in those days after some time, the king of Egypt died. 19 And the Lord said to Moses in Madiam, Go; depart into Egypt, for all that sought thy life are dead. 20 And Moses took his wife and his children, and mounted them on the beasts, and returned to Egypt; and Moses took the rod, which he had, from God in his hand.

21 And the Lord said to Moses, When thou goes and returns to Egypt, see, all the miracles I put into thine hands, thou shall perform them before Pharaoh; and I will harden his heart, and he shall certainly not send away the people.

Exodus 5

22 And thou shall say to Pharaoh, These things saith the Lord, Israel is my firstborn. 23 And I said to thee, Send away my people that they may serve me: now if thou wilt not send them away, see, I will kill thy firstborn son. 24 And it came to pass that the angel of the Lord met him by the way in the inn, and sought to kill him. 25 and Sepphora having taken a stone cut off the foreskin of her son, and fell at his feet and said, The blood of the circumcision of my son is staunched: 26 and he departed from him, because she said, The blood of the circumcision of my son is staunched. 27 And the Lord said to Aaron, Go into the wilderness to meet Moses; and he went and met him in the mount of God, and they kissed each other. 28 And Moses reported to Aaron all the words of the Lord, which he sent, and all the things, which he charged him. 29 And Moses and Aaron went and gathered the elders of the sons of Israel.

30 And Aaron spoke all these words, which God spoke to Moses, and wrought the miracles before the people. 31 and the people believed and rejoiced, because God visited the sons of Israel, and because He saw their affliction; and the people bowed and worshipped.

Chapter 5

And after this went in Moses and Aaron to Pharaoh, and they said to him, These things says the Lord God of Israel, Send my people away, that they may keep a feast to me in the wilderness. 2 And Pharaoh said, Who is he that I should hearken to his voice, so that I should send away the sons of Israel? I do not know the Lord, and I will not send out Israel. 3 And they say to him, The God of the Hebrews has called us to him; we will go therefore a three days' journey into the wilderness, that we may sacrifice to the Lord our God, lest at any time death or slaughter happen to us. 4 And the King of Egypt said to them, Why do ye, Moses and Aaron, turn the people from their works? Depart each of you to your works. 5 And Pharaoh said, Behold now, the people is very numerous; let us not then give them rest from their work.

6 And Pharaoh gave orders to the task-masters of the people and the accountants, saying, 7 Ye shall no longer give straw to the people for brick making as yesterday and the third day; but let them go themselves, and collect straw for themselves. 8 And thou shall impose on them daily the rate of brick-making which they perform; thou shall not abate anything, for they are idle; therefore have they cried, saying, Let us arise and do sacrifice to our God. 9 Let the works of these men be made grievous, and let them care for these things, and not care for vain words. 10 And the taskmasters and the accountants hastened them, and they spoke to the people, saying, thus says Pharaoh; I will give you straw no longer. 11 Go ye, yourselves, get for yourselves straw wherever ye can find it, for nothing is diminished from your rate.

12 So the people were dispersed in all the land of Egypt, to gather stubble for straw. 13 and the taskmasters hastened them, saying, Fulfill your regular daily tasks, even as when straw was given you. 14 And the accountants of the race of the sons of Israel, who were set over them by the masters of Pharaoh, were scourged, and questioned, men saying, Why have ye not fulfilled your rates of brickwork as yesterday and the third day, today also? 15 And the accountants of the sons of Israel went in and cried to Pharaoh, saying, Why does thou act thus to thy servants? 16 Straw is not given to thy servants, and they tell us to make brick; and behold thy servants have been scourged; thou will therefore injure thy people. 17 And he said to them, Ye are idle, ye are idlers; therefore ye say, Let us go and do sacrifice to our God. 18 Now then go and work, for straw shall not be given to you, yet ye shall return the rate of bricks. 19 And the accountants of the sons of Israel saw themselves in an evil plight, men saying, Ye shall not fail from the brick making that belongs to each day.

20 And they met Moses and Aaron coming forth to meet them, as they came forth from Pharaoh. 21 And they said to them, The Lord look upon you and judge you, for ye have made our savor abominable before Pharaoh, and before his servants, to put a sword into his hands to kill us. 22 And Moses turned to the Lord, and said, I pray, Lord, why hast thou afflicted this people? And wherefore hast thou sent me? 23 For from the time that I went to Pharaoh to speak in thy name, he has afflicted this people, and thou hast not delivered thy people.

Chapter 6

And the Lord said to Moses, Now thou shall see what I will do to Pharaoh; for he shall send them forth with a mighty hand, and with a high arm shall he cast them out of his land.

2 And God spoke to Moses and said to him, I am the Lord. 3 And I appeared to Abraham and Isaac and Jacob, being their God, but I did not manifest to them my name: Lord. 4 And I established my covenant with them, to give them the land of the Canaanites, the land wherein they traveled, in which also they lived as strangers. 5 And I hearkened to the groaning of the sons of Israel (the affliction with which the Egyptians enslave them) and I remembered your covenant. 6 Go, speak to the sons of Israel, saying, I am the Lord; and I will lead you forth from the tyranny of the Egyptians, and I will deliver you from slavery, and I will ransom you with a high arm, and great judgment. 7 And I will take you to me a people for myself, and will be your God; and ye shall know that I am the Lord your God, who brought you out from the tyranny of the Egyptians. 8 And I will bring you into the land concerning which I stretched out my hand to give it to Abraham and Isaac and Jacob, and I will give it you for an inheritance: I am the Lord.

Exodus 6

9 And Moses spoke thus to the sons of Israel, and they hearkened not to Moses for faintheartedness, and for their hard tasks. 10 And the Lord spoke to Moses, saying, 11 Go in, speak to Pharaoh King of Egypt that he send forth the sons of Israel out of his land. 12 And Moses spoke before the Lord, saying, Behold, the sons of Israel hearkened not to me, and how shall Pharaoh hearken to me? And I am not eloquent. 13 And the Lord spoke to Moses and Aaron, and gave them a charge to Pharaoh King of Egypt, that he should send forth the sons of Israel out of the land of Egypt.

14 And these are the heads of the houses of their families: the sons of Ruben the firstborn of Israel; Enoch and Phallus, Asron, and Harmi, this is the kindred of Ruben. 15 And the sons of Simon, Jemuel and Jamin, and Aod, and Jahin and Saar, and Saul the son of a Phoenician woman, these are the families of the sons of Simon. 16 And these are the names of the sons of Levi according to their kindred, Gedson, Kaath, and Merari; and the years of the life of Levi were a hundred and thirty-seven. 17 And these are the sons of Gedson, Lobeni and Semei, the houses of their family. And the sons of Kaath, 18 Ambram and Issaar, Hebron, and Oziel, and the years of the life of Kaath were * a hundred and thirty-three years. 19 And the sons of Merari, Mooli, and Omusi, these are the houses of the families of Levi, according to their kindred. 20 And Ambram took to wife Johabed the daughter of his father's brother, and she bore to him both Aaron and Moses, and Mariam their sister: and the years of the life of Ambram were * a hundred and thirty-two years. 21 And the sons of Issaar, Core, and Naphek, and Zehri. 22 And the sons of Oziel, Misael, and Elisaphan, and Segri. 23 And Aaron took to himself to wife Elisabeth daughter of Aminadab sister of Naasson, and she bore to him both Nadab and Abiud, and Eleazar and Ithamar. 24 And the sons of Kore, Asir, and Elkana, and Abiasar, these are the generations of Kore. 25 And Eleazar the son of Aaron took to himself for a wife one of the daughters of Phutiel, and she bore to him Phinees. These are the rulers of the family of the Levites, according to their generations. 26 This is Aaron and Moses, whom God told to bring out the sons of Israel out of the land of Egypt with their forces. 27 These are they that spoke with Pharaoh king of Egypt, and Aaron himself and Moses brought out the sons of Israel from the land of Egypt,

28 in the day in which the Lord spoke to Moses in the land of Egypt; 29 then the Lord spoke to Moses, saying, I am the Lord; speak to Pharaoh King of Egypt whatever I say to thee. 30 And Moses said before the Lord, Behold, I am not able in speech, and how shall Pharaoh hearken to me?

---

* *Codex Alexandrinus* reads verse eighteen: a hundred and thirty years.
* *Codex Alexandrinus* reads verse twenty-one: a hundred and thirty-six years

Chapter 7

And the Lord spoke to Moses, saying, Behold, I have made thee a god to Pharaoh, and Aaron thy brother shall be thy prophet. 2 And thou shall say to him all things that I charge thee, and Aaron thy brother shall speak to Pharaoh, that he should send forth the sons of Israel out of his land. 3 And I will harden the heart of Pharaoh, and I will multiply My signs and wonders in the land of Egypt. 4 And Pharaoh will not hearken to you, and I will lay My hand upon Egypt; and will bring out My people the sons of Israel with My power out of the land of Egypt with great vengeance. 5 And all the Egyptians shall know that I am the Lord, stretching out My hand upon Egypt, and I will bring out the sons of Israel out of the midst of them. 6 And Moses and Aaron did as the Lord commanded them, so did they. 7 And Moses was eighty years old, and Aaron his brother was eighty-three years old, when he spoke to Pharaoh.

8 And the Lord spoke to Moses and Aaron, saying, 9 Now if Pharaoh should speak to you, saying, Give us a sign or a wonder, then shall thou say to thy brother Aaron, Take thy rod and cast it upon the ground before Pharaoh, and before his servants, and it shall become a serpent. 10 And Moses and Aaron went in before Pharaoh, and before his servants, and they did so, as the Lord commanded them; and Aaron cast down his rod before Pharaoh, and before his servants, and it became a serpent. 11 But Pharaoh called together the wise men of Egypt, and the sorcerers, and the charmers also of the Egyptians did likewise with their sorceries. 12 And they cast down each their rod, and they became serpents, but the rod of Aaron swallowed up their rods. 13 and the heart of Pharaoh was hardened, and he hearkened not to them, as the Lord charged them.

14 and the Lord said to Moses, The heart of Pharaoh is made hard, so that he should not let the people go. 15 Go to Pharaoh early in the morning; behold, he goes forth to the water; and thou shall meet him on the bank of the river, and thou shall take in thine hand the rod that was turned into a serpent. 16 And thou shall say to him, The Lord God of the Hebrews has sent me to thee, saying, Send my people away, that they may serve me in the wilderness and behold hitherto thou has not hearkened. 17 These things said the Lord, Hereby shall thou know that I am the Lord, behold, I strike with the rod that is in my hand on the water, which is in the river, and it shall change it into blood. 18 And the fish that are in the river shall die, and the river shall stink thereupon, and the Egyptians shall not be able to drink water from the river. 19 And the Lord said to Moses, Say to thy brother Aaron, Take thy rod in thy hand, and stretch forth thy hand over the waters of Egypt, and over their rivers, and over their canals, and over their ponds, and over all their standing water, and it shall become blood: and there

Exodus 8

was blood in all the land of Egypt, both in vessels of wood and of stone. 20 and Moses and Aaron did so, as the Lord commanded them; and Aaron having lifted up his hand with his rod, struck the water in the river before Pharaoh, and before his slaves, and changed all the water in the river into blood. 21 And the fish in the river died, and the river stank thereupon; and the Egyptians could not drink water from the river, and the blood was in all the land of Egypt. 22 And the charmers also of the Egyptians did so with their sorceries; and the heart of Pharaoh was hardened, and he did not hearken to them, even as the Lord said. 23 And Pharaoh turned and entered into his house, nor did he fix his attention even on this thing. 24 And all the Egyptians dug round about the river, so as to drink water, for they could not drink water from the river.

25 and seven days were fulfilled after the Lord has smitten the river. 26 And the Lord said to Moses, Go in to Pharaoh, and thou shall say to him, These things say the Lord, Send forth my people that they may serve me. 27 And if thou will not send them forth, behold, I afflict all thy borders with frogs; 28 and the river shall teem with frogs, and they shall go up and enter into thy houses, and into thy bed chambers, and upon thy beds, and upon the houses of thy slaves, and of thy people and on thy dough, and on thine ovens. 29 And upon thee, and upon thy servants, and upon thy people, shall the frogs come up.

Chapter 8

And the Lord said to Moses, Say to Aaron thy brother, Stretch forth with the hand thy rod over the rivers, and over the canals, and over the pools, and bring up the frogs. 2 And Aaron stretched forth his hand over the waters of Egypt, and brought up the frogs; and the frog was brought up, and covered the land of Egypt. 3 And the charmers of the Egyptians also did likewise with their sorceries, and brought up the frogs on the land of Egypt. 4 And Pharaoh called Moses and Aaron, and said, Pray for me to the Lord, and let him take away the frogs from me and from my people; and I will send them away, and they shall sacrifice to the Lord. 5 And Moses said to Pharaoh, Appoint me a time when I shall pray for thee, and for thy slaves, and for thy people, to cause the frogs to disappear from thee, and from thy people, and from your houses, only in the river shall they be left behind. 6 And he said, Tomorrow; he said therefore, As thou has said; that thou may know, that there is no other God but the Lord. 7 And the frogs shall be removed away from thee, and from your houses and from the villages, and from thy slaves, and from thy people, only in the river they shall be left. 8 And Moses and Aaron went forth from Pharaoh, and Moses cried to the Lord concerning the restriction of the frogs, as Pharaoh appointed him. 9 And the Lord did as Moses said, and the frogs died out of the houses, and out of the villages, and out of the fields.

Exodus 8

10 And they gathered them together in heaps, and the land stank. 11 And when Pharaoh saw that there was relief, his heart was hardened, and he did not hearken to them, as the Lord spoke. 12 And the Lord said to Moses, Say to Aaron, Stretch forth thy rod with thy hand and strike the dust of the earth; and there shall be lice both upon man, and upon quadrupeds, and in all the land of Egypt. 13 So Aaron stretched out his rod with his hand, and struck the dust of the earth; and the lice were on men and on quadrupeds, and in all the dust of the earth there were lice. 14 And the charmers also did so with their sorceries, to bring forth the louse, and they could not. And the lice were both on the men and on the quadrupeds. 15 So the charmers said to Pharaoh, This is the finger of God. But the heart of Pharaoh was hardened, and he did not hearken unto them, as the Lord said.

16 And the Lord said to Moses, Arise early in the morning, and stand before Pharaoh; and behold, he will go forth to the water, and thou shall say to him, These things says the Lord, Send away my people, that they may serve me in the wilderness. 17 And if thou will not let my people go, behold, I send upon thee, and upon thy servants, and upon thy people, and upon your houses, the dog fly; and the houses of the Egyptians shall be filled with the dog fly, even throughout the land upon which they are. 18 and I will distinguish marvelously in that day the land of Gesem, in which my people live, in which the dog fly shall not be; that thou may know that I am the Lord the God of all the earth. 19 And I will put a difference between my people and thy people, and on the morrow shall this be on the land. And the Lord did thus. 20 And the dog fly came in abundance into the houses of Pharaoh and into the houses of his slaves, and into all the land of Egypt; and the dog fly destroyed the land.

21 And Pharaoh called Moses and Aaron, saying, Go and sacrifice to the Lord your God in the land. 22 And Moses said, It could not be so, for we shall sacrifice to the Lord our God the abominations of the Egyptians; for if we sacrifice the abominations of the Egyptians before them, we shall be stoned. 23 We will go a journey of three days into the wilderness, and we will sacrifice to the Lord our God, as the Lord said to us. 24 And Pharaoh said, I will let you go, and do ye sacrifice to your God in the wilderness, but do not go very far away: pray then for me to the Lord. 25 And Moses said, I then will go forth from thee and pray to God, and the dog fly shall depart both from thy slaves, and from thy people tomorrow. Do not thou, Pharaoh, deceive again, so as not to send the people away to do sacrifice to the Lord. 26 And Moses went out from Pharaoh, and prayed to God. 27 And the Lord did as Moses said, and removed the dog fly from Pharaoh, and from his slaves, and from his people, and there was not one left. 28 And Pharaoh hardened his heart, even on this occasion, and he would not send the people away.

Exodus 9

Chapter 9

And the Lord said to Moses, Go in to Pharaoh, and thou shall say to him, These things says the Lord God of the Hebrews; Send my people away that they may serve me. 2 If however thou will not send my people away, but yet detain them: 3 behold, the hand of the Lord shall be upon thy cattle in the fields, both on the horses, and on the asses, and on the camels and oxen and sheep, a very great death. 4 And I will make a marvelous distinction in that time between the cattle of the Egyptians, and the cattle of the sons of Israel; nothing shall die of all that is of the sons of Israel. 5 And God fixed a limit, saying; Tomorrow the Lord will do this thing on the land. 6 And the Lord did this thing on the next day, and all the cattle of the Egyptians died, but of the cattle of the sons of Israel not one died. 7 And when Pharaoh saw, that of all the cattle of the sons of Israel not one died, the heart of Pharaoh was hardened, and he did not let the people go.

8 And the Lord spoke to Moses and Aaron, saying, Take you handfuls of ashes of the furnace, and let Moses scatter it toward heaven before Pharaoh, and before his slaves. 9 And let it become dust over all the land of Egypt, and there shall be upon men and upon beast sores, boils breaking forth both on men and on beasts, in all the land of Egypt. 10 So he took of the ashes of the furnace before Pharaoh, and Moses scattered it toward heaven, and it became sores, boils breaking forth both on men and on beasts. 11 And the sorcerers could not stand before Moses because of the sores, for the sores were on the sorcerers, and in all the land of Egypt. 12 And the Lord hardened Pharaoh's heart, and he hearkened not to them, as the Lord appointed.

13 And the Lord said to Moses, Rise up early in the morning, and stand before Pharaoh; and thou shall say to him, These things said the Lord God of the Hebrews, Send away my people that they may serve me. 14 For at this present time do I send forth all my occurrences into thine heart, and the heart of thy slaves and of thy people; that thou may know that there is not another such as I in all the earth. 15 For now I will stretch forth my hand and strike thee and kill thy people, and thou shall be consumed from off the earth. 16 And for this purpose has thou been preserved, that I might display in thee my strength, and that my name might be published in all the earth. 17 Does thou then yet exert thyself to hinder my people, so as not to let them go? 18 Behold, tomorrow at this hour I will rain a very great hail, such as has not been in Egypt, from the time it was created until this day. 19 Now then hasten to gather thy cattle, and all that thou has in the fields; for all the men and cattle as many as shall be found in the fields, and shall not enter into a house, (but the hail shall fall upon them), shall die. 20 He of the servants of Pharaoh that feared the word of the Lord gathered his cattle into the houses.

21 And he that did not attend in his mind to the word of the Lord left the cattle in the fields. 22 And the Lord said to Moses, Stretch out thine hand to heaven, and there shall be hail on all the land of Egypt, both on the men and on the cattle, and on all the herbage on the land. 23 And Moses stretched forth his hand to heaven, and the Lord sent a *thundering* voice and hail; and the fire ran along upon the ground, and the Lord rained hail on all the land of Egypt. 24 So there was hail and flaming fire mingled with hail, and the hail was very great, such as was not in Egypt, from the time there was a nation upon it. 25 And the hail struck in all the land of Egypt both man and beast, and the hail struck all the grass in the field, and the hail broke in pieces all the trees in the field. 26 Only in the land of Gesem where the sons of Israel were, the hail was not. 27 And Pharaoh sent and called Moses and Aaron, and said to them, I have sinned this time: the Lord is righteous, and my people and I are wicked. 28 Pray then for me to the Lord, and let him cause the *thundering* voice of God to cease from being, and the hail and the fire, and I will send you forth and ye shall remain no longer. 29 And Moses said to him, When I shall have departed from the city, I will stretch out my hands to the Lord, and the *thundering* voices shall cease, and the hail and the rain shall be no longer, that thou may know that the earth is the Lord's. 30 But as for thee and thy servants, I know that ye have not yet feared the Lord.

31 And the flax and the barley were struck, for the barley was ripe, and the flax was seeding. 32 But the wheat and the rye were not struck, for they were late. 33 And Moses went forth from Pharaoh out of the city, and stretched out his hands to the Lord, and the thunders ceased and the hail and the rain did not drop on the earth. 34 And when Pharaoh saw that the rain and the hail and the thunders ceased, he continued to sin; and he hardened his heart, and the heart of his servants. 35 And the heart of Pharaoh was hardened, and he did not send forth the sons of Israel, as the Lord said to Moses.

Chapter 10

And the Lord spoke to Moses, saying, Go in to Pharaoh; for I have hardened his heart and the heart of his slaves, that these signs may come upon them; in order 2 that ye may relate in the ears of your children, and to your children's children, in how many things I have mocked the Egyptians, and My wonders which I wrought among them; and ye shall know that I am the Lord. 3 And Moses and Aaron went in before Pharaoh, and they said to him, These things said the Lord God of the Hebrews, How long does thou refuse to reverence Me? Send My people away, that they may serve Me. 4 But if thou will not send My people away, behold, at this hour tomorrow I will bring an abundance of locusts upon all thy coasts.

Exodus 10

5 And they shall cover the face of the earth, and thou shall not be able to see the earth; and they shall devour all that is left of the abundance of the earth, which the hail has left you, and shall devour every tree that grows for you on the land. 6 And thy houses shall be filled, and the houses of thy servants, and all the houses in all the land of the Egyptians; things which thy fathers have never seen, nor their forefathers, from the day that they were upon the earth until this day. And Moses turned away and departed from Pharaoh. 7 And the servants of Pharaoh say to him, How long shall this be a snare to us? Send away the men that they may serve their God; will thou know that Egypt is destroyed? 8 And they brought back both Moses and Aaron to Pharaoh; and he said to them, Go and serve the Lord your God; but who are they that are going with you? 9 And Moses said, We will go with the young and the old, with our sons, and daughters, and sheep, and oxen, for it is a feast of the Lord. 10 And he said to them, So let the Lord be with you; as I will send you away, must I send away your store also? * Be aware that evil lies near to you. 11 Not so, but let the men go and serve God, for this ye yourselves seek; and they cast them out from the presence of Pharaoh.

12 And the Lord said to Moses, Stretch out thine hand over the land of Egypt, and let the locust come up on the land, and it shall devour every herb of the land, and all the fruit of the trees, which the hail left. 13 And Moses lifted up his rod towards heaven, and the Lord brought a south wind upon the earth, all that day and all that night; the morning dawned, and the south wind brought up the locusts, 14 and brought them up over all the land of Egypt. And they rested in very great abundance over all the borders of Egypt. Before them there were not such locusts, neither after them shall there be. 15 And they covered the face of the earth, and the land was wasted, and they devoured all the herbage of the land, and all the fruit of the trees, which was left by the hail: there was no green thing left on the trees, nor on all the herbage of the field, in all the land of Egypt.

16 And Pharaoh hasted to call Moses and Aaron, saying, I have sinned before the Lord your God, and against you; 17 accept therefore my sin yet this time, and pray to the Lord your God, and let him take away from me this death. 18 And Moses went forth from Pharaoh, and prayed to God. 19 And the Lord brought in the opposite direction a strong wind from the sea, and took up the locusts and cast them into the Red Sea, and there was not one locust left in all the land of Egypt. 20 And the Lord hardened the heart of Pharaoh, and he did not send away the sons of Israel. 21 And the Lord said to Moses, Stretch out thy hand to heaven, and let there be darkness over the land of Egypt; darkness that may be felt. 22 And Moses stretched out his hand to heaven, and there was darkness, blackness, even a storm over all the land of Egypt three days. 23 And for three days no man saw his brother, and no man rose up from his bed for three days; but all the sons of Israel had light in all the places where they were.

24 And Pharaoh called Moses and Aaron, saying, Go, serve the Lord your God, only leave behind your sheep and your oxen, and let your store depart with you. 25 And Moses said, Nay, but thou shall give to us whole burnt offerings and sacrifices, which we will sacrifice to the Lord our God. 26 And our cattle shall go with us, and we will not leave a hoof behind, for of them we will take to serve the Lord our God; but we know not in what manner we shall serve the Lord our God, until we arrive there. 27 But the Lord hardened the heart of Pharaoh, and he would not let them go. 28 And Pharaoh says, Depart from me, beware of seeing my face again, for in what day thou shall appear before me, thou shall die. 29 And Moses says, Thou hast said, I will not appear in thy presence again.

* *Codex Alexandrinus* reads: "Be aware, you have an evil purpose."

Chapter 11

And the Lord said to Moses, I would yet bring one plague upon Pharaoh and upon Egypt, and after that he will send you forth thence; and whenever he sends you forth with every thing, he will indeed drive you out. 2 Speak therefore secretly in the ears of the people, and let every one ask of his neighbor jewels of silver and gold, and raiment. 3 And the Lord gave his people favor in the sight of the Egyptians, and they lent to them; and the man Moses was very great before the Egyptians, and before Pharaoh, and before his slaves.

4 And Moses said, These things said the Lord, About midnight I go forth into the midst of Egypt. 5 And every firstborn in the land of Egypt shall die, from the firstborn of Pharaoh that sits on the throne, even to the firstborn of the female slave that is by the mill, and to the firstborn of all cattle. 6 And there shall be a great cry through all the land of Egypt, such as has not been, and such shall not be repeated any more. 7 But among all the sons of Israel shall not a dog snarl with his tongue, either at man or beast; that thou may know how wide a distinction the Lord will make between the Egyptians and Israel. 8 And all these thy servants shall come down to me, and do me reverence, saying, Go forth, thou and all the people over whom thou presides, and afterwards I will go forth. 9 And Moses went forth from Pharaoh with wrath. And the Lord said to Moses, Pharaoh would not hearken to you, that I may greatly multiply my signs and wonders in the land of Egypt. 10 And Moses and Aaron wrought all these signs and wonders in the land of Egypt before Pharaoh; and the Lord hardened the heart of Pharaoh, and he did not hearken to send forth the sons of Israel out of the land of Egypt.

Exodus 12

Chapter 12

And the Lord spoke to Moses and Aaron in the land of Egypt, saying, 2 This month shall be to you the beginning of months; it is the first to you among the months of the year. 3 Speak to the entire congregation of the sons of Israel, saying, On the tenth of this month let them take each man a sheep according to the houses of their families, * every man a sheep for his household. 4 And if they be few in a household, so that there are not enough for a sheep, he shall take with himself his neighbor that lives near to him, as to the number of souls, every one according to that which suffices him shall make a reckoning for the sheep. 5 It shall be to you a sheep unblemished, a male of a year old; ye shall take it of the lambs and the kids. 6 And you shall keep it till the fourteenth of this month, and the entire multitude of the congregation of the sons of Israel shall kill it toward evening. 7 And they shall take some of the blood, and shall put it on the two doorposts, and on the lintel, in the houses in which ever they shall eat it. 8 And they shall eat the flesh in this night roast with fire, and they shall eat unleavened bread with bitter herbs. 9 Ye shall not eat of it raw nor boiled in water, but only roasted with fire, the head with the feet and the entrails. 10 Nothing shall be left of it till the morning, and a bone of it ye shall not break; but that which is left of it till the morning ye shall burn up with fire. 11 And thus shall ye eat it; your loins girded, and your sandals on your feet, and your staves in your hands, and ye shall eat it in haste. It is a Passover to the Lord.

12 and I will go throughout the land of Egypt in that night, and will kill every firstborn in the land of Egypt both man and beast, and on all the gods of Egypt will I execute vengeance: I am the Lord. 13 And the blood shall be for a sign to you on the houses, in which ye are, and I will see the blood, and will protect you, and there shall not be on you the plague of destruction, when I strike the land of Egypt. 14 And this day shall be to you a memorial, and ye shall keep it a feast to the Lord through all your generations; ye shall keep it a feast for a perpetual ordinance. 15 Seven days ye shall eat unleavened bread, and from the first day ye shall utterly remove leaven from your houses: whoever shall eat leaven, that soul shall be utterly destroyed from Israel, from the first day until the seventh day. 16 And the first day shall be called holy, and the seventh day shall be named holy to you: ye shall do no servile work on them, only as many things as will necessarily be done by every soul, this only shall be done by you. 17 And ye shall keep this commandment, for on this day will I bring out your force out of the land of Egypt; and ye shall make this day a perpetual ordinance for you throughout your generations. 18 Beginning the fourteenth day of the first month, ye shall eat unleavened bread from evening, till the twenty-first day of the month, till evening.

19 Seven days leaven shall not be found in your houses; whoever shall eat anything leavened, that soul should be cut off from the congregation of Israel, both among the occupiers of the land and the original inhabitants. 20 Ye shall eat nothing leavened, but in every habitation of yours ye shall eat unleavened bread.

21 And Moses called all the elders of the sons of Israel, and said to them, Go away and take to yourselves a lamb according to your kindred, and kill the Passover. 22 And ye shall take a bunch of hyssop, and having dipped it into some of the blood that is by the door, ye shall touch the lintel, and shall put it upon both doorposts, even of the blood which is by the door; but ye shall not go out every one from the door of his house till the morning. 23 And the Lord shall pass by to kill the Egyptians, and shall see the blood upon the lintel, and upon both the doorposts; and the Lord shall pass by the door, and shall not suffer the destroyer to enter into your houses to kill you. 24 And keep ye this thing as an ordinance for thyself and for thy children forever. 25 And if ye should enter into the land, which the Lord shall give you, as he has spoken, keep this service. 26 And it shall come to pass, if your sons say to you, What is this service? 27 that ye shall say to them, This Passover is a sacrifice to the Lord, as he defended the houses of the sons of Israel in Egypt, when he killed the Egyptians, but delivered our houses. 28 And the people bowed and worshipped. And the sons of Israel departed and did as the Lord commanded Moses and Aaron so did they.

29 And it came to pass at midnight that the Lord killed all the firstborn in the land of Egypt, from the firstborn of Pharaoh that sat on the throne, to the firstborn of the captive maid in the dungeon, and the firstborn of all cattle. 30 And Pharaoh rose up by night, and his slaves, and all the Egyptians; and there was a great cry in all the land of Egypt, for there was not a house in which there was not one dead. 31 And Pharaoh called Moses and Aaron by night, and said to them, Arise and depart from my people, both ye and the sons of Israel. Go and serve the Lord your God, even as ye say. 32 And take with you your sheep, and your oxen; bless me also, I pray you. 33 And the Egyptians constrained the people, so that they cast them out of the land with haste, for they said, We all shall die. 34 And the people took their dough before their kneaded meal was leavened, wrapped up as it was in their garments, on their shoulders. 35 And the sons of Israel did as Moses commanded them, and they asked of the Egyptians articles of silver and gold and apparel. 36 And the Lord gave his people favor in the sight of the Egyptians, and they lent to them; and they spoiled the Egyptians.

37 And the sons Israel having departed from Ramesse to Succoth, to the full number of six hundred thousand footmen, even men, besides the baggage. 38 And a great mixed company went up with them, and sheep and oxen and very much cattle.

Exodus 13

39 And they baked the dough which they brought out of Egypt, unleavened cakes, for it had not been leavened; for the Egyptians cast them out, and they could not remain, neither did they prepare provision for themselves for the journey. 40 And the traveling of the sons of Israel, which they traveled in the land of Egypt and the land of Canaan, was four hundred and thirty years. 41 And it came to pass after the four hundred and thirty years; all the forces of the Lord came forth out of the land of Egypt by night. 42 It is a vigil unto the Lord, so that he should bring them out of the land of Egypt; that very night is a vigil unto the Lord, so that it should be to all the sons of Israel to their generations.

43 And the Lord said to Moses and Aaron, This is the law of the Passover; no stranger shall eat of it. 44 And every slave or servant bought with money; him thou shall circumcise, and then shall he eat of it. 45 A traveler or hireling shall not eat of it. 46 In one house shall it be eaten, and ye shall not carry of the flesh out from the house; and a bone of it ye shall not break. 47 All the congregation of the sons of Israel shall keep it. 48 And if any proselyte shall come to you to keep the Passover to the Lord, thou shall circumcise every male of him, and then shall he approach to sacrifice it, and he shall be even as the original inhabitant of the land; no uncircumcised person shall eat of it. 49 There shall be one law to the native, and to the proselyte coming among you. 50 And the sons of Israel did as the Lord commanded Moses and Aaron for them, so they did. * 51 And it came to pass on that day that the Lord brought out the sons of Israel from the land of Egypt with their forces.

* The phrase: "every man a sheep for his household" is omitted from Chapter Twelve verse three for the Third Reading of vespers on Holy and Great Saturday for the Holy Week of *Pascha*. However, this phase is found in *Codex Vaticanus* and the Apostoliki Diakonia and Zoe Brotherhood biblical texts.

Chapter 13

* And the Lord spoke to Moses, saying, 2 Sanctify to me every firstborn, first produced, opening every womb among the sons of Israel both of man and beast; it is mine. 3 And Moses said to the people, Remember this day, in which ye came forth out of the land of Egypt, out of the house of slavery, for with a strong hand the Lord brought you forth thence; and leaven shall not be eaten. 4 For on this day ye go forth in the month of new corn. 5 And it shall come to pass when the Lord thy God shall have brought thee into the land of the Canaanites, and the Hittites, and Amorites, and Evites, and Jebusites, and Gergesites, and Pherezites, which he swore to thy fathers to give thee, a land flowing with milk and honey, that thou shall perform this service in this month. 6 Six days ye shall eat unleavened bread, and on the seventh day is a feast to the Lord.

Exodus 13

7 Seven days shall ye eat unleavened bread; nothing leavened shall be seen with thee, neither shall thou have leaven in all thy borders. 8 And thou shall tell thy son in that day, saying, Therefore the Lord did thus to me, as I was going out of Egypt. 9 And it shall be to thee a sign upon thy hand and a memorial before thine eyes that the law of the Lord may be in thy mouth, for with a strong hand the Lord God brought thee out of Egypt. 10 And preserve ye this law according to the times of the seasons, from days to days. 11 And it shall come to pass when the Lord thy God shall bring thee into the land of the Canaanites, as he swore to thy fathers, and shall give it thee, 12 that thou shall separate every offspring opening the womb, the males to the Lord, every one that opens the womb out of the herds or among thy cattle, as many as thou shall have; thou shall sanctify the males to the Lord. 13 Every offspring opening the womb of the donkey thou shall change for a sheep; and if thou will not change it, thou shall redeem it; every firstborn of man of thy sons shall thou redeem. 14 And if thy son should ask thee hereafter, saying, What is this? Then thou shall say to him, With a strong hand the Lord brought us out of Egypt, out of the house of slavery. 15 And when Pharaoh hardened his heart so as not to send us away, He killed every firstborn in the land of Egypt, both the firstborn of man and the firstborn of beast; therefore do I sacrifice every offspring that opens the womb, the males to the Lord, and every firstborn of my sons I will redeem. 16 And it shall be for a sign upon thy hand, and immovable before thine eyes, for with a strong hand the Lord brought thee out of Egypt.

17 And when Pharaoh sent forth the people, God led them not by the way of the land of the Philistines, because it was near; for God said, Lest at any time the people repent when they see war, and return to Egypt. 18 And God led the people round by the way to the wilderness, to the Red Sea; and in the fifth generation the sons of Israel went up out of the land of Egypt. 19 And Moses took the bones of Joseph with him, for he had solemnly adjured the sons of Israel, saying, God will surely visit you, and ye shall carry up my bones hence with you. 20 And the sons of Israel departed from Succoth, and encamped in Othom by the wilderness. 21 And God led them, in the day by a pillar of cloud, to show them the way, and in the night by a pillar of fire. 22 And the pillar of cloud failed neither by day, nor the pillar of fire by night, before all the people.

* The February vesper reading for Chapter Twelve verse fifty-one through Chapter Thirteen verse sixteen for The Meeting of Our Lord and Savior Jesus Christ from the *Greek Menaion* and *Prophetologion* is somewhat different than what is present in the biblical text as published by the Apostoliki Diakonia and Zoe Brotherhood. The reading is translated as follows:

"The Lord spoke to Moses on that day that the Lord brought out the sons of Israel from the land of Egypt, saying, Sanctify to Me every firstborn, first produced, opening every womb among the sons of Israel.

Exodus 14

And Moses said to the people, Remember this day, in which ye came forth out of the land of Egypt, out of the house of slavery, for with a strong hand the Lord brought you forth thence. And preserve ye His law. And it shall come to pass that when the Lord *thy* God shall bring thee into the land of the Canaanites, as He swore to thy fathers, that thou shall separate every *offspring* opening the womb, the males to the Lord. And if thy son should ask thee hereafter, saying, What is this? Then thou shall say to him, With a strong hand the Lord brought us out of Egypt, out of the house of slavery. And when Pharaoh hardened his heart so as not to send us away, the Lord killed every firstborn in the land of Egypt, both the firstborn of man and the firstborn of beast; therefore do I sacrifice every *offspring* that opens the womb, the males to the Lord, and every firstborn of my sons I will redeem. And it shall be for a sign upon thy hand, and immovable before thine eyes, because thus said the Lord Almighty, The firstborn of thy sons you shall give to Me.

Chapter 14

And the Lord spoke to Moses, saying, 2 Speak to the sons of Israel, and let them turn and encamp before the village, between Magdol and the sea, opposite Beelsepphon; before them shall thou encamp by the sea. 3 And Pharaoh will say to his people, As for these sons of Israel, they are wandering in the land, for the wilderness has shut them in. 4 And I will harden the heart of Pharaoh, and he shall pursue after them; and I will be glorified in Pharaoh, and in all his host, and all the Egyptians shall know that I am the Lord. And they did so. 5 And it was reported to the king of the Egyptians that the people had fled; and the heart of Pharaoh was turned, and that of his servants against the people; and they said, What is this that we have done, to let the sons of Israel go, so that they should not serve us? 6 So Pharaoh yoked his chariots, and led off all his people with himself; 7 having also taken six hundred chosen chariots, and all the cavalry of the Egyptians, and rulers over all. 8 And the Lord hardened the heart of Pharaoh King of Egypt, * and of his servants, and he pursued after the sons of Israel; and the sons of Israel went forth with a high hand. 9 And the Egyptians pursued after them, and found them encamped by the sea; and all the cavalry and the chariots of Pharaoh, and the horsemen, and his host were before the village, over against Beelsepphon.

10 And Pharaoh approached, and the sons of Israel having looked up, beheld with their eyes, and the Egyptians encamped behind them; and they were very greatly terrified, and the sons of Israel cried to the Lord; 11 and said to Moses, Because there were no graves in the land of Egypt, has thou brought us forth to kill us in the wilderness? What is this that thou have done to us, having brought us out of Egypt? 12 Is not this the word, which we spoke to thee in Egypt, saying, Let us alone that we may serve the Egyptians? For it is better for us to serve the Egyptians than to die in this wilderness.

13 And Moses said to the people, Take courage; stand and see the salvation that is from the Lord, which He will work for us this day; for as ye have seen the Egyptians today, ye shall see them again forever. 14 The Lord shall fight for you, and ye shall hold your peace.

15 The Lord said to Moses, Why cry thou to me? Speak to the sons of Israel, and let them break camp. 16 And do thou lift up thy rod, and stretch forth thy hand over the sea, and divide it, and let the sons of Israel enter into the midst of the sea on the dry land. 17 And behold! I will harden the heart of Pharaoh and of all the Egyptians, and they shall go in after them; and I will be glorified upon Pharaoh, and on his entire host, and on his chariots and his horses. 18 And all the Egyptians shall know that I am the Lord, when I am glorified upon Pharaoh and upon his chariots and his horses. 19 And the angel of God that went before the camp of the sons of Israel removed and went behind, and the pillar of the cloud also removed from before them and stood behind them. 20 And it went between the camp of the Egyptians and the camp of Israel, and stood; and there was darkness and blackness; and the night passed, and they came not near to one another during the whole night. 21 And Moses stretched forth his hand over the sea, and the Lord carried back the sea with a strong south wind all the night, and made the sea dry land, and the water was divided. 22 And the sons of Israel went into the midst of the sea on the dry land, and the water of it was a wall on the right hand and a wall on the left.

23 And the Egyptians pursued them and went in after them, and every horse of Pharaoh, and his chariots, and his horsemen, into the midst of the sea. 24 And it came to pass in the morning watch that the Lord looked forth on the camp of the Egyptians through the pillar of fire and cloud, and troubled the camp of the Egyptians, 25 and bound the axles of their chariots, and caused them to go with difficulty; and the Egyptians said, Let us flee from the face of Israel, for the Lord fights for them against the Egyptians. 26 And the Lord said to Moses, Stretch forth thine hand over the sea, and let the water be turned back to its place, and let it cover the Egyptians coming both upon the chariots and the riders. 27 And Moses stretched forth his hand over the sea, and the water returned to its place when day came; and the Egyptians fled *from* under the water, and the Lord shook off the Egyptians in the midst of the sea. 28 and the water returned and covered the chariots and the riders, and all the forces of Pharaoh, who had entered after them into the sea: and there was not left of them even one. 29 But the sons of Israel went along dry land in the midst of the sea, and the water was to them a wall on the right hand, and a wall on the left. 30 So the Lord delivered Israel in that day from the hand of the Egyptians, and Israel saw the Egyptians dead by the shore of the sea.

Exodus 15

31 And Israel saw the mighty hand, the things that the Lord did to the Egyptians; and the people feared the Lord, and they believed God and Moses his servant.

* The reading for Chapter Fourteen verse eight for the Sixth Reading on Holy and Great Saturday from the Holy Week of *Pascha* omits the phrase: "and of his servants". However, this phase is found in *Codex Vaticanus* and the Apostoliki Diakonia and Zoe Brotherhood biblical texts.

Chapter 15

Then sang Moses and the sons of Israel this song to God, and spoke, saying, Let us sing to the Lord, for he is very greatly glorified; horse and rider He has thrown into the sea. 2 He was to me a helper and protector for salvation; this is my God and I will glorify him; my father's God, and I will exalt Him. 3 The Lord bringing wars to naught, the Lord is His name. 4 He has cast the chariots of Pharaoh and his forces into the sea, the chosen mounted captains; they were swallowed up in the Red Sea. 5 He covered them with the sea; they sank to the depth like a stone. 6 Thy right hand, O God, has been glorified in strength; thy right hand, O God, has broken the enemies. 7 And in the abundance of thy glory thou have broken the adversaries to pieces; thou sends forth thy wrath it devoured them as stubble. 8 And by the breath of thine anger the water parted asunder; the waters were fixed as a wall; the waves were congealed in the midst of the sea. 9 The enemy said, I will pursue, I will overtake, I will divide the spoils; I will satisfy my soul, I will destroy with my sword, my hand shall have dominion. 10 Thou sends forth thy spirit, the sea covered them; they sank like lead in the mighty water. 11 Who is like to thee among the gods, O Lord? Who is like to thee? Glorified in holiness, marvelous in glories, doing wonders. 12 Thou stretched forth thy right hand, and the earth swallowed them up. 13 Thou have guided in thy righteousness this people of yours whom thou has redeemed, by thy strength thou has called them into thy holy resting place. 14 The nations heard and were angry, pangs have seized on the dwellers among the Philistines.

15 Then the rulers of Edom, and the rulers of the Moabites hasted; trembling took hold upon them, all the inhabitants of Canaan melted away. 16 Let trembling and fear fall upon them; by the greatness of thine arm, let them become as stone; till thy people pass over, O Lord, till this thy people pass over, whom thou has purchased. 17 Bring them in and plant them in the mountain of their inheritance, in thy prepared habitation, which thou, O Lord, have prepared the sanctuary, O Lord, which thine hands have made ready. 18 The Lord reigning over the ages and forever and ever.

19 For the horse of Pharaoh went in with the chariots and horsemen into the sea, and the Lord brought upon them the water of the sea, but the sons of Israel walked through dry land in the midst of the sea. 20 And Miriam the prophetess, the sister of Aaron, having taken a timbrel in her hand; then there went forth all the women after her with timbrels and dances. 21 And Miriam led them, saying, Let us sing to the Lord, for he has been very greatly glorified; the horse and rider has He cast into the sea. 22 So Moses brought up the sons of Israel from the Red Sea, and brought them into the wilderness of Sur; and they marched three days in the wilderness, and found no water to drink. 23 They came to Merrha, and could not drink of Merrha, for it was bitter; therefore he named the name of that place, Bitterness. 24 And the people murmured against Moses, saying, What shall we drink? 25 Moses cried to the Lord, and the Lord showed him a piece of wood, and he cast it into the water, and the water was sweetened; there He established to him ordinances and judgments, and there He tested him, 26 and said, If thou will indeed hear the voice of the Lord thy God, and do what is well-pleasing before him, and will hearken to his commands, and keep all his ordinances, no disease which I have brought upon the Egyptians will I bring upon thee, for I am the Lord * thy God that heals thee.

27 And they came to Eleim, and there were there twelve fountains of water, and seventy stems of palm trees; and they encamped there by the waters.

* The January vesper reading for Chapter Fifteen verse twenty-six from the *Greek Menaion* omits "thy God" and this phrase is only found in *Codex Vaticanus* and the Apostoliki Diakonia and Zoe Brotherhood biblical texts.

Chapter 16

And they departed from Elim, and the entire congregation of the sons of Israel came to the wilderness of Sin, which is between Elim and Sinai; and on the fifteenth day, in the second month after their departure from the land of Egypt, 2 the entire congregation of the sons of Israel murmured against Moses and Aaron. 3 And the sons of Israel said to them, Would we had died struck by the Lord in the land of Egypt, when we sat by the flesh pots, and ate bread to satiety! For ye have brought us out into this wilderness, to kill this entire congregation with hunger. 4 And the Lord said to Moses, Behold, I will rain bread upon you out of heaven: and the people shall go forth, and they shall gather their daily portion for the day, that I may try them whether they will walk in my law or not. 5 And it shall come to pass on the sixth day that they shall prepare whatever they have brought in, and it shall be double of what they shall have gathered for the day, daily. 6 And Moses and Aaron said to all the congregation of the sons of Israel, At even ye shall know that the Lord has brought you out of the land of Egypt;

Exodus 16

7 and in the morning ye shall see the glory of the Lord, inasmuch as He hears your murmuring against God; and who are we, that ye continue to murmur against us? 8 And Moses said, This shall be when the Lord gives you in the evening flesh to eat, and bread in the morning to satiety, because the Lord has heard your murmuring, which ye murmur against us; and what are we? For your murmuring is not against us, but against God. 9 And Moses said to Aaron, Say to all the congregation of the sons of Israel, Come near before God, for He has heard your murmuring. 10 And when Aaron spoke to the entire congregation of the sons of Israel, and they turned toward the wilderness, then the glory of the Lord appeared in a cloud. 11 And the Lord spoke to Moses, saying, 12 I have heard the murmuring of the sons of Israel; speak to them, saying, Towards evening ye shall eat flesh, and in the morning ye shall be satisfied with bread; and ye shall know that I am the Lord your God. 13 And it was evening, and quails came up and covered the camp; 14 in the morning it came to pass as the dew ceased around the camp, that, behold, on the face of the wilderness was a small thing like white coriander seed, as frost upon the earth. 15 And when the sons of Israel saw it, they said one to another, What is this? For they knew not what it was; and Moses said to them, 16 This is the bread which the Lord has given you to eat. This is that which the Lord has appointed; gather of it each man for his family, a homer for each person, by the head, according to the number of your souls, gather each of you with his fellow lodgers. 17 And the sons of Israel did so, and gathered some much and some less. 18 And having measured the homer full, he that gathered much had nothing over, and he that had gathered less had no lack; each gathered just sufficient for the need of those who belonged to him. 19 And Moses said to them, Let no man leave of it till the morning.

20 But they did not hearken to Moses, but some left of it till the morning; and it bred worms and stank; and Moses was irritated with them. 21 And they gathered it every morning, each man what he needed, and when the sun waxed hot it melted. 22 And it came to pass on the sixth day, they gathered double what was needed, two homers for one man; and all the rulers of the synagogue went in and reported it to Moses. 23 And Moses said to them, Is not this the word, which the Lord spoke? Tomorrow is the Sabbath, a holy rest to the Lord; bake that ye will bake, and see that ye will see, and all that is over leave to be laid by for the morrow. 24 And they left of it till the morning, as Moses commanded them; and it stank not, neither was there a worm in it. 25 And Moses said, Eat that today, for today is a Sabbath to the Lord; it shall not be found in the plain. 26 Six days ye shall gather it, and on the seventh day is a Sabbath, for there shall be none on that day. 27 And it came to pass on the seventh day that some of the people went forth to gather, and found none.

28 And the Lord said to Moses, How long are ye unwilling to hearken to my commands and my law? 29 See, for the Lord has given you this day as the Sabbath, therefore he has given you on the sixth day the bread of two days; ye shall sit each of you in your houses; let no one go forth from his place on the seventh day. 30 And the people kept Sabbath on the seventh day. 31 And the sons of Israel called the name of it Man; and it was as white coriander seed, and the taste of it as a wafer with honey. 32 And Moses said, This is the thing which the Lord hath commanded, Fill an homer with manna, to be laid up for your generations; that they may see the bread which ye ate in the wilderness, when the Lord led you forth out of the land of Egypt. 33 And Moses said to Aaron, Take a golden pot, and cast into it one full homer of manna; and thou shall lay it up before God, to be kept for your generations, 34 as the Lord commanded Moses; and Aaron laid it up before the testimony to be kept. 35 And the sons of Israel ate manna forty years; until they came to the land *they were to* inhabit they ate the manna, until they came to the region of Phoenicia. 36 Now the homer was the tenth part of three measures.

Chapter 17

And the entire congregation of the sons of Israel departed from the wilderness of Sin, according to their encampments, by the word of the Lord; and they encamped in Raphidin; and there was no water for the people to drink. 2 And the people reviled Moses, saying, Give us water that we may drink; and Moses said to them, Why do ye revile me, and why tempt ye the Lord? 3 And the people thirsted there for water, and there the people murmured against Moses, saying, Why is this? Have thou brought us up out of Egypt to kill us and our children and our cattle with thirst? 4 And Moses cried to the Lord, saying, What shall I do to this people? Yet a little while and they will stone me. 5 And the Lord said to Moses, Go before this people, and take to thyself of the elders of the people; and the rod with which thou struck the river, take in thine hand, and thou shall go. 6 Behold, I stand there before thou come, on the rock in Horeb, and thou shall strike the rock, and water shall come out from it, and the people shall drink. And Moses did so before the sons of Israel. 7 And he called the name of that place, Temptation, and Reviling, because of the reviling of the sons of Israel, and because they tempted the Lord, saying, Is the Lord among us or not? 8 And Amalek came and fought with Israel in Raphidin. 9 And Moses said to Jesus, Choose out for thyself mighty men, and go forth and set the army in array against Amalek tomorrow; and, behold, I shall stand on the top of the hill, and the rod of God will be in my hand. 10 And Jesus did as Moses said to him, and he went out and set the army in array against Amalek, and Moses and Aaron and Or went up to the top of the hill.

Exodus 18

11 And it came to pass, when Moses lifted up his hands, Israel prevailed; and when he let down his hands, Amalec prevailed. 12 But the hands of Moses were heavy, and they took a stone and put it under him, and he sat upon it; and Aaron and Or supported his hands one on this side and the other on that, and the hands of Moses were supported till the going down of the sun. 13 And Jesus routed Amalek and all his people with the slaughter of the sword. 14 And the Lord said to Moses, Write this for a memorial in a book, and give this in the ears of Jesus for I will utterly blot out the memorial of Amalek from under heaven. 15 And Moses built an altar to the Lord, and called the name of it, The Lord my Refuge. 16 For with a secret hand the Lord wages war upon Amalek from generation to generation.

Chapter 18

And Jethro the priest of Madiam, the father-in-law of Moses, heard of all that the Lord did to his people Israel; for the Lord brought Israel out of Egypt. 2 And Jethro the father-in-law of Moses, took Sepphora the wife of Moses after she had been sent away, 3 and her two sons; the name of the one was Gersam, his father saying, I was a traveler in a strange land; 4 and the name of the second Eliezer, saying, For the God of my father is my helper, and he has rescued me out of the hand of Pharaoh. 5 And Jethro the father-in-law of Moses, and his sons and his wife, went forth to Moses into the wilderness, where he encamped on the mount of God. 6 And it was told Moses, saying, Behold, thy father-in-law Jethro is coming to thee, and thy wife and two sons with him. 7 And Moses went forth to meet his father-in-law, and did him reverence, and kissed him, and they embraced each other, and he brought them into the tent. 8 And Moses related to his father-in-law all things that the Lord did to Pharaoh and all the Egyptians for Israel's sake, and all the labor that had befallen them in the way, and that the Lord had rescued them out of the hand of Pharaoh, and out of the hand of the Egyptians. 9 And Jethro was amazed at all the good things, which the Lord did to them, forasmuch as he rescued them out of the hand of the Egyptians and out of the hand of Pharaoh. 10 And Jethro said, Blessed be the Lord, because he has rescued them out of the hand of the Egyptians and out of the hand of Pharaoh. 11 Now know I that the Lord is great above all gods, because of this, wherein they attacked them.

12 And Jethro the father-in-law of Moses took whole burnt offerings and sacrifices for God, for Aaron and all the elders of Israel came to eat bread with the father-in-law of Moses before God. 13 And it came to pass after tomorrow that Moses sat to judge the people, and all the people stood by Moses from morning till evening.

14 And Jethro having seen all that Moses was doing to the people, said, What is this that thou does to the people? Wherefore thou sits alone, and all the people stand by thee from morning till evening? 15 And Moses says to his father-in-law, Because the people come to me to seek judgment from God. 16 For whenever there is a dispute among them, and they come to me, I give judgment upon each, and I teach them the ordinances of God and his law. 17 And the father-in-law of Moses said to him, Thou does not this thing rightly, 18 thou will wear away with intolerable weariness, both those and all this people which is with thee; this thing is hard, thou will not be able to endure it thyself alone. 19 Now then hearken to me, and I will advise thee, and God shall be with thee; be thou to the people in the things pertaining to God, and thou shall bring their words to God. 20 And thou shall testify to them the ordinances of God and his law, and thou shall show to them the ways in which they shall walk, and the works, which they shall do. 21 And do thou look out for thyself out of all the people able men, fearing God, righteous men, hating pride, and thou shall set over them captains of thousands and captains of hundreds, and captains of fifties, and captains of tens. 22 And they shall judge the people at all times, and the too burdensome matter they shall bring to thee, but they shall judge the smaller cases; so they shall relieve thee and help thee. 23 If thou will do this thing, God shall strengthen thee, and thou shall be able to attend, and this entire people shall come with peace into their own place.

24 And Moses hearkened to the voice of his father-in-law, and did whatever he said to him. 25 And Moses chose out able men out of all Israel, and he made them captains of thousands and captains of hundreds, and captains of fifties and captains of tens over them. 26 And they judged the people at all times; and every too burdensome matter they brought to Moses, but every light matter they judged themselves. 27 And Moses dismissed his father-in-law, and he returned to his own land.

Chapter 19

And in the third month of the departure of the sons of Israel out of the land of Egypt, on the same day, they came into the wilderness of Sinai. 2 And they departed from Raphidin, and came into the wilderness of Sinai, and there Israel encamped before the mountain. 3 And Moses went up to the mount of God, and God called him out of the mountain, saying, These things shall thou say to the house of Jacob, and thou shall report them to the sons of Israel. 4 Ye have seen all that I have done to the Egyptians, and I took you up as upon eagles' wings, and I brought you near to myself. 5 And now if ye will indeed hear my voice, and keep my covenant, ye shall be to me a peculiar people above all nations, for the whole earth is mine.

Exodus 19

6 And ye shall be to me a royal priesthood and a holy nation; these words shall thou speak to the sons of Israel. 7 And Moses came and called the elders of the people, and he set before them all these words, which God appointed them. 8 And all the people answered with one accord, and said, All things that God has spoken, we will do and hearken to; and Moses reported these words to God. 9 And the Lord said to Moses, Behold! I come to thee in a pillar of a cloud that the people may hear me speaking to thee, and may believe thee forever; and Moses reported the words of the people to the Lord. 10 The Lord said to Moses, Go down and solemnly charge the people, and sanctify them today and tomorrow, and let them wash their garments. 11 And let them be ready against the third day, for on the third day the Lord will descend upon Mount Sinai before all the people. 12 And thou shall separate the people around, saying, Take heed to yourselves that ye go not up into the mountain, nor touch any part of it: every one that touches the mountain shall die the death. 13 A hand shall not touch it, for *every one that touches* shall be stoned with stones or shot through with an arrow, whether beast or whether man, it shall not live; when the voices and trumpets and cloud depart from off the mountain, they shall come up on the mountain.

14 And Moses went down from the mountain to the people, and sanctified them, and they washed their clothes. 15 And he said to the people, Be ready, for three days come not near to a woman. 16 It came to pass on the third day, as the morning drew near, there were voices and lightning and a dark cloud on Mount Sinai; the voice of the trumpet sounded loud, and all the people in the camp trembled. 17 And Moses led the people forth out of the camp to meet God, and they stood by under the mountain. 18 The entire Mount Sinai smoked because God had descended upon it in fire; and the smoke went up as the smoke of a furnace, and the people were exceedingly amazed. 19 And the sounds of the trumpet were growing louder and louder. Moses spoke, and God answered him with a voice. 20 And the Lord came down upon Mount Sinai on the top of the mountain; and the Lord called Moses to the top of the mountain, and Moses went up.

21 And God spoke to Moses, saying, Go down, and solemnly charge the people, lest at any time they draw near to God to gaze, and a multitude of them fall. 22 And let the priests that draw near to the Lord God sanctify themselves, lest the Lord remove some of them. 23 And Moses said to God, The people will not be able to approach to the mount of Sinai, for thou has solemnly charged us, saying, Set bounds to the mountain and sanctify it. 24 And the Lord said to him, Go, descend, and come up thou and Aaron with thee; but let not the priests and the people force their way to come up to God, lest the Lord destroy some of them. 25 And Moses went down to the people, and spoke to them.

Chapter 20

And the Lord spoke all these words, saying, 2 I am the Lord thy God, who brought thee out of the land of Egypt, out of the house of slavery. 3 Thou shall have no other gods beside me. 4 Thou shall not make to thyself an idol, nor likeness of anything, whatever things are in the heaven above, and whatever is in the earth beneath, and whatever is in the waters under the earth. 5 Thou shall not bow down to them, nor serve them; for I am the Lord thy God, a jealous God, recompensing the sins of the fathers upon the children, to the third and fourth generation to them that hate me, 6 and bestowing mercy on them that love me to thousands of them, and on them that keep my commandments. 7 Thou shall not take the name of the Lord thy God in vain; for the Lord thy God will not acquit him that takes his name in vain. 8 Remember the Sabbath day to keep it holy. 9 Six days thou shall labor, and shall perform all thy work. 10 But on the seventh day is the Sabbath of the Lord thy God; on it thou shall do no work, thou, nor thy son, nor thy daughter, thy servant nor thy female slave, thine ox nor thine ass, nor any cattle of thine, nor the stranger that travels with thee. 11 For in six days the Lord made the heaven and the earth, and the sea and all things in them, and rested on the seventh day; therefore the Lord blessed the seventh day, and hallowed it. 12 Honor thy father and thy mother, that it may be well with thee, and that thou may live long on the good land, which the Lord thy God gives to thee. 13 Thou shall not commit adultery. 14 Thou shall not steal. 15 Thou shall not kill. 16 Thou shall not bear false witness against thy neighbor. 17 Thou shall not covet thy neighbor's wife; thou shall not covet thy neighbor's house; or his field, or his servant, or his maid, or his ox, or his donkey, or any of his cattle, or whatever belongs to thy neighbor.

18 And all the people perceived the thundering voice, and the flashes of light, and the voice of the trumpet, and the mountain smoking; and all the people feared and stood afar off, 19 and said to Moses, Speak thou to us, and let not God speak to us, lest we die. 20 And Moses says to them, Be of good courage, for God is come to you to try you, that his fear may be among you that ye sin not. 21 And the people stood afar off, and Moses went into the darkness where God was. 22 And the Lord said to Moses, Thus shall thou say to the house of Jacob, and thou shall report it to the children of Israel, Ye have seen that I have spoken to you from heaven. 23 Ye shall not make to yourselves gods of silver, and gods of gold ye shall not make to yourselves. 24 Ye shall make to me an altar of earth; and upon it ye shall sacrifice your whole burnt offerings, and your peace offerings, and your sheep and your calves in every place, where I shall record my name; and I will come to thee and bless thee.

Exodus 21

25 And if thou will make to me an altar of stones, thou shall not build them hewn stones, for thou hast lifted up thy tool upon them, and they are defiled. 26 Thou shall not go up to my altar by steps, that thou may not uncover thy nakedness upon it.

Chapter 21

And these *are* the ordinances that thou shall set before them. 2 If thou buy a Hebrew slave, six years shall he serve thee, and in the seventh year he shall go forth free for nothing. 3 If he should have come in alone, he shall also go forth alone; and if his wife should have gone in together with him, his wife also shall go out. 4 Moreover, if his master give him a wife, and she have him sons or daughters, the wife and the children shall be his master's; and he shall go forth alone. 5 And if the slave should answer and say, I love my master and wife and children, I will not run away free; 6 his master shall bring him to the judgment-seat of God, and then shall he bring him to the door, to the door post, and his master shall bore his ear through with an awl, and he shall serve him forever. 7 And if any one sells his daughter as a domestic, she shall not depart as the female slaves depart. 8 If she be not pleasing to her master, who has betrothed herself to him, he shall let her go free; but he is not at liberty to sell her to a foreign nation, because he has trifled with her. 9 And if he should have betrothed her to his son, he shall do to her according to the right of daughters. 10 And if he takes another to himself, he shall not deprive her of necessaries and her apparel, and her companionship. 11 And if he will not do these three things to her, she shall go out free without money.

12 And if any man strikes another and he die, let him be certainly put to death. 13 But as for him that did it not willingly, but God delivered him into his hands, I will give thee a place whither the killer may flee. 14 And if any one lie in wait for his neighbor to kill him by craft, and he go for refuge, thou shall take him from my altar to put him to death. 15 Whoever strikes his father or his mother let him be certainly put to death. 16 He that reviles his father or his mother shall surely die. 17 Whoever shall steal one of the sons of Israel, and prevail over him and sell him, and he be found with him, let him certainly die. 18 And if two men revile each other and strike the one the other with a stone or his fist, and he die not, but be laid upon his bed; 19 if the man arise and walk abroad on his staff, he that struck him shall be clear; only he shall pay for his loss of time, and for his healing. 20 And if a man strikes his male slave or his female slave, with a rod, and die under his hands, he shall be surely punished. 21 But if *he* continues to live a day or two, let *there* not be punished for he is his money.

22 And if two men strive and strike a woman with child, and her child be born imperfectly formed, he shall be forced to pay a penalty; as the woman's husband may lay upon him, he shall pay with a valuation. 23 But if it be perfectly formed, he shall give life for life, 24 eye for eye, tooth for tooth, hand for hand, foot for foot, 25 burning for burning, wound for wound, stripe for stripe. 26 And if one strike the eye of his male servant, or the eye of his female slave, and put it out, he shall let them go free for their eye's sake. 27 And if he should strike out the tooth of his male servant, or the tooth of his female servant, he shall send them away free for their tooth's sake.

28 And if a bull gore a man or woman and *they* die, the bull shall be stoned with stones, and his flesh shall not be eaten; but the owner of the bull shall be clear. 29 But if the bull should have been given to goring in former time, and men should have told his owner, and he have not removed him, but he should have killed a man or woman, the bull shall be stoned, and his owner shall die also. 30 And if a ransom should be imposed on him, he shall pay for the ransom of his soul as much as they shall lay upon him. 31 And if *it* gores a son or daughter, let them do to him according to this ordinance. 32 And if the bull gores a male slave or female slave, he shall pay to their master thirty silver didrachms, and the bull shall be stoned. 33 And if any one open a pit or dig a cavity in stone, and cover it not, and an ox or an ass fall in there, 34 the owner of the pit shall make compensation; he shall give money to their owner, and the dead shall be his own. 35 And if any man's bull gore the bull of his neighbor, and it die, they shall sell the living bull and divide the money, and they shall divide the dead bull. 36 But if the bull be known to have been given to goring in time past, and they have testified to his owner, and he have not removed him, he shall repay bull for bull, but the dead shall be his own.

Chapter 22

And if one steal a calf or a sheep, and kill it or sell it, he shall pay five calves for a calf, and four sheep for a sheep. 2 And if the thief be found in the breach and be smitten and die, there shall not be blood spilled for him. 3 But if the sun were raised upon him, he is guilty, he shall die instead; and if he has nothing, let him be sold in compensation for what he has stolen. 4 And if the thing stolen be left and be in his hand alive, whether ox or sheep, he shall restore them two-fold. 5 And if any one should feed down a field or a vineyard, and should send in his beast to feed down another field, he shall make compensation of his own field according to his produce; and if he shall have fed down the whole field, he shall pay for compensation the best of his own field and the best of his vineyard.

Exodus 22

6 And if fire have gone forth and caught thorns, and should also set on fire threshing floors or ears of corn or a field, he that kindled the fire shall make compensation. 7 And if any one gives to his neighbor money or goods to keep, and they be stolen out of the man's house, if the thief be found he shall repay double. 8 But if the thief be not found, the master of the house shall come forward before God, and shall swear that surely he has not wrought wickedly against any part of his neighbor's deposit, 9 according to every injury alleged, both concerning a calf, and an ass, and a sheep, and a garment, and every alleged loss, whatever in fact it may be, the judgment of both shall proceed before God, and he that is convicted by God shall repay to his neighbor double. 10 And if any one give to his neighbor to keep a calf or sheep or any beast, and it be wounded or die or be taken, and no one know, 11 an oath of God shall be between both, that he has surely not at all been guilty in the matter of his neighbor's deposit; and so his master shall accept him guiltless, and he shall not make compensation. 12 And if it were stolen from him, he shall make compensation to the owner. 13 And if it were seized of beasts, he shall bring him to the prey, and he shall not make compensation. 14 And if any one borrow of his neighbor, and it be wounded or die or be carried away, and the owner of it be not with it, he shall make compensation. 15 But if the owner were with it, he shall not make compensation: but if he were a hired worker, there shall be *compensation* to him instead of his wages.

16 And if any one deceives a virgin that is not betrothed, and lie with her, he shall surely endow her for a wife to himself. 17 And if her father positively refuse, and will not consent to give her to him for a wife, he shall pay silver to her father according to the amount of the dowry of virgins. 18 Ye shall not save the lives of sorcerers. 19 Every one that lies with a beast ye shall surely put to death. 20 He that sacrifices to any gods but to the Lord alone shall be destroyed by death. 21 And ye shall not hurt a stranger, nor afflict him, for ye were strangers in the land of Egypt. 22 Ye shall hurt no widow or orphan. 23 And if ye should afflict them by ill treatment, and they should cry aloud to me, I will surely hear their voice. 24 And I will be very angry, and will kill you with the sword, and your wives shall be widows and your children orphans. 25 And if thou should lend money to thy poor brother who is by thee, thou shall not be hard upon him thou shall not exact usury of him. 26 And if thou take thy neighbor's garment for a pledge, thou shall restore it to him before sunset. 27 For this is his clothing, this is the only covering of his nakedness; wherein shall he sleep? If then he shall cry to me, I will hearken to him, for I am merciful. 28 Thou shall not revile the gods, nor speak ill of the ruler of thy people. 29 Thou shall not keep back the first fruits of thy threshing floor and press. The firstborn of thy sons thou shall give to me.

30 So shall thou do with thy calf and thy sheep and thine donkey; seven days shall it be under the mother, and the eighth day thou shall give it to me. 31 And ye shall be holy men to me; and ye shall not eat flesh taken of beasts, ye shall cast it to the dog.

Chapter 23

Thou shall not receive a vain report, thou shall not agree with the unjust to become an unjust witness. 2 Thou shall not associate with the multitude for evil; thou shall not join thyself with a multitude to turn aside with the majority so as to shut out judgment. 3 And thou shall not spare a poor man in judgment. 4 And if thou meet thine enemy's ox or his ass going astray, thou shall turn them back and restore them to him. 5 And if thou see thine enemy's ass fallen under its burden, thou shall not pass by it, but shall help to raise it with him. 6 Thou shall not wrest the sentence of the poor in his judgment. 7 Thou shall abstain from every unjust thing; thou shall not kill the innocent and just, and thou shall not justify the wicked for gifts. 8 And thou shall not receive gifts, for gifts blind the eyes of the seeing, and corrupt just words. 9 And ye shall not afflict a stranger, for ye know the heart of a stranger, for ye were yourselves strangers in the land of Egypt.

10 Six years thou shall sow thy land, and gather in the fruits of it. 11 But in the seventh year thou shall let it rest, and leave it, and the poor of thy nation shall feed; and the wild beasts of the field shall eat that which remains; thus shall thou do to thy vineyard and to thine olive yard. 12 Six days shall thou do thy works, and on the seventh day there shall be rest, that thine ox and thine ass may rest, and that the son of thy female slave and the stranger may be refreshed.

13 Observe all things whatever I have commanded you; and ye shall make no mention of the name of other gods, neither shall they be heard out of your mouth. 14 Keep you a feast to me three times in the year. 15 Take heed to keep the feast of unleavened bread: seven days ye shall eat unleavened bread, as I charged thee at the season of the month of new, for in it thou came out of Egypt; thou shall not appear before me empty. 16 And thou shall keep the feast of the harvest of first fruits of thy labors, whatever thou shall have sown in thy field, and the feast of completion at the end of the year in the gathering in of thy works out of thy field. 17 Three times in the year shall all thy males appear before the Lord thy God. 18 For when I shall have cast out the nations from before thee, and shall have widened thy borders, thou shall not offer the blood of my sacrifice with leaven, neither must the fat of my feast abide till the morning. 19 Thou shall bring the first offerings of the first fruits of thy land into the house of the Lord thy God. Thou shall not boil a lamb in its mother's milk.

Exodus 24

20 And, behold, I send my angel before thy face, that he may keep thee in the way, that he may bring thee into the land which I have prepared for thee. 21 Take heed to thyself and hearken to him, and disobey him not, for he will not give way to thee, for my name is on him. 22 If ye will indeed hear my voice, and if thou will do all the things I shall charge thee with, and keep my covenant, ye shall be to me a peculiar people above all nations, for the whole earth is mine; and ye shall be to me a royal priesthood, and a holy nation; these words shall ye speak to the sons of Israel, If ye shall indeed hear my voice, and do all the things I shall tell thee, I will be an enemy to thine enemies, and an adversary to thine adversaries. 23 For my angel shall go as thy leader, and shall bring thee to the Amorite, and Hittite, and Pherezite, and Canaanite, and Gergesite, and Evite, and Jebusite, and I will destroy them. 24 Thou shall not worship their gods, nor serve them; thou shall not do according to their works, but shall utterly destroy them, and break to pieces their pillars.

25 And thou shall serve the Lord thy God, and I will bless thy bread and thy wine and thy water, and I will turn away sickness from you. 26 There shall not be on thy land one that is impotent or barren. I will surely fulfill the number of thy days. 27 And I will send terror before thee, and I will strike with amazement all the nations to which thou shall come, and I will make all thine enemies to flee. 28 And I will send hornets before thee, and thou shall cast out the Amorites and the Evites, and the Canaanites and the Hittites from thee. 29 I will not cast them out in one year, lest the land become desolate and the beasts of the field multiply against thee. 30 By little I will cast them out from before thee, until thou shall be increased and inherit the earth. 31 And I will set thy borders from the Red Sea, to the sea of the Philistines, and from the wilderness to the great river Euphrates; and I will give into your hand those that live in the land, and will cast them out from thee. 32 Thou shall make no covenant with them and their gods. 33 And they shall not live in thy land, lest they cause thee to sin against me; for if thou should serve their gods, these will be an offence to thee.

Chapter 24

And to Moses he said, Go up to the Lord, thou and Aaron and Nadav and Abiud, and seventy of the rulers of Israel; and they shall worship the Lord from a distance. 2 And Moses alone shall draw near to God; and they shall not draw near, and the people shall not come up with them. 3 And Moses went in and related to the people all the words of God and the ordinances; and all the people answered with one voice, saying, All the words, which the Lord has spoken, we will do and hear.

4 And Moses wrote all the words of the Lord; and Moses rose up early in the morning, and built an altar under the mountain and twelve stones for the twelve tribes of Israel. 5 And he sent forth the young men of the sons of Israel, and they offered whole burnt offerings, and they sacrificed young calves as a peace offering to God. 6 And Moses took half the blood and poured it into bowls, and half the blood he poured out upon the altar. 7 And he took the book of the covenant and read it in the ears of the people, and they said, All things whatever the Lord has spoken we will do and hearken therein. 8 And Moses took the blood and sprinkled it upon the people, and said, Behold the blood of the covenant, which the Lord has made with you concerning all these words.

9 And Moses went up, and Aaron, and Nadav and Abiud, and seventy of the elders of Israel. 10 And they saw the place where the God of Israel stood; and under his feet was as it were a work of sapphire slabs, and as it were the appearance of the firmament of heaven in its purity. 11 And of the chosen ones of Israel there was not even one missing, and they appeared where God was, and did eat and drink.

12 And the Lord said to Moses, Come up to me into the mountain, and wait there; and I will give thee the tables of stone, the law and the commandments, which I have written to give them laws. 13 And Moses arose and Jesus his attendant and they went up onto the mountain of God. 14 And to the elders they said, Rest here till we return to you; and behold, Aaron and Or are with you; if any man has a cause to be tried, let them go to them. 15 And Moses * and Jesus went up onto the mountain, and the cloud covered the mountain. 16 And the glory of God came down upon Mount Sinai, and the cloud covered it six days, and the Lord called Moses on the seventh day out of the midst of the cloud. 17 And the appearance of the glory of the Lord was as burning fire on the top of the mountain, before the sons of Israel. 18 And Moses went into the midst of the cloud, and went up to the mountain, and was there in the mountain forty days and forty nights.

* In the *Greek Menaion* the words "and Jesus" are omitted from the vesper reading for August for the Holy Transfiguration of Our Lord and Savior Jesus Christ.

Chapter 25

And the Lord spoke to Moses, saying, 2 Speak to the sons of Israel, and take first fruits of all, who may be disposed in their heart to give; and ye shall take my first fruits. 3 And this is the offering, which ye shall take of them, gold and silver and brass, 4 and blue, and purple, and double red, and fine-spun linen, and goats' hair,

Exodus 25

5 and rams' skins dyed red, and blue skins, and incorruptible wood, 6 and oil for the light, incense for anointing oil, and for the composition of incense, and Sardis stones, and stones for the carved work of the shoulder-piece, and the full-length robe. 7 And thou shall make me a sanctuary, and I will appear among you. 8 And thou shall make for me according to all things, which I show thee in the mountain; even the pattern of the tabernacle, and the pattern of all its furniture; so shall thou make it.

9 And thou shall make the ark of testimony of incorruptible wood, the length of two cubits and a half, and the breadth of a cubit and a half, and the height of a cubit and a half. 10 And thou shall gild it with pure gold, thou shall gild it within and without; and thou shall make for it golden wreaths twisted around. 11 And thou shall cast for it four golden rings, and shall put them on the four sides; two rings on the one side, and two rings on the other side. 12 And thou shall make staves *of* incorruptible wood, and shall gild them with gold. 13 And thou shall put the staves into the rings on the sides of the ark, to bear the ark with them. 14 The staves shall remain fixed in the rings of the ark. 15 And thou shall put into the ark the testimonies, which I shall give thee. 16 And thou shall make a propitiatory, a lid of pure gold, the length of two cubits and a half, and the breadth of a cubit and a half. 17 And thou shall make two cherubs graven in gold, and thou shall put them on both sides of the propitiatory. 18 They shall be made, one cherub on this side, and another cherub on the other side of the propitiatory; and thou shall make the two cherubs on the two sides. 19 The cherubs shall stretch forth their wings above, overshadowing the propitiatory with their wings; and their faces shall be toward each other, the faces of the cherubs shall be toward the propitiatory. 20 And thou shall set the propitiatory on the ark above, and thou shall put into the ark the testimonies, which I shall give thee. 21 And I will make myself known to thee from thence, and I will speak to thee above the propitiatory between the two cherubs, which are upon the ark of testimony, even in all things, which I shall charge thee concerning the sons of Israel.

22 And thou shall make a golden table of pure gold, in length two cubits, and in breadth a cubit, and in height a cubit and a half. 23 And thou shall make for it golden wreaths twisted around, and thou shall make for it a crown of a handbreadth around. 24 And thou shall make a twisted wreath for the crown around. 25 And thou shall make four golden rings; and thou shall put the four rings upon the four parts of its feet under the crown. 26 And the rings shall be for bearings for the staves, that they may bear the table with them. 27 And thou shall make the staves of incorruptible wood, and thou shall gild them with pure gold; and the table shall be borne with them. 28 And thou shall make its dishes and its censers, and its bowls, and its cups, with which thou shall offer drink offerings; of pure gold shall thou make them.

29 And thou shall set upon the table showbread before me continually. 30 And thou shall make a candlestick of pure gold; thou shall make the candlestick of graven work; its stem and its branches, and its bowls and its knops and its lilies shall be of one piece. 31 And six branches proceeding sideways, three branches of the candlestick from one side of it, and three branches of the candlestick from the other side. 32 And three bowls fashioned like almonds, on each branch a knop and a lily; so to the six branches proceeding from the candlestick, 33 and in the candlestick four bowls fashioned like almonds, in each branch knops and the flowers of the same. 34 A knop under two branches out of it, and a knop under four branches out of it; so to the six branches proceeding from the candlestick; 35 and in the candlestick four bowls fashioned like almonds. 36 Let the knops and the branches be of it one piece, altogether graven of one piece of pure gold. 37 And thou shall make its seven lamps: and thou shall set on *it* the lamps, and they shall shine from one front. 38 And thou shall make its funnel and its snuff-dishes of pure gold. 39 All these articles *shall be* a talent of pure gold. 40 See thou shall make them according to the pattern showed thee in the mount.

Chapter 26

And thou shall make the tabernacle, ten curtains of fine linen spun and blue and purple and red spun *with* cherubs; thou shall make them with work of a weaver. 2 The length of one curtain shall be eight and twenty cubits, and one curtain shall be the breadth of four cubits; there shall be the same measure to all the curtains. 3 And the five curtains shall be joined one to another, and *the other* five curtains shall be closely connected the one with the other. 4 And thou shall make for them loops of blue on the edge of one curtain, on one side for the coupling, and so shall thou make on the edge of the outer curtain for the second coupling. 5 Fifty loops shall thou make for one curtain, and fifty loops shall thou make on the part of the curtain answering to the coupling of the second, opposite, corresponding to each other at each point. 6 And thou shall make fifty golden rings; and thou shall join the curtains to each other with the rings, and it shall be one tabernacle. 7 And thou shall make for a covering of the tabernacle skins with the hair on; thou shall make them eleven skins. 8 The length of one skin thirty cubits, and the breadth of one skin four cubits; there shall be the same measure to the eleven skins. 9 And thou shall join the five skins together, and the six skins together; and thou shall double the sixth skin in front of the tabernacle. 10 And thou shall make fifty loops on the border of one skin, which is in the midst for the joining; and thou shall make fifty loops on the edge of the second skin that joins it.

Exodus 26

11 And thou shall make fifty brazen rings; and thou shall join the rings by the loops, and thou shall join the skins, and they shall be one. 12 And thou shall fix at the end that which is over in the skins of the tabernacle; the half of the skin that is left shall thou fold over, according to the surplus of the skins of the tabernacle; thou shall fold it over behind the tabernacle. 13 A cubit an this side, and a cubit on that side of that which remains of the skins, of the length of the skins of the tabernacle; it shall be folding over the sides of the tabernacle on this side and that side, that it may cover it. 14 And thou shall make for a covering of the tabernacle rams' skins dyed red and blue skins as coverings above.

15 And thou shall make the posts of the tabernacle of incorruptible wood. 16 Of ten cubits shall thou make one post, and the breadth of one post of a cubit and a half. 17 Two joints shall thou make in one post, answering the one to the other; so shall thou do to all the posts of the tabernacle. 18 And thou shall make posts to the tabernacle, twenty posts on the north side. 19 And thou shall make to the twenty posts forty silver sockets; two sockets to one post on both its sides, and two sockets to the other post on both its sides. 20 And for the next side, toward the south, twenty posts, 21 and their forty silver sockets; two sockets to one post on both its sides, and two sockets to the other post on both its sides. 22 And on the back of the tabernacle at the part that is toward the *west* thou shall make six posts. 23 And thou shall make two posts on the corners of the tabernacle behind. 24 And it shall be equal below, they shall be equal toward the same part from the heads to one joining; so shall thou make to both the two corners, let them be equal. 25 And there shall be eight posts, and their sixteen silver sockets; two sockets to one post on both its sides, and two sockets to the other post. 26 And thou shall make bars of incorruptible wood, five to one post on one side of the tabernacle, 27 and five bars to one post on the second side of the tabernacle, and five bars to the hinder posts, on the side of the tabernacle toward the sea. 28 And let the bar in the middle between the posts go through from the one side to the other side. 29 And thou shall gild the posts with gold; and thou shall make golden rings, into which thou shall introduce the bars, and thou shall gild the bars with gold. 30 And thou shall set up the tabernacle according to the pattern showed thee in the mount.

31 And thou shall make a veil of blue and purple and red woven, and fine linen spun; thou shall make it cherubs *in* woven work. 32 And thou shall set it upon four posts of incorruptible wood overlaid with gold; and their tops gold, and their four sockets of silver. 33 And thou shall put the veil on the posts, and thou shall carry in thither within the veil the ark of the testimony; and the veil shall make a separation for you between the holy and the holy of holies. 34 And thou shall screen with the veil the ark of the testimony in the holy of holies.

35 And thou shall set the table outside the veil, and the candlestick opposite the table on the south side of the tabernacle; and thou shall put the table on the north side of the tabernacle. 36 And thou shall make a screen for the door of the tabernacle of blue, and purple, and spun scarlet and fine linen spun the work of the embroiderer. 37 And thou shall make for the veil five posts, and thou shall gild them with gold; and their tops shall be gold; and thou shall cast for them five brazen sockets.

Chapter 27

And thou shall make an altar of incorruptible wood, of five cubits in the length, and five cubits in the breadth; the altar shall be square, and the height of it shall be of three cubits. 2 And thou shall make the horns on the four corners; the horns shall be of it, and thou shall overlay them with brass. 3 And thou shall make a rim for the altar; and its covering and its cups, and its flesh hooks, and its fire pan, and all its vessels shall thou make of brass. 4 And thou shall make for it a brazen grate with net work; and thou shall make for the grate four brazen rings under the four sides. 5 And thou shall put them below under the grate of the altar, and the grate shall extend to the middle of the altar. 6 And thou shall make for the altar staves of incorruptible wood, and thou shall overlay them with brass. 7 And thou shall put the staves into the rings; and let the staves be on the sides of the altar to carry it. 8 Thou shall make it hollow with boards; according to what was showed thee in the mount, so thou shall make it.

9 And thou shall make a court for the tabernacle, curtains of the court of fine linen spun on the south side, the length of a hundred cubits for one side. 10 And their pillars twenty, and twenty brazen sockets of them, and their rings and their clasps of silver. 11 Thus to the side toward the north curtains of a hundred cubits in length, and their pillars twenty, and their sockets twenty of brass, and the rings and the clasps of the pillars, and their sockets overlaid with silver. 12 And in the breadth of the tabernacle toward the west curtains of fifty cubits, there are ten pillars and their ten sockets. 13 And in the breadth of the tabernacle toward the south, curtains of fifty cubits, there are ten pillars, and their ten sockets. 14 And the height of the curtains of fifty cubits for the one side, their pillars three, and their sockets three. 15 And the second side the height of the curtains of fifteen cubits, their pillars three, and their sockets three. 16 And a veil for the door of the court, the height of twenty cubits of blue linen, and of purple, and spun red, and of fine linen spun with the art of the embroiderer; their pillars four, and their sockets four. 17 All the pillars of the court round about overlaid with silver, and their tops silver and their brass sockets.

Exodus 28

18 And the length of the court a hundred *cubits* on each side, and the breadth fifty on each side, and the height five cubits of fine linen spun, and their sockets of brass. 19 And all the furniture and all the instruments and the pins of the court, of brass. 20 And do thou charge the sons of Israel, and let them take for thee refined pure olive oil beaten to burn for light, that a lamp may burn continually 21 in the Tabernacle of the Testimony, without the veil that is over the covenant, shall Aaron and his sons burn it from evening until morning, before the Lord; it is a perpetual ordinance to your generations of the sons of Israel.

Chapter 28

And do thou take to thyself both Aaron thy brother, and his sons, even of the sons of Israel; so that Aaron, and Nadav and Abiud, and Eleazar and Ithamar, sons of Aaron, may minister to me. 2 And thou shall make holy apparel for Aaron thy brother, for honor and glory. 3 And speak thou to all those who are wise in understanding, whom I have filled with the spirit of wisdom and perception; and they shall make the holy apparel of Aaron for the sanctuary, in which he shall minister to me as priest. 4 And these are the garments which they shall make: the breastplate, and the shoulder piece, and the full-length robe, and the tunic with a fringe, and the tire, and the girdle; and they shall make holy garments for Aaron and his sons to minister to me as priests.

5 And they shall take the gold, and the blue, and the purple, and the red, and the fine linen. 6 And they shall make the shoulder piece of fine linen spun, the woven work of the embroiderer. 7 It shall have two shoulder pieces joined together, fastened on the two sides. 8 And the woven work of the shoulder pieces, which is upon him, shall be of one piece according to the work, of pure gold and blue and purple, and spun red and fine twined linen. 9 And thou shall take the two stones, the stones of emerald, and thou shall grave on them the names of the sons of Israel.

10 Six names on the first stone, and the other six names on the second stone, according to their births. 11 The work of the stone engraver's art, as the graving of a seal thou shall engrave the two stones with the names of the sons of Israel. 12 And thou shall put the two stones on the shoulders of the shoulder piece; they are memorial stones for the sons of Israel; and Aaron shall bear the names of the sons of Israel before the Lord on his two shoulders, a memorial for them. 13 And thou shall make discs of pure gold; 14 and thou shall make two fringes of pure gold, variegated with flowers wreathen work; and thou shall put the wreathen fringes on the circlets, fastening them on their shoulder pieces in front.

Exodus 28

15 And thou shall make the oracle of judgment, the work of the embroiderer; in keeping with the ephod, thou shall make it of gold, and blue and purple, and spun red, and fine linen spun. 16 Thou shall make it square; it shall be double, of a span the length of it, and of a span the breadth. 17 And thou shall interweave with it a texture of four rows of stone; there shall be a row of stones, a sardius, a topaz, and emerald, the first row. 18 And the second row, a carbuncle, a sapphire, and jasper. 19 And the third row, a ligure, an agate, an amethyst; 20 and the fourth row, a chrysolite, and a beryl, and an onyx stone, set round with gold, bound together with gold; let them be according to their row. 21 And let the stones of the names of the sons of Israel be twelve according to their names, engravings as of seals; let them be for the twelve tribes each according to the name. 22 And thou shall make on the oracle woven fringes, a chain work of pure gold. 23 And Aaron shall take the names of the sons of Israel, on the oracle of judgment on his breast, a memorial before God for him as he goes into the sanctuary. 24 And thou shall put the fringes on the oracle of judgment; thou shall put the wreaths on both sides of the oracle, 25 and thou shall put the two circlets on both the shoulders of the ephod in front.

26 And thou shall put the Manifestation and the Truth on the oracle of judgment; and it shall be on the breast of Aaron, when he goes into the holy place before the Lord; and Aaron shall bear the judgments of the sons of Israel on his breast before the Lord continually. 27 And thou shall make the full-length tunic all of blue. 28 And the opening of it shall be in the middle having a fringe round about the opening, the work of the weaver, woven together in the joining of the same piece that it might not be rent. 29 And under the fringe of the robe below thou shall make as it were pomegranates of a flowering pomegranate tree, of blue, and purple, and spun red, and fine linen spun, under the fringe of the robe around; golden pomegranates of the same shape, and bells round about between these. 30 A bell by the side of a golden pomegranate, and flower work on the fringe of the robe around. 31 And the sound of Aaron shall be audible when he ministers, as he goes into the sanctuary before the Lord, and has he goes out, that he dies not.

32 And thou shall make a plate pure gold, and thou shall grave on it the graving of a signet, Holiness of the Lord. 33 And thou shall put it on the spun blue cloth, and it shall be on the miter; it shall be in the front of the miter. 34 And it shall be on the forehead of Aaron; and Aaron shall bear away the sins of their holy things, all that the sons of Israel shall sanctify of every gift of their holy things, and it shall be on the forehead of Aaron continually acceptable for them before the Lord. 35 And the fringes of the garments of fine linen; and thou shall make a tire of fine linen, and thou shall make a girdle, the work of the embroiderer.

Exodus 29

36 And for the sons of Aaron thou shall make tunics and girdles, and thou shall make for them tires for honor and glory. 37 And thou shall put them on Aaron thy brother, and his sons with him, and thou shall anoint them and fill their hands: and thou shall sanctify them that they may minister to me in the priest's office. 38 And thou shall make for them linen drawers to cover the nakedness of their flesh; they shall reach from the loins to the thighs. 39 And Aaron shall have them, and his sons, whenever they enter into the tabernacle of witness, or when they shall advance to the altar of the sanctuary to minister, so they shall not bring sin upon themselves, lest they die; a perpetual statute for him, and for his seed after him.

Chapter 29

And these are the things, which thou shall do to them; thou shall sanctify them, so that they shall serve me in the priesthood; and thou shall take one young calf from the herd, and two unblemished rams; 2 and unleavened loaves kneaded with oil, and unleavened cakes anointed with oil; thou shall make them *of* fine flour of wheat. 3 And thou shall put them in one basket, and thou shall offer them in the basket, and the young calf and the two rams. 4 And thou shall bring Aaron and his sons to the doors of the tabernacle of testimony, and thou shall wash them with water. 5 And having taken the garments, thou shall put on Aaron thy brother both the full-length robe and the ephod and the oracle; and thou shall join for him the oracle to the ephod. 6 And thou shall put the miter on his head; and thou shall put the plate, the Holiness, on the miter. 7 And thou shall take of the anointing oil, and thou shall pour it on his head, and shall anoint him, 8 and thou shall bring his sons, and put garments on them. 9 And thou shall gird them with the girdles, and put the tires upon them, and they shall have a priestly office to me forever; and thou shall fill the hands of Aaron and the hands of his sons.

10 And thou shall bring the calf to the door of the tabernacle of witness; and Aaron and his sons shall lay their hands on the head of the calf, before the Lord, by the doors of the tabernacle of witness. 11 And thou shall kill the calf before the Lord, by the doors of the tabernacle of witness. 12 And thou shall take of the blood of the calf, and put it on the horns of the altar with thy finger, but all the rest of the blood thou shall pour out at the foot of the altar. 13 And thou shall take all the fat that is on the belly, and the lobe of the liver, and the two kidneys, and the fat that is upon them, and shall put them upon the altar. 14 But the flesh of the calf, and his skin, and his dung, shall thou burn with fire outside the camp, for it is for *an offering of* sin.

Exodus 29

15 And thou shall take one ram, and Aaron and his sons shall lay their hands on the head of the ram. 16 And thou shall kill it, and take the blood and pour it on the altar round about.

17 And thou shall divide the ram by his several limbs, and thou shall wash the inward parts and the feet with water, and thou shall put them on the divided parts with the head. 18 And thou shall offer the whole ram on the altar, a whole burnt offering to the Lord for a sweet smelling savor; it is an offering of incense to the Lord. 19 And thou shall take the second ram, and Aaron and his sons shall lay their hands on the head of the ram. 20 And thou shall kill it, and take of the blood of it, and put it on the tip of Aaron's right ear, and on the thumb of his right hand, and on the great toe of his right foot, and on the tips of the right ears of his sons, and on the thumbs of their right hands, and on the great toes of their right feet. 21 And thou shall take of the blood from the altar, and of the anointing oil; and thou shall sprinkle it upon Aaron and on his garments, and on his sons and on his sons' garments with him; and he shall be sanctified and his apparel, and his sons and his sons' apparel with him; but the blood of the ram thou shall pour round about upon the altar. 22 And thou shall take from the ram its fat, both the fat that covers the belly, and the lobe of the liver, and the two kidneys, and the fat that is upon them, and the right shoulder, for this is a validation. 23 And one cake with oil and one cake from the basket of unleavened bread set forth before the Lord. 24 And thou shall put them all on the hands of Aaron, and on the hands of his sons, and thou shall separate them as for a separation *offering* before the Lord. 25 And thou shall take them from their hands, and shall offer them up on the altar of whole burnt offering for a sweet smelling savor before the Lord; it is an offering to the Lord. 26 And thou shall take the breast from the ram of consecration, which is Aaron's, and thou shall separate it as a separate offering before the Lord, and it shall be to thee for a portion.

27 And thou shall sanctify the separated breast and the shoulder of removal which has been separated, and which has been removed from the ram of consecration, of the portion of Aaron and of his sons. 28 And it shall be a perpetual statute of the sons of Israel to Aaron and his sons, for this is a separation *offering*; and it shall be a special offering from the sons of Israel, from the peace offerings of the sons of Israel, a special offering to the Lord. 29 And the apparel of the sanctuary, which is Aaron's, shall be his son's after him, for them to be anointed in them, and to fill their hands. 30 The priest his successor from among his sons who shall go into the Tabernacle of Witness to minister in the holies, shall put them on seven days. 31 And thou shall take the ram of consecration, and thou shall boil the flesh in the holy place. 32 And Aaron and his sons shall eat the flesh of the ram, and the loaves in the basket, by the doors of the tabernacle of witness.

Exodus 30

33 They shall eat the offerings with which they were sanctified to fill their hands, to sanctify them; and a stranger shall not eat of them, for they are holy.

34 And if the flesh of the sacrifice of consecration was left and of the loaves until the morning, thou shall burn the remainder with fire; it shall not be eaten, for it is a holy thing. 35 And thus shall thou do for Aaron and for his sons according to all things that I have commanded thee; seven days shall thou fill their hands. 36 And thou shall sacrifice the calf of the sin offering on the day of purification, and thou shall purify the altar when thou do sanctify upon it, and thou shall anoint it so as to sanctify it. 37 Seven days shall thou purify the altar and sanctify it; and the altar shall be most holy, every one that touches the altar shall be hallowed. 38 And these are the offerings which thou shall offer upon the altar; two unblemished lambs of a year old daily on the altar continually, a constant offering. 39 One lamb thou shall offer in the morning, and the second lamb thou shall offer in the evening. 40 And a tenth measure of fine flour mingled with the fourth part of a hin of beaten oil, and a drink offering the fourth part of a hin of wine for one lamb. 41 And thou shall offer the second lamb in the evening, after the manner of the morning offering, and according to the drink offering of it the morning lamb; thou shall offer it an offering to the Lord for a sweet smelling savor, 42 a perpetual sacrifice to your generations, at the door of the tabernacle of witness before the Lord; wherein I will be known to thee from thence, so as to speak to thee.

43 And I will there give orders to the sons of Israel, and I will be sanctified in my glory. 44 And I will sanctify the Tabernacle of Testimony and the altar, and I will sanctify Aaron and his sons, to minister as priests to me. 45 And I will be invoked among the sons of Israel, and will be their God. 46 And they shall know that I am the Lord their God, who brought them forth out of the land of Egypt, to be called upon by them, and to be their God.

Chapter 30

And thou shall make the altar of incense of incorruptible wood. 2 And thou shall make it a cubit in length, and a cubit in breadth; it shall be square; and the height of it shall be of two cubits, its horns shall be of it the same piece. 3 And thou shall gild its grate with pure gold, and its sides round about, and its horns; and thou shall make for it a wreathen border of gold roundabout. 4 And thou shall make under its wreathen border two rings of pure gold; thou shall make it to the two corners on the two sides, and they shall be bearings for the staves, so as to bear it with them. 5 And thou shall make the staves of incorruptible wood, and shall gild them with gold.

6 And thou shall set it before the veil that is over the ark of the testimonies, wherein I will make myself known to thee from thence. 7 And Aaron shall burn upon it fine compound incense every morning; whenever he trims the lamps he shall burn incense upon it.

8 And when Aaron lights the lamps in the evening, he shall burn incense upon it, a constant incense offering always before the Lord for their generations. 9 And thou shall not offer strange incense upon it, and offering made by fire, *nor* a sacrifice; and thou shall not pour a drink offering upon it. 10 And once in the year Aaron shall make atonement on it, on its horns, he shall purge it with the blood of purification for their generations: it is most holy to the Lord. 11 And the Lord spoke to Moses, saying, 12 If thou take account of the sons of Israel in the surveying of them, and they shall give every one a ransom for his soul to the Lord, then there shall not be among them destruction in the visiting of them. 13 And this is what they shall give, as many as pass the survey, half a didrachm which is according to the didrachm of the sanctuary; twenty oboli the didrachm, but the half of the didrachm is the offering to the Lord. 14 Every one that passes the survey from twenty years old and upward shall give the offering to the Lord.

15 The rich shall not give more, and the poor shall not give less than the half didrachm in giving the offering to the Lord, to make atonement for your souls. 16 And thou shall take the silver of the offering from the sons of Israel, and shall give it for the service of the tabernacle of testimony; and it shall be to the sons of Israel a memorial before the Lord, to make atonement for your souls. 17 And the Lord spoke to Moses, saying, 18 Make a brazen laver, and a brazen base for it, so as to wash one's self; and thou shall put it between the tabernacle of witness and the altar, and thou shall pour forth water into it.

19 And Aaron and his sons shall wash their hands and their feet with water from it. 20 Whenever they shall go into the tabernacle of witness, they shall wash themselves with water, so they shall not die, whenever they advance to the altar to do service and to offer the whole burnt offerings to the Lord. 21 They shall wash their hands and feet with water, whenever they shall go into the Tabernacle of Witness; they shall wash themselves with water, that they die not; and it shall be for them a perpetual statute, for him and his generations after him. 22 And the Lord spoke to Moses, saying, 23 Do thou also take sweet herbs, the flower of choice myrrh five hundred shekels, and the half of this two hundred and fifty shekels of sweet smelling cinnamon, and two hundred and fifty shekels of sweet smelling calamus, 24 and of iris five hundred shekels of the sanctuary, and a hin of olive oil. 25 And thou shall make it holy anointing oil, a perfumed ointment by the art of the perfumer; it shall be holy anointing oil. 26 And thou shall anoint with it the tabernacle of witness, and the ark of the Tabernacle of Witness, 27 and all its furniture, and the candlestick and all its furniture, and the altar of incense,

Exodus 31

28 and the altar of whole burnt offerings and all its furniture, and the table and all its furniture, and the laver. 29 And thou shall sanctify them, and they shall be most holy; every one that touches them shall be hallowed. 30 And thou shall anoint Aaron and his sons, and sanctify them that they may minister to me as priests. 31 And thou shall speak to the sons of Israel, saying, This shall be to you holy anointing oil throughout your generations. 32 On man's flesh it shall not be poured, and ye shall not make for yourselves according to this composition: it is holy, and shall be holiness to you. 33 Whoever shall make it in like manner, and whoever shall give of it to a stranger, shall be destroyed from among his people. 34 And the Lord said to Moses, Take for thyself sweet herbs, stacte, onycha, sweet galbanum, and transparent frankincense; there shall be an equal to equal *weight* of each. 35 And they shall make with it perfumed incense, tempered with the art of a perfumer, a pure holy work. 36 And of these thou shall beat some small, and thou shall put it before the testimonies in the Tabernacle of Testimony, whence I will make myself known to thee; it shall be to you a most holy incense. 37 Ye shall not make any for yourselves according to this composition; it shall be to you a holy thing for the Lord. 38 Whoever shall make any in like manner, so as to smell of it, shall perish from his people.

Chapter 31

And the Lord spoke to Moses, saying, 2 Behold, I have called by name Beseleel the son of Urias the son of Or, of the tribe of Judah. 3 And I have filled him *with* a godly spirit of wisdom, and understanding, and knowledge, to invent in every work, 4 and to frame works, to labor in gold, and silver, and brass, and blue, and purple, and spun scarlet, 5 and works in stone, and for artificers' work in wood, to work at all works. 6 And I have given him and Eliav the *son* of Ahisamah of the tribe of Dan, and to every one understanding in heart I have given understanding; and they shall work in all things as many as I have appointed thee, 7 the Tabernacle of Witness, and the Ark of the Covenant, and the propitiatory that is upon it, and the furniture of the tabernacle, 8 and the altars, and the table and all its furniture, 9 and the pure candlestick and all its furniture, and the laver and its base, 10 and Aaron's robes of ministry, and the robes of his sons to minister to me as priests, 11 and the anointing oil and the compound incense of the sanctuary; according to all that I have commanded thee shall they make them. 12 And the Lord spoke to Moses, saying, 13 Do thou also charge the sons of Israel, saying, Take heed and keep my Sabbaths; they are a sign with Me and among you throughout your generations, that ye may know that I am the Lord that sanctifies you.

14 And ye shall keep the Sabbaths, because this is holy to the Lord for you; he that profanes it shall surely be put to death; every one who shall do a work on it, that soul shall be destroyed from the midst of his people. 15 Six days thou shall do works, but the seventh day is the Sabbath, a holy rest to the Lord; every one who shall do a work on the seventh day shall be put to death.

16 And the sons of Israel shall keep the Sabbaths, to observe them through all their generations. 17 It is a perpetual covenant with me and the sons of Israel, it is a perpetual sign with me; for in six days the Lord made the heaven and the earth, and on the seventh day he ceased, and rested. 18 And he gave to Moses when he left off speaking to him on Mount Sinai the two tables of testimony, tables of stone written with the finger of God.

Chapter 32

And when the people saw that Moses delayed to come down from the mountain, the people combined against Aaron, and said to him, Arise and make us gods who shall go before us; for this Moses, the man who brought us forth out of the land of Egypt we do not know what is become of him. 2 And Aaron says to them, Take off the golden earrings, which are in the ears of your wives and daughters, and bring them to me. 3 And all the people took off the golden earrings that were in their ears, and brought them to Aaron. 4 And he received them at their hands, and formed them with a graving tool; and he made them a molten calf, and said, These *are* thy gods, O Israel, which have brought thee up out of the land of Egypt. 5 And Aaron having seen it built an altar before it, and Aaron made proclamation saying, Tomorrow *is* a feast of the Lord. 6 And having risen early in the morning, he placed upon the alter whole burnt offerings, and offered a peace offering; and the people sat down to eat and drink, and rose up to play.

7 And the Lord spoke to Moses, saying, Go quickly, *and* descend hence, for thy people whom thou brought out of the land of Egypt have transgressed. 8 They have quickly gone out of the way which thou commanded; they have made for themselves a calf, and worshipped it, and sacrificed to it, and said, These are thy gods, O Israel, who brought thee up out of the land of Egypt. And now leave me alone, and I will be very angry with them and consume them, 10 and I will make thee a great nation. 11 And Moses prayed before the Lord God, and said, Wherefore, O Lord, art thou very angry with thy people, whom thou brought out of the land of Egypt with great strength, and with thy high arm? 12 Lest at any time the Egyptians speak, saying, With evil intent he brought them out to kill them in the mountains, and to consume them from off the earth; cease from thy wrathful anger, and be merciful to the sin of thy people,

Exodus 32

13 remembering Abraham and Isaac and Jacob thy servants, to whom thou hast sworn by thyself, and has spoken to them, saying, I will greatly multiply your seed as the stars of heaven for multitude, and all this land which thou spoke of to give to them, so that they shall possess it forever. 14 And the Lord was propitiated to preserve his people.

15 And Moses turned and went down from the mountain, and the two tables of testimony were in his hands, tables of stone written on both their sides; they were written within and without. 16 And the tables were the work of God, and the writing the writing of God written on the tables. 17 And Jesus having heard the voice of the people crying says to Moses, There is a noise of war in the camp. 18 And *Moses* says, It is not the voice of them that begin the battle, nor the voice of them that begin of defeat, but the voice of them that begin of wine do I hear. 19 And when he drew near to the camp, he sees the calf and the dances; and Moses being very angry cast the two tables out of his hands, and broke them to pieces under the mountain. 20 And having taken the calf, which they made, he consumed it with fire, and ground it very small, and sowed it under the water, and made the sons of Israel to drink it. 21 And Moses said to Aaron, What have this people done to thee, that thou hast brought upon them a great sin? 22 And Aaron said to Moses, Be not angry lord, for thou know the impulse of this people. 23 For they say to me, Make us gods, which shall go before us, for as for this man Moses, who brought us out of Egypt, we do not know what has happened to him. 24 And I said to them, If any one has golden ornaments, take them off; and they gave them me, and I cast them into the fire, and there came out this calf.

25 And when Moses saw that the people were scattered, for Aaron scattered them, a rejoicing to their enemies, 26 then stood Moses at the gate of the camp, and said, Who is on the Lord's side? Let him come to me. Then all the sons of Levi came to him. 27 And he says to them, Thus saith the Lord God of Israel, Put every one his sword on his thigh, and go through and return from gate to gate through the camp, and kill every one his brother, and every one his neighbor, and every one him that is nearest to him. 28 And the sons of Levi did as Moses spoke to them, and there fell of the people in that day to the three thousand men. 29 And Moses said to them, Ye have filled your hands this day to the Lord each one on his son or on his brother, so that blessing should be given to you.

30 And it came to pass after the morning, that Moses said to the people, Ye have sinned a great sin; and now I will go up to God, that I may make atonement for your sin. 31 And Moses returned to the Lord and said, I pray, O Lord, this people has sinned a great sin, and they have made for themselves golden gods. 32 And now if thou do forgive their sin, forgive; and if not, blot me out of thy book, which thou have written.

Exodus 33

33 And the Lord said to Moses, If any one has sinned against me, I would blot them out of my book. 34 and now go, descend, and lead this people into the place of which I spoke to thee; behold, my angel shall go before thy face; and in the day when I shall visit I will bring upon them their sin. 35 And the Lord struck the people for the making of the calf, which Aaron made.

Chapter 33

And the Lord said to Moses, Go forward, go up hence, thou and thy people, whom thou brought out of the land of Egypt, into the land which I swore to Abraham, and Isaac, and Jacob, saying, I will give it to your seed. 2 And I will send at the same time my angel before thy face, and he shall cast out the Amorite and the Hittite, and the Pherezite and Gergesite, and Evite, and Jebusite, and Canaanite. 3 And I will bring thee into a land flowing with milk and honey, for I will not go up with thee, because thou art a stiff necked people, lest I consume thee by the way. 4 And the people having heard this harsh saying, mourned in mourning clothes. 5 For the Lord said to the sons of Israel, Ye are a stiff necked people; take heed lest I bring on you another plague, and destroy you; now then put off your glorious apparel, and ornaments, and I will show thee what I will do to thee. 6 So the sons of Israel took off their ornaments and their array at the mount of Horeb.

7 And Moses took his tabernacle and pitched it outside the camp, at a distance from the camp; and it was called the Tabernacle of Testimony, and it came to pass every one that sought the Lord went forth to the tabernacle which was outside the camp. 8 And whenever Moses went into the tabernacle outside the camp, all the people stood every one watching by the doors of his tent; and when Moses departed, they took notice until he entered into the tabernacle. 9 And when Moses entered into the tabernacle, the pillar of the cloud descended, and stood at the door of the tabernacle, and talked to Moses. 10 And all the people saw the pillar of the cloud standing by the door of the tabernacle, and all the people stood and worshipped every one from the door of his tent. 11 And the Lord spoke to Moses face to face, as if one should speak to his friend; and he retired into the camp; but his servant Jesus the son of Naue, a young man, departed not forth from the tabernacle.

12 And Moses said to the Lord, Behold! Thou says to me, Bring up this people; but thou has not showed me whom thou will send with me, but thou has said to me, I know thee above all, and thou has found favor with me. 13 If then I have found favor in thy sight, reveal thyself to me, that I may evidently see thee that I may find favor in thy sight, and that I may know that this great nation *is* thy people. 14 And He says, I myself will go before thee, and give thee rest.

Exodus 34

15 And he said to him; if thou go not up with us thyself, bring me not up hence. 16 And how shall it be surely known, that both this people and I have found favor with thee, except only if thou go with us? So both thy people and I shall be glorified beyond all the nations, as many as are upon the earth. 17 And the Lord said to Moses, I would also do for thee this thing, which thou have spoken, for thou has found grace before me, and I know thee above all.

18 And * *Moses* said, Manifest Thyself to me. 19 And *God* said, I will pass by before thee with My glory, and I will call by My name, the Lord, before thee; and I will have mercy on whom I will have mercy, and will have pity on whom I will have pity. 20 And *God* said, Thou should not be able to see My face; for no man shall see My face, and live. 21 And the Lord said, Behold, a place by Me; thou shall stand upon the rock, 22 and when My glory shall pass by, then I will put thee into a hole of the rock; and I will cover thee over with my hand, until I shall have passed by. 23 And I will remove My hand, and then shall thou see My back; but My face shall not appear to thee.

* The August vesper reading for Chapter Thirty-Three verse eighteen from the *Greek Menaion* reads differently as it is present in the biblical text as published by the Apostoliki Diakonia and Zoe Brotherhood. The phrase is translated as follows: "Moses said, Manifest to me Thy glory".

Chapter 34

And the Lord said to Moses, carve for thyself two tables of stone, as also the first were, and come up to me to the mountain; and I will write upon the tables the words, which were on the first tables, which thou broke. 2 And be ready by the morning, and thou shall go up to the Mount Sinai, and shall stand there for me on the top of the mountain. 3 And let no one go up with thee, nor be seen in the entire mountain; and let not the sheep and oxen feed near that mountain. 4 And *Moses* carved two tables of stone, as also the first were; and Moses having arisen early in the morning went up to the Mount Sinai, as the Lord appointed him; and Moses took the two tables of stone. 5 And the Lord descended in a cloud, and stood near him there, and called by the name of the Lord. 6 And the Lord passed by before his face, and proclaimed, * The Lord God, pitiful and merciful, longsuffering and very compassionate, and true, 7 and keeping justice and mercy for thousands, taking away iniquity, and unrighteousness, and sins; and he will not clear the guilty; bringing the iniquity of the fathers upon the children, and to the children's children, to the third and fourth generation. * 8 And Moses hurried, and bowed to the earth and worshipped

Exodus 34

9 and said, If I have found grace before thee, let my Lord go with us; for the people are stiff necked; and thou shall take away our sins and our iniquities, and we will be thine. 10 And the Lord said to Moses, Behold, I establish a covenant for thee in the presence of all thy people; I will do glorious things, which have not been done in all the earth, or in any nation; and all the people among whom thou art shall see the works of the Lord, that they are wonderful, which I will do for thee.

11 Do thou take heed to all things whatever I command thee; behold, I cast out before your face the Amorite and the Canaanite and the Pherezite, and the Hittite, and Evite, and Gergesite and Jebusite: 12 take heed to thyself, lest at any time thou make a covenant with the dwellers on the land, into which thou art entering, lest it be to thee a stumbling block among you. 13 Ye shall destroy their altars, and break in pieces their pillars, and ye shall cut down their groves, and the graven images of their gods ye shall burn with fire. 14 For ye shall not worship strange gods, for the Lord God, a jealous name, is a jealous God, 15 lest at any time thou make a covenant with the dwellers on the land, and they go a whoring after their gods, and sacrifice to their gods, and they call thee, and thou should eat of their feasts, 16 and thou should take of their daughters to thy sons, and thou should give of thy daughters to their sons; and thy daughters should go a whoring after their gods, and thy sons should go a whoring after their gods. 17 And thou shall not make to thyself molten gods. 18 And thou shall keep the feast of unleavened bread; seven days shall thou eat unleavened bread, as I have charged thee, at the season in the month of new; for in the month of new thou came out from Egypt. 19 The males *are* mine, everything that opens the womb, every first-born of a calf, and firstborn of sheep. 20 And the firstborn of an mule thou shall redeem with a sheep, and if thou will not redeem it thou shall pay a price; every firstborn of thy sons shall thou redeem; thou shall not appear before me empty.

21 Six days thou shall work, but on the seventh day thou shall rest; rest in seedtime and harvest. 22 And thou shall make to Me the feast of weeks, the beginning of wheat harvest, and the feast of ingathering in the middle of the year. 23 Three times in the year shall every male of thine appear before the Lord the God of Israel. 24 For when I shall have cast out the nations before thy face, and shall have enlarged thy coasts, no one shall desire thy land, whenever thou may go up to appear before the Lord thy God, three times in the year. 25 Thou shall not slay the blood of my sacrifices upon leaven; neither shall the sacrifices of the feast of the Passover sleep until the morning. 26 The first fruits of thy land shall thou put into the house of the Lord thy God; thou shall not boil a lamb in his mother's milk.

27 And the Lord said to Moses, Write these words for thyself, for on these words I have established a covenant with thee and with Israel.

Exodus 35

28 And Moses was there before the Lord forty days, and forty nights; he did not eat bread, and he did not drink water; and he wrote upon the tables these words of the covenant, the ten sayings. 29 And when Moses went down from the mountain, and the two tables in the hands of Moses, as he was coming down from the mountain; Moses knew not that the appearance of the color of his face was glorified, when He spoke to him.

30 And Aaron and all the elders of Israel saw Moses, and the appearance of the skin of his face was made glorious, and they feared to approach him. 31 And Moses called them, and Aaron and all the rulers of the synagogue turned towards him, and Moses spoke to them. 32 And afterwards all the sons of Israel came to him, and he commanded them all things, whatever the Lord had commanded him on the Mount of Sinai. 33 And when he ceased speaking to them, he put a veil on his face. 34 And whenever Moses went in before the Lord to speak to him, he took off the veil till he went out, and he went forth and spoke to all the sons of Israel whatever the Lord commanded him. 35 And the sons of Israel saw the face of Moses that it was glorified; and Moses put the veil over his face, till he went in to speak with him.

* The August vesper reading for Chapter Thirty-Four verses six and eight from the *Greek Menaion* reads differently as it is present in the biblical text as published by the Apostoliki Diakonia and Zoe Brotherhood. The phrase is translated as follows:

"The Lord, the Lord, God pitiful and merciful, longsuffering and very compassionate, and true. And Moses hurried, and bowed to the earth and worshipped the Lord."

Chapter 35

And Moses gathered the entire congregation of the sons of Israel together, and said; These are the words, which the Lord has spoken for to do them. 2 Six days shall thou perform works, but on the seventh day rest, a Holy Sabbath, a rest for the Lord; every one that does work on it, let him die. 3 Ye shall not burn a fire in any of your dwellings on the Sabbath day; I *am* the Lord.

4 And Moses spoke to all the congregation of the sons of Israel, saying, This *is* the thing, which the Lord has appointed you, saying, 5 Take of yourselves an offering for the Lord; every one that engages in his heart they shall bring the first fruits to the Lord; gold, silver, brass, 6 blue, purple, double red spun, and fine linen spun, and goats' hair, 7 and rams' skins dyed red, and skins blue, and incorruptible wood, 8 and sardine stones, and stones for engraving for the ephod and full-length robe. 9 And every man that is wise in heart among you, let him come and work all things whatsoever the Lord has commanded.

Exodus 35

10 The tabernacle, and the cords, and the coverings, and the rings, and the bars, and the posts, 11 and the ark of the testimony, and its staves, and its propitiatory, and the veil, 12 and the curtains of the court, and its posts, 13 and the emerald stones, 14 and the incense, and the anointing oil, 15 and the table and all its furniture, 16 and the candlestick for the light and all its furniture, 17 and the altar and all its furniture; 18 and the holy garments of Aaron the priest, and the garments in which they shall do service, 19 and the garments of priesthood for the sons of Aaron and the anointing oil, and the compound incense. 20 And all the congregation of the sons of Israel went out from Moses. And they brought, they whose heart prompted them, and they to whomever it seemed good in their mind, each and offering: 21 and they brought an offering to the Lord for all the works of the tabernacle of witness, and all its services, and for all the robes of the sanctuary. 22 And the men, even every one to whom it seemed good in his heart, brought from the women, brought seals and earrings, and finger rings, and hair clasps, and bracelets, every article of gold. 23 And all as many as brought ornaments of gold to the Lord, and with whomever fine linen was found; and they brought skins blue, and rams' skins dyed red. 24 And every one that offered an offering brought silver and brass, the offerings to the Lord; and with who was found incorruptible wood; and they brought for all the works of the preparation.

25 And every woman skilled in her heart to spin with her hands, they brought spun *works of* the blue, and purple, and red and fine linen. 26 And all the women, to whom it seemed good in their heart in their wisdom, spun the goats' hair. 27 And the rulers brought the emerald stones and the stones for setting in the ephod, and the oracle, 28 and the compounds both for the anointing oil, and the composition of the incense. 29 And every man and woman whose mind inclined them to come in and do all the works as many as the Lord appointed them to do by Moses, the sons of Israel brought an offering to the Lord.

30 And Moses said to the sons of Israel, Behold, God has called by name Beseleel the *son* of Urias the *son of* Or, of the tribe of Judah, 31 and has filled him with a divine spirit of wisdom and understanding, and knowledge of all things, 32 to labor skillfully in all works of cunning workmanship, to form the gold and the silver and the brass, 33 and to work in stone, and to fashion the wood, and to work in every work of wisdom. 34 And *God* gave improvement in understanding both to him, and to Eliav the *son* of Ahisamah of the tribe of Dan. 35 And *God* filled them with wisdom, understanding *and* perception, to understand to work all the works of the sanctuary, and to weave the woven and embroidered work with red and fine linen, to do all work of curious workmanship embroidery.

Exodus 36

Chapter 36

And Beseleel wrought, and Eliav and every one wise in understanding, to whom was given wisdom and knowledge, to understand to do all the works according to the holy offices, according to all things which the Lord appointed. 2 And Moses called Beseleel and Eliav, and all that had wisdom, to whom God gave knowledge in *the* heart, and all who were freely willing to come forward to the works, to perform them.

3 And they received from Moses all the offerings, which the sons of Israel brought for all the works of the sanctuary to do them; and they continued to receive the gifts brought, from those who brought them in the morning. 4 And there came all the wise men that wrought the works of the sanctuary, each according to his own work, which they wrought. 5 And * they said to Moses, The people bring abundance in proportion to all the works, which the Lord has appointed to do. 6 And Moses commanded, and proclaimed in the camp, saying, Let neither man nor woman any longer labor for the offerings of the sanctuary; and the people were restrained from bringing any more. 7 And the works were sufficient for making the furniture, and there were things left over. 8 And every wise one among those that wrought made the robes of the holy places, which belong to Aaron the priest, as the Lord commanded Moses. 9 And they made the ephod of gold, and blue, and purple, and spun red, and fine linen twined. 10 And the plates were divided, the threads of gold, so as to interweave with the blue and purple, and with the spun scarlet, and the fine linen twined, they made it a woven work; 11 shoulder pieces joined from both sides, a work woven by mutual twisting of the parts into itself. 12 They made it of the same material according to the making of it, of gold, and blue, and purple, and spun scarlet, and fine linen twined, as the Lord commanded Moses; 13 and they made the two emerald stones clasped together and set in gold, graven and cut after the cutting of a seal with the names of the sons of Israel; 14 and he put them on the shoulder pieces of the ephod, stones of memorial of the sons of Israel, as the Lord appointed Moses.

15 And they made the oracle, a work woven with embroidery, according to the work of the ephod, of gold, and blue, and purple, and spun scarlet, and fine linen twined. 16 They made the oracle square *and* double, the length of a span, and the breadth of a span, double. 17 And there was interwoven with it a woven work of four rows of stones, a series of stones, the first row, a sardius and topaz and emerald; 18 and the second row, a carbuncle and sapphire and jasper; 19 and the third row, a ligure and agate and amethyst; 20 and the fourth row a chrysolite and beryl and onyx set round about with gold, and fastened with gold.

21 And the stones were twelve according to the names of the sons of Israel, graven according to their names for seals, each according to his own name for the twelve tribes. 22 And they made on the oracle turned wreaths, wreathen work, of pure gold, 23 and they made two golden circlets and two golden rings, and they put the two golden rings on both the corners of the oracle; 25 and they put the golden wreaths on the rings on both sides of the oracle, and the two wreaths into the two couplings. 26 And they put them on the two circlets, and they put them on the shoulders of the ephod opposite in front. 27 And they made two golden rings, and put them on the two projections on the top of the oracle, and on the top of the hinder part of the ephod within. 28 And they made two golden rings, and put them on both the shoulders of the ephod under it, in front by the coupling above the connection of the ephod. 29 And he fastened the oracle by the rings that were on it to the rings of the ephod, which were fastened with *a string* of blue, joined together with the woven work of the ephod; that the oracle should not be loosed from the ephod, as the Lord commanded Moses.

30 And they made the tunic under the ephod, woven work, all of blue. 31 And the opening of the tunic in the midst woven closely together, the opening having a fringe around, that it might not be rent. 32 And they made on the border of the tunic below pomegranates as of a flowering pomegranate tree, of blue, and purple, and spun red, and fine linen twined. 33 And they made golden bells, and put the bells on the border of the tunic round about between the pomegranates; 34 a golden bell and a pomegranate on the border of the tunic around, for the ministration, as the Lord commanded Moses.

35 And they made vestments of fine linen, a woven work, for Aaron and his sons, 36 and the tires of fine linen, and the miter of fine linen, and the drawers of fine linen twined; 37 and their girdles of fine linen, and blue, and purple, and red spun, the work of an embroiderer, according as the Lord commanded Moses. 38 And they made the golden plate, a dedicated thing of the sanctuary, of pure gold; 39 and he wrote upon it graven letters of a seal, Holiness to the Lord. 40 And they put it on the border of blue, so that it should be on the miter above, as the Lord commanded Moses.

* Some copies of *Codex Vaticanus* read: "one said", while other copies of *Codex Vaticanus* read: "they said". The Apostoliki Diakonia and Zoe Brotherhood biblical texts read: "they said".

Chapter 37

And they made ten curtains for the tabernacle; 2 of eight and twenty cubits the length of one curtain; the same was to all, and the breadth of one curtain was of four cubits.

Exodus 38

3 And they made the veil of blue, and purple, and spun red, and fine linen twined the woven work with cherubs. 4 And they put it on four posts of incorruptible *wood* overlaid with gold; and their tops were gold, and their four sockets were silver. 5 And they made the veil of the door of the tabernacle of witness of blue, and purple, and spun red, and fine linen twined, woven work with cherubs, 6 and their posts five, and the rings; and they gilded their tops and their clasps with gold, and they had five sockets of brass. 7 And they made the court toward the south; the curtains of the court of fine linen twined, a hundred *cubits* on each side, 8 and their posts twenty, and their sockets twenty; 9 and on the north side a hundred every way, and on the south side a hundred every way, and their posts twenty and their sockets twenty. 10 And on the west side curtains of fifty cubits, there are ten posts and their ten sockets. 11 And on the east side curtains of fifty cubits of fifteen cubits behind, 12 and their pillars three, and their sockets three. 13 And at the second back on this side and on that by the gate of the court, curtains of fifteen cubits, their pillars three and their sockets three; 14 all the curtains of the tabernacle of fine linen twined. 15 And the sockets of their pillars of brass, and their hooks of silver, and their tops overlaid with silver, and all the posts of the court overlaid with silver; 16 and the veil of the gate of the court, the work of an embroiderer of blue, and purple, and spun scarlet, and fine linen twined; the length of twenty cubits, and the height and the breadth of five cubits, made equal to the curtains of the court; 17 and their pillars four, and their sockets four of brass, and their hooks of silver, and their tops overlaid with silver. 18 And all the pins of the court around with brass, and they *were* overlaid with silver.

19 And this was the arrangement of the Tabernacle of Witness, accordingly as it was appointed to Moses; so that the public service should belong to the Levites, through Ithamar the son of Aaron the priest. 20 And Beseleel the son of Urias of the tribe of Judah did as the Lord commanded Moses. 21 And Eliav the son of Ahisamah of the tribe of Dan, who was chief artificer in the woven works and needle works and embroideries, to weave with the red and fine linen.

Chapter 38

And Beseleel made the ark, 2 and overlaid it with pure gold within and without, 3 and he cast for it four golden rings, two on the one side, and two on the other, 4 wide for the staves, so that men should bear it with them. 5 And he made the propitiatory over the ark of pure gold, 6 and the two cherubs of gold; 7 one cherub on the one end of the propitiatory, and another cherub on the other end of the propitiatory,

8 overshadowing the propitiatory with their wings. 9 And he made the table of showbread of pure gold, 10 and cast for it four rings: two on the one side and two on the other side, broad, so that *men* should lift it with the staves in them. 11 And he made the staves of the ark and of the table, and gilded them with gold. 12 And he made the furniture of the table, both the dishes, and the censers, and the cups, and the bowls with which he will offer drink offerings, of gold. 13 And he made the candlestick which gives light, of gold; 14 the stem solid, and the branches from both its sides; 15 and blossoms proceeding from its branches, three on this side, and three on the other, made equal to each other. 16 And their lamps, which are on the ends, knops like almonds from them; and sockets proceeding from them, that the lamps might be upon them; and the seventh socket, on the top of the candlestick, on the summit above, entirely of solid gold. 17 And on it seven golden lamps, and its snuffers of gold, and its oil funnels of gold. 18 He overlaid the posts, and cast for the post golden rings, and gilded the bars with gold; and he gilded the posts of the veil with gold, and made the hooks of gold. 19 He made also the rings of the tabernacle of gold; and the rings of the court, and the rings for drawing out the veil above of brass. 20 He cast the silver tops of the tabernacle and the brazen tops of the door of the tabernacle, and the gate of the court; and he made silver hooks for the posts, he overlaid them with silver on the posts. 21 He made the pins of the tabernacle and the pins of the court of brass. 22 He made the brazen altar of the brazen censers, which belonged to the men engaged in sedition with the gathering of Core. 23 He made all the vessels of the altar and its fire pan, and its base, and its bowls, and the brazen flesh hooks. 24 He made an appendage for the altar of network under the grate, beneath it as far as the middle of it; and he fastened to it four brazen rings on the four parts of the appendage of the altar, wide for the bars, so as to bear the altar with them.

25 He made the holy anointing oil and the composition of the incense, the pure work of the perfumer. 26 He made the brazen laver, and the brazen base of it of the mirrors of the women that fasted, which fasted by the doors of the tabernacle of witness, in the day in which he set it up. 27 And he made the laver, that of it Moses and Aaron and his sons might wash their hands and their feet; when they went into the Tabernacle of Witness, or whenever they should advance to the altar to do service, they washed at it, as the Lord commanded Moses.

Chapter 39

All the gold that was employed for the works according to all the fabrication of the holy things was of the gold of the first fruits, twenty-nine talents, and * seven hundred and twenty shekels according to the holy shekel.

Exodus 39

2 And the offering of silver from the men that were numbered of the congregation a hundred talents, and a thousand seven hundred and seventy-five shekels, one drachma apiece, even the half shekel, according to the holy shekel. 3 Every one that passed the survey from twenty years old and up to six hundred thousand, and three thousand five hundred and fifty. 4 And the hundred talents of silver went to the casting of the hundred tops of the tabernacle, and to the tops of the veil; 5 a hundred tops to the hundred talents, a talent to a top. 6 And the thousand seven hundred and seventy-five shekels he formed into hooks for the pillars, and he gilt their tops and adorned them. 7 And the brass of the offering *was* * seventy talents, and * a thousand five hundred shekels; 8 and they made of it the bases of the door of the tabernacle of witness, 9 and the bases of the court round about, and the bases of the gate of the court, and the pins of the tabernacle, and the pins of the court round about; 10 and the brazen appendage of the altar, and all the vessels of the altar, and all the instruments of the tabernacle of witness. 11 And the sons of Israel did as the Lord commanded Moses, so did they.

12 And of the gold that remained of the offering they made vessels to minister with before the Lord. 13 And the blue that was left, and the purple, and the red they made garments of ministry for Aaron, so that he should minister with them in the sanctuary.

14 And they brought the garments to Moses, and the tabernacle, and its furniture, its bases and its bars and the posts; 15 and the Ark of the Covenant, and its bearers, and the altar and all its furniture. 16 And they made the anointing oil, and the incense of composition, and the pure candlestick, 17 and its lamps, lamps for burning, and oil for the light, 18 and the table of showbread, and all its furniture, and the showbread upon it, 19 and the garments of the sanctuary, which belong to Aaron, and the garments of his sons, for the priestly ministry; 20 and the curtains of the court, and the posts, and the veil of the door of the tabernacle, and the gate of the court, 21 and all the vessels of the tabernacle and all its instruments: and the skins, even rams' skins dyed red, and the blue coverings, and the coverings of the other things, and the pins, and all the instruments for the works of the Tabernacle of Witness. 22 whatever things the Lord appointed Moses so did the sons of Israel to make all the preparations. 23 And Moses saw all the works; and they had done them all as the Lord commanded Moses, so had they made them; and Moses blessed them.

* *Codex Alexandrinus* reads verse one: "seven hundred and thirty shekels."
* *Codex Alexandrinus us* reads verse seven: "four hundred and seventy shekels."
* *Codex Alexandrinus* reads verse seven: "two thousand four hundred shekels."

Exodus 40

Chapter 40

And the Lord spoke to Moses, saying, 2 On the first day of the first month, at the new moon, thou shall set up the Tabernacle of Witness, 3 and thou shall place *in it* the Ark of the Testimony, and shall cover the ark with the veil, 4 and thou shall bring in the table and shall set forth that which is to be set forth on it; and thou shall bring in the candlestick and place its lamps on it. 5 And thou shall place the golden altar, to burn incense before the ark; and thou shall put a covering of a veil on the door of the Tabernacle of Witness. 6 And thou shall put the altar of burnt offerings by the doors of the Tabernacle of Witness, and thou shall set up the tabernacle around, and thou shall hallow all that belongs to it around. 7 And thou shall take the anointing oil, and shall anoint the tabernacle, and all things in it; and shall sanctify it, and all its furniture, and it shall be holy. 8 And thou shall anoint the altar of burnt offerings, and all its furniture; 9 and thou shall hallow the altar, and the altar shall be most holy. 10 And thou shall bring Aaron and his sons to the doors of the tabernacle of witness, and thou shall wash them with water. 11 And thou shall put on Aaron the holy garments, and thou shall anoint him, and thou shall sanctify him, and he shall minister to me as priest. 12 And thou shall bring up his sons, and shall put garments on them. 13 And thou shall anoint them as thou didst anoint their father, and they shall minister to me as priests; and it shall be that they shall have an everlasting anointing of priesthood, throughout their generations. 14 And Moses did all things whatever the Lord commanded him, so did he.

15 And it came to pass in the first month, in the second year after their going forth out of Egypt, at the new moon, that the tabernacle was set up. 16 And Moses set up the tabernacle, and put on the tops, and put the bars into their places, and set up the posts. 17 And he stretched out the curtains over the tabernacle, and put the veil of the tabernacle on it above as the Lord commanded Moses. 18 And he took the testimonies, and put them into the ark; and he put the staves under the sides of the ark. 19 And he brought the ark into the tabernacle, and put on the covering of the veil, and covered the Ark of the Testimony, as the Lord commanded Moses. 20 And he put the table in the tabernacle of witness, on the north side without the veil of the tabernacle. 21 And he put on it the showbread before the Lord, as the Lord commanded Moses. 22 And he put the candlestick into the tabernacle of witness, on the side of the tabernacle toward the south. 23 And he put on it its lamps before the Lord, as the Lord had commanded Moses. 24 And he put the golden altar in the tabernacle of witness before the veil; 25 and he burnt on it incense of composition, as the Lord commanded Moses. 26 And he put the altar of the burnt offerings by the doors of the tabernacle.

Exodus 40

27 And he set up the court around the * tabernacle and the altar; and Moses accomplished all the works. 28 And the cloud covered the tabernacle of witness, and the tabernacle was filled with the glory of the Lord. 29 And Moses was not able to enter into the Tabernacle of Testimony, because the cloud overshadowed it, and the tabernacle was filled with the glory of the Lord. 30 And when the cloud ascended from the tabernacle, the sons of Israel *would* break camp with their baggage. 31 And if the cloud did not ascend, they did not break camp, until the day when the cloud *would* ascend.

32 For a cloud was on the tabernacle by day, and fire was on it by night before all Israel, in all their travels.

* The October vesper reading from Chapter Forty verse twenty-seven from the *Greek Menaion* and *Prophetologion* reads: "Tabernacle of Testimony".

The Book of
Leviticus

Chapter 1

And the Lord again called Moses and spoke to him outside of the Tabernacle of Witness, saying, Speak to the sons of Israel, and thou shall say to them, 2 If *any* man of you shall bring gifts to the Lord, ye shall bring your gifts of the cattle and of the oxen and of the sheep.

3 If his gift is a whole burnt offering, he shall bring an unblemished male of the herd to the door of the Tabernacle of Witness; he shall bring it as acceptable before the Lord. 4 And he shall lay his hand on the head of the burnt offering as a thing acceptable for him, to make atonement for him. 5 And they shall kill the calf before the Lord; and the sons of Aaron the priests shall bring the blood, and they shall pour the blood around on the altar, which *is* at the doors of the Tabernacle of Witness. 6 And having flayed the whole burnt offering, they shall divide it by its limbs. 7 And the sons of Aaron the priests shall put fire on the altar, and shall pile wood on the fire. 8 And the sons of Aaron the priests shall pile up the divided parts, and the head, and the fat on the wood on the fire, which is on the altar. 9 And the entrails and the feet they shall wash in water and the priests shall put all on the altar; it is a burnt offering, a sacrifice, *and* a smell of sweet savor to the Lord.

10 And if his gift of the sheep to the Lord, or of the lambs, or of the kids for whole burnt offerings, he shall bring it a male without blemish. 11 And he shall lay his hand on its head; and they shall kill it by the side of the altar, toward the north before the Lord, and the sons of Aaron the priests shall pour its blood on the altar around. 12 And they shall divide it by its limbs, and its head and its fat, and the priests shall pile them up on the wood, which is on the fire, on the altar. 13 And they shall wash the entrails and the feet with water, and the priest shall bring all and put them on the altar: it is a burnt offering, a sacrifice, a smell of sweet savor to the Lord.

14 And if he brings his gift, a burnt offering to the Lord, of birds, then shall he bring his gift of doves or pigeons. 15 And the priest shall bring it to the altar, and shall pluck off its head; and the priest shall put it on the altar, and shall squeeze out the blood at the bottom of the altar. 16 And he shall take away the crop with the feathers, and shall cast it forth by the altar toward the east to the place of the ashes. 17 And he shall break it off from the wings and shall not separate it, and the priest shall place it on the altar on the wood, which is on the fire; it is a burnt offering, a sacrifice, *and* a sweet smelling savor to the Lord.

Chapter 2

And if a soul brings a gift, a sacrifice to the Lord, his gift shall be fine flour; and he shall pour oil upon it, and shall put frankincense on it; it is a sacrifice. 2 And he shall bring it to the priests the sons of Aaron; and having taken from it a handful of the fine flour with the oil, and all its frankincense, then the priest shall put the memorial of it on the altar; a sacrifice, an odor of sweet savor to the Lord. 3 And the remainder of the sacrifice shall be for Aaron and his sons, a most holy portion from the sacrifices of the Lord. 4 And if he bring as a gift a sacrifice baked from the oven, a gift to the Lord of fine flour, unleavened bread kneaded with oil, and unleavened cakes anointed with oil. 5 And if thy gift *be* a sacrifice from a pan, it is fine flour mingled with oil, unleavened. 6 And thou shall break them into fragments and pour oil upon them; it is a sacrifice to the Lord. 7 And if thy gift be a sacrifice from the hearth, it shall be made of fine flour with oil. 8 And he shall offer the sacrifice, which he shall make of these to the Lord, and shall bring it to the priest. 9 And the priest shall approach the altar, and shall take away from the sacrifice a memorial of it, and the priest shall place it on the altar: a burnt offering, a smell of sweet savor to the Lord. 10 And that which is left of the sacrifice *shall be* for Aaron and his sons, most holy from the burnt offerings of the Lord.

11 Ye shall not leaven any sacrifice, which ye shall bring to the Lord; for any leaven, or any honey, ye shall not bring of it to offer a gift to the Lord. 12 Ye shall bring them in the way of fruits to the Lord, but they shall not be offered on the altar for a sweet smelling savor to the Lord. 13 And every gift of your sacrifice shall be seasoned with salt; omit not the salt of the covenant of the Lord from your sacrifices: on every gift of yours ye shall offer salt to the Lord your God. 14 And if thou would offer a sacrifice of first fruits to the Lord, new grains ground *and* roasted for the Lord; so shall thou bring the sacrifice of the first fruits. 15 And thou shall pour oil upon it, and shall put frankincense on it: it is a sacrifice. 16 And the priest shall offer the memorial of it from the grains with the oil, and all its frankincense; it is a burnt offering to the Lord.

Chapter 3

And if his gift to the Lord were a peace offering, if he should bring it of the oxen, whether it is male or whether it is female, he shall bring it unblemished before the Lord. 2 And he shall lay his hands on the head of the gift, and shall kill it before the Lord, by the doors of the Tabernacle of Witness. And the priests the sons of Aaron shall pour the blood on the altar of burnt offerings around.

3 And they shall bring of the peace offering a burnt sacrifice to the Lord, the fat covering the belly, and all the fat on the belly. 4 And the two kidneys and the fat that is upon them; he shall take away that which is on the thighs, and the caul above the liver together with the kidneys. 5 And the priests the sons of Aaron shall offer them on the altar on the burnt offering, on the wood, which is on the fire upon the altar; a burnt offering, a smell of sweet savor to the Lord.

6 And if his gift be of the sheep, a peace offering to the Lord, male or female, he shall bring it unblemished. 7 If he brings a lamb for his gift, he shall bring it before the Lord. 8 And he shall lay his hands on the head of his offering, and shall kill it by the doors of the Tabernacle of Witness; and the priests the sons of Aaron shall pour out the blood on the altar around. 9 And he shall bring of the peace offering a burnt sacrifice to the Lord; the fat and the hinder part unblemished he shall take away with the loins, and having taken away all the fat that covers the belly, and all the fat that is on the belly, 10 and both the kidneys and the fat that is upon them, that which is on the thighs, and the caul which is on the liver with the kidneys, 11 the priest shall offer these on the altar; a sacrifice of sweet savor, a burnt offering to the Lord.

12 And if his offering were of the goats, then shall he bring it before the Lord. 13 And he shall lay his hands on its head; and they shall slay it before the Lord by the doors of the tabernacle of witness; and the priests the sons of Aaron shall pour out the blood on the altar round about. 14 And he shall offer of it a burnt offering to the Lord, *even* the fat that covers the belly, and all the fat that is on the belly. 15 And both the kidneys and all the fat that is upon them, that which is upon the thighs, and the caul of the liver with the kidneys, shall he take away. 16 And the priest shall offer it upon the altar; a burnt offering, a smell of sweet savor to the Lord. All the fat to the Lord *is His*. 17 A perpetual statute throughout your generations, in all your habitations; ye shall eat no fat and no blood.

Chapter 4

And the Lord spoke to Moses, saying, 2 Speak to the sons of Israel, saying, If a soul shall sin unwillingly before the Lord, from any of the commandments of the Lord concerning things which he ought not to do, and shall do some of them; 3 if the anointed priest sins by reason of the people sinning, then shall he bring for his sin, which he has sinned, an unblemished calf of the herd to the Lord for his sin. 4 And he shall bring the calf to the door of the Tabernacle of Witness before the Lord, and he shall put his hand on the head of the calf before the Lord, and shall kill the calf in the presence of the Lord.

Leviticus 4

5 And the anointed priest, whose hands have been perfected from receiving the blood of the calf, shall then bring it into the Tabernacle of Witness. 6 And the priest shall dip his finger into the blood, and sprinkle the blood seven times before the Lord, over against the holy veil. 7 And the priest shall put of the blood of the calf on the horns of the altar of the compound incense that is before the Lord, which is in the Tabernacle of Witness; and all the blood of the calf shall he pour out by the foot of the altar of whole burnt offerings, which is by the doors of the Tabernacle of Witness. 8 and all the fat of the calf of the sin offering shall he take off from it; the fat that covers the inwards, and all the fat that is on the inwards, 9 and the two kidneys, and the fat that is upon them, which is on the thighs, and the caul that is on the liver with the kidneys, *of* it shall he take away, 10 as he takes it away from the calf of the sacrifice of peace offering, so shall the priest offer it on the altar of burnt offering. 11 And the skin of the calf, and all his flesh with the head and the extremities and the belly and the dung, 12 and they shall carry out the whole calf out of the camp into a clean place, where they *will* pour out the ashes, and they shall consume it there upon wood with fire; it shall be burnt on the out poured ashes.

13 And if the whole congregation of Israel should be ignorant *or* unwilling, and a thing should escape the notice of the congregation, and they commit one of any forbidden thing of any of the commands of the Lord, and they should transgress: 14 and the sin wherein they have sinned should become known to them, then shall the congregation bring an unblemished calf of the herd for a sin offering, and they shall bring it to the doors of the tabernacle of witness. 15 And the elders of the congregation shall lay their hands on the head of the calf before the Lord, and they shall kill the calf before the Lord. 16 And the anointed priest shall bring in of the blood of the calf into the Tabernacle of Witness. 17 And the priest shall dip his finger into some of the blood of the calf, and shall sprinkle it seven times before the Lord, in front of the veil of the sanctuary. 18 And the priest shall put some of the blood on the horns of the altar of the incense of composition that is before the Lord, which is in the tabernacle of witness; and he shall pour out all the blood at the bottom of the altar of whole burnt offerings, which is by the door of the Tabernacle of Witness. 19 And he shall take away all the fat from it, and shall offer it up on the altar. 20 And he shall do to the calf as he did to the calf of the sin offering, so shall it be done; and the priest shall make atonement for them, and the trespass shall be forgiven them. 21 And they shall carry forth the calf whole outside the camp, and they shall burn the calf as they burned the former calf; it is the sin offering of the congregation.

22 And if a ruler sin, and commit one of all the commands of the Lord his God, that ought not to be done, unwillingly, and shall sin and trespass,

23 and his trespass wherein he has sinned is known to him, then shall he offer for his gift a kid of the goats, a male without blemish. 24 And he shall lay his hand on the head of the kid, and they shall kill it in the place where they kill the whole burnt offerings before the Lord; it is a sin offering. 25 And the priest shall put some of the blood of the sin offering with his finger on the horns of the altar of whole burnt offering; and he shall pour out all *of* its blood by the bottom of the altar of whole burnt offerings. 26 And he shall offer up all his fat on the altar, as the fat of the sacrifice of peace offering; and the priest shall make atonement for him concerning his sin, and it shall be forgiven him.

27 And if a soul of the people of the land should sin unwillingly, in doing a thing any of the commandments of the Lord, which ought not to be done, and shall transgress, 28 and his sin should be known to him, wherein he has sinned, then shall he bring a kid of the goats, a female without blemish shall he bring for his sin, which he has sinned. 29 And he shall lay his hand on the head of his sin offering, and they shall kill the kid of the sin offering in the place where they kill the whole burnt offerings. 30 And the priest shall take of its blood with his finger, and shall put it on the horns of the altar of whole burnt offerings; and all its blood he shall pour forth by the foot of the altar. 31 And he shall take away all the fat, as the fat is taken away from the sacrifice of peace offering, and the priest shall offer it on the altar for a smell of sweet savor to the Lord; and the priest shall make atonement for him, and shall be forgiven him.

32 And if he should offer a lamb for his sin offering, he shall offer it a female without blemish. 33 And he shall lay his hand on the head of the sin offerings, and they shall kill it in the place where they kill the whole burnt offerings. 34 And the priest shall take of the blood of the sin offering with his finger, and shall put it on the horns of the altar of whole burnt offerings, and he shall pour out all its blood by the bottom of the altar of whole burnt offering. 35 And he shall take away all his fat, as the fat of the lamb of the sacrifice of peace offering is taken away, and the priest shall put it on the altar for a whole burnt offering to the Lord; and the priest shall make atonement for him for the sin which he sinned, and it shall be forgiven him.

Chapter 5

And if a soul sin, and hear the voice of swearing and he is a witness or has seen or been conscious, if he do not report it, he shall bear his iniquity. 2 That soul which shall touch any unclean thing, or carcass, or unclean being taken of beasts or the dead bodies of abominable which are unclean, or carcass of unclean cattle,

Leviticus 5

3 or should touch the uncleanness of a man, or whatever kind, which he may touch and be defiled by, and it should have escaped him, but afterwards he should know, then he shall have transgressed. 4 That unrighteous soul, which determines with his lips to do evil or to do good according to whatever a man may determine with an oath, and it shall have escaped his notice, and he shall know, and he should sin in some one of these things; 5 then shall he declare his sin in the things wherein he has sinned by that sin. 6 And he shall bring for his transgressions against the Lord, for his sin, which he has sinned, an ewe lamb of the flock, or a kid of the goats, for a sin offering; and the priest shall make atonement for him for his sin, which he has sinned, and his sin shall be forgiven him.

7 And if his hand is not sufficiently strong for a sheep, he shall bring for his sin which he has sinned, two turtledoves or two young pigeons to the Lord; one for a sin offering, and the other for a burnt offering. 8 And he shall bring them to the priest, and the priest shall bring the sin offering first; and the priest shall pinch off the head from the neck, and shall not divide the body. 9 And he shall sprinkle of the blood of the sin offering on the side of the altar, but the rest of the blood he shall drop at the foot of the altar, for it is a sin offering. 10 And he shall make the second a whole burnt offering, as it is fit; and the priest shall make atonement for his sin, which he has sinned, and it shall be forgiven him.

11 And if his hand cannot find a pair of turtledoves, or two young pigeons, then shall he bring as his gift for his sin, the tenth part of an ephah of fine flour for a sin offering; he shall not pour oil upon it, nor shall he put frankincense upon it, because it is a sin offering. 12 And he shall bring it to the priest; and the priest having taken a handful of it shall lay the memorial of it on the altar of whole burnt offerings to the Lord; it is a sin offering. 13 And the priest shall make atonement for him for his sin, which he has sinned in one of these things, and it shall be forgiven him; and that which is left shall be the priest's, as an offering of fine flour.

14 And the Lord spoke to Moses, saying, 15 The soul which shall be really unconscious, and shall sin unwillingly in any of the holy things of the Lord, shall even bring to the Lord for his transgression, a ram of the flock without blemish, valued according to shekels of silver according to the shekel of the sanctuary, for his wherein he transgressed. 16 And he shall make compensation for that wherein he has sinned in the holy things; and he shall add the fifth part to it, and give it to the priest; and the priest shall make atonement for him with the ram of transgression, and shall be forgiven him.

17 And the soul which shall sin, and do one thing any of the commandments of the Lord, which it is not right to do, and has not known it, and shall have transgressed, and shall have contracted guilt,

18 he shall even bring a ram without blemish from the flock, at a price of silver for his transgression to the priest; and the priest shall make atonement for his trespass of ignorance, wherein he ignorantly trespassed, and he knew it not; and it shall be forgiven him. 19 For he has surely been guilty of transgression before the Lord. 20 And the Lord spoke to Moses, saying, 21 If a soul sins, and by overlooking disregards the commandments of the Lord, and deals falsely in the affairs of his neighbor in the matter of a deposit, or concerning fellowship, or concerning plunder, 22 or has in anything wronged his neighbor, 23 or has found that which was lost, and shall have lied concerning it, and shall have sworn unjustly concerning one of all the things, whatever a man may do, so as to sin hereby; 24 it shall come to pass, whenever he shall have sinned, and transgressed, that he shall restore the plunder which he has seized, or the injury which he has committed, or restore the deposit which was entrusted to him, or the lost article which he has found of any thing, about which he swore unjustly, he shall even restore it in full; and he shall add to it a fifth part besides; he shall restore it to him whose it is in the day in which he happens to be convicted.

25 And he shall bring to the Lord for his trespass, a ram of the flock, without blemish, of value to the amount of the thing in which he trespassed. 26 And the priest shall make atonement for him before the Lord, and he shall be forgiven for any one of all the things, which he did and trespassed in it.

Chapter 6

And the Lord spoke to Moses, saying, 2 Charge Aaron and his sons, saying, This *is* the law of whole burnt offering; this is the whole burnt offering on its burning on the altar all the night till the morning; and the fire of the altar shall burn on it, it shall not be put out. 3 And the priest shall put on the linen tunic, and he shall put the linen drawers on his body; and shall take away that which has been thoroughly burned, which the fire shall have consumed, even the whole burnt offering from the altar, and he shall put it near the altar. 4 And he shall put off his robe, and put on another robe, and he shall take forth the offering that has been burned outside the camp into a clean place. 5 And the fire on the altar shall be kept burning on it, and shall not be extinguished; and the priest shall burn on it wood every morning, and shall heap on it the whole burnt offering, and shall lay on it the fat of the peace offering. 6 And the fire shall always burn on the altar; it shall not be extinguished. 7 This is the law of the sacrifice, which the sons of Aaron shall bring near before the Lord, before the altar.

Leviticus 7

8 And he shall take from it a handful of the fine flour of the sacrifice with its oil, and with all its frankincense, which are upon the sacrifice; and he shall offer up on the altar a burnt offering as a sweet smelling savor, a memorial of it to the Lord. 9 And Aaron and his sons shall eat that which is left of it; it shall be eaten without leaven in a holy place; they shall eat it in the court of the tabernacle of witness. 10 It shall not be baked with leaven. I have given it as a portion to them of the burnt offerings of the Lord; it is most holy, as the offering for sin, and as the offering for trespass. 11 Every male of the priests shall eat it; it is a perpetual ordinance throughout your generations of the burnt offerings of the Lord; whoever shall touch them shall be hallowed. 12 And the Lord spoke to Moses, saying, 13 This is the gift of Aaron and of his sons, which they shall offer to the Lord in the day in which thou shall anoint him; the tenth of an ephah of fine flour for a sacrifice continually, the half of it in the morning, and the half of it in the evening.

14 It shall be made with oil on a frying pan; he shall offer it kneaded *and* rolled an offering of fragments, an offering of a sweet savor unto the Lord. 15 The anointed priest who is in his place, of his sons, shall offer it, it is a perpetual statute, and it shall all be consumed. 16 And every sacrifice of a priest shall be thoroughly burnt, and shall not be eaten. 17 And the Lord spoke to Moses, saying, 18 Speak to Aaron and to his sons, saying, This is the law of the sin offering; in the place where they kill the whole burnt offering, they shall kill the sin offerings before the Lord; they are most holy.

19 The priest that offers it shall eat it; in a holy place it shall be eaten, in the court of the tabernacle of witness. 20 Every one that touches the flesh of it shall be holy, and on whosoever garment any of its blood shall have been sprinkled, that on which it is sprinkled shall be washed in the holy place. 21 And the earthen vessel, in whichever it shall have been boiled, shall be broken; and if it shall have been boiled in a brazen vessel, he shall scour it and wash it with water. 22 Every male among the priests shall eat it; it is most holy to the Lord. 23 And no offerings for sin, of whose blood there shall be brought any into the Tabernacle of Witness to make atonement in the holy place, shall be eaten; they shall be burned with fire.

Chapter 7

And this law of the ram for the trespass offering, it is most holy. 2 In the place where they kill the whole burnt offering, they shall kill the ram of the trespass offering before the Lord, and he shall pour out the blood at the bottom of the altar around. 3 And he shall offer all the fat from it; and the hind-quarters, and all the fat that covers the inwards, and all the fat that is upon the inwards,

4 and the two kidneys, and the fat that is upon them, that which is upon the thighs, and the caul upon the liver with the kidney, he shall take them away. 5 And the priest shall offer them on the altar a burnt offering to the Lord; it is for trespass. 6 Every male of the priest shall eat them, in the holy place they shall eat them; they are most holy. 7 As the sin offering, so also the trespass offering. There is one law of them; the priest who shall make atonement with it, his it shall be. 8 And the priest who offers a man's whole burnt offering, the skin of the whole burnt offering, which he offers, shall be his. 9 And every sacrifice, which shall be made in the oven, and every one, which shall be made on the hearth, or on a frying pan, it is the property of the priest that offers it; it shall be his. 10 And every sacrifice made up with oil, or not made up, shall belong to the sons of Aaron, an equal portion to each.

11 This *is* the law of the sacrifice of peace offering, which they shall bring to the Lord. 12 If a man should offer it for praise, then shall he bring, for the sacrifice of praise, loaves of fine flour made up with oil, and unleavened cakes anointed with oil, and fine flour kneaded with oil. 13 With leavened bread he shall offer his gifts, with the peace offering of praise. 14 And he shall bring one of all his gifts, a separate offering to the Lord; shall belong to the priest who pours forth the blood of the peace offering. 15 And the flesh of the sacrifice of the peace offering of praise shall be his, and it shall be eaten in the day in which it is offered; shall not leave of it till the morning. 16 And if it be a vow, or he offer his gift of his own will, on whatever day he shall offer his sacrifice, it shall be eaten, tomorrow. 17 And that which is left of the flesh of the sacrifice till the third day, shall be consumed with fire. 18 And if he does at all eat of the flesh on the third day, it shall not be accepted for him that offers; it shall not be reckoned to him, it is pollution; and whatever soul shall eat of it, shall bear his iniquity.

19 And whatever flesh shall have touched any unclean thing, it shall not be eaten, it shall be consumed with fire; every one that is clean shall eat the flesh. 20 And whatever soul shall eat of the flesh of the sacrifice of the peace offering, which is the Lord's, and his uncleanness is upon him, that soul shall perish from his people. 21 And whatever soul shall touch any unclean thing, either of the uncleanness of a man, or of unclean quadrupeds, or any unclean abomination, and shall eat of the flesh of the sacrifice of the peace offering, which is the Lord's, that soul shall perish from his people.

22 And the Lord spoke to Moses, saying, 23 Speak to the sons of Israel, saying, Ye shall eat no fat of oxen or sheep or goats. 24 And the fat of such animals as have died of themselves, or have been seized of beasts, may be employed for any work; but it shall not be eaten for food. 25 Every one that eats fat off the beasts, from which he will bring a burnt offering to the Lord, that soul shall perish from his people. 26 Ye shall eat no blood in all your habitations, either of beasts or of birds.

Leviticus 8

27 Every soul that shall eat blood, that soul shall perish from his people. 28 And the Lord spoke to Moses, saying, 29 Thou shall also speak to the sons of Israel, saying, He that offers a sacrifice of peace offering, shall bring his gift to the Lord also from the sacrifice of peace offering. 30 His hands shall bring the burnt offerings to the Lord; the fat, which is on the breast and the lobe of the liver, he shall bring them, so as to set them for a gift before the Lord. 31 And the priest shall offer the fat upon the altar, and the breast shall be Aaron's and his sons, 32 and ye shall give the right shoulder for a choice piece to the priest of your sacrifices of peace offering. 33 He that offers the blood of the peace offering, and the fat, of the sons of Aaron, his shall be the right shoulder for a portion. 34 For I have taken the breast *offering and* placed *it* upon *the alter* and shoulder of separation from the sons of Israel from the sacrifices of your peace offerings, and I have given them to Aaron the priest and his sons, a perpetual ordinance from the sons of Israel.

35 This is the anointing of Aaron, and the anointing of his sons, of the burnt offerings of the Lord, in the day in which he brought them forward to minister as priests to the Lord; 36 as the Lord commanded to give to them in the day in which he anointed them of the sons of Israel, a perpetual statute through their generations.

37 This *is* the law of the whole burnt offerings, and of sacrifice, and of sin offering, and of offering for transgression, and of the sacrifice of consecration, and of the sacrifice of peace offering; 38 as the Lord commanded Moses in the mount Sinai, in the day in which he commanded the sons of Israel to offer their gifts before the Lord in the wilderness of Sinai.

Chapter 8

And the Lord spoke to Moses, saying, 2 Take Aaron and his sons, and his robes and the anointing oil, and the calf for the sin offering, and the two rams, and the basket of unleavened bread, 3 and assemble the whole congregation at the door of the tabernacle of witness. 4 And Moses did as the Lord appointed him, and he assembled the congregation at the door of the tabernacle of witness.

5 And Moses said to the congregation, This is the thing, which the Lord has commanded you to do. 6 And Moses brought near Aaron and his sons, and washed them with water, 7 and put on him the coat, and girded him with the girdle, and clothed him with the tunic, and put on him the ephod; 8 and girded him according to the make of the ephod, and clasped him closely with it, and put upon it the oracle, and put upon the oracle the Manifestation and the Truth. 9 And he put the turban on his head, and put upon the turban on *the* front the golden plate, the sanctified holy object, as the Lord commanded Moses.

Leviticus 8

10 And Moses took of the anointing oil, 11 and sprinkled of it seven times on the altar; and anointed the altar, and hallowed it, and all things in it, and the washbasin, and its base, and sanctified them; and anointed the tabernacle and all its items, and hallowed it. 12 And Moses poured of the anointing oil on the head of Aaron; and he anointed him and sanctified him. 13 And Moses brought the sons of Aaron near, and put on them coast and girded them with girdles, and put on them bonnets, as the Lord commanded Moses.

14 And Moses brought near the calf for the sin offering, and Aaron and his sons laid their hands on the head of the calf of the sin offering. 15 And he killed it; and Moses took of the blood, and put it on the horns of the altar around with his finger; and he purified the altar, and poured out the blood at the bottom of the altar, and sanctified it, to make atonement upon it. 16 And Moses took all the fat that was upon the inwards, and the lobe on the liver, and both the kidneys, and the fat that was upon them, and Moses offered them on the altar. 17 But the calf, and his hide, and his flesh, and his dung, he burnt with fire without the camp, as the Lord commanded Moses.

18 And Moses brought near the ram for a whole burnt offering, and Aaron and his sons laid their hands on the head of the ram. And Moses killed the ram; and Moses poured the blood on the altar round about. 19 And he divided the ram by its limbs, and Moses offered the head, and the limbs, and the fat; and he washed the belly and the feet with water. 20 And Moses offered up the whole ram on the altar; it is a whole burnt offering for a sweet smelling savor; it is a burnt offering to the Lord, as the Lord commanded Moses. 21 And Moses brought the second ram; the ram of consecration, and Aaron and his sons laid their hands on the head of the ram, and killed him.

22 and Moses took of his blood, and put it upon the tip of Aaron's right ear, and on the thumb of his right hand, and on the great toe of his right foot. 23 And Moses brought near the sons of Aaron; and Moses put of the blood on the tips of their right ears, and on the thumbs of their right hands, and on the great toes of their right feet, and Moses poured out the blood on the altar around. 24 And he took the fat, and the rump, and the fat on the belly, and the lobe of the liver, and the two kidneys, and the fat that is upon them, and the right shoulder. 25 And from the basket of consecration, which was before the Lord, he also took one unleavened loaf, and one loaf made with oil, and one cake; and put upon the fat, and the right shoulder; 26 and put them all on the hands of Aaron, and upon the hands of his sons, and offered them up for a wave offering before the Lord. 27 And Moses took them at their hands, and Moses offered them on the altar, on the whole burnt offering of consecration, which is a smell of sweet savor; it is a burnt offering to the Lord. 28 And Moses took the breast, and separated it for a heave offering before the Lord, from the ram of consecration; and it became Moses' portion, as the Lord commanded Moses.

Leviticus 9

29 And Moses took of the anointing oil, and of the blood that was on the altar, and sprinkled it on Aaron, and on his garments, and his sons, and the garments of his sons with him. 30 And he sanctified Aaron and his garments, and his sons, and the garments of his sons with him.

31 And Moses said to Aaron and to his sons, Boil the flesh in the tent of the tabernacle of witness in the holy place; and there ye shall eat it and the loaves in the basket of consecration, as it has been appointed me, saying, Aaron and his sons shall eat them. 32 And that which is left of the flesh and of the loaves burn ye with fire. 33 And ye shall not go out from the door of the Tabernacle of Witness for seven days, until the day be fulfilled, the day of your consecration; for in seven days shall he consecrate your hands, 34 as he did in this day on which the Lord commanded me to do so, to make an atonement for you. 35 And ye shall sit seven days at the door of the Tabernacle of Witness, day and night; ye shall observe the ordinances of the Lord that ye do not die, for so has the Lord God commanded me. 36 And Aaron and his sons performed all the words which the Lord commanded *to* Moses.

Chapter 9

And it came to pass on the eighth day, that Moses called Aaron and his sons, and the council of elders of Israel, 2 and Moses said to Aaron, Take to thyself a young calf of the herd for a sin offering, and a ram for a whole burnt offering, unblemished, and offer them before the Lord. 3 And speak to the rulers of Israel, saying, Take one kid of the goats for a sin offering, and a young calf, and a lamb of a year old for a whole burnt offering, spotless, 4 and a calf and a ram for a peace offering before the Lord, and fine flour mingled with oil, for today the Lord will appear among you. 5 And they took as Moses commanded them before the Tabernacle of Witness, and the entire congregation drew near, and they stood before the Lord. 6 And Moses said, This is the thing, which the Lord has spoken; do *it*, and the glory of the Lord shall appear among you. 7 And Moses said to Aaron, Draw near to the altar, and offer thy sin offering, and thy whole burnt offering, and make atonement for thyself, and for thy house; and offer the gifts of the people, and make atonement for them, as the Lord commanded Moses.

8 And Aaron drew near to the altar, and killed the calf of his sin offering. 9 And the sons of Aaron brought the blood to him, and he dipped his finger into the blood, and put it on the horns of the altar, and he poured out the blood at the bottom of the altar. 10 And he offered up on the altar the fat and the kidneys and the lobe of the liver of the sin offering, according as the Lord commanded Moses. 11 And the flesh and the hide he burned with fire outside of the camp.

12 And he killed the whole burnt offering; and the sons of Aaron brought the blood to him, and he poured it on the altar around. 13 And they brought the whole burnt offering, according to its pieces; them and the head he put upon the altar. 14 And he washed the belly and the feet with water, and he put them on the whole burnt offering on the altar.

15 And he brought the gift of the people, and took the goat of the sin offering of the people, and killed it, and purified it as also the first. 16 And he brought the whole burnt offering, and offered it as is proper. 17 And he brought the sacrifice and filled his hands with it, and laid it on the altar, besides the morning whole burnt offering. 18 And he killed the calf, and the ram of the sacrifice of peace offering of the people; and the sons of Aaron brought the blood to him, and he poured it out on the altar around. 19 And the fat of the calf, and the hind quarters of the ram, and the fat covering the belly, and the two kidneys, and the fat upon them, and the caul on the liver. 20 And he put the fat on the breasts, and offered the fat on the altar. 21 And Aaron separated the breast and the right shoulder as a choice offering before the Lord, as the Lord commanded Moses.

22 And Aaron lifted up his hands on the people and blessed them; and after he had offered the sin offering, and the whole burnt offerings, and the peace offerings, he came down. 23 And Moses and Aaron entered into the tabernacle of witness. And they came out and blessed all the people and the glory of the Lord appeared to all the people. 24 And fire came forth from the Lord, and devoured the offerings on the altar, both the whole burnt offerings and the fat; and all the people saw, and were amazed, and fell upon their faces.

Chapter 10

And the two sons of Aaron, Nadab and Abiud, took each his censer, and put fire therein, and threw incense thereon, and offered strange fire before the Lord, which the Lord did not command them, 2 and fire came forth from the Lord, and devoured them, and they died before the Lord. 3 And Moses said to Aaron, This is the thing, which the Lord spoke, saying, I will be sanctified among them that draw near to me, and I will be glorified in the whole congregation; and Aaron was disturbed. 4 And Moses called Misadae, and Elisaphan, sons of Oziel, sons of the brother of Aaron's father, and said to them, Come near and take your brothers from before the Holiness, outside of the camp. 5 And they came near and took them in their coats outside of the camp, as Moses said. 6 And Moses said to Aaron, and Eleazar and Ithamar his sons that were left, Ye shall not make bare your head, and ye shall not tear your garments; that ye die not, and there shall be wrath on the entire congregation; but your brothers, all the house of Israel, shall lament for the burning, with which they were burned by the Lord. 7 And ye shall not go forth from the door of the Tabernacle of Witness that ye die not; for the Lord's anointing oil *is* upon you; and they did according to the word of Moses.

8 And the Lord spoke to Aaron, saying, 9 Ye shall not drink wine nor strong drink, thou and thy sons with thee, whenever ye enter into the tabernacle of witness, or when ye approach the altar, so shall ye not die; a perpetual statute for your generations, 10 to distinguish between sacred and profane, and between clean and unclean, 11 and to teach the sons of Israel all the statutes, which the Lord spoke to them by the hand of Moses.

12 And Moses said to Aaron, and to Eleazar and Ithamar, the sons of Aaron who survived, Take the sacrifice that is left of the burnt offerings of the Lord, and ye shall eat unleavened bread by the altar; it is most holy. 13 And ye shall eat it in the holy place; for this is a statute for thee and a statute for thy sons, of the burnt offerings to the Lord; for so it has been commanded me. 14 And ye shall eat the breast of separation, and the shoulder of the choice offering in the holy place, thou and thy sons and thy house with thee; for it has been given as an ordinance for thee and an ordinance for thy sons, of the sacrifices of peace offering of the children of Israel. 15 They shall bring the shoulder of the choice offering, and the breast of the separation upon the burnt offerings of the fat, to separate for a separation before the Lord; and it shall be a perpetual ordinance for thee and thy sons and thy daughters with thee, as the Lord commanded Moses.

16 And Moses diligently sought the goat of the sin offering, but it had been consumed by fire; and Moses was angry with Eleazar and Ithamar the sons of Aaron that were left, saying, 17 Why did ye not eat the sin offering in the holy place? For because it is most holy he has given you this to eat, that ye might take away the sin of the congregation, and make atonement for them before the Lord. 18 For the blood of it were not brought into the holy place; ye shall eat it within, before the face *of the Lord*, as the Lord commanded me. 19 And Aaron spoke to Moses, saying, If they have brought near today their sin offerings, and their whole burnt offerings before the Lord, and these events have happened to me, and I should eat today of the sin offerings, will it be pleasing to the Lord? 20 And Moses heard, and it pleased him.

Chapter 11

And the Lord spoke to Moses and Aaron, saying,

Leviticus 11

2 Speak ye to the sons of Israel, saying, These are the beasts, which ye shall eat of all beasts that are upon the earth. 3 Every beast parting the hoof and making divisions of two claws, and chewing the cud among beasts, these ye shall eat. 4 But of these ye shall not eat, of those that chew the cud, and of those that part the hoofs, and divide claws; the camel, because it chews the cud, but does not divide the hoof, this is unclean to you. 5 And the rabbit, because it chews the cud, but does not divide the hoof, this is unclean to you. 6 And the hare, because it does * not chew the cud, and does not divide the hoof, this is unclean to you. 7 And the swine, because this divides the hoof, and makes claws of the hoof, and it does not chew the cud, is unclean to you. 8 Ye shall not eat of their flesh, and ye shall not touch their carcasses; these are unclean to you. 9 And these what ye shall eat of all that are in the waters: all things that have fins and scales in the waters, and in the seas, and in the brooks, these ye shall eat. 10 And all things which have not fins or scales in the water, or in the seas, and in the streams, of all which the waters yield up, and of every soul living in the water, are an abomination; and they shall be abominations to you. 11 Ye shall not eat of their flesh, and ye shall abhor their carcasses. 12 And all things that have not fins or scale of those that are in the waters, these are an abomination to you.

13 And these are the things, which ye shall abhor of birds, and they shall not be eaten, they are an abomination: the eagle and the ossifrage, and the sea eagle. 14 And the vulture, and the kite, and the like to it; 15 and the sparrow, and the owl, and the sea mew, and the like to it: 16 and every raven, and the birds like it, and the hawk and his like, 17 and the night raven and the cormorant and the stork, 18 and the red bill, and the pelican, and swan, 19 and the heron, and the sealark, and the like to it, and the hoopoe and the bat.

20 And all winged creatures that creep, which go upon four feet, are abominations to you. 21 But these ye shall eat of the creeping winged animals, which go upon four feet, which have legs above their feet, to leap with on the earth. 22 And these of them ye shall eat; the locust and his like, and the bald locust and his like, and the cricket and his like, and the snake-fighting grasshopper and his like. 23 Every creeping thing from among the birds, having four feet, is an abomination to you.

24 And by these shall ye be defiled; every one that touches their carcasses shall be unclean till the evening. 25 And every one that takes of their dead bodies shall wash his garments, and shall be unclean till the evening. 26 And whichever among the beasts divides the hoof and makes claws, and does not chew the cud, shall be unclean to you; every one that touches their dead bodies shall be unclean till evening. 27 And every one among all the wild beasts that moves upon its fore feet, which goes on all four, they are unclean to you; every one that touches their dead bodies shall be unclean till evening.

Leviticus 11

28 And he that takes of their dead bodies shall wash his garments, and shall be unclean till evening; these are unclean to you. 29 And these unclean to you of reptiles upon the earth, the weasel, and the mouse, and the land crocodile, 30 the ferret, and the chameleon, and the gecko, and the lizard, and the mole. 31 These are unclean to you of all the reptiles, which are on the earth; every one who touches their carcasses shall be unclean till evening. 32 And on whatever one of their dead bodies shall fall it shall be unclean; from every wooden vessel, or garment, or skin, or sackcloth it may be, every vessel in which work should be done, shall be dipped in water, and shall be unclean till evening; and it shall be clean. 33 And every earthen vessel into which one of these things shall fall, whatever is inside it shall be unclean, and it shall be broken. 34 And all food that is eaten, on which water shall come, shall be unclean; and every beverage, which is drunk in any *such* vessel, shall be unclean. 35 And every thing on which there shall fall of their dead bodies shall be unclean; ovens and stands for jars shall be broken down; these are unclean, and they shall be unclean to you. 36 Only of fountains of water, or a pool, or confluence of water, it shall be clean; but he that touches their carcasses shall be unclean. 37 And if one of their carcasses should fall upon any sowing seed, which shall be sown, it shall be clean. 38 But if water be poured on any seed, and one of their dead bodies fall upon it, it is unclean to you.

39 And if one of the cattle dies, which it is lawful for you to eat, he that touches their carcasses shall be unclean till evening. 40 And he that eats of their carcasses shall wash his garments, and be unclean till evening; and he that carries any of their carcasses shall wash his garments, and bathe himself in water, and be unclean till evening.

41 And every reptile that creeps on the earth, this shall be an abomination to you; it shall not be eaten. 42 And every *thing* that creeps on its belly, and every one that goes on fours continually, which abounds with feet among all the reptiles creeping upon the earth ye shall not eat it, for it is an abomination to you. 43 And ye shall not make your souls abominable with any of those that creep, that creep upon the earth, and ye shall not be polluted with them, and ye shall not be unclean by them. 44 For I am the Lord your God; and ye shall be sanctified, and ye shall be holy, because I the Lord your God am holy; and ye shall not defile your souls with any of the reptiles creeping upon the earth. 45 For I am the Lord who brought you up out of the land of Egypt to be your God; and ye shall be holy, for I the Lord am holy.

46 This is the law concerning beasts and birds and every living creature moving in the water, and every living creature creeping on the earth,

Leviticus 12

47 to discern between the unclean and the clean; and between those that bring forth *things* alive, such as should be eaten, and those that bring forth *things* alive, such as should not be eaten.

* *Codex Alexandrinus* omits the word "not".

Chapter 12

And the Lord spoke to Moses, saying, 2 Speak to the sons of Israel, and thou shall say to them, * Whatever woman shall have conceived and born a male child shall be unclean seven days, she shall be unclean according to the days of separation for her monthly courses. 3 And on the eighth day she shall circumcise the flesh of his foreskin. 4 And for thirty-three days she shall continue in her unclean blood; she shall touch nothing holy, and shall not enter the sanctuary, until the days of her purification be fulfilled. 5 But if she should have born a female child, then she shall be unclean twice seven days, according to the time of her monthly courses; and for sixty-six days shall she remain in her unclean blood.
6 And when the days of her purification shall have been fulfilled for a son or a daughter, she shall bring a lamb of a year old without blemish for a whole burnt offering, and a young pigeon or turtle dove for a sin offering to the door of the Tabernacle of Witness, to the priest. 7 And he shall present it before the Lord, and the priest shall make atonement for her, and shall purge her from the fountain of her blood; this is the law of her who bears a male or a female. 8 And if her hand cannot find what is sufficient for a lamb, then shall she take two turtle doves or two young pigeons, one for a whole burnt offering, and one for a sin offering; and the priest shall make atonement for her, and she shall be purified.

* The February 2nd reading of Chapter Twelve for great vespers in the *Greek Menaion* reads somewhat differently than what is present in the biblical text as published by the Apostoliki Diakonia and Zoe Brotherhood. Of particular significance is that it renders certain words masculine, which in the great *Septuagint* biblical codices of *Vaticanus*, *Alexandrinus* and *Sinaiticus* are rendered in the feminine. Thus, the liturgical reading is translated as follows:

"And it shall be that every man who shall have conceived and born a male child shall circumcise the flesh of its foreskin on the eighth day. And for thirty-three days he shall not enter the sanctuary of God *and go* to the priest, until the days of purification be fulfilled. And after this he shall bring a lamb a year old to the Lord without blemish for a whole burnt offering, and a young pigeon or turtle dove to the door of the Tabernacle of Witness, to the priest. O instead of these he will offer two turtle doves or two young pigeons. And the priest shall make atonement for him."

Chapter 13

And the Lord spoke to Moses and Aaron, saying, 2 If any man should have in the skin of his flesh a bright clear spot, and there should be in the skin of his flesh a plague of leprosy, he shall be brought to Aaron the priest, or to one of his sons the priests. 3 And the priest shall view the spot in the skin of his flesh; and *if* the hair in the spot is changed white, and the appearance of the spot is deep in the skin of the flesh, it is a plague of leprosy; and the priest shall look upon it, and pronounce him defiled. 4 But if the spot be clear and white in the skin of his flesh, yet the appearance of it be not deep in the skin, and its hair have not changed *into* white hair, but it is dark, then the priest shall separate *him with* the spot seven days; 5 and the priest shall look on the spot the seventh day; and, behold, *if* the spot remains before him, *and* the spot has not spread in the skin, then the priest shall separate him the second time seven days. 6 And the priest shall look upon him the second time on the seventh day; and, behold, *if* the spot be dark, *and* the spot have not spread in the skin, then the priest shall pronounce him clean; for it is *only* a mark, and the man shall wash his garments and be clean. 7 But if the bright spot should have changed and spread in the skin, after the priest has seen him for the purpose of purifying him, then shall he appear the second time to the priest, 8 and the priest shall look upon him; and, behold, *if* the mark have spread in the skin, then the priest shall pronounce him unclean; it is a leprosy.

9 And if a man has a plague of leprosy, then he shall come to the priest, 10 and the priest shall look, and, behold, if it is a white spot in the skin, and it has changed the hair to white, and some of the sound part of the quick flesh in the sore 11 it is a leprosy waxing old in the skin of the flesh; and the priest shall pronounce him defiled, and shall separate him, because he is unclean. 12 And if the leprosy should have come out very evidently in the skin, and the leprosy should cover all the skin of the infection from the head to the feet, according to *the* entire vision of priest, 13 then the priest shall look, and, behold, the leprosy has covered all the skin of the flesh; and the priest shall pronounce him clean of the plague, because it has changed all to white, it is clean. 14 But on whatever day living flesh shall appear on him, he shall be pronounced defiled. 15 And the priest shall look upon the healthy flesh, and the healthy flesh shall prove him to be defiled; for it is unclean, it is leprosy. 16 But if the healthy flesh be restored and changed white, then shall he come to the priest; 17 and the priest shall see, and, behold, *if* the plague is turned white, then the priest shall pronounce the patient clean; he is clean.

18 And if the flesh should have become an ulcer in his skin, and should be healed,

Leviticus 13

19 and there should be in the place of the ulcer a white sore, or looking white and bright, or fiery, and it shall be seen by the priest; 20 then the priest shall look, and, behold, if the appearance be deeper *in* the skin, and its hair has changed to white, then the priest shall pronounce him defiled; because it is a leprosy, it has broken out in the ulcer. 21 But if the priest look, and behold there is no white hair on it, and it be not below the skin of the flesh, and it be dark colored; then the priest shall separate him seven days. 22 But if it manifestly spread over the skin, then the priest shall pronounce him defiled; it is a plague of leprosy; it has broken out in the ulcer. 23 But if the bright spot should remain in its place and not spread, it is merely an ulcerous sore; and the priest shall pronounce him clean.

24 And if the flesh be in his skin *a* fiery inflammation, and there should be in his skin the part which is healed of the inflammation, bright, clear, and white, suffused with red or very white; 25 then the priest shall look upon him, and, behold, *if* the hair being white is changed to a bright color, and its appearance is lower than the skin, it is a leprosy; it has broken out in the inflammation, and the priest shall pronounce him defiled; it is a plague of leprosy. 26 But if the priest should look, and, behold, there is not in the bright spot any white hair, and it should not be deeper than the skin, and it should be dark, then the priest shall separate him seven days. 27 And the priest shall look upon him on the seventh day; and if the spot were much spread in the skin, then the priest shall pronounce him defiled; it is a plague of leprosy; it has broken out in the ulcer. 28 But if the bright spot remain stationary, and has not spread in the skin, but should be dark, it is a scar of inflammation; and the priest shall pronounce him clean, for it is the mark of the inflammation.

29 And if a man or a woman have in them a plague of leprosy in the head or the beard; 30 then the priest shall look on the plague, and, behold, *if* the appearance of it be deep in the skin, and in it there be thin yellowish hair, then the priest shall pronounce him defiled: it is a scurf, it is a leprosy of the head or a leprosy of the beard. 31 And if the priest should see the plague of the rupture, and, behold, the appearance of it be not deep in the skin, and there is no yellowish hair in it, then the priest shall set *him* apart *for he has* the plague of the rupture seven days. 32 And the priest shall look at the plague on the seventh day; and, behold, *if* the rupture has not spread, and there be no yellowish hair on it, and the appearance of the rupture is not hollow under the skin; 33 then the skin shall be shaven, but the rupture shall not be shaven; and the priest shall set aside the person having the rupture a second time for seven days. 34 And the priest shall see the rupture on the seventh day; and, behold, *if* the rupture has not spread in the skin after the man has been shaved, and the appearance of the rupture is not hollow deep in the skin, then the priest shall pronounce him clean; and he shall wash his garments, and be clean.

Leviticus 13

35 But if the rupture be indeed spread in the skin after he has been purified, 36 then the priest shall look, and, behold, *if* the rupture has spread in the skin, the priest shall not examine concerning the yellow hair, for he is defiled. 37 But if the rupture remains before *him* in its place, and a dark hair should have arisen in it, the rupture is healed; he is clean, and the priest shall pronounce him clean.

38 And if a man or woman should have in the skin of their flesh spots of a bright whiteness, 39 then the priest shall look; and, behold, there bright spots of a bright whiteness in the skin of their flesh, it is a tatter; it burst forth in the skin of his flesh; he is clean.

40 And if any one's head should lose the hair, he is *only* bald he is clean. 41 And if his head should lose the hair in front, he is forehead bald; he is clean. 42 And if there should be in his baldness of head, or his baldness of forehead, a white or fiery plague, it is leprosy in his baldness of head, or baldness of forehead. 43 And the priest shall look upon him, and, behold, if the appearance of the plague be white or inflamed in his baldness of head or baldness in front, as the appearance of leprosy in the skin of his flesh, 44 he is a leprous man; with defilement the priest shall pronounce him defiled; his plague is in his head.

45 And the leper in whom the plague is, let his garments be loosened, and his head uncovered; and let him have a covering put upon his mouth, and he shall be called unclean. 46 All the days in which the plague shall be upon him, being unclean, he shall be *deemed* unclean; he shall stay apart, his place of travel shall be outside the camp.

47 And if a garment have in it the plague of leprosy, a garment of wool, or a garment of flax, 48 either in the warp or in the woof, or in the linen, or in the woolen threads, or in a skin, or in any workmanship of skin, 49 and the plague be greenish or reddish in the skin, or in the garment, either in the warp, or in the woof, or in any workmanship of skin, it is a plague of leprosy, and he shall show it to the priest. 50 And the priest shall look upon the plague, and the priest shall set apart *him that has* the plague seven days. 51 And the priest shall look upon the plague on the seventh day; and if the plague be spread in the garment, either in the warp or in the woof, or in the skin, in whatever things skins may be used in their workmanship, the plague is a confirmed leprosy; it is unclean. 52 He shall burn the garment, either the warp or woof in woolen garments or in flaxen, or in any utensil of skin, in which there may be the plague; because it is a confirmed leprosy; it shall be burned with fire.

53 And if the priest should see, and the plague be not spread in the garments, either in the warp or in the woof, or in any utensil of skin, 54 then the priest shall give directions, and *one* shall wash that on which there may have been the plague, and the priest shall set it aside a second time for seven days.

55 And the priest shall look upon it after the plague has been washed; and *if* this, even the plague, has not changed its appearance, and the plague does not spread, it is unclean; it shall be burnt with fire; it is fixed in the garment, in the warp, or in the woof. 56 And if the priest should look, and the spot is dark after it has been washed, he shall tear it off from the garment, either from the warp or from the woof, or from the skin. 57 And if it should still appear in the garment, either in the warp or in the woof, or in any article of skin, it is a leprosy bursting forth; that wherein the plague is, *it* shall be burned with fire. 58 And the garment, or the warp, or the woof, or any article of skin, which shall be washed, and the plague depart from it, shall also be washed again, and shall be clean.

59 This is the law of the plague of leprosy of a woolen or linen garment, either of the warp, or woof, or any leathern article, to pronounce it clean or unclean.

Chapter 14

And the Lord spoke to Moses, saying, 2 This is the law of the leper; in whatever day he shall have been cleansed, *and* then shall he be brought to the priest. 3 And the priest shall come forth out of the camp, and the priest shall look, and, behold, the plague of the leprosy is healed from the leper. 4 And the priest shall give directions, and they shall take for him that is cleansed two clean live birds, and cedar wood, and spun red, and hyssop. 5 And the priest shall give direction, and they shall kill one bird into an earthen vessel over living water. 6 And as for the living bird he shall take it, and the cedar wood, and the spun red, and the hyssop, and he shall dip them and the living bird into the blood of the bird that was killed over living water. 7 And he shall sprinkle seven times upon him that was cleansed of his leprosy, and he shall be clean; and he shall let go the living bird into the field. 8 and the man that has been cleansed shall wash his garments, and shall shave off all his hair, and shall wash himself in water, and shall be clean; and after that he shall go into the camp, and shall remain out of his house seven days. 9 And it shall come to pass on the seventh day, he shall shave off all his hair, his head and his beard, and his eyebrows, even all his hair shall he shave; and he shall wash his garments, and wash his body with water, and shall be clean.

10 And on the eighth day he shall take two lambs without spot of a year old, and one sheep without spot of a year old, and three-tenths of fine flour for sacrifice kneaded with oil, and one small cup of oil. 11 And the priest that cleanses shall stand the man under purification, and these *offerings* before the Lord, at the door of the Tabernacle of Witness.

Leviticus 14

12 And the priest shall take one lamb, and offer him for a trespass offering, and the cup of oil, and set them apart for a special offering before the Lord. 13 and they shall kill the lamb in the place where they kill the whole burnt offerings, and the sin offerings, in the holy places; for it is a sin offering; as the trespass offering, it belongs to the priest, it is most holy. 14 And the priest shall take of the blood of the trespass offering, and the priest shall put it on the tip of the right ear of the person under purification, and on the thumb of his right hand, and on the great toe of his right foot. 15 And the priest shall take of the cup of oil, and shall pour it upon the left hand of the priest. 16 And moisten his right finger with the olive oil that is in his left hand, and sprinkle seven times with his finger before the Lord. 17 And the remaining oil that is in his hand, the priest shall put on the tip of the right ear of him that is under purification, and on the thumb of his right hand, and on the great toe of his right foot, on the place of the blood of the trespass *offering*. 18 And the remaining oil that is on the hand of the priest, the priest shall put on the head of the cleansed, and the priest shall make atonement for him before the Lord. 19 And the priest shall sacrifice the sin offering, and the priest shall make atonement for the person under purification from his sin, and afterwards the priest shall kill the whole burnt offering. 20 And the priest shall offer the whole burnt offering and the sacrifice upon the altar before the Lord; and the priest shall make atonement for him, and he shall be cleansed.

21 And if he should be poor, and his hand does not find, he shall take one lamb for his transgression for a separate offering, so as to make propitiation for him, and a tenth deal of fine flour mingled with oil for a sacrifice, and one cup of oil, 22 and two turtle doves, or two young pigeons, as many as his hand has found; and the one shall be for a sin offering, and the other for a whole burnt offering. 23 And he shall bring them on the eighth day, to purify him, to the priest, to the door of the tabernacle of witness before the Lord. 24 And the priest shall take the lamb of the trespass offering, and the cup of oil, and place them for a set offering before the Lord. 25 And he shall kill the lamb of the trespass *offering*; and the priest shall take of the blood of the trespass offering, and put it on the tip of the right ear of him that is under purification, and on the thumb of his right hand, and on the great toe of his right foot. 26 And the priest shall pour of the olive oil on his own left hand. 27 And the priest shall sprinkle with his right finger of his right hand the olive oil that is in his left hand seven times before the Lord. 28 And the priest shall put of the olive oil that is on his hand on the tip of the right ear of him that is under purification, and on the thumb of his right hand, and on the great toe of his right foot, on the place of the blood of the trespass *offering*. 29 And that which is left of the olive oil which is on the hand of the priest he shall put on the head of him that is purged, and the priest shall make atonement for him before the Lord.

30 And he shall offer one of the turtledoves or of the young pigeons, as his hand has found, 31 the one for a sin offering, the other for a whole burnt offering with the meat offering, and the priest shall make atonement before the Lord for him that is under purification. 32 This is the law for him in who the plague of leprosy is, and who cannot find with his hand for his purification.

33 And the Lord spoke to Moses and Aaron, saying, 34 Whenever ye shall enter into the land of the Canaanites, which I give you for a possession, and I shall give the plague of leprosy in the houses of the land of your possession; 35 then the owner of the house shall come and report to the priest, saying, I have seen as it were a plague in the house. 36 And the priest shall give orders to remove the furniture of the house, before the priest comes in to see the plague, and none of the things in the house shall become unclean; and afterwards the priest shall go in to examine the house. 37 And he shall look on the plague, and, behold, *if* the plague is in the walls of the house, greenish or reddish cavities, and the appearance of them beneath the surface of the walls. 38 And the priest shall come out of the house to the door of the house, and the priest shall separate the house seven days. 39 And the priest shall return on the seventh day and view the house; and, behold, *if* the plague is spread in the walls of the house, 40 then the priest shall give orders, and they shall take away the stones in which the plague is, and shall cast them out of the city into an unclean place. 41 And they shall scrape the house within around, and shall pour out the dust scraped off outside the city into an unclean place. 42 And they shall take other scraped stones, and put them in the place of the *former* stones, and they shall take other plaster and plaster the house.

43 And if the plague should return again, and break out in the house after they have taken away the stones and after the house is scraped, and after it has been plastered, 44 then the priest shall go in and see if the plague is spread in the house: it is a confirmed leprosy in the house, it is unclean. 45 And they shall take down the house, and its timbers and its stones, and they shall carry out all the mortar without the city into an unclean place. 46 And he that goes into the house at any time, during its separation, shall be unclean until evening. 47 And he that sleeps in the house shall wash his garments, and be unclean until evening; and he that eats in the house shall wash his garments, and be unclean until evening.

48 and if the priest shall arrive and enter and see, and behold the plague be not at all spread in the house after the house has been plastered, then the priest shall declare the house clean, because the plague is healed. 49 And he shall take to purify the house two clean living birds, and cedar wood, and spun scarlet, and hyssop. 50 And he shall kill one bird into an earthen vessel over living water. 51 And he shall take the cedar wood, and the spun red, and the hyssop, and the living bird; and shall dip it into the blood of the bird killed over living water, and with them he shall sprinkle the house seven times.

Leviticus 15

52 and he shall purify the house with the blood of the bird, and with the living water, and with the living bird, and with the cedar wood, and with the hyssop, and with the spun red. 53 And he shall let the living bird go out of the city into the field, and shall make atonement for the house, and it shall be clean.

54 This *is* the law concerning every plague of leprosy and rupture, 55 and of the leprosy of a garment, and of a house, 56 and of a sore, and of a clear spot, and of a shining one, 57 and of declaring in what day it is unclean, and in what day it shall be purged; this *is* the law of the leprosy.

Chapter 15

And the Lord spoke to Moses and Aaron, saying, 2 Speak to the sons of Israel, and thou shall say to them, Whatever man shall have a flow out of his body his flow is unclean. 3 And this *is* the law of his uncleanness when he *has an* ejaculation *of* semen out of his body, this is his uncleanness in him by reason of the flow, by which, his body is affected through the flow: all the days of the flow of his body, by which his body is affected through the flow, there is his uncleanness. 4 Every bed on which he that has the ejaculation *of* semen shall happen to sleep is unclean; and every item on which he that has the ejaculation *of* semen may happen to sit, shall be unclean.

5 And the man who shall touch his bed, shall wash his garments, and bathe himself in water, and shall be unclean till evening. 6 And whoever sits on the seat, on which he that has the issue may have sat, shall wash his garments, and bathe himself in water, and shall be unclean until evening. 7 And he that touches the skin of him that has the ejaculation *of* semen, shall wash his garments and washes himself in water, and shall be unclean till evening. 8 And if he that has the ejaculation *of* semen should spit upon one that is clean, shall wash his garments, and washes himself in water, and be unclean until evening. 9 And every donkey's saddle, on which the man with the ejaculation *of* semen shall have mounted, shall be unclean till evening.

10 And every one that touches whatever shall have been under him shall be unclean until evening; and he that takes them up shall wash his garments, and wash himself in water, and shall be unclean until evening. 11 And whomever he that has the ejaculation *of* semen shall touch, if he has not rinsed his hands in water, he shall wash his garments, and wash his body in water, and shall be unclean until evening. 12 And the earthen vessel, which he that has the ejaculation *of* semen shall happen to touch, shall be broken; and a wooden vessel shall be washed with water, and shall be clean.

Leviticus 15

13 and if he that has the ejaculation *of* semen should be cleansed of his issue, then shall he number to himself seven days for his purification; and he shall wash his garments, and bathe his body in water, and shall be clean. 14 And on the eighth day he shall take to himself two turtle doves or two young pigeons, and he shall bring them before the Lord to the doors of the Tabernacle of Witness, and shall give them to the priest. 15 And the priest shall offer them one for a sin offering, and the other for a whole burnt offering; and the priest shall make atonement for him before the Lord for his ejaculation *of* semen.

16 And the man whose semen shall happen to go forth from him, shall then wash his whole body, and shall be unclean until evening. 17 And every garment, and every skin on which there shall be semen shall both be washed with water, and be unclean until evening. 18 And *with* a woman, if a man shall sleep with her in a bed of semen they shall both wash themselves in water and shall be unclean until evening.

19 And a woman whoever shall be flowing of blood, when her floe shall be in her body, *she* shall be seven days in her menstruation; every one that touches her shall be unclean until evening. 20 And every thing she shall sleep upon in her menstruation shall be unclean; and whatever she shall sit upon, shall be unclean. 21 And whoever shall touch her bed shall wash his garments, and wash his body in water, and shall be unclean until evening. 22 and every one that touches any item on which she shall sit, shall wash his garments and bathe himself in water, and shall be unclean until evening. 23 And whether it is while she is on her bed, or on an item, which she may happen to sit upon when he touches her, he shall be unclean till evening. 24 And if any one shall sleep with her, and her uncleanness is upon him, he shall be unclean seven days; and every bed on which he shall have slept shall be unclean.

25 And if a woman has a flow of blood many days, not in the time of her menstruation; if the blood should also flow after her menstruation, all the days of the flow of her uncleanness as the days of her menstruation; she shall be unclean. 26 And every bed on which she shall sleep all the days of her flow shall be to her as the bed of her menstruation, and every item whereon she shall sit shall be unclean according to the uncleanness of her menstruation. 27 Every one that touches it shall be unclean; and he shall wash his garments, and wash his body in water, and shall be unclean till evening. 28 But if she shall be cleansed from her flow, then she shall number to herself seven days, and afterwards she shall be purged clean. 29 And on the eighth day she shall take two turtledoves, or two young pigeons, and shall bring them to the priest, to the door of the Tabernacle of Witness. 30 And the priest shall offer one for a sin offering, and the other for a whole burnt offering, and the priest shall make atonement for her before the Lord because of the flow of her uncleanness.

Leviticus 16

31 And ye shall cause the sons of Israel to beware of their uncleanness; so they shall not die for their uncleanness, in polluting my tabernacle that is among them.

32 This is the law of the man who has an ejaculation *of* semen, and if one *should* discharge semen *on a* bed, so that he should be defiled by it. 33 And for her that has the flow of blood in her menstruation, and as to the one who has an ejaculation *of* semen, in his flow; to the male or the female, and for the man who shall have slept with *the* one who sits apart.

Chapter 16

And the Lord spoke to Moses after the two sons of Aaron died in bringing strange fire before the Lord, so they died. 2 And the Lord said to Moses, Speak to Aaron thy brother, and let him not come in at all times into the holy place within the veil before the propitiatory, which is upon the ark of the testimony, and he shall not die; for I will appear in a cloud on the propitiatory. 3 Thus shall Aaron enter into the holy place with a calf of the herd for a sin offering, and a ram for a whole burnt offering. 4 And he shall put on the consecrated linen tunic, and he shall have on his flesh the linen drawers, and shall gird himself with a linen girdle, and shall put on the linen cap, they are holy garments; and he shall bathe his entire body in water, and shall put them on. 5 And he shall take of the congregation of the sons of Israel two kids of the goats for a sin offering, and one lamb for a whole burnt offering. 6 And Aaron shall bring the calf for his own sin offering, and shall make atonement for himself and for his house. 7 And he shall take the two goats, and place them before the Lord by the door of the tabernacle of witness. 8 and Aaron shall cast lots upon the two goats, one lot for the Lord, and the other for the scapegoat. 9 And Aaron shall bring forward the goat on which the lot for the Lord fell, and shall offer him for a sin offering. 10 and the goat upon which the lot of the scapegoat came, he shall present alive before the Lord, to make atonement upon him, so as to send him away for the dismissal, and he shall send him into the wilderness.

11 And Aaron shall bring the calf for his sin, and he shall make atonement for himself and for his house, and he shall kill the calf for his sin offering. 12 And he shall take his censer full of coals of fire off the altar, which is before the Lord; and he shall fill his hands with fine compound incense, and shall bring it within the veil. 13 And he shall put the incense on the fire before the Lord, and the smoke of the incense shall cover the mercy seat over the testimonies, and he shall not die.

14 And he shall take of the blood of the calf, and sprinkle with his finger on the mercy seat to the east; before the mercy seat shall he sprinkle seven times of the blood with his finger. 15 and he shall kill the goat for the sin offering that is for the people, before the Lord; and he shall bring in of its blood within the veil, and shall do with its blood as he did with the blood of the calf, and shall sprinkle its blood on the mercy seat, in front of the mercy seat. 16 and he shall make atonement for the sanctuary on account of the uncleanness of the sons of Israel, and for their trespasses in the matter of all their sins; and thus shall he do to the Tabernacle of Witness established among them in the midst of their uncleanness. 17 and there shall be no man in the Tabernacle of Witness, when he goes in to make atonement in the holy place, until he shall have come out; and he shall make atonement for himself, and for his house, and for the entire congregation of the sons of Israel. 18 And he shall come forth to the altar that is before the Lord, and he shall make atonement upon it; and he shall take of the blood of the calf, and of the blood of the goat, and shall put it on the horns of the altar around. 19 And he shall sprinkle some of the blood upon it seven times with his finger, and shall purge it, and hallow it from the uncleanness of the sons of Israel.

20 And he shall finish making atonement for the sanctuary and for the Tabernacle of Witness, and for the altar; and he shall make a cleansing for the priests, and he shall bring the living goat; 21 and Aaron shall lay his hands on the head of the live goat, and he shall declare over him all the iniquities of the sons of Israel, and all their unrighteousness, and all their sins; and he shall lay them upon the head of the live goat, and shall send him by the hand of a ready man into the wilderness. 22 And the goat shall bear their unrighteousness upon him into a desert land; and Aaron shall send away the goat into the wilderness.

23 And Aaron shall enter into the Tabernacle of Witness, and shall put off the linen garment, which he had put on, as he entered into the holy place, and shall lay it by there. 24 And he shall bathe his body in water in the holy place, and shall put on his raiment, and shall go out and offer the whole burnt offering for himself and the whole burnt offering for the people; and shall make atonement for himself and for his house, and for the people, as for the priests. 25 And he shall offer the fat for the sin offering on the altar. 26 And he that sends forth the goat that has been set apart to be let go, shall wash his garments, and wash his body in water, and afterwards shall enter into the camp. 27 And the calf for the sin offering, and the goat for the sin offering, whose blood was brought in to make atonement in the holy place, they shall carry forth out of the camp, and burn them with fire, even their skins and their flesh and their dung. 28 And he that burns them shall wash his garments, and wash his body in water, and afterwards he shall enter into the camp.

Leviticus 17

29 And this shall be a perpetual statute for you; in the seventh month, on the tenth day of the month, ye shall humble your souls, and shall do no work, the native and the stranger who attaches himself to you. 30 For in this day he shall make atonement for you, to cleanse you from all your sins before the Lord, and ye shall be cleansed. 31 A Sabbath of sabbaths, a rest, and ye shall humble your souls; it is a perpetual ordinance. 32 The priest whomever they shall anoint shall make atonement, and whosever hands they shall perfect to exercise the office of priest after his father; and he shall put on the linen robe, the holy garment. 33 And he shall make atonement for the most holy place, and the tabernacle of witness; and he shall make atonement for the altar, and for the priests; and he shall make atonement for the entire congregation. 34 And this shall be to you a perpetual statute to make atonement for the sons of Israel from all their sins; it shall be done once in the year, as the Lord commanded Moses.

Chapter 17

And the Lord spoke to Moses, saying, 2 Speak to Aaron and to his sons, and to all the sons of Israel, and thou shall say to them, This is the word which the Lord has commanded, saying, 3 Every man of the sons of Israel, or of the strangers abiding among you, who shall kill a calf, or a sheep, or a goat in the camp, or who shall kill it outside of the camp, 4 and shall not bring it to the door of the Tabernacle of Witness, so as to sacrifice it for a whole burnt offering or peace offering to the Lord to be acceptable for a sweet smelling savor; and whoever shall kill it outside, and shall not bring it to the door of the Tabernacle of Witness, so as to offer it as a gift to the Lord before the tabernacle of the Lord; blood shall be imputed to that man, he has shed blood; that soul shall be cut off from his people. 5 That the sons of Israel may offer their sacrifices, all that they shall kill in the fields, and bring them to the Lord unto the doors of the tabernacle of witness to the priest, and they shall sacrifice them as a peace offering to the Lord. 6 And the priest pours the blood on the altar around before the Lord by the doors of the Tabernacle of Witness, and shall offer the fat for a sweet smelling savor to the Lord. 7 And they shall no longer offer their sacrifices to vain after which they go a whoring; it shall be a perpetual statute to you for your generations.

8 And thou shall say to them, Whatever man of the sons of Israel, or of the sons of the proselytes abiding among you, shall offer a whole burnt offering or a sacrifice, 9 and shall not bring it to the door of the Tabernacle of Witness to sacrifice it to the Lord, that man shall be destroyed from among his people.

10 And whatever man of the sons of Israel, or of the strangers abiding among you, shall eat any blood, I will even set My face against that soul that eats blood, and will destroy it from its people. 11 For the life of flesh is its blood, and I have given it to you on the altar to make atonement for your souls; for its blood shall make atonement for the soul. 12 Therefore I said to the sons of Israel, No soul of you shall eat blood, and the stranger that attaches himself to you shall not eat blood. 13 And whatever man of the sons of Israel, or of the strangers that attach themselves to you shall take any animal in hunting, beast, or bird, which is eaten, *and* then shall he pour out the blood, and cover it in the dust. 14 For the blood of all flesh is its life; and I said to the sons of Israel, Ye shall not eat the blood of any flesh, for the life of all flesh is its blood; every one that eats it shall be destroyed. 15 And every soul which eats that which has died of itself, or is taken of beasts, either among the natives or among the strangers, shall wash his garments, and bathe himself in water, and shall be unclean until evening; then shall he be clean. 16 But if he does not wash his garments, and does not wash his body in water, then shall he bear his iniquity.

Chapter 18

And the Lord spoke to Moses, saying, 2 Speak to the sons of Israel, and thou shall say to them, I *am* the Lord your God. 3 Ye shall not do according to the devices of Egypt, in which ye lived; and according to the devices of the land of Canaan, into which I bring you, ye shall not do; and ye shall not walk in their ordinances. 4 Ye shall observe My judgments, and shall keep My ordinances, and shall walk in them; I *am* the Lord your God. 5 So ye shall keep all My ordinances, and all My judgments, and do them, which if a man do, he shall live in them; I *am* the Lord your God.

6 No man shall draw near to any of his near kindred to uncover their nakedness; I *am* the Lord. 7 Thou shall not uncover the nakedness of thy father, or the nakedness of thy mother, for she is thy mother; thou shall not uncover her nakedness. 8 Thou shall not uncover the nakedness of thy father's wife; it is thy father's nakedness. 9 The nakedness of thy sister by thy father or by thy mother, born at home or abroad, their nakedness thou shall not uncover. 10 The nakedness of thy son's daughter, or thy daughter's daughter, their nakedness thou shall not uncover because it is thy nakedness. 11 Thou shall not uncover the nakedness of the daughter of thy father's wife; she is thy sister by the same father: thou shall not uncover her nakedness. 12 Thou shall not uncover the nakedness of thy father's sister, for she is near akin to thy father. 13 Thou shall not uncover the nakedness of thy mother's sister, for she is near akin to thy mother.

Leviticus 19

14 Thou shall not uncover the nakedness of thy father's brother, and thou shall not go in to his wife for she is thy relation. 15 Thou shall not uncover the nakedness of thy daughter-in-law, for she is thy son's wife, thou shall not uncover her nakedness. 16 Thou shall not uncover the nakedness of thy brother's wife; it is thy brother's nakedness. 17 The nakedness of a woman and her daughter shall thou not uncover; her son's daughter, and her daughter's daughter, shall thou not take, to uncover their nakedness, for they are thy kinswomen: it is impiety. 18 Thou shall not take a wife in addition to her sister, as a rival, to uncover her nakedness in opposition to her, while she is yet living.

19 And thou shall not go in to a woman under separation for her uncleanness, to uncover her nakedness. 20 And thou shall not lie with thy neighbor's wife, to defile thyself with her. 21 And thou shall not give of thy seed to serve a ruler; and thou shall not profane my holy name; I *am* the Lord. 22 And thou shall not sleep with a man, as with a woman, for it is an abomination. 23 Neither shall thou give your bed to any quadruped for copulation, to be defiled with it; neither shall a woman present herself before any quadruped to be mounted by it; for it is an abomination.

24 Do not defile yourselves with any of these things; for in all these things the nations are defiled, which I drive out before you, 25 and the land is defiled; and I have recompensed their iniquity to them because of it, and the land is aggrieved with them that live upon it. 26 And ye shall keep all my statutes and all my ordinances, and ye shall do none of these abominations; neither the native, nor the stranger that joins himself with you; 27 (for all these abominations the men of the land did who were before you, and the land was defiled,) 28 and lest the land be aggrieved with you in your defilement of it, as it was angered with the nations before you. 29 For whoever shall do any of these abominations; the souls that do them shall be destroyed from among their people. 30 And ye shall keep Mine ordinances, that ye may not do any of the abominable practices, which have taken place before your time; and ye shall not be defiled in them for I *am* the Lord your God.

Chapter 19

And the Lord spoke to Moses, saying, 2 Speak to the congregation of the sons of Israel, and thou shall say to them, Ye shall be holy; for I the Lord your God *am* holy. 3 Let every one of you fear his father and his mother; and ye shall keep my Sabbaths; I the Lord your God. 4 Ye shall not follow idols, and ye shall not make to yourselves molten gods: I the Lord your God. 5 And if ye will sacrifice a peace offering to the Lord, ye shall offer it acceptable from yourselves.

Leviticus 19

6 In what day so ever ye shall sacrifice it, it shall be eaten; and on the following day, and if any of it should be left till the third day, it shall be thoroughly burnt with fire. 7 And if it should be at all eaten on the third day, it is unfit for sacrifice: it shall not be accepted. 8 And he that eats it shall bear his iniquity, because he has profaned the holy things of the Lord; and the souls that eat it shall be destroyed from among their people.

9 And when ye reap the harvest of your land, ye shall not complete the reaping of your field with exactness, and thou shall not gather that which falls from thy reaping. 10 And thou shall not go over the gathering of thy vineyard, neither shall thou gather the grape stones of thy vineyard: thou shall leave them for the poor and the stranger: I am the Lord your God.

11 Ye shall not steal, ye shall not lie, nor shall each bear false witness as an informer against his neighbor. 12 And ye shall not swear unjustly by my name, and ye shall not profane the holy name of your God; I am the Lord your God.

13 Thou shall not injure thy neighbor, nor do thou rob, nor shall the wages of thy hireling remain with thee until the morning. 14 Thou shall not revile the deaf, nor shall thou put an obstacle in the way of the blind; and thou shall fear the Lord thy God; I am the Lord your God.

15 Thou shall not act unjustly in judgment; thou shall not accept the person of the poor, nor admire the person of the mighty; with justice shall thou judge thy neighbor.

16 Thou shall not walk deceitfully among thy people; thou shall not rise up against the blood of thy neighbor; I am the Lord your God.

17 Thou shall not hate thy brother in thine heart; with rebuke you shall reprove thy neighbor, so thou shall not bear sin on his account. 18 And thy hand shall not avenge thee; and thou shall not be angry with the sons of thy people; and thou shall love thy neighbor as thyself; I am the Lord.

19 Ye shall observe My law: thou shall not let thy cattle gender with one of a different kind, and thou shall not sow thy vineyard with diverse seed; and thou shall not put upon thyself a mingled garment woven of two.

20 And if any one sleep carnally with a woman in a bed of semen, and she should be a household slave being guarded for a man, and she has not been ransomed, her freedom has not been given to her, they shall be visited; but they shall not die, because she was not set at liberty. 21 And he shall bring for his trespass to the Lord to the door of the Tabernacle of Witness, a ram for a trespass offering. 22 And the priest shall make atonement for him with the ram of the trespass offering, before the Lord, for the sin, which he sinned; and the sin, which he sinned, shall be forgiven him.

Leviticus 20

23 And whenever ye shall enter into the land which the Lord your God gives you, and shall plant any fruit tree, then shall ye purge away its uncleanness; its fruit shall be three years uncleanness to you, it shall not be eaten. 24 And in the fourth year all its fruit shall be holy, laudable to the Lord. 25 And in the fifth year ye shall eat the fruit, its produce is an increase to you. I am the Lord your God.

26 Eat not on the mountains, nor shall ye divine from omens, nor divine by inspection of birds. 27 Ye shall not make a round cutting of the hair of your head, nor spoil the appearance of your beard. 28 And ye shall not make cuttings of a soul on your body, and ye shall not inscribe on yourselves any marks. I am the Lord your God.

29 Thou shall not profane thy daughter to prostitute her; so the land shall not go a whoring, and the land be filled with iniquity. 30 Ye shall keep My Sabbaths, and fear My holy *sanctuaries*; I am the Lord.

31 Ye shall not attend to those who deliver oracles, nor attach yourselves to enchanters, to defile yourselves with them; I am the Lord your God.

32 Thou shall arise before the face of *one who is* grey, and honor the face of the old man, and shall fear thy God; I am the Lord your God.

33 And if there should come to you a stranger in your land, ye shall not afflict him. 34 The stranger that comes to you shall be among you as the native, and thou shall love him as thyself; for ye were strangers in the land of Egypt; I am the Lord your God.

35 Ye shall not act unrighteous in judgment, in measures and weights and scales. 36 There shall be among you just balances and just weights and just liquid measure. I am the Lord your God, who brought you out of the land of Egypt. 37 And ye shall keep all my law and all my ordinances, and ye shall do them; I am the Lord your God.

Chapter 20

And the Lord spoke to Moses, saying, 2 Thou shall also say to the sons of Israel, If any of the sons of Israel, or of those who have become proselytes in Israel, who shall give of his seed to the ruler, by death let him be put to death; the nation upon the land shall stone him with stones. 3 And I will set My face against that man, and will cut him off from his people, because he has given of his seed to the ruler, to defile My holy *sanctuaries*, and profane the name of them that are consecrated to me. 4 And if the natives of the land should in anywise overlook that man in giving of his seed to the ruler, so as not to put him to death;

5 then will I set My face against that man and his family, and I will destroy him, and all who have been of one mind with him, so that he should go a whoring to the rulers, from their people.

6 And the soul that shall follow those who have in them divining spirits, or enchanters, so as to go a whoring after them; I will set my face against that soul, and will destroy it from among its people.

7 And ye shall be holy, for I the Lord your God *am* holy.

8 And ye shall observe my ordinances, and do them: I the Lord that sanctifies you.

9 Every man who shall speak evil of his father or of his mother let him die the death; has he spoken evil of his father or his mother? He shall be guilty.

10 Whatever man shall commit adultery with the wife of a man, or whoever shall commit adultery with the wife of his neighbor, let them die the death, the adulterer and the adulteress. 11 And if any one should lie with his father's wife, he has uncovered his father's nakedness: let them both die the death they are guilty. 12 And if any one should sleep with his daughter-in-law, let them both by die the death; for they have wrought impiety, they are guilty.

13 And whoever shall sleep with a man in a bed for a woman, they have both wrought abomination, let them die the death they are guilty.

14 Whoever shall take a woman and her mother, it is iniquity; they shall burn him and them with fire; so there shall not be iniquity among you.

15 And whoever shall sleep with a quadruped, let him die the death; and ye shall kill the beast. 16 And whatever woman shall approach any beast, so as to be mounted by it, ye shall kill the woman and the beast; let them die the death they are guilty.

17 Whoever shall take his sister by his father or by his mother, and shall see her nakedness and she see his nakedness, it is a reproach; they shall be destroyed before the children of their family; he has uncovered his sister's nakedness, they shall bear their sin.

18 And whatever man shall sleep with a woman that is set apart, and shall uncover her nakedness, he has uncovered her fountain, and she has uncovered the flow of her blood; they shall both be destroyed from among their generation. 19 And thou shall not uncover the nakedness of thy father's sister, or of the sister of thy mother; for that man has uncovered the nakedness of one near akin: they shall bear their iniquity. 20 Whoever shall sleep with his near kinswoman, has uncovered the nakedness of one near akin to him; they shall die childless. 21 Whoever shall take his brother's wife, it is uncleanness; he has uncovered his brother's nakedness; they shall die childless.

22 And safeguard you all My ordinances, and My judgments; and ye shall do them, and the land shall not be aggrieved with you, into which I bring you to live upon it.

Leviticus 21

23 And walk ye not in the customs of the nations which I drive out from before you; for they have done all these things, and I have abhorred them; 24 and I said to you, Ye shall inherit their land, and I will give it to you for a possession, a land flowing with milk and honey; I the Lord your God, who have separated you from all people. 25 And ye shall separate them: between the clean and the unclean cattle, and between clean and unclean birds; and ye shall not defile your souls with cattle, or with birds, or with any creeping things of the earth, which I have separated for you by reason of uncleanness. 26 And ye shall be holy to Me; because I the Lord your God *am* holy, who separated you from all nations, to be Mine.

27 And *for* a man or woman whoever of them shall have in them a divining spirit, or be an enchanter, let them both die the death; ye shall stone them with stones, they are guilty.

Chapter 21

And the Lord spoke to Moses, saying, Speak to the priests the sons of Aaron, and thou shall tell them they shall not defile themselves in their nation for the dead, 2 but for a relative who is very near to them, for a father and mother, and sons and daughters, for a brother, 3 and for a virgin sister that is near to one, that is not espoused to a man; for these one shall defile himself. 4 He shall not defile himself suddenly among his people to profane himself. 5 And ye shall not shave your head for the dead with baldness on the top; and they shall not shave the appearance of their beard, neither shall they make gashes on their flesh. 6 They shall be holy to their God, and they shall not profane the name of their God for they offer the sacrifices of the Lord as the gifts of their God, and they shall be holy. 7 They shall not take a female prostitute and one who has been profaned, and a woman put away from her husband for he is holy to the Lord his God. 8 And He shall sanctify him; he offers the gifts of the Lord your God: he shall be holy, for I the Lord that sanctify them *am* holy. 9 And if the daughter of a man, a priest should be profaned to go a whoring, she profanes the name of her father: she shall be burned with fire.

10 And the priest that is great among his brothers, the olive oil having been poured upon the head of the anointed one, and he having been consecrated to put on the garments, shall not take the turban off his head, and shall not rend his garments: 11 neither shall he go in to any dead body; neither shall he defile himself for his father or his mother. 12 And he shall not go forth out of the sanctuary, and he shall not profane the sanctuary of his God, because the holy anointing oil of God *is* upon him: I *am* the Lord. 13 He shall take for a wife a virgin of his own race.

14 But a widow, or one that is put away, or profaned, or a harlot, these he shall not take; but he shall take for a wife a virgin of his own people. 15 And he shall not profane his seed among his people: I *am* the Lord that sanctifies him.

16 And the Lord spoke to Moses, saying, 17 Say to Aaron, A man of thy tribe throughout your generations, who shall have a blemish on him, shall not draw near to offer the gifts of his God. 18 No man who has a blemish on him shall draw near; a man blind, lame, with his nose disfigured, or his ears cut, 19 a man who has a broken hand or a broken foot, 20 or humpbacked, or blear-eyed, or that has lost his eyelashes, or a man who has a malignant ulcer, or tatter, or one that has lost a testicle. 21 Whoever of the seed of Aaron the priest has a blemish on him, shall not draw near to offer sacrifices to thy God, because he has a blemish on him; he shall not draw near to offer the gifts of God. 22 The gifts of God *are* most holy, and he shall eat of the holy things. 23 Only he shall not approach the veil, and he shall not draw near to the altar, because he has a blemish; and he shall not profane the holy *sanctuary* of his God, for I am the Lord that sanctifies them. 24 And Moses spoke to Aaron and his sons, and to all the sons of Israel.

Chapter 22

And the Lord spoke to Moses, saying, 2 Speak to Aaron and to his sons, and let them take heed concerning the holy *things* of the sons of Israel, so they shall not profane My holy name in any of the things which they consecrate to Me; I *am* the Lord. 3 Say to them, Every man throughout your generations, whoever of all your seed shall approach to the holy things, whatever the sons of Israel shall consecrate to the Lord, and his uncleanness be upon him, that soul shall be cut off from Me; I *am* the Lord your God. 4 And the man of the seed of Aaron the priest, if he should have leprosy or issue of the reins, shall not eat of the holy things, until he be cleansed; and he that touches any uncleanness of a dead body, or the man whose ejaculation *of* semen shall have gone out from him, 5 or whoever shall touch any unclean reptile, which will defile him, or a man, whereby he shall defile himself according to all his uncleanness; 6 whatever soul shall touch them shall be unclean until evening; he shall not eat of the holy *things*, unless he bathe his body in water, 7 and the sun go down, and then he shall be clean; and then shall he eat of all the holy *things*, for they are his bread. 8 He shall not eat that which dies of itself, or is taken of beasts, so that they should pollute him; I *am* the Lord. 9 And they shall keep My ordinances, that they do not bear iniquity because of them, and die because of them, if they shall profane them; I *am* the Lord God that sanctifies them.

Leviticus 22

10 And no stranger shall eat the holy *things*; one that travels with a priest, or a hireling, shall not eat the holy *things*. 11 But if a priest should have a soul purchased for money, he shall eat of his bread; and they that are born in his house, they also shall eat of his bread. 12 And if the daughter of a priest should marry a * foreigner, she shall not eat of the first fruits of the holy *sanctuary*. 13 And if the daughter of priest should be a widow, or put away, and have no seed, she shall return to her father's house, as in her youth; she shall eat of her father's bread, but no stranger shall eat of it. 14 And the man, who shall ignorantly eat holy *things*, shall add the fifth part to it, and give the holy *thing* to the priest. 15 And they shall not profane the holy *things* of the sons of Israel, which they offer to the Lord. 16 So shall they bring upon themselves the iniquity of trespass in their eating their holy *things*; for I *am* the Lord that sanctifies them.

17 And the Lord spoke to Moses, saying, 18 Speak to Aaron and his sons, and to the entire congregation of Israel, and thou shall say to them, Any man of the sons of Israel, or of the strangers that attach themselves to them in Israel, who shall offer his gifts according to all their confession and according to all their choice, whatever they may bring to the Lord for whole burnt offerings, 19 your acceptable offerings *shall* be males without blemish of the herds, or of the sheep, or of the goats. 20 They shall not bring to the Lord anything that has a blemish in it, for it shall not be acceptable for you. 21 And whatever man shall offer a peace offering to the Lord, discharging a vow, or in the way of a choice offering, or an offering in your feasts, of the herds or of the sheep, it shall be without blemish for acceptance; there shall be no blemish in it. 22 One that is blind, or broken, or has its tongue cut out, or is troubled with warts, or has a malignant ulcer, or tatters, they shall not offer these to the Lord; neither shall ye offer any of them for a burnt offering on the altar of the Lord. 23 And a calf or a sheep with the ears cut off, or that has lost its tail, thou shall kill them for thyself; but they shall not be accepted for thy vow. 24 That which has crushed testicles, or being squeezed out or emasculated or drawn away, thou shall not offer them to the Lord, nor shall ye sacrifice them upon your land. 25 Neither shall ye offer the gifts of your God of all these things by the hand of a stranger, because there are corruptions in them, a blemish in them; these shall not be accepted for you.

26 And the Lord spoke to Moses, saying, 27 As for a calf, or a sheep, or a goat, whenever it is born, then shall it be seven days under its mother; and on the eighth day and after they shall be accepted for sacrifices, a burnt offering to the Lord. 28 And a calf and a sheep, it and its young, thou shall not kill in one day. 29 And if thou should offer a sacrifice, a vow of rejoicing to the Lord, ye shall offer it so as to be accepted for you. 30 In that same day it shall be eaten; ye shall not leave of the flesh till tomorrow: I am the Lord.

31 And ye shall keep My commandments and do them.

32 And ye shall not profane the name of the Holy One, and I will be sanctified in the midst of the sons of Israel. I *am* the Lord that sanctifies you, 33 who brought you out of the land of Egypt, to be your God; I the Lord.

* This word is used in the *Septuagint* as a distinct reference to "Philistines", but is literally translated as "foreigners", or "those of another people or tribe"

Chapter 23

And the Lord spoke to Moses, saying, 2 Speak to the sons of Israel, and thou shall say unto them, The feasts of the Lord which ye shall call holy assemblies, these are my feasts.

3 Six days shall thou do works, but on the seventh day is the Sabbath; a rest, a holy convocation to the Lord; thou shall not do any work; it is a Sabbath to the Lord in all your habitations.

4 These *are* the feasts to the Lord, holy convocations, which ye shall call in their seasons. 5 In the first month, on the fourteenth day of the month, between the evening times is the Lord's Passover. 6 And on the fifteenth day of this month is the feast of unleavened bread to the Lord; seven days shall ye eat unleavened bread. 7 And the first day shall be a holy convocation to you; ye shall do no servile work. 8 And ye shall offer whole burnt offerings to the Lord seven days; and the seventh day shall be a holy convocation to you; ye shall do no servile work.

9 And the Lord spoke to Moses, saying, 10 Speak to the sons of Israel, and thou shall say to them, When ye shall enter into the land which I give you, and reap the harvest of it, then shall ye bring a sheaf, the first fruits of your harvest, to the priest; 11 and he shall lift up the sheaf before the Lord, to be accepted for you. On the morning of the first day the priest shall lift it up. 12 And ye shall offer on the day on which ye bring the sheaf, a lamb without blemish of a year old for a whole burnt offering to the Lord. 13 And its meat offering two tenth portions of fine flour mingled with oil; it is a sacrifice to the Lord, a smell of sweet savor to the Lord, and its drink offering the fourth part of a hin of wine. 14 And ye shall not eat bread, or the new parched corn, until this same day, until ye offer the sacrifices to your God, a perpetual statute throughout your generations in all your habitations.

15 And ye shall number to yourselves from the day after the Sabbath, from the day on which ye shall offer the sheaf of the heave offering, seven full weeks; 16 until tomorrow after the last week ye shall number fifty days, and shall bring a new meat offering to the Lord. 17 Ye shall bring from your habitation loaves, as a heave offering, two loaves; they shall be of two tenth portions of fine flour; they shall be baked with leaven of the first fruits to the Lord.

Leviticus 23

18 And ye shall bring with the loaves seven unblemished lambs of a year old, and one calf of the herd, and two rams without blemish, and they shall be a whole burnt offering to the Lord; and their meat offerings and their drink offerings a sacrifice, a smell of sweet savor to the Lord. 19 And they shall sacrifice one kid of the goats for a sin offering, and two lambs of a year old for a peace offering, with the loaves of the first fruits. 20 And the priest shall place them with the loaves of the first fruits an offering before the Lord with the two lambs, they shall be holy to the Lord; they shall belong to the priest that brings them. 21 And ye shall call this day convocation; it shall be holy to you; ye shall do no servile work on it; it is a perpetual ordinance throughout your generations in all your habitations.

22 And when ye shall reap the harvest of your land, ye shall not fully reap the remainder of the harvest of your field when thou reap, and thou shall not gather that which falls from thy reaping; thou shall leave it for the poor and the stranger; I *am* the Lord your God.

23 And the Lord spoke to Moses, saying, 24 Speak to the sons of Israel, saying, In the seventh month, on the first day of the month, ye shall have a rest, a memorial of trumpets; it shall be to you a holy convocation. 25 Ye shall do no servile work, and ye shall offer a whole burnt offering to the Lord.

26 And the Lord spoke to Moses, saying, 27 Also on the tenth day of this seventh month is a day of atonement; it shall be a holy convocation to you; and ye shall humble your souls, and offer a whole burnt offering to the Lord. 28 Ye shall do no work on this self same day; for this is a day of atonement for you, to make atonement for you before the Lord your God. 29 Every soul that shall not be humbled in that day shall be cut off from among its people. 30 And every soul which shall do work on that day, that soul shall be destroyed from among its people. 31 Ye shall do no manner of work; it is a perpetual statute throughout your generations in all your habitations. 32 It shall be a holy Sabbath to you; and ye shall humble your souls, from the ninth day of the month; from evening to evening ye shall keep your Sabbaths.

33 And the Lord spoke to Moses, saying, 34 Speak to the sons of Israel, saying, On the fifteenth day of this seventh month, there shall be a feast of tabernacles seven days to the Lord. 35 And on the first day shall be a holy convocation; ye shall do no servile work. 36 Seven days shall ye offer whole burnt offerings to the Lord, and the eighth day shall be a holy convocation to you; and ye shall offer whole burnt offerings to the Lord; it is a time of release, ye shall do no servile work.

37 These *are* the feasts to the Lord, which ye shall call holy convocations, to offer burnt offerings to the Lord, whole burnt offerings and their meat offerings, and their drink offerings, that for each day on its day;

38 besides the Sabbaths of the Lord, and besides your gifts, and besides all your vows, and besides your free will offerings, which ye shall give to the Lord. 39 And on the fifteenth day of this seventh month, when ye shall have completely gathered in the fruits of the earth, ye shall keep a feast to the Lord seven days; on the first day there shall be a rest, and on the eighth day a rest. 40 And on the first day ye shall take goodly fruit of trees, and branches of palm trees, and thick boughs of trees, and willows, and branches of osiers from the brook, to rejoice before the Lord your God seven days in the year. 41 A perpetual statute for your generations; in the seventh month ye shall keep it. 42 Seven days ye shall live in tabernacles; every native in Israel shall live in tents, 43 that your generations may see, that I made the sons of Israel to live in tents, when I brought them out of the land of Egypt; I *am* the Lord your God.

44 And Moses spoke *concerning* the feasts of the Lord to the sons of Israel.

Chapter 24

And the Lord spoke to Moses, saying, 2 Charge the sons of Israel, and let them take for thee pure olive oil beaten for the light, to burn a lamp continually, 3 outside the veil in the Tabernacle of Witness; and Aaron and his sons shall burn it from evening until morning before the Lord continually, a perpetual statute throughout your generations. 4 Ye shall burn the lamps on the pure lamp stand before the Lord till tomorrow.

5 And ye shall take fine flour, and make of it twelve loaves; each loaf shall be of two tenth parts. 6 And ye shall put them *in* two rows, each row six loaves, on the pure table before the Lord. 7 And ye shall put on *each* row pure frankincense and salt; and shall be for loaves for a memorial, set forth before the Lord. 24 On the Sabbath day they shall be set forth before the Lord continually before the sons of Israel, for an everlasting covenant. 9 And they shall be for Aaron and his sons, and they shall eat them in the holy place: for this is their most holy portion of the offerings made to the Lord, a perpetual statute.

10 And there went forth a son of an Israelite woman, and he was son of an Egyptian man among the sons of Israel; and they fought in the camp, the son of the Israelite woman, and a man who was an Israelite. 11 And the son of the Israelite woman named THE NAME and cursed; and they brought him to Moses; and his mother's name was Salomith, daughter of Dabri of the tribe of Dan. 12 And they put him in ward, to judge him by the command of the Lord.

13 And the Lord spoke to Moses, saying, 14 Bring forth him that cursed outside the camp, and all who heard shall lay their hands upon his head, and the entire congregation shall stone him. 15 And speak to the sons of Israel, and thou shall say to them, Whoever shall curse God shall bear his sin.

Leviticus 25

16 And he that names the name of the Lord, let him die the death; let all the congregation of Israel stone him with stones; whether he be a stranger or a native, let him die for naming the name of the Lord. 17 And whoever shall throw away the soul of a man and he dies, let him die the death. 18 And whoever shall discard a beast, and it shall die, let him render life for life. 19 And whoever shall inflict a blemish on his neighbor, as he has done to him, so shall it be done to him in return; 20 bruise for bruise, eye for eye, tooth for tooth; as any one may inflict a blemish on a man, so shall it be rendered to him. 21 Whoever shall strike a man, and he shall die, let him die the death. 22 There shall be one judgment for the stranger and the native, for I *am* the Lord your God. 23 And Moses spoke to the sons of Israel, and they brought him that had cursed outside of the camp, and stoned him with stones; and the sons of Israel did as the Lord commanded Moses.

Chapter 25

And the Lord spoke to Moses on the mountain *of* Sinai, saying, 2 Speak to the sons of Israel, and thou shall say to them, Whenever ye shall have entered into the land that I give to you, then the land shall rest which I give to you, for its Sabbaths to the Lord. 3 Six years thou shall sow thy field, and six years thou shall prune thy vine, and gather in its fruit. 4 But in the seventh year a Sabbath, it shall be a rest to the land, a Sabbath to the Lord; thou shall not sow thy field, and thou shall not prune thy vine. 5 And thou shall not gather the spontaneous produce of thy field, and thou shall not gather fully the grapes of thy dedication; it shall be a year of rest to the land. 6 And the Sabbaths of the land shall be food for thee, and for thy male slave, and for thy female slave, and thy hireling, and the stranger that abides with thee. 7 And for thy cattle, and for the wild beats that are in thy land, shall every fruit of it be for food.

8 And thou shall reckon to thyself seven Sabbaths of years, seven times seven years; and they shall be to thee seven weeks of years, nine and forty years. 9 In the seventh month, on the tenth day of the month, ye shall make a proclamation with the sound of a trumpet in all your land; on the Day of Atonement ye shall make a proclamation with a trumpet in all your land. 10 And ye shall sanctify the year, the fiftieth year, and ye shall proclaim a release upon the land to all that inhabit it; it shall be given a year of release, an indication for you; and each one shall depart to his possession, and ye shall go each to his family. 11 This is a jubilee of release, the year shall be to you the fiftieth year: ye shall not sow, nor reap the produce that comes of itself from the land; neither shall ye gather its dedicated fruits. 12 For it is an indication of release it shall be holy to you, ye shall eat its fruits off the fields.

Leviticus 25

13 In the year of the release, *in* the indication of it shall one return to his possession. 14 And if thou should sell a sold *item* to thy neighbor, or if thou should buy of thy neighbor, let not a man oppress his neighbor. 15 According to the number of years after the indication shall thou buy of thy neighbor; according to the number of years of the fruits shall he sell to thee. 16 According as a greater number of years he shall increase his possession, and according as a less number of years he shall lessen his possession; for according to the number of his crops, so shall he sell to thee. 17 Let not a man oppress his neighbor, and thou shall fear the Lord thy God; I am the Lord thy God.

18 And ye shall keep all My ordinances, and all My judgments; and do ye observe them, and ye shall keep them, and live securely in the land. 19 And the land shall yield her increase, and ye shall eat to fullness, and shall live securely in it. 20 And if ye should say, What shall we eat in this seventh year, if we do not sow nor gather in our fruits? 21 Then will I send My blessing upon you in the sixth year, and the land shall produce its fruits for three years. 22 And ye shall sow in the eighth year, and eat old fruits till the ninth year; until its fruit come, ye shall eat old fruits of the old. 23 And the land shall not be sold for permanence for the land is Mine, because ye are strangers and travelers before Me. 24 And in every land of your possession, ye shall pay ransoms for the land.

25 And if thy brother who is with thee be poor, and should have sold of his possession, and his kinsman who is near to him come, *and* then he shall redeem the possession which his brother has sold. 26 And if one have no near kinsman, and he *shall* prosper with his hand, and he find sufficient money, his ransom; 27 then shall he calculate the years of his sale, and he shall give what is over to the man to whom he sold it, and he shall return to his possession. 28 But if his hand has not prospered sufficiently, so as that he should restore the money to him, then he that bought the possessions shall have them till the sixth year of the release; and it shall go out in the release, and the owner shall return to his possession.

29 And if any one should sell an inhabited house in a walled city, then there shall be the ransom of it, until *the time* is fulfilled; its time of ransom shall be a full year. 30 And if it be not ransomed until there be completed of it a full year, the house which is in the walled city shall be surely confirmed to him that bought it, throughout his generations; and it shall not go out in the release. 31 But the houses in the villages that have not a wall around them shall be reckoned to the fields of the country; they shall always be redeemable, and they shall go out in the release. 32 And the cities of the Levites, the houses of the cities in their possession, shall be always redeemable to the Levites. 33 And if any one shall redeem a house of the Levites, then shall their sale of the houses of their possession go out in the release because the houses of the cities of the Levites are their possession in the midst of the sons of Israel.

Leviticus 25

34 And the lands set apart for their cities shall not be sold, because this is their perpetual possession. 35 And if thy brother who is with thee becomes poor and he become powerless in the hands with thee, thou shall help him as a stranger and a traveler, and thy brother shall live with thee. 36 Thou shall not receive from him interest, or increase; and thou shall fear thy God; I *am* the Lord; and thy brother shall live with thee. 37 Thou shall not lend thy money to him at interest, and thou shall not lend thy foods to him to be returned with interest. 38 I the Lord your God, who brought you out of the land of Egypt, to give you the land of Canaan, so as to be your God. 39 And if thy brother by thee be lowered, and be sold to thee, he shall not serve thee with the servitude of a slave. 40 He shall be with thee as a hireling or a traveler, he shall work for thee till the year of release; 41 and he shall go out in the release and his children with him; and he shall go to his family, he shall hasten back to his patrimony. 42 Because these are My servants, whom I brought out of the land of Egypt such a one, shall not be sold as a slave. 43 Thou shall not violently strain him with labor, and shall fear the Lord thy God. 44 And whatever number of male slaves and female slaves thou shall have, thou shall purchase male and female servants from the nations that are round about thee. 45 And of the sons of the travelers that are among you, of these ye shall buy and of their relations, all that shall be in your lands; let them be to you for a possession. 46 And ye shall distribute them to your children after you, and they shall be to you *as* permanent possessions forever; but of your brothers, the sons of Israel, one shall not oppress his brother in labors.

47 And if the hand of a stranger or traveler with thee find wealth, and thy brother in distress be sold to the stranger or the traveler that is with thee, or to a proselyte by extraction; 48 after he is sold to him there shall be redemption for him; one of his brothers shall redeem him. 49 A brother of his father, or a son of his father's brother shall redeem him; or let one of his near kin of his tribe redeem him, and if he should be rich and redeem himself, 50 then shall he calculate with his purchaser from the year that he sold himself to him until the year of release: and the money of his purchase shall be as that of a hireling, he shall be with him from year to year. 51 And if any have a greater number of years, according to these he shall pay his ransom out of his purchase money. 52 And if but a little time be left of the years to the year of release, then shall he reckon to him according to his years, and shall pay his ransom 53 as a hireling; he shall be with him from year to year; thou shall not violently oppress him with labor before thee. 54 And if he does not pay his ransom accordingly, he shall go out in the year of his release, he and his children with him. 55 For the sons of Israel are My servants; they are My attendants, whom I brought out of the land of Egypt. I *am* the Lord your God.

Chapter 26

Ye shall not make to yourselves gods made with hands, or graven; neither shall ye rear up a pillar for yourselves, neither shall ye set up a stone *as* an object in your land to worship it; I am the Lord your God. 2 Ye shall keep my Sabbaths, and reverence my sanctuaries: I am the Lord.

* 3 If ye will walk in my ordinances, and keep my commandments, and do them, 4 then will I give you the rain in its season, and the land shall produce its fruits, and the trees of the field shall yield their fruit. 5 And your threshing time shall overtake the vintage, and your vintage shall overtake your seedtime; and ye shall eat your bread to the full; and ye shall live safely upon your land, and war shall not go through your land. 6 And I will give peace in your land, and ye shall sleep, and none *shall* make you afraid; and I will destroy the evil beasts out of your land, 7 and ye shall pursue your enemies, and they shall fall before you with slaughter. 8 And five of you shall chase a hundred, and a hundred of you shall chase tens of thousands; and your enemies shall fall before you by the sword. 9 And I will look upon you, and increase you, and multiply you, and establish My covenant with you. 10 And ye shall eat that which is old and very old, and bring forth the old from the face of the new. 11 And I will set My tabernacle among you, and My soul shall not abhor you. 12 And I will walk among you, and be your God, and ye shall be My people. 13 I am the Lord your God, who brought you out of the land of Egypt, where ye were slaves; and I broke the band of your yoke, and brought you forth openly.

* 14 But if ye will not hearken to Me, nor obey these My ordinances, 15 but disobey them, and your soul should loathe My judgments, so that ye should not keep all My commands, so as to break My covenant, 16 then will I do thus to you; I will even bring upon you distress and the scab, and the fever that causes your eyes to waste away, and that consumes your life; and ye shall sow your seeds in vain, and your enemies shall eat them. 17 And I will set my face against you, and ye shall fall before your enemies, and they that hate you shall pursue you; and ye shall flee, *with* no one pursuing you. 18 And if ye still will not to hearken to me, then will I chasten you yet more even seven times for your sins. * 19 And I will break down the haughtiness of your pride; and I will make your heaven iron, and your earth, as it was brass. 20 And your strength shall be in vain; and your land shall not yield its seed, and the trees of your field shall not yield its fruit. 21 And if after this ye should walk perversely, and not be willing to obey me, I will further bring upon you seven plagues according to your sins. * 22 And I will send upon you the wild beasts of the land, and they shall devour you, and shall consume your cattle; and I will make you few in number, and your ways shall be desolate.

Leviticus 26

* 23 And if hereupon ye are not corrected, but walk perversely towards me, 24 I also will walk with you with a perverse anger, and I also will strike you seven times for your sins. 25 And I will bring upon you a sword avenging the cause of *my* covenant, and ye shall flee for refuge to your cities; and I will send out death against you, and ye shall be delivered into the hands of your enemies. 26 When I afflict you with famine of bread, then ten women shall bake your loaves in one oven, and they shall render your loaves by weight; and ye shall eat, and not be satisfied.

27 And if hereupon ye will not obey me, but walk perversely towards me, 28 then will I walk with you with a forward mind, and I will chasten you sevenfold according to your sins. 29 And ye shall eat the flesh of your sons, and the flesh of your daughters shall ye eat. 30 And I will render your pillars desolate, and will utterly destroy your wood made with hands; and I will lay your carcasses on the carcasses of your idols, and my soul shall loathe you. 31 And I will lay your cities waste, and I will make your sanctuaries desolate, and I will not smell the savor of your sacrifices. 32 And I will lay your land desolate, and your enemies who live in it shall wonder at it.

* 33 And I will scatter you among the nations, and the sword shall come upon you and consume you; and your land shall be a desert, and your cities shall be a desert.

34 Then the land shall enjoy its Sabbaths all the days of its desolation. 35 And ye shall be in the land of your enemies; then the land shall keep its Sabbaths, and the land shall enjoy its Sabbaths all the days of its desolation; it shall keep Sabbaths that it kept not among your Sabbaths, when ye lived in it. 36 And to those who are left of you I will bring slavery into their heart in the land of their enemies; and the sound of a shaken leaf shall chase them, and they shall flee as fleeing from war, and shall fall when none pursues them. 37 And brother shall disregard brother as in war, when none pursues; and ye shall not be able to withstand your enemies. 38 And ye shall perish among the Gentiles, and the land of your enemies shall devour you. 39 And those who are left of you shall perish, because of their sins, and because of the sins of their fathers; in the land of their enemies shall they consume away.

40 And they shall confess their sins, and the sins of their fathers, that they have transgressed and neglected me, and that they have walked perversely before me, 41 and I walked with them with a perverse mind; and I will destroy them in the land of their enemies: then shall their uncircumcised heart be ashamed, and then shall they acquiesce in their sins. 42 And I will remember the covenant of Jacob, and the covenant of Isaac, and the covenant of Abraham will I remember.

Leviticus 26

43 And I will remember the land, and the land shall be left of them; then the land shall enjoy her Sabbaths, when it is deserted through them; and they shall accept their iniquities, because they neglected my judgments, and in their soul loathed my ordinances. 44 And yet not even thus, while they were in the land of their enemies, did I overlook them, neither did I loathe them so as to consume them, to break My covenant made with them; for I am the Lord their God. 45 And I will remember their former covenant, when I brought them out of the land of Egypt, out of the house of slavery before the nation, to be their God; I am the Lord.

46 These are My judgments and My ordinances, and the law, which the Lord gave between Himself and the sons of Israel, on the Mountain *of* Sinai, by the hand of Moses.

* The September vesper reading of Chapter Twenty-Six verses three through twelve, fourteen through seventeen, nineteen through twenty, twenty-two, thirty-three and twenty-three through twenty-five as found in the *Greek Menaion* and the *Prophetologion* is somewhat different as it is found in the biblical text as published by the Apostoliki Diakonia and the Zoe Brotherhood, and it reads as follows:

"The Lord spoke to the sons of Israel saying, If ye will walk in My ordinances, and keep My commandments, and do them, then will I give you the rain in its season, and the land shall produce its fruits, and the trees of the field shall yield their fruit. And your threshing time shall overtake the vintage, and your vintage shall overtake your seedtime; and ye shall eat your bread to the full; and ye shall live safely upon your land; and none *shall* make you afraid; and I will destroy the evil beasts out of your land, and war shall not pass through your land, and your enemies shall fall before you. Five of you shall chase a hundred, and a hundred of you shall chase tens of thousands. And I will look upon you, and bless you and increase you, and multiply you, and establish My covenant with you. And ye shall eat that which is old and very old, and bring forth the old from the face of the new. And My soul shall not abhor you. And I will walk among you, and be your God, and ye shall be My people. But if ye will not hearken to Me, nor obey these My ordinances, but disobey them, and your soul should loathe My judgments, so that ye should not keep all My commands, then will I do thus to you; I will even bring upon you distress, and ye shall sow your seeds in vain, and your enemies shall eat them. And I will set My face against you, and ye shall fall before your enemies, and they shall pursue you; and ye shall flee, *with* no one pursuing you; and I will break down the haughtiness of your pride; and I will make your heaven iron, and your earth, as it was brass. And your strength shall be in vain; and your land shall not yield its seed, and the trees of your field shall not yield its fruit. And I will send upon you the wild beasts of the land, and they shall consume your cattle, and the sword shall come upon you and make you few in number. And your land shall be a desert, and your farms shall be a desert; because you have walked perversely towards Me, I also will walk with you with a perverse anger, says the Lord God, the Holy One of Israel."

Chapter 27

And the Lord spoke to Moses, saying, 2 Speak to the sons of Israel, and thou shall say to them, Whoever shall vow a vow as the valuation of his soul for the Lord, 3 the valuation of a male from twenty years old to sixty years old shall be his valuation shall be fifty didrachms of silver by the holy standards of the sanctuary. 4 And the valuation of a female shall be thirty didrachms. 5 And if it be from five years old to twenty, the valuation of a male shall be twenty didrachms, and of a female ten didrachms. 6 And from a month old to five years old, the valuation of a male shall be five didrachms, and of a female, three didrachms of silver. 7 And if from sixty years and upward, if it be a male, his valuation shall be fifteen didrachms of silver, and if a female, *then* ten didrachms. 8 And if the man is too poor for the valuation, he shall stand before the priest; and the priest shall value him: according to what the man who has vowed can afford, the priest shall value him.

9 And if it were from the cattle that are offered as a gift to the Lord, whoever shall offer one of these to the Lord, it shall be holy. 10 He shall not change it, a good for a bad, or a bad for a good; and if he do at all change it, a beast for a beast, it and the substitute shall be holy. 11 And if it were any unclean beast, of which none are offered as a gift to the Lord, he shall set the beast before the priest. 12 And the priest shall make a valuation between the good and the bad, and accordingly as the priest shall value it, so shall it stand. 13 And if will at all redeem it, he shall add the fifth part to its value.

14 And whatever man shall consecrate his house as holy to the Lord, the priest shall make a valuation of it between the good and the bad; as the priest shall value it, so shall it stand. 15 And if he that has sanctified it should redeem his house, he shall add to it the fifth part of the money of the valuation, and it shall be his.

16 And if a man should hallow to the Lord a part of the field of his possession, then the valuation shall be according to its seed, fifty didrachms of silver for a homer of barley. 17 And if he should sanctify his field from the year of release, it shall stand according to his valuation. 18 And if he should sanctify his field in the latter time after the release, the priest shall reckon to him the money for the remaining years, until the year of release, and it shall be deducted as an equivalent from his full valuation. 19 And if he that sanctified the field would redeem it, he shall add to its value the fifth part of the money, and it shall be his. 20 And if he do not redeem the field, but should sell the field to another man, he shall not after redeem it. 21 But the field shall be holy to the Lord after the release, as separated land; the priest shall have possession of it.

Leviticus 27

22 And if he should consecrate to the Lord of a field, which he has bought, which is not of the field of his possession, 23 the priest shall reckon to him the full valuation from the year of release, and he shall pay the valuation in that day *as* holy to the Lord. 24 And in the year of release the land shall be restored to the man of whom the other bought it, to who the possession of the land was. 25 And every valuation shall be by holy weights; the didrachm shall be twenty oboli.

26 And every first-born which shall be produced among thy cattle shall be the Lord's, and no man shall sanctify it; whether calf or sheep, it is the Lord's. 27 But if he should exchange an unclean beast, according to its valuation, then he shall add the fifth part to it, and it shall be his; and if he redeems it not, it shall be sold according to its valuation.

28 And every dedicated thing which a man shall dedicate to the Lord of all that he has, whether man or beast, or of the field of his possession, he shall not sell it, nor redeem it; every devoted thing shall be most holy to the Lord. 29 And whatever shall be dedicated of men, shall not be ransomed, but shall surely die the death.

30 Every tithe of the land, both of the seed of the land, and of the fruit of trees, is the Lord's, holy to the Lord. 31 And if a man should at all redeem his tithe, he shall add the fifth part to it, and it shall be his. 32 And every tithe of oxen, and of sheep, and whatever may come in numbering under the rod, the tenth shall be holy to the Lord. 33 Thou shall not change a good for a bad, or a bad for a good; and if thou should at all change it its equivalent also shall be holy, it shall not be redeemed. 34 These are the commandments which the Lord commanded Moses for the sons of Israel on *the* Mountain *of* Sinai.

The Book of
Numbers

Chapter 1

And the Lord spoke to Moses in the wilderness of Sinai, in the tabernacle of witness, on the first day of the second month, in the second year of their departure from the land of Egypt, saying, 2 Take the sum of all the congregation of Israel according to their kindred, according to their fathers' houses, according to their number by their names, according to their heads; every male 3 from twenty years old and upward, every one that goes forth in the force of Israel, take account of them with their strength; thou and Aaron take account of them. 4 And with you there shall be each one of the rulers according to the tribe of each; they shall be according to the houses of their fathers'. 5 And these are the names of the men who shall be present with you; of the tribe of Ruben, Elisur the son of Sediur. 6 Of Simon, Salamiel the son of Surisadai. 7 Of Judah, Naasson the son of Aminadab. 8 Of Issahar, Nathaniel the son of Sogar. 9 Of Zabulon, Eliab the son of Haelon. 10 Of the sons of Joseph, of Ephraim, Elisama the son of Emiud; have Manasse, Gamaliel the son of Phadasur. 11 Of Benjamin, Abidan the son of Gadeoni. 12 Of Dan, Ahiezer the son of Amisadai. 13 Of Aser, Phagaiel the son of Ehran. 14 Of Gad, Elisaph the son of Raguel. 15 Of Nephthali, Ahire the son of Aenan. 16 These were famous men of the congregation, rulers of the tribes according to their paternal lineage; these are leaders of thousands in Israel.

17 And Moses and Aaron took these men who were called by name. 18 And they assembled the entire congregation on the first day of the month in the second year; and they registered them after their birth, after their paternal lineage, after the number of their names, from twenty years old and upwards, every male according to their head; 19 as the Lord commanded Moses, so they were numbered in the wilderness of Sinai.

20 And the sons of Ruben the firstborn of Israel according to their kindred, according to their divisions, according to their fathers' houses, according to the number of their names, according to their head, were all males from twenty years old and upward, every one that went out with the force 21 the numbering of them of the tribe of Ruben, was forty-six thousand and four hundred.

22 For the sons of Simon according to their kindred, according to their divisions, according to their fathers' houses, according to the number of their names, according to their head, all males from twenty years old and upward, every one that goes out with the force, 23 the numbering of them of the tribe of Simon, was fifty-nine thousand and three hundred.

Numbers 1

24 For the sons of Judah according to their kindred, according to their divisions, according to their fathers' houses, according to the number of their names, according to their head, all males from twenty years old and upward, every one that goes forth with the host, 25 the numbering of them of the tribe of Judah, was seventy-four thousand and six hundred.

26 For the sons of Issahar according to their kindred, according to their divisions, according to their fathers' houses, according to the number of their names, according to their head, all males from twenty years old and upward, every one that goes forth with the force, 27 the numbering of them of the tribe of Issahar, was fifty-four thousand and four hundred.

28 For the sons of Zabulon according to their kindred, according to their divisions, according to their fathers' houses, according to the number of their names, according to their head, all males from twenty years old and upward, every one that goes out with the force, 29 the numbering of them of the tribe of Zabulon, was fifty-seven thousand and * four hundred.

30 For the sons of Joseph, the sons of Ephraim, according to their kindred, according to their divisions, according to their fathers' houses, according to the number of their names, according to their head, all males from twenty years old and upward, every one that goes out with the force, 31 the numbering of them of the tribe of Ephraim, was forty thousand and five hundred.

32 For the sons of Manasse according to their kindred, according to their divisions, according to their fathers' houses, according to the number of their names, according to their head, all males from twenty years old and upward, every one that goes out with the force, 33 the numbering of them of the tribe of Manasse, was thirty-two thousand and two hundred.

34 For the sons of Benjamin according to their kindred, according to their divisions, according to their fathers' houses, according to the number of their names, according to their head, every male from twenty years old and upward, every one that goes forth with the force, 35 the numbering of them of the tribe of Benjamin, was thirty-five thousand and four hundred.

36 For the sons of Gad according to their kindred, according to their divisions, according to their fathers' houses, according to the number of their names, according to their head, all males from twenty years old and upward, every one that goes forth with the force, 37 the numbering of them of the tribe of Gad, was forty and five thousand and six hundred and fifty.

38 For the sons of Dan according to their kindred, according to their divisions, according to their fathers' houses, according to the number of their names, according to their head, all males from twenty years old and upward, every one that goes forth with the force, 39 the numbering of them of the tribe of Dan, was sixty and two thousand and seven hundred.

40 For the sons of Aser according to their kindred, according to their divisions, according to their fathers' houses, according to the number of their names, according to their head, every male from twenty years old and upward, every one that goes forth with the force, 41 the numbering of them of the tribe of Aser, was forty and one thousand and five hundred.

42 For the sons of Nephthali according to their kindred, according to their divisions, according to their fathers' houses of their families, according to the number of their names, according to their head, every male from twenty years old and upward, every one who goes forth with the force, 43 the numbering of them of the tribe of Nephthali, was fifty-three thousand and four hundred.

44 This is the numbering which Moses and Aaron and the rulers of Israel, being twelve men, conducted; there was one man for each tribe, they were according to the tribe of their fathers' houses. 45 And the whole numbering of the sons of Israel with their force from twenty years old and upward, every one that goes out to do battle in Israel, came to 46 six hundred thousand and three thousand and five hundred and fifty.

47 But the Levites from their fathers' tribe were not counted among the sons of Israel. 48 And the Lord spoke to Moses, saying, 49 See, thou shall not consider the tribe of Levi, and thou shall not take their numbers, in the midst of the sons of Israel. 50 And do thou set the Levites over the Tabernacle of Witness, and over all its items, and over all as many *that are* in it; and they shall perform *the* liturgy in it, and they shall encamp around the tabernacle. 51 And in removing the tabernacle, the Levites shall take it down, and in pitching the tabernacle they shall set it up; and let the stranger that advances die. 52 And the sons of Israel shall encamp, every man in his own order, and every man according to his own rank, with their force. 53 But let the Levites encamp opposite, around the Tabernacle of Witness, and there shall be no sin among the sons of Israel; and the Levites themselves shall keep the guard of the Tabernacle of Witness. 54 And the sons of Israel did according to all that the Lord commanded Moses and Aaron so they did.

* *Codex Alexandrinus* reads: "five hundred".

Chapter 2

And the Lord spoke to Moses and Aaron, saying, 2 Let the sons of Israel encamp, every man keeping his own rank, according to standards, according to their paternal houses; opposite around the Tabernacle of Witness. 3 And they that encamp first toward the east *shall be* the order of the camp of Judah with their force, and the rulers of the sons of Judah, Naasson the son of Aminadab. 4 His forces that were numbered were seventy-four thousand and six hundred.

Numbers 2

5 And they that encamp next of the tribe of Issahar, and the ruler of the sons of Issahar, Nathaniel the son of Sogar. 6 His forces that were numbered were fifty-four thousand and four hundred. 7 And they that encamp next of the tribe of Zabulon, and the ruler of the sons of Zabulon Eliab the son of Haelon. 8 His forces that were numbered were fifty-seven thousand and four hundred. 9 All that were numbered of the camp of Judah were a hundred and eighty thousand and six thousand and four hundred; they shall move first with their forces.

10 The order of the camp of Ruben; their forces toward the south, and the rulers of the sons of Ruben Elisur the son of Sediur. 11 His forces that were numbered were forty-six thousand and five hundred. 12 And they that encamp next to him of the tribe of Simon, and the rulers of the sons of Simon Salamiel the son of Surisadai. 13 His forces that were numbered were fifty-nine thousand and three hundred. 14 And they that encamp next to them the tribe of Gad; and the rulers of the sons of Gad, Elisaph the son of Raguel. 15 His forces that were numbered were forty-five thousand and six hundred and fifty. 16 All who were numbered of the camp of Ruben were a hundred and fifty-one thousand and four hundred and fifty; they with their forces shall proceed in the second place.

17 And the Tabernacle of Witness shall be set forward, and the camp of the Levites between the camps; as they shall encamp, so also shall they commence their march, each one next in order to his fellow according to their companies.

18 The station of the camp of Ephraim *shall be* by the sea with their forces, and the rulers of the sons of Ephraim Elisama the son of Emiud. 19 His forces that were numbered are forty thousand and five hundred. 20 And they that encamp next of the tribe of Manasse, and the ruler of the sons of Manasse, Gamaliel the son of Phadassur. 21 His forces that were numbered were thirty-two thousand and two hundred. 22 And they that encamp next of the tribe of Benjamin, and the ruler of the sons of Benjamin, Abidan the son of Gideon. 23 His forces that were numbered were thirty-five thousand and four hundred. 24 All that were numbered of the camp of Ephraim were one hundred and eight thousand and one hundred; they with their forces shall set out third.

25 The order of the camp of Dan to the north with their forces; and the rulers of the sons of Dan, Ahiezer the son of Amisadai. 26 His forces that were numbered were sixty-two thousand and seven hundred. 27 And they that encamp next to him the tribe of Aser; and the ruler of the sons of Aser, Phagiel the son of Ehran. 28 His forces that were numbered were forty-one thousand and five hundred. 29 And they that encamp next of the tribe of Nephthali; and the ruler of the sons of Nephthali, Ahire son Aenan. 30 His forces that were numbered were fifty-three thousand and four hundred.

31 All that were numbered of the camp of Dan, a hundred and fifty-seven thousand and six hundred; they shall set out last according to their order.

32 This *is* the numbering of the sons of Israel according to their fathers' houses; all the numbering of the camps with their forces *was* six hundred and three thousand, five hundred and fifty. 33 But the Levites were not numbered with them, as the Lord commanded Moses.

34 And the sons of Israel did all things that the Lord commanded Moses; thus they encamped in their order, and thus they began their march in succession each according to their divisions, according to their fathers' houses.

Chapter 3

And these *are* the generations of Aaron and Moses, in the day in which the Lord spoke to Moses on Mount Sinai. 2 And these *are* the names of the sons of Aaron; Nadab the firstborn; and Abiud, Eleazar and Ithamar. 3 These *are* the names of the sons of Aaron, the anointed priests whose hands they confirmed to serve in the priesthood. 4 And Nadab and Abiud died before the Lord, when they offered strange fire before the Lord, in the wilderness of Sinai; and they had no children; and Eleazar and Ithamar served in the priesthood with Aaron their father.

5 And the Lord spoke to Moses, saying, 6 Take the tribe of Levi, and thou shall set them before Aaron the priest, and they shall minister to him, 7 and shall keep his charges, and the charges of the sons of Israel, before the Tabernacle of Witness, to do the works of the tabernacle. 8 And they shall keep all the items of the Tabernacle of Witness, and the charges of the son of Israel as to all the works of the tabernacle. 9 And thou shall give the Levites to Aaron, and to his sons the priests; they are given for a gift to me of the sons of Israel. 10 And thou shall appoint Aaron and his sons over the Tabernacle of Witness; and they shall keep their charge of priesthood, and all things belonging to the altar, and within the veil; and the stranger that touches them shall die.

11 And the Lord spoke to Moses, saying, 12 Behold, I have taken the Levites from the midst of the sons of Israel, instead of every male that opens the womb from among the sons of Israel; they shall be their ransom, and the Levites shall be Mine. 13 For every firstborn *are* Mine; in the day in which I killed every firstborn in the land of Egypt, I sanctified to Myself every firstborn in Israel; both of man and beast, they shall be Mine; I *am* the Lord.

14 And the Lord spoke to Moses in the wilderness of Sinai, saying, 15 Take the number of the sons of Levi, according to their fathers' houses, according to their people; number ye them every male from a month old and upwards.

Numbers 3

16 And Moses and Aaron numbered them by the voice of the Lord, as the Lord commanded them. 17 And these were the sons of Levi by their names, Gedson, Kaath, and Merari. 18 And these *are* the names of the sons of Gedson according to their people; Lobeni and Semei: 19 and the sons of Kaath according to their people; Amram and Issaar, Hebron and Oziel: 20 and the sons of Merari according to their people, Mooli and Musi; these are the people of the Levites according to their fathers' houses.

21 To Gedson belong the people of Lobeni, and the people of Semei; these are the people of Gedson. 22 The numbering of them according to the number of every male from a month old and upward, their numbering seven thousand and five hundred. 23 And the sons of Gedson shall encamp to the west behind the tabernacle. 24 And the ruler of *their* fathers' houses of the people of Gedson Elisaph the son of Dael. 25 And the charge of the sons of Gedson in the Tabernacle of Witness the tent and the veil, and the covering of the door of the Tabernacle of Witness, 26 and the curtains of the court, and the veil of the door of the court, which is by the tabernacle, and the remainder of its entire works.

27 To Kaath *belongs* one people, that of Amram, and another people, that of Issaar, and another people, that of Hebron, and another people, that of Oziel, these are the people of Kaath, according to number. 28 Every male from a month old and upward, eight thousand and six hundred, keeping the charges of the holy things. 29 The people of the sons of Kaath, shall encamp beside the tabernacle toward the south. 30 And the ruler of *their* fathers' houses of the people of Kaath, Elisaphan the son of Oziel. 31 And their charge is: the ark, and the table, and the candlestick, and the altars, and all the items of the holy *sanctuary* wherewith they perform *the* holy liturgy, and the veil, and all their works. 32 And the ruler over the ruler of the Levites, Eleazar the son of Aaron the priest, appointed to keep the charges of the holy things.

33 To Merari the people of Mooli, and the people of Musi, these are the people of Merari. 34 The mustering of them according to number, every male from a month old and upward, six thousand and fifty. 35 And the rulers of their fathers' houses of the people of Merari were Suriel the son of Abihail; they shall encamp by the side of the tabernacle to the north. 36 The oversight of the charge of the sons of Merari *was* the tops of the tabernacle, and its bars, and its pillars, and its sockets, and all their items, and their works, 37 and the pillars of the court around, and their bases, and their pins, and their cords.

38 They that encamp before the face of the Tabernacle of Witness on the east *shall be* Moses and Aaron and his sons, keeping the charges of the holy *sanctuary* according to the charges of the sons of Israel, and the stranger that touches them, shall die. 39 All the numbering of the Levites, whom Moses and Aaron numbered by the voice of the Lord, according to their people, every male from a month old and upward, two and twenty thousand.

40 And the Lord spoke to Moses, saying, Count every firstborn male of the sons of Israel from a month old and upward, and take the number by name. 41 And thou shall take the Levites for me I *am* the Lord instead of all the firstborn of the sons of Israel, and the cattle of the Levites instead of all the firstborn among the cattle of the sons of Israel. 42 And Moses counted, as the Lord commanded him, every firstborn among the sons of Israel. 43 And all the male firstborn in number by name, from a month old and upward, were according to their numbering twenty-two thousand and two hundred and seventy-three.

44 And the Lord spoke to Moses, saying, 45 Take the Levites instead of all the firstborn of the sons of Israel, and the cattle of the Levites instead of their cattle, and the Levites shall be Mine; I *am* the Lord. 46 And for the ransoms of the two hundred and seventy-three, which exceed the Levites in number of the firstborn of the sons of Israel; 47 thou shall even take five shekels a head; thou shall take them according to the holy didrachm, twenty oboli to the shekel. 48 And thou shall give the money to Aaron and to his sons, the ransom of those who exceed in number among them. 49 And Moses took the silver, the ransom of those that exceeded in number the redemption of the Levites. 50 He took the silver from the firstborn of the sons of Israel, a thousand three hundred and sixty-five shekels, according to the holy shekel. 51 And Moses gave the ransom of them that were over to Aaron and his sons, by the voice of the Lord, as the Lord commanded Moses.

Chapter 4

And the Lord spoke to Moses and Aaron, saying, 2 Take *a full count of the* heads of the sons of Kaath from the midst of the sons of Levi, after their people, according to their fathers' houses; 3 from twenty-five years old and upward until fifty years, every one that goes in to perform the official duties, to do all the works in the Tabernacle of Witness. 4 And these are the works of the sons of Kaath in the Tabernacle of Witness; it is the holy of holies.

5 And Aaron and his sons shall go in, when the camp is about to move, and shall take down the shadowing veil, and shall cover with it the Ark of the Testimony. 6 And they shall put on it a cover, even a blue skin, and put on it above a garment all of blue, and shall put the staves through. 7 And they shall put on the table set forth for showbread a cloth all of purple, and the dishes, and the censers, and the cups, and the vessels with which one offers drink offerings; and the continual loaves shall be upon it. 8 And they shall put upon it a red cloth, and they shall cover it with a blue covering of skin, and they shall put the staves into it.

Numbers 4

9 And they shall take a blue covering, and cover the candlestick that gives light, and its lamps, and its snuffers, and its funnels, and all the vessels of oil with which they *shall use to perform the* liturgy. 10 And they shall put it, and all its items, into a blue skin cover; and they shall put it on bearers. 11 And they shall put a blue cloth for a cover on the golden altar, and shall cover it with a blue skin cover, and put in its staves. 12 And they shall take all the items of the liturgy, with which they *use to perform the* liturgy in the holy *sanctuary*; and shall place them in a cloth of blue, and shall cover them with blue skin covering, and put them upon staves. 13 And he shall put the covering on the altar, and they shall cover it with a cloth all of purple. 14 And they shall put upon it all the items with which they perform the liturgy upon it, and the fire pans, and the flesh hooks, and the cups, and the cover, and all the items of the altar; and they shall put on it a blue cover of skins, and shall put in its staves; and they shall take a purple cloth, and cover the laver and its foot, and they shall put it into a blue cover of skin, and put it on bars. 15 And Aaron and his sons shall finish covering the holy *things*, and all the holy items, when the camp begins to move; and afterwards the sons of Kaath shall go in to take up; but shall not touch the holy *things*, lest they die; these shall the sons of Kaath bear in the Tabernacle of Witness.

16 Eleazar, the son of Aaron the priest, is the overseer of the oil of the light, and the incense of composition, and the daily meat offering and the anointing oil, are his charge; even the oversight of the whole tabernacle, and as many *things* that are in it in the holy *place*, in all the works.

17 And the Lord spoke to Moses and Aaron, saying, 18 Ye shall not destroy the tribe of the people of Kaath from out of the midst of the Levites. 19 This do ye to them, and they shall live and not die, when they approach the holy of holies; Let Aaron and his sons advance, and they shall place them each in his post for bearing. 20 And they shall by no means go in to look suddenly upon the holy things, and die.

21 And the Lord spoke to Moses, saying, 22 Take the rulers of the sons of Gedson, and these according to their fathers' houses, according to their people. 23 Take the number of them from five and twenty years old and upwards until the age of fifty, every one that goes in to perform his official duties, to do His work in the Tabernacle of Witness. 24 This *is* the public service of the people of Gedson, to do their official duties and to carry. 25 And they shall bear the skins of the tabernacle, and the Tabernacle of Witness, and its veil, and the blue cover that was on it above, and the cover of the door of the Tabernacle of Witness. 26 And all the curtains of the court, which were upon the Tabernacle of Witness, and the appendages, and all the items of the liturgy that they perform the liturgy with they shall attend to. 27 By the mouth of Aaron and his sons shall be the official duties of the sons of Gedson, in all their services, and in all their works; and thou shall take account of them by name in all things borne by them.

Numbers 4

28 These are the official duties of the sons of Gedson in the Tabernacle of Witness, and their charge by the hand of Ithamar the son of Aaron the priest.

29 The sons of Merari according to their people, according to their fathers' houses, take you the number of them. 30 Take the number of them from five and twenty years old and upwards until fifty years old, every one that enters to officiate the works of the Tabernacle of Witness. 31 And these are the charges of the things borne by them according to all their works in the Tabernacle of Witness; they shall bear the tops of the tabernacle, and the bars, and its pillars, and its sockets, and the veil, and their sockets, and their pillars, and the curtain of the door of the tabernacle. 32 And they shall bear the pillars of the court around, and their sockets, and the pillars of the veil of the door of the court, and their sockets and their pins, and their cords, and all their items, and all their liturgical instruments; take ye their number by name, and all the articles of the charge of the things borne by them. 33 These are the official duties of the people of the sons of Merari in all their works in the Tabernacle of Witness, by the hand of Ithamar the son of Aaron the priest.

34 And Moses and Aaron and the rulers of Israel took the number of the sons of Kaath according to their people, according to their fathers' houses; 35 from five and twenty years old and upwards to the age of fifty years, every one that enters to officiate the works in the Tabernacle of Witness. 36 And the numbering of them according to their families was two thousand, * seven hundred and fifty. 37 This is the numbering of the people of Kaath, every one that performs his official duties in the Tabernacle of Witness, as Moses and Aaron numbered them by the voice of the Lord, by the hand of Moses.

38 And the sons of Gedson were numbered according to their people, according to their fathers' houses, 39 from five and twenty years old and upward till fifty years old, every one that enters to officiate and to do the works in the Tabernacle of Witness. 40 And the numbering of them according to their people, according to their fathers' houses, *was* two thousand six hundred and thirty. 41 This *is* the numbering of the people of the sons of Gedson, every one who performs his official duties in the Tabernacle of Witness; whom Moses and Aaron numbered by the voice of the Lord, by the hand of Moses.

42 And also the people of the sons of Merari were numbered according to their people, according to their fathers' houses; 43 from five and twenty years old and upward till fifty years old, every one that enters to officiate in the works of the Tabernacle of Witness. 44 And the numbering of them according to their people, according to their fathers' houses, three thousand and two hundred. 45 This *is* the numbering of the people of the sons of Merari, whom Moses and Aaron numbered by the voice of the Lord, by the hand of Moses. 46 All that were numbered, whom Moses and Aaron and the rulers of Israel numbered, the Levites, according to their people and according to their fathers' houses,

Numbers 5

47 from five and twenty years old and upward till fifty years old, every one that enters to *do* the work of the works, and the work of the things that are carried in the tabernacle of witness. 48 And they that were numbered were eight thousand * five hundred and eighty. 49 He reviewed them by the voice of the Lord by the hand of Moses, appointing each man severally over their work, and over their burdens; and they were numbered, as the Lord commanded Moses.

* *Codex Alexandrinus* reads: "Three hundred and fifty."
* *Codex Alexandrinus* reads: "Four hundred and fifty."

Chapter 5

And the Lord spoke to Moses, saying, 2 Charge the sons of Israel, and let them send forth out of the camp every leper, and every one who has a discharge, and every one who is unclean from *touching* a *dead* soul. 3 Whether male or female, send them away outside of the encampment; and they shall not defile their camps in which I live among them. 4 And the sons of Israel did so, and sent them outside of the encampment; as the Lord said to Moses, so did the sons of Israel.

5 And the Lord spoke to Moses, saying, 6 Speak to the sons of Israel, saying, Every man or woman who shall commit any sin that is common to man, or if that soul shall in anywise have neglected the commandment and transgressed 7 Shall confess the sin which he has committed, and shall make satisfaction for his trespass; he *shall compensate* the principal, and shall add to it the fifth part, and shall make restoration to him against whom he has trespassed. 8 But if a man has no near kinsman, so as to make satisfaction for his trespass to him, the trespass offering paid to the Lord shall be for the priest, besides the ram of atonement, by which he shall make atonement with it for him. 9 And every first fruit in all the sanctified things among the sons of Israel, whatever they shall offer to the Lord, shall be for the priest himself. 10 And the sanctified things of every man shall be his; and whatever man shall give to the priest, the gift shall be his.

11 And the Lord spoke to Moses, saying, 12 Speak to the sons of Israel, and thou shall say to them, Whosever wife shall transgress against him, and slight and despise him, 13 and *if* any one shall sleep with her in a bed of semen, and the thing shall be hid from the eyes of her husband, and she should conceal it and be herself defiled, and there be no witness with her, and she should not be taken; 14 and there should come upon him a spirit of jealousy, and he should be jealous of his wife, and she be defiled; or there should come upon him a spirit of jealousy, and he should be jealous of his wife, and she should not be defiled;

15 then shall the man bring his wife to the priest, and shall bring his gift for her, the tenth part of an ephah of barley meal; he shall not pour oil upon it, neither shall he put frankincense upon it; for it is a sacrifice of jealousy, a sacrifice of memorial, recalling sin to remembrance.

16 And the priest shall bring her, and cause her to stand before the Lord. 17 And the priest shall take pure living water in an earthen vessel, and he shall take of the earth that is on the floor of the Tabernacle of Witness, and the priest having taken it shall cast it into the water. 18 And the priest shall cause the woman to stand before the Lord, and shall uncover the head of the woman, and shall put into her hands the sacrifice of memorial, the sacrifice of jealousy; and in the hand of the priest shall be the water of this rebuke *that brings* this curse. 19 And the priest shall adjure her, and shall say to the woman, If no one has slept with thee, and if thou has not transgressed so as to be defiled, being under the power of thy husband, be free from this water of rebuke *that causes* this curse. 20 But if being a married woman thou has transgressed, or been defiled, and any one has gone to bed with thee, beside thy husband; 21 then the priest shall adjure the woman by the oaths of this curse, and the priest shall say to the woman, The Lord bring thee into a curse and under an oath in the midst of thy people, in that the Lord should cause thy thigh to rot and thy stomach to swell; 22 and this water bringing the curse shall enter into thy womb to cause thy belly to swell, and thy thigh to rot. And the woman shall say, So be it, So be it.

23 And the priest shall write these curses in a book, and shall blot them out in the water of rebuke *that brings* this curse. 24 And he shall cause the woman to drink the water of rebuke *that brings* this curse; and the water of rebuke *that brings* this curse shall enter into her. 25 And the priest shall take from the hand of the woman the sacrifice of jealousy, and shall present the sacrifice before the Lord, and shall bring it to the altar. 26 And the priest shall take a handful of the sacrifice as a memorial of it, and shall offer it up upon the altar; and afterwards he shall cause the woman to drink the water. 27 And it shall come to pass, if she be defiled, and have altogether escaped the notice of her husband, then the water of rebuke *that brings* this curse shall enter into her; and she shall swell in her belly, and her thigh shall rot, and the woman shall be for a curse in the midst of her people. 28 But if the woman have not been defiled, and be clean, then shall she be guiltless and shall bring forth seed.

29 This is the law of jealousy, wherein a married woman should happen to transgress, and be defiled, 30 or in the case of a man on whomever the spirit of jealousy should come, and he should be jealous of his wife, and he should place his wife before the Lord, and the priest shall execute towards her all this law. 31 Then the man shall be clear from sin, and that woman shall bear her sin.

Chapter 6

And the Lord spoke to Moses, saying, 2 Speak to the sons of Israel, and thou shall say to them, Whatever man or woman shall specially vow a vow to separate oneself with purity to the Lord, 3 he shall purely abstain from wine and strong drink; and he shall drink no vinegar of wine or vinegar of strong drink; and whatever is made of the grape he shall not drink; neither shall he eat fresh grapes or raisins, 4 all the days of his vow: he shall eat not one of all the things that come from the vine, wine from pressed grapes to the grape stone,

5 all the days of his separation: a razor shall not come upon his head, until the days be fulfilled which he vowed to the Lord; he shall be holy, cherishing *the* lock of hair *on his* head, 6 all the days of his vow to the Lord; he shall not go near to any soul that has departed, 7 to his father or his mother, or to his brother or his sister; he shall not defile himself for them, when they have died, because the vow of God is upon him on his head. 8 All the days of his vow he shall be holy to the Lord. 9 And if any one should die suddenly by him, immediately the head of his vow shall be defiled; and he shall shave his head in whatever day he shall be purified; on the seventh day he shall be shaved. 10 And on the eighth day he shall bring two turtledoves, or two young pigeons, to the priest, to the doors of the tabernacle of witness. 11 And the priest shall offer one for a sin offering; and the other for a whole burnt offering; and the priest shall make atonement for him in the things wherein he sinned concerning the *touching of a dead* soul, and he shall sanctify his head in that day, 12 in which he was consecrated to the Lord, *all* the days of his vow; and he shall bring a lamb of a year old for a trespass offering; and the former days shall not be reckoned, because the head of his vow was polluted.

13 And this is the law of him that has vowed; in whatever day he shall have fulfilled the days of his vow; he shall himself bring his gift to the doors of the Tabernacle of Witness. 14 And he shall bring his gift to the Lord; one male lamb of a year old without blemish for a whole burnt offering, and one ewe-lamb of a year old without blemish for a sin offering, and one ram without blemish for a peace offering; 15 and a basket of unleavened bread of fine flour, loaves kneaded with oil, and unleavened cakes anointed with oil, and their meat offering, and their drink offering. 16 And the priest shall bring them before the Lord, and shall offer his sin offering, and his whole burnt offering. 17 And he shall offer the ram as a sacrifice of peace offering to the Lord with the basket of unleavened bread; and the priest shall offer its meat offering and its drink offering. 18 And he that has made the vow shall shave the head of his vow by the doors of the Tabernacle of Witness, and shall put the hairs on the fire, which is under the sacrifice of peace offering.

19 And the priest shall take the cooked shoulder of the ram, and one unleavened loaf from the basket, and one unleavened cake, and shall put them on the hands of the one making a vow, after he has shaved off his vow. 20 And the priest shall present them as an offering before the Lord; it shall be holy for the priest beside the breast of the heave offering and beside the shoulder of the wave offering; and afterwards the one making a vow shall drink wine.

21 This is the law of the one making a vow who shall have vowed to the Lord his gift to the Lord, concerning his vow, besides what he may be able to afford according to the value of his vow, which he may have vowed according to the law of separation.

22 And the Lord spoke to Moses, saying, 23 Speak to Aaron and to his sons, saying, Thus ye shall bless the sons of Israel, saying to them,

24 The Lord bless thee and keep thee; 25 the Lord make his face to shine upon thee, and have mercy upon thee; 26 the Lord lift up his face upon thee, and give thee peace.

27 And they shall put My name upon the sons of Israel, and I the Lord will bless them.

Chapter 7

And it came to pass in the day in which Moses finished the setting up of the tabernacle, that he anointed it, and consecrated it, and all its items, and the altar and all its items, he even anointed them, and consecrated them. 2 And the rulers of Israel brought *gifts*, twelve rulers of their fathers' houses: these were the rulers of tribes; these are they that presided over the numbering. 3 And they brought their gift before the Lord, six covered wagons, and twelve oxen; a wagon from two rulers, and a calf from each, and they brought them before the tabernacle. 4 And the Lord spoke to Moses, saying, 5 Take of them, and they shall be for the works of the liturgy of the Tabernacle of Witness; and thou shall give them to the Levites, to each one according to his official duties. 6 And Moses took the wagons and the oxen, and gave them to the Levites. 7 And he gave two wagons and four oxen to the sons of Gedson, according to their official duties. 8 And four wagons and eight oxen he gave to the sons of Merari according to their official duties, by Ithamar the son of Aaron the priest. 9 But to the sons of Kaath he gave them not, because they have the official duties *over* the holy things; they shall bear them on their shoulders. 10 And the rulers brought for the dedication of the altar, in the day in which he anointed it, and the rulers brought their gifts before the altar. 11 And the Lord said to Moses, One ruler each day, they shall offer their gifts *to* a ruler each day for the dedication of the altar.

Numbers 7

12 And he that offered his gift on the first day was Naasson the son of Aminadab, ruler of the tribe of Judah. 13 And he brought his gift, one silver charger of a hundred and thirty shekels was its weight, one silver bowl, of seventy shekels according to the holy shekel; both full of fine flour kneaded with oil for a meat offering. 14 One golden censer of ten golden *weights* full of incense. 15 One calf of the herd, one ram, one male lamb of a year old for a whole burnt offering; 16 and one kid of the goats for a sin offering. 17 And for a sacrifice of peace offering, two heifers, five rams, five he goats, five ewe-lambs of a year old; this gift of Naasson the son of Aminadab.

18 On the second day Nathaniel son of Sogar, the ruler of the tribe of Issahar, brought *an offering*. 19 And he brought his gift, one silver charger, its weight *being* a hundred and thirty, one silver bowl of seventy shekels according to the holy shekel; both full of fine flour kneaded with oil for a meat offering. 20 One censer of ten golden *weights*, full of incense. 21 One calf of the herd, one ram, one male lamb of a year old for a whole burnt offering, 22 and one kid of the goats for a sin offering. 23 And for a sacrifice, a peace offering, two heifers, five rams, five male goats, five ewe-lambs of a year old; this gift of Nathaniel the son of Sogar.

24 On the third day the ruler of the sons of Zabulon, Eliab the son of Haelon. 25 His gift, one silver charger, its weight was a hundred and thirty, one silver bowl of seventy shekels according to the holy shekel; both full of fine flour kneaded with oil for a meat offering. 26 One golden censer of ten *weights*, full of incense. 27 One calf of the herd, one ram, one male lamb of a year old for a whole burnt offering, 28 and one kid of the goats for a sin offering. 29 And for a sacrifice of peace offering, two heifers, five rams, five male goats, five ewe-lambs of a year old: this gift of Eliab the son of Haelon.

30 On the fourth day Elisur the son of Sediur, the ruler of the sons of Ruben. 31 His gift, one silver charger, its weight was a hundred and thirty, one silver bowl of seventy shekels according to the holy shekel; both full of fine flour kneaded with oil for a meat offering. 32 One golden censer of ten *weights*, full of incense. 33 One calf of the herd, one ram, one male lamb of a year old for a whole burnt offering, 34 and one kid of the goats for a sin offering. 35 And for a sacrifice of peace offering, two heifers, five rams, five male goats, five ewe-lambs of a year old; this the gift of Elisur the son of Seedier.

36 On the fifth day the ruler of the sons of Simon, Salamiel the son of Surisadai. 37 His gift, one silver charger, its weight was a hundred and thirty, one silver bowl of seventy shekels according to the holy shekel; both full of fine flour kneaded with oil for a meat offering. 38 One golden censer of ten shekels, full of incense. 39 One calf of the herd, one ram, one male lamb of a year old for a whole burnt offering, 40 and one kid of the goats for a sin offering.

41 And for a sacrifice of peace offering, two heifers, five rams, five male goats, five ewe-lambs of a year old; this gift of Salamiel the son of Surisadai.

42 On the sixth day the ruler of the sons of Gad, Elisaph the son of Raguel. 43 His gift, one silver charger, its weight was a hundred and thirty, one silver bowl of seventy shekels according to the holy shekel; both full of fine flour kneaded with oil for a meat offering. 44 One golden censer of ten *weights*, full of incense. 45 One calf of the herd, one ram, one male lamb of a year old for a whole burnt offering, 46 and one kid of the goats for a sin offering. 47 And for a sacrifice of peace offering, two heifers, five rams, five male goats, five ewe-lambs of a year old; this gift of Elisaph the son of Raguel.

48 On the seventh day the rulers of the sons of Ephraim, Elisama the son of Emiud. 49 His gift, one silver charger, its weight was a hundred and thirty, one silver bowl of seventy shekels according to the holy shekel; both full of fine flour kneaded with oil for a meat offering. 50 One golden censer of ten shekels, full of incense. 51 One calf of the herd, one ram, one male lamb of a year old for a whole burnt offering, 52 and one kid of the goats for a sin offering. 53 And for a sacrifice of peace offering, two heifers, five rams, five male goats, five ewe-lambs of a year old; this gift of Elisama the son of Emiud.

54 On the eighth day the ruler of the sons of Manasse, Gamaliel the son of Phadassur. 55 His gift, one silver charger, its weight was a hundred and thirty, one silver bowl of seventy shekels according to the holy shekel; both full of fine flour mingled with oil for a meat offering. 56 One golden censer of ten *weights*, full of incense. 57 One calf of the herd, one ram, one male lamb of a year old for a whole burnt offering, 58 and one kid of the goats for a sin offering. 59 And for a sacrifice of peace offering two heifers, five rams, five male goats, five ewe-lambs of a year old; this gift of Gamaliel the son of Phadassur.

60 On the ninth day the prince of the sons of Benjamin, Abidan the son of Gadeoni. 61 His gift, one silver charger, its weight was a hundred and thirty, one silver bowl of seventy shekels according to the holy shekel; both full of fine flour mingled with oil for a meat offering. 62 One golden censer of ten *weights*, full of incense. 63 One calf of the herd, one ram, one male lamb of a year old for a whole burnt offering, 64 and one kid of the goats for a sin offering. 65 And for a sacrifice of peace offering, two heifers, five rams, five male goats, five ewe-lambs of a year old; this *gift* of Abidan the son of Gadeoni.

66 On the tenth day the ruler of the sons of Dan, Achiezer the son of Amisadai. 67 His gift, one silver charger, its weight was a hundred and thirty, one silver bowl of seventy shekels according to the holy shekel; both full of fine flour kneaded with oil for a meat offering. 68 One golden censer of ten *weights*, full of incense. 69 One calf of the herd, one ram, one male lamb of a year old for a whole burnt offering, 70 and one kid of the goats for a sin offering.

Numbers 8

71 And for a sacrifice of peace offering, two heifers, five rams, five male goats, five ewe-lambs of a year old. This *was the* gift of Ahiezer the son of Amisadai.

72 On the eleventh day the ruler of the sons of Aser, Phageel the son of Ehran. 73 His gift, one silver charger, its weight was a hundred and thirty, one silver bowl of seventy shekels according to the holy shekel; both full of fine flour mingled with oil for a meat offering. 74 One golden censer of ten *weights*, full of incense. 75 One calf of the herd, one ram, one male lamb of a year old for a whole burnt offering, 76 and one kid of the goats for a sin offering. 77 And for a sacrifice of peace offering, two heifers, five rams, five male goats, five ewe-lambs of a year old; this gift of Phageel the son of Ehran.

78 On the twelfth day the ruler of the sons of Nephthali, Ahire the son of Aenan. 79 His gift, one silver charger, its weight was a hundred and thirty; one silver bowl of seventy shekels according to the holy shekel; both full of fine flour mingled with oil for a meat offering. 80 One golden censer of ten *weights*, full of incense. 81 One calf of the herd, one ram, one male lamb of a year old for a whole burnt offering, 82 and one kid of the goats for a sin offering. 83 And for a sacrifice of peace offering, two heifers, five rams, five male goats, five ewe-lambs of a year old; this gift of Ahire the son of Aenan.

84 This was the dedication of the altar in the day in which *it was* anointed, by the rulers of the sons of Israel; twelve silver chargers, twelve silver bowls, *and* twelve golden censers: 85 one charger of a hundred and thirty shekels, and each bowl of seventy shekels; all the silver of the vessels two thousand four hundred shekels, the shekels according to the holy shekel. 86 Twelve golden censers full of incense; all the gold of the censers was a hundred and twenty *weights of* gold. 87 All the cows for whole burnt offerings, twelve calves, twelve rams, twelve male lambs of a year old, and their meat offerings, and their drink offerings; and twelve kids of the goats for sin offering. 88 All the cattle for a sacrifice of peace offering, twenty-four heifers, sixty rams, sixty male goats of a year old, sixty ewe-lambs of a year old without blemish; this is the dedication of the altar, after that he filled his hands, and after he anointed him.

89 When Moses went into the Tabernacle of Witness to speak to Him, then he heard the voice of the Lord speaking to him from off the mercy seat, which is upon the Ark of the Testimony, between the two cherubs; and he spoke to him.

Chapter 8

And the Lord spoke to Moses, saying, 2 Speak to Aaron, and thou shall say to him, Whenever thou shall set the lamps in order, the seven lamps shall give light opposite the candlestick.

3 And Aaron did so; on one side opposite the candlestick he lighted its lamps, as the Lord appointed Moses. 4 And this *is* the arrangement of the candlestick: *it is to be* solid, its stem golden, and its lilies entirely solid; according to the pattern that the Lord showed Moses, so he made the candlestick.

5 And the Lord spoke to Moses, saying, 6 Take the Levites out of the midst of the sons of Israel, and thou shall purify them. 07 And thus shall thou perform their purification; thou shall sprinkle them with water of purification, and a razor shall come upon the whole of their body, and they shall wash their garments, and shall be clean. 8 And they shall take one calf of the herd, and its meat offering, fine flour mingled with oil; and thou shall take a calf of a year old of the herd for a sin offering. 9 And thou shall bring the Levites before the Tabernacle of Witness; and thou shall assemble the entire congregation of the sons of Israel. 10 And thou shall bring the Levites before the Lord; and the sons of Israel shall lay their hands upon the Levites. 11 And Aaron shall separate the Levites for a gift before the Lord from the sons of Israel, and they shall be prepared so as to perform the works of the Lord. 12 The Levites shall lay their hands on the heads of the calves; and thou shall offer one for a sin offering, and the other for a whole burnt offering to the Lord, to make atonement for them. 13 And thou shall set the Levites before the Lord, and before Aaron, and before his sons; and thou shall give them as a gift before the Lord. 14 And thou shall separate the Levites from the midst of the sons of Israel, and they shall be Mine. 15 And afterwards the Levites shall enter to work the works of the Tabernacle of Witness; and thou shall purify them, and present them before the Lord. * 16 For these are given back to Me as a gift out of the midst of the son of Israel; I have taken them to Myself instead of all the firstborn of the sons of Israel that open every womb. 17 For every firstborn among the sons of Israel *are* Mine, whether of man or beast; in the day in which I killed every firstborn in the land of Egypt, I sanctified them to Myself. 18 And I took the Levites in the place of every firstborn among the sons of Israel. 19 And I gave the Levites presented as a gift to Aaron and his sons out of the midst of the sons of Israel, to work the works of the sons of Israel in the Tabernacle of Witness, and to make atonement for the sons of Israel; thus there shall be none among the sons of Israel to draw near to the holy things.

20 And Moses and Aaron, and the entire congregation of the sons of Israel, did to the Levites as the Lord commanded Moses concerning the Levites, so the sons of Israel did to them. 21 So the Levites purified themselves and washed their garments; and Aaron presented them as a gift before the Lord, and Aaron made atonement for them to purify them. 22 And afterwards the Levites went in to officiate in their liturgy in the Tabernacle of Witness before Aaron, and before his sons; as the Lord appointed Moses concerning the Levites, so they did to them. 23 And the Lord spoke to Moses, saying,

Numbers 9

24 This is for the Levites; From five and twenty years old and upward, they shall go to work in the Tabernacle of Witness. 25 And from fifty years old they shall cease from the ministry, and shall not work any longer. 26 And his brother shall serve in the Tabernacle of Witness to keep charge, but he shall not perform works; so shall thou do to the Levites in their charge.

* The February Second reading for Chapter Eight verses sixteen through seventeen for great vespers in the *Greek Menaion* is considerably different and reads as follows:

"For these are given to Me as a gift out of the son of Israel. And I have taken them and sanctified them to Myself instead of all the firstborn of the Egyptians, on the day when I killed every firstborn in the land of Egypt from man to beast of burden, said God the Most High, the Holy One of Israel."

Chapter 9

And the Lord spoke to Moses in the wilderness of Sinai in the second year after they had gone forth from the land of Egypt, in the first month, saying, 2 Speak, and let the sons of Israel keep the Passover in its season. 3 On the fourteenth day of the first month at even, thou shall keep it in its season; thou shall keep it according to its law, and according to its ordinance. 4 And Moses ordered the sons of Israel to sacrifice the Passover, 5 on the fourteenth day of the first month in the wilderness of Sinai, as the Lord appointed Moses, so the children of Israel did. 6 And there came men, who were unclean by reason of *touching* the *dead* soul of a man, and they were not able to keep the Passover on that day; and they came before Moses and Aaron on that day. 7 And those men said to him, We are unclean by reason of *touching* the *dead* soul of a man; shall we therefore fail to offer the gift to the Lord in its season in the midst of the sons of Israel? 8 And Moses said to them, stand there, and I will hear what charge the Lord will give concerning you.

9 And the Lord spoke to Moses, saying, 10 Speak to the sons of Israel, saying, Whatever man shall be unclean by reason of *touching* a *dead* soul, or on a journey far off, among you, or among your posterity; he shall then keep the Passover to the Lord, 11 in the second month, on the fourteenth day, in the evening they shall offer it, with unleavened bread and bitter herbs shall they eat it. 12 They shall not leave of it until the morning, and they shall not break a bone of it; they shall sacrifice it according to the ordinance of the Passover. 13 And whatever man shall be clean, and is not far off on a journey, and shall fail to keep the Passover that soul shall be cut off from his people, because he has not offered the gift to the Lord in its season; that man shall bear his iniquity.

14 And if there should come to you a stranger in your land, and should keep the Passover to the Lord, he shall keep it according to the law of the Passover and according to its ordinance; there shall be one law for you, both for the stranger, and for the native of the land.

* 15 And in the day in which the tabernacle was pitched the cloud covered the tabernacle, the house of the testimony; and in the evening there was upon the tabernacle as the appearance of fire till the morning. 16 So it was continually; the cloud covered it by day, and the appearance of fire by night. 17 And when the cloud went up from the tabernacle, then after that the sons of Israel departed; and in whatever place the cloud rested, there the sons of Israel encamped. 18 The sons of Israel shall encamp by the command of the Lord, and by the command of the Lord they shall leave; all the days, in which the cloud overshadows the tabernacle, the sons of Israel shall encamp. 19 And whenever the cloud shall be drawn over the tabernacle for many days, then the sons of Israel shall keep the charge of God, and they shall not leave. 20 And it shall be, whenever the cloud overshadows the tabernacle *for* a number of days, they shall encamp by the voice of the Lord, and shall leave by the command of the Lord. 21 And it shall come to pass, whenever the cloud shall remain from the evening till the morning, and in the morning the cloud shall go up, *and* then shall they leave by day or by night. 22 When the cloud continues *for* more than a month overshadowing the tabernacle, the sons of Israel shall encamp, and shall not depart. 23 For they shall depart by the command of the Lord, they kept the charge of the Lord by the command of the Lord by the hand of Moses.

---

* The October reading of Chapter Nine verses fifteen through twenty-three for great vespers in the *Greek Menaion* and *Prophetologion* is somewhat different than what is present in the biblical text as published by the Apostoliki Diakonia and the Zoe Brotherhood, and reads as follows:

"In the day in which the tabernacle was pitched the cloud covered the tabernacle, the house of the testimony; and in the evening there was upon the tabernacle as the appearance of fire till the morning. So it was continually; the cloud covered it by day, and the appearance of fire by night. And when the cloud went up from the tabernacle, then after that the people of Israel departed; and in whatever place the cloud rested, there the people of Israel encamped. 18 The people of Israel shall encamp by the command of the Lord, and by the command of the Lord they shall leave; all the days, in which the cloud overshadows the tabernacle, the sons of Israel shall encamp. And whenever the cloud shall be drawn over the tabernacle for many days, then the sons of Israel shall keep the charge of the Lord, and they shall not leave. And it shall be, whenever the cloud overshadows the tabernacle *for* a number of days, they shall encamp by the word of the Lord, and shall leave by the command of the Lord. And it shall come to pass, whenever the cloud shall remain from the evening till the morning, and in the morning the cloud shall go up, *and* then shall they leave by day or by night. When the cloud continues *for* more than a month overshadowing the tabernacle, the sons of Israel shall encamp, and shall not depart.

Numbers 10

For they shall depart by the command of the Lord, they kept the charge of the Lord by the command of the Lord by Moses."

Chapter 10

And the Lord spoke to Moses, saying, 2 Make to thyself two silver trumpets: thou shall make them of beaten work; and they shall be to thee for the purpose of calling the assembly, and of removing the camps. 3 And thou shall sound with them, and the entire congregation shall be gathered to the door of the Tabernacle of Witness. 4 And if they shall sound with one, all the rulers even the leaders of Israel shall come to thee. 5 And ye shall sound an alarm, and the camps pitched to the east shall begin to move. 6 And ye shall sound a second alarm, and the camps pitched to the south shall move; and ye shall sound a third alarm, and the camps pitched to the west shall move forward; and ye shall sound a fourth alarm, and they that encamp toward the north shall move forward; they shall sound an alarm at their departure. 7 And whenever ye shall gather the assembly, ye shall sound, but not an alarm. 8 And the priests the sons of Aaron shall sound with the trumpets; and it shall be a perpetual ordinance for you throughout your generations. 9 And if ye shall go forth to war in your land against your enemies that are opposed to you, then shall ye sound with the trumpets; and ye shall be had in remembrance before the Lord, and ye shall be saved from your enemies. 10 And in the days of your gladness, and in your feasts, and in your new moons, ye shall sound with the trumpets at your whole burnt offerings, and at the sacrifices of your peace offerings; and there shall be a memorial for you before your God; I *am* the Lord your God.

11 And it came to pass in the second year, in the second month, on the twentieth day of the month the cloud went up from the Tabernacle of Witness. 12 And the sons of Israel set forward with their baggage in the wilderness of Sinai; and the cloud rested in the wilderness of Pharan. 13 And the first rank departed by the voice of the Lord by the hand of Moses. 14 And they first set in motion the order of the camp of the sons of Judah with their forces; and over their forces Naasson, son of Aminadab. 15 And over the forces of the tribe of the sons of Issahar, Nathaniel son of Sogar. 16 And over the forces of the tribe of the sons of Zabulon, Eliab the son of Haelon.

17 And they shall take down the tabernacle, and the sons of Gedson shall set forward, and the sons of Merari, who bear the tabernacle. 18 And the order of the camp of Ruben set forward with their forces and over their forces Elisur the son of Sediur. 19 And over the forces of the tribe of the sons of Simon, Salamiel son of Surisadai. 20 And over the forces of the tribe of the sons of Gad, Elisaph the son of Raguel.

21 And the sons of Kaath shall set forward bearing the holy things, and shall set up the tabernacle until they arrive. 22 And the order of the camp of Ephraim shall set forward with their forces and over their forces Elisama the son of Semiud. 23 And over the forces of the tribes of the sons of Manasse, Gamaliel of Phadassur. 24 And over the forces of the tribe of the sons of Benjamin, Abidan of Gideon.

25 And the order of the camp of the sons of Dan shall set forward the last of all the camps, with their forces, and over their forces Ahiezer of Amisadai. 26 And over the forces of the tribe of the sons of Aser, Phageel the son of Ehran. 27 And over the forces of the tribe of the sons of Nephthali, Ahire the son of Aenan. 28 These *are* the armies of the sons of Israel; and they set forward with their forces.

29 And Moses said to Obab the son of Raguel the Madianite, the father-in-law of Moses, We are going forward to the place concerning which the Lord said, This will I give to you, Come with us, and we will do thee good, for the Lord has spoken good concerning Israel. 30 And he said to him, I will not go, but to my land and to my kindred. 31 And he said, Leave us not, because thou have been with us in the wilderness, and thou shall be a ruler among us. 32 And it shall come to pass if thou will go with us, it shall even come to pass that in whatever things the Lord shall do us good, we will also do thee good.

33 And they departed from the mountain of the Lord a three days' journey; and the ark of the covenant of the Lord went before them a three days' journey to provide rest for them. 34 And the cloud overshadowed them by day, when they departed from the camp.

35 And it came to pass when the ark set forward, that Moses said, Arise, O Lord, and let thine enemies be scattered; let all that hate thee flee. 36 And in the resting he said, Turn again, O Lord, the thousands *and* tens of thousands in Israel.

Chapter 11

And the people murmured sinfully before the Lord; and the Lord heard and was very angry; and fire was kindled among them from the Lord, and devoured a part of the camp. 2 And the people cried to Moses; and Moses prayed to the Lord, and the fire was quenched. 3 And the name of that place was called Burning; for a fire was kindled among them from the Lord.

4 And the mixed multitude among them lusted a lust; and they and the sons of Israel sat down and wept and said, Who shall give us flesh to eat? 5 We remember the fish, which we ate in Egypt freely; and the cucumbers, and the cantaloupes, and the leeks, and the garlic, and the onions.

Numbers 11

6 But now our soul is dried up, our eyes to nothing but to the manna. 7 And the manna is as coriander seed and the appearance of it the appearance of crystal. 8 And the people went through the field, and gathered, and ground it in the mill, or pounded it in a mortar, and baked it in a pan, and made cakes of it; and the sweetness of it was as the taste *of* wafer made with oil. 9 And when the dew came upon the camp by night, the manna came down upon it.

10 And Moses heard them weeping by their families, every one in his door: and the Lord was very angry; and the thing was evil in the sight of Moses. 11 And Moses said to the Lord, Why have thou afflicted thy servant, and why have I not found grace in thy sight, that thou should lay the weight of this people upon me? 12 Have I conceived this entire people, or have I born them? That thou say to me, Take them into thy bosom, as a nurse would take her suckling, into the land which thou swore to their fathers? 13 Where have I flesh to give to this entire people? For they weep to me, saying, Give us flesh that we may eat. 14 I shall not be able to bear this people alone, for this thing is too heavy for me. 15 And if thou does thus to me, kill me utterly, if I have found favor with thee, that I may not see my affliction.

* 16 And the Lord said to Moses, Gather me seventy men from the elders of Israel, whom thou thyself knows that they are the elders of the people, and their scribes; and thou shall bring them to the Tabernacle of Witness, and they shall stand there with thee. 17 And I will go down, and speak there with thee; and I will take of the spirit that is upon thee, and will put it upon them; and they shall bear together with thee the burden of the people, and thou shall not bear them alone. 18 And to the people thou shall say, Purify yourselves for tomorrow, and ye shall eat flesh; for ye wept before the Lord, saying, Who shall give us flesh to eat? For it is well with us in Egypt, and the Lord shall allow you to eat flesh, and ye shall eat flesh. 19 Ye shall not eat one day, or two, or five days, or ten days, or twenty days, 20 ye shall eat for a month of days, until *the flesh* come out at your nostrils; and it shall be cholera to you, because ye disobeyed the Lord, who is among you, and wept before him, saying, What had we to do to come out of Egypt? 21 And Moses said, The people among whom I am are six hundred thousand footmen; and thou said, I will give them flesh to eat, and they shall eat a whole month. 22 Shall sheep and oxen be killed for them, and shall it suffice them? Or shall all the fish of the sea be gathered together for them, and shall it suffice them? 23 And the Lord said to Moses, Should not the hand of the Lord be fully sufficient? Now shall thou know whether My word will overtake thee or not.

* 24 And Moses went out, and spoke the words of the Lord to the people; and he gathered seventy men of the elders of the people, and he set them around the tabernacle.

Numbers 11

25 And the Lord came down in a cloud, and spoke to him, and took of the spirit that was upon him, and put it upon the seventy men that were elders, but when the spirit rested upon them, they prophesied and then ceased.

26 And there were two men left in the camp, the name of the one was Eldad, and the name of the second was Modad; and the spirit rested upon them, and these were of the number of them that were enrolled, but they did not come to the tabernacle; and they prophesied in the camp. 27 And a young man ran and told Moses, and spoke, saying, Eldad and Modad prophesy in the camp. 28 And Jesus the son of Naue, who attended on Moses, his chosen one, said, lord Moses, stop them. 29 And Moses said to him, Art thou jealous on my account? And who would not give that all the Lord's people were prophets whenever the Lord shall put his spirit upon them. 30 And Moses departed into the camp, himself and the rulers of Israel.

31 And there went forth a wind from the Lord, and brought quails over from the sea; and it brought them down upon the camp a day's journey on this side, and a day's journey on that side, round about the camp, as it were two cubits from the earth. 32 And the people rose up all the day, and all the night, and all the next day, and gathered quails; he that gathered little, gathered ten kors; and they refreshed for themselves with refreshments around the camp. 33 The flesh was yet between their teeth, before it failed, when the Lord was angry with the people, and the Lord struck the people with a very great plague. 34 And the name of that place was called the Graves of Lust, for there they buried the people that lusted. 35 The people departed from the Graves of Lust to Aseroth; and the people were in at Aseroth.

* The reading of Chapter Eleven verses sixteen through seventeen and verses twenty-four through twenty-nine for the Sunday of *Holy Pentecost* for Saturday evening at great vespers is somewhat different than what is present in the biblical text as published by the Apostoliki Diakonia and the Zoe Brotherhood, and reads as follows:

"The Lord said to Moses, Gather Me seventy men from the elders of the people, whom thou thyself knows that they are the elders of the people, and their scribes; and thou shall bring them to the Tabernacle of Witness, and they shall stand there with thee. And I will go down, and speak there with thee; and I will take of the spirit that is upon thee, and will put it upon them; and they shall bear together with thee the burden of the people, and thou shall not bear them alone. And Moses gathered seventy men of the elders of the people, and he set them around the tabernacle. And the Lord came down in a cloud, and spoke to Moses, and took of the spirit that was upon him, and put it upon the seventy men that were elders. But when the spirit rested upon them, they prophesied in the camp and then ceased. And there were two men left in the camp, the name of the one was Eldad, and the name of the second was Modad; and the spirit rested upon them, and these were of the number of them that were enrolled, but they did not come to the tabernacle; and they prophesied in the camp. And a young man ran and told Moses, and said to him, Eldad and Modad prophesy in the camp. And Jesus the son of Naue, who attended on Moses, his chosen one, said, lord Moses, stop them.

Numbers 12

And Moses said to him, Art thou jealous on my account? And who would not give that all the Lord's people were prophets whenever the Lord shall put his spirit upon them."

Chapter 12

And Mariam and Aaron spoke against Moses, because of the Ethiopian woman whom Moses took for he had taken an Ethiopian woman. 2 And they said, Has the Lord spoken to Moses only? Has he not also spoken to us? And the Lord heard it. 3 And the man Moses was very meek beyond all the men that were upon the earth. 4 And the Lord said immediately to Moses and Aaron and Mariam, Come forth the three of you to the Tabernacle of Witness. 5 And the three came forth to the Tabernacle of Witness; and the Lord descended in a pillar of a cloud, and stood at the door of the Tabernacle of Witness; and Aaron and Mariam were called; and both came forth. 6 And He said to them, Hear My words; If there should be of you a prophet to the Lord, I will be made known to him in a vision, and in sleep will I speak to him. 7 My servant Moses *is* not so; he is faithful in My entire house. 8 I will speak to him mouth to mouth apparently, and not in dark speeches; and he has seen the glory of the Lord; and why were ye not afraid to speak against My servant Moses?

9 And the great anger of the Lord *was* upon them, and He departed. 10 And the cloud departed from the tabernacle; and, behold, Mariam was leprous, as snow; and Aaron looked upon Mariam, and, behold, she *was* leprous. 11 And Aaron said to Moses, I beseech thee, my lord; do not lay sin upon us, for we were ignorant wherein we sinned. 12 Let her not be as it were like death, as an abortion coming out of his mother's womb, when *the disease* devours the half of the flesh. 13 And Moses cried to the Lord, saying, O God, I beseech thee; heal her. 14 And the Lord said to Moses, If her father had only spit in her face, will she not be ashamed seven days? Let her be set apart seven days outside the camp, and afterwards she shall come in. 15 And Mariam was separated outside the camp seven days; and the people did not moved forward till Mariam was cleansed.

Chapter 13

And afterwards the people set forth from Aseroth, and encamped in the wilderness of Pharan. 2 And the Lord spoke to Moses, saying, 3 Send for thee men, and let them spy the land of the Canaanites, which I give to the sons of Israel for a possession; one man for a tribe, thou shall send them away according to their families, every one of them a ruler. 4 And Moses sent them out of the wilderness of Pharan by the word of the Lord; all these *were* the rulers of the sons of Israel.

Numbers 13

5 And these *are* their names, of the tribe of Ruben, Samuel the son of Zahur. 6 Of the tribe of Simon, Saphat the son of Suri. 7 Of the tribe of Judah, Caleb the son of Jephonne. 8 Of the tribe of Issahar, Ilaal the son of Joseph. 9 Of the tribe of Ephraim, Ause the son of Naue. 10 Of the tribe of Benjamin, Phalti the son of Raphu. 11 Of the tribe of Zabulon, Gudiel the son of Sudi. 12 Of the tribe of Joseph of the sons of Manasse, Gaddi the son of Susi. 13 Of the tribe of Dan, Amiel the son of Gamali. 14 Of the tribe of Aser, Sathur the son of Michael. 15 Of the tribe of Nephthali, Nabi the son of Sabi. 16 Of the tribe of Gad, Gudiel the son of Makhi.

17 These *are* the names of the men whom Moses sent to spy out the land; and Moses called Ause the son of Naue, Jesus. 18 And Moses sent them to spy out the land of Canaan, and said to them, Go up by this wilderness; and ye shall go up to the mountain, 19 and ye shall see the land, what it is, and the people that live on it, whether it is strong or weak, or they are few or many. 20 And what the land is on which they live, *whether* it is good or bad; and what the cities are wherein these live, whether they live in walled or unwalled.

21 And what the land is, whether rich or neglected; whether there are trees in it or no; and ye shall persevere and take of the fruits of the land, and the days *were* the days of spring, the forerunners of the grape. 22 And they went up and surveyed the land from the wilderness of Sin to Rhoob, as men go in to Aemath. 23 And they went up by the wilderness, and departed as far as Hebron; and there Achiman, and Sessi, and Thelami, the progeny of Enah. Now Hebron was built seven years before Tanin of Egypt. 24 And they came to the valley of the cluster and surveyed it; and they cut down thence a bough and one cluster of grapes upon it, and bore it on staves, and *they took* of the pomegranates and the figs.

25 And they called that place, The Valley of the Cluster, because of the cluster which the sons of Israel cut down from thence. 26 And they returned from thence, having surveyed the land, after forty days. 27 And they proceeded and came to Moses and Aaron and the entire congregation of the sons of Israel, to the wilderness of Pharan Kades; and they brought word to them and to the entire congregation, and they showed the fruit of the land; 28 and they reported to him, and said, We came into the land into which thou sent us, a land flowing with milk and honey; and this is the fruit of it. 29 Only the nation that lives upon it is bold, and they have very great and strong walled towns, and we saw there the sons of Enah.

30 And Amalek lives in the land toward the south, and the Hittite and the Evite, and the Jebusite, and the Amorite live in the hill country; and the Canaanite lives by the sea, and by the river Jordan. 31 And Kaleb stayed the people from speaking to Moses, and said to him, Nay, but we will go up by all means, and will inherit it, for we shall surely prevail against them.

Numbers 14

32 But the men that went up together with him said, We will not go up, for we shall not by any means be able to go up against the nation, for it is much stronger than we. 33 And they brought a horror of that land which they surveyed upon the sons of Israel, saying, The land which we passed by to survey it, is a land that eats up its inhabitants; and all the people whom we saw in it are men of extraordinary stature. 34 And there we saw the giants; and we were before them as locusts, yea even so were we before them.

Chapter 14

And the entire congregation lifted up their voice and cried; and the people wept all that night. 2 And all the sons of Israel murmured against Moses and Aaron; and the entire congregation said to them, 3 Would we have died in the land of Egypt! Or in this wilderness, would we have died! And why does the Lord bring us into this land to fall in war? Our wives and our children shall be for a prey: now then it is better to return into Egypt.

4 And they said one to another, Let us make a ruler, and return into Egypt. 5 And Moses and Aaron fell upon their face before the entire congregation of the sons of Israel. 6 But Jesus of Naue, and Kaleb of Jephonne, of them that spied out the land, rent their garments, 7 and spoke to the entire congregation of the sons of Israel, saying, The land which we surveyed is indeed extremely good. 8 If the Lord choose us, he will bring us into this land, and give it us; a land that flows with milk and honey. 9 Only depart not from the Lord; and fear ye not the people of the land, for they are meat for us; for the season is departed from them, but the Lord *is* among us: fear them not. 10 And the entire congregation bade stone them with stones; and the glory of the Lord appeared in the cloud on the tabernacle of witness to all the sons of Israel.

11 And the Lord said to Moses, How long do this people provoke Me? And how long do they not believe Me for all the signs that I have wrought among them? 12 I will strike them with death, and destroy them; and I will make of thee and of thy father's house a great nation, and much greater than this. 13 And Moses said to the Lord, So Egypt shall hear, for thou have brought up this people from them by thy might. 14 Moreover all those that live upon this land have heard that Thou art Lord in the midst of this people, who, O Lord, art seen face to face, and thy cloud rests upon them, and thou goes before them by day in a pillar of a cloud, and by night in a pillar of fire. 15 And Thou shall destroy this nation as one man; then all the nations that have heard Thy name shall speak, saying, 16 Because the Lord could not bring this people into the land which He swore to them, He has overthrown them in the wilderness. 17 And now, O Lord, let Thy strength be exalted, as thou speaks, saying,

18 The Lord *is* long-suffering and merciful, and true, removing transgressions and iniquities and sins, and He will by no means clear the guilty, visiting the sins of the fathers upon the children to the third and fourth generation. 19 Forgive this people their sin according to Thy great mercy, as Thou was favorable to them from Egypt until now.

20 And the Lord said to Moses, I am gracious to them according to thy word. 21 But *as* I live and My name is living, so the glory of the Lord shall fill all the earth. 22 For all the men who see My glory, and the signs that I performed in Egypt, and in the wilderness, and have tempted Me this tenth time, and have not hearkened to My voice, 23 surely they shall not see the land, which I swore to their fathers; but their children which are with Me here, as many as know not good or evil, every inexperienced youth, to them will I give the land; but none who have provoked Me shall see it. 24 But My servant Kaleb, because there was another spirit in him, and he followed Me, I will bring him into the land into which he entered, and his seed shall inherit it. 25 But Amalek and the Canaanite live in the valley; tomorrow turn and depart for the wilderness by the way of the Red Sea.

26 And the Lord spoke to Moses and Aaron, saying, 27 How long *shall I endure* this wicked congregation? I have heard their murmurings against Me, the murmuring of the sons of Israel, which they have murmured concerning you. 28 Say to them, I live, saith the Lord; surely as ye spoke into My ears, so will I do to you. 29 Your carcasses shall fall in this wilderness; and all those of you that were reviewed, and those of you that were numbered from twenty years old and upward, all that murmured against Me, 30 ye shall not enter into the land for which I stretched out My hand to establish you upon it; except only Kaleb the son of Jephonne, and Jesus *the son* of Naue. 31 And your little ones, who ye said should be a prey, they will I bring into the land; and they shall inherit the land from which ye turned away. 32 And your carcasses shall fall in this wilderness. 33 Your sons shall be fed in the wilderness forty years, and they shall bear your fornication, until your carcasses be consumed in the wilderness. 34 According to the number of the days during which ye spied the land, forty days, a day for a year, ye shall bear your sins forty years, and ye shall know My fierce anger. 35 I the Lord have spoken, Surely will I do thus to this evil congregation that has risen up together against Me; in this wilderness they shall be utterly consumed, and there they shall die.

36 And the people whom Moses sent to spy out the land, and who came and murmured against it to the assembly so as to bring out evil words concerning the land, 37 the men that spoke evil reports against the land, died of the plague before the Lord. 38 And Jesus the son of Naue and Kaleb the son of Jephonne lived of those men that went to spy out the land.

Numbers 15

39 And Moses spoke these words to all the sons of Israel; and the people mourned exceedingly. 40 And they rose early in the morning and went up to the top of the mountain, saying, Behold, we that are here will go up to the place of which the Lord has spoken, because we have sinned. 41 And Moses said, Why do ye transgress the word of the Lord? Ye shall not prosper. 42 Go not up, for the Lord is not with you; so shall ye fall before the face of your enemies. 43 For Amalek and the Canaanite *are* there before you, and ye shall fall by the sword; because ye have disobeyed the Lord and turned aside, and the Lord will not be among you.

44 And having forced their passage, they went up to the top of the mountain; but the Ark of the Covenant of the Lord and Moses stirred not out of the camp. 45 And Amalek and the Canaanite that lived in that mountain came down, and routed them, and destroyed them unto Herman; and they returned to the camp.

Chapter 15

And the Lord spoke to Moses, saying, 2 Speak to the sons of Israel, and thou shall say to them, When ye are come into the land of your habitation, which I give to you, 3 and thou will offer whole burnt offerings to the Lord, a whole burnt offering or a meat offering to magnify a vow, or a free will offering, or to offer in your feasts a sacrifice of sweet savor to the Lord, whether of the herd or the flock; 4 then he that offers his gift to the Lord shall bring a meat offering of fine flour, a tenth part of an ephah mingled with oil, even with the fourth part of a hin. 5 And for a drink offering ye shall offer the fourth part of a hin on the whole burnt offering, or on the meat offering; for every lamb thou shall offer so much, as a sacrifice, a smell of sweet savor to the Lord. 6 And for a ram, when ye offer it as a whole burnt offering or as a sacrifice, thou shall prepare as a meat offering two tenths of fine flour mingled with oil, the third part of a hin. 7 And ye shall offer for a smell of sweet savor to the Lord wine for a drink offering, the third part of a hin. 8 If ye sacrifice from the herd for a whole burnt offering or for a sacrifice, to perform a vow or a peace offering to the Lord, 9 then shall *one* offer upon the calf a meat offering, three tenth deals of fine flour mingled with oil, the half of a hin. 10 And wine for a drink offering, the half of a hin, a sacrifice for a smell of sweet savor to the Lord.

11 Thus shall thou do to one calf or to one ram, or to one lamb of the sheep or kid of the goats. 12 According to the number of what ye shall offer, so shall ye do to each one, according to their number. 13 Every native of the country shall do thus to offer such things as sacrifices for a smell of sweet savor to the Lord.

14 And if there should be a stranger among you in your land, or one who should be born to you among your generations, and he will offer a sacrifice, a smell of sweet savor to the Lord as ye do, so the congregation shall offer to the Lord. 15 There shall be one law for you and for the strangers abiding among you, a perpetual law for your generations: as ye, so shall the stranger be before the Lord. 16 There shall be one law and one ordinance for you, and for the stranger that abides among you.

17 And the Lord spoke to Moses, saying, 18 Speak to the sons of Israel, and thou shall say to them, When ye are entering into the land, into which I bring you, 19 then it shall come to pass, when ye shall eat of the bread of the land, ye shall separate a wave offering, a special offering to the Lord, the first fruits of your dough. 20 Ye shall offer your bread as a heave offering; as a heave offering from the threshing floor, so shall ye separate it, 21 even the first fruits of your dough, and ye shall give the Lord a heave offering throughout your generations. 22 But whenever ye shall transgress, and not perform all these commands, which the Lord spoke to Moses; 23 as the Lord appointed you by the hand of Moses, from the day that the Lord appointed you and forward throughout your generations, 24 then it shall come to pass, if a trespass be committed unwillingly, unknown to the congregation, then shall all the congregation offer a calf of the herd without blemish for a whole burnt offering of sweet savor to the Lord, and its meat offering and its drink offering according to the ordinance, and one kid of the goats for a sin offering. 25 And the priest shall make atonement for the entire congregation of the sons of Israel, and shall be forgiven them, because it is involuntary; and they have brought their gift, a burnt offering to the Lord for their trespass before the Lord, even for their involuntary sins. 26 And it shall be forgiven as respects all the congregation of the sons of Israel, and the stranger that is abiding among you, because *it is* involuntary to the entire people.

27 If one soul sins unwillingly, he shall bring one she-goat of a year old as a sin offering. 28 The priest shall make atonement for the soul that committed the trespass unwillingly, and that sinned unwillingly before the Lord, to make atonement for him. 29 There shall be one law for the native among the sons of Israel, and for the stranger that abides among them, whoever shall commit a trespass unwillingly. 30 And whatever soul either of the natives or of the strangers shall do any thing with a presumptuous hand, he will provoke God; that soul shall be cut off from his people, 31 for he has set at nothing the word of the Lord and broken his commands; that soul shall be utterly destroyed, his sin *is* upon him.

32 And the sons of Israel were in the wilderness, and they found a man gathering sticks on the day of the Sabbath.

Numbers 16

33 And they who found him gathering sticks on the day of the Sabbath brought him to Moses and Aaron, and to the entire congregation of the sons of Israel. 34 And they placed him in custody, for they did not determine what they should do to him. 35 And the Lord spoke to Moses, saying, Let the man by all means die the death; the entire congregation, stone him with stones. 36 And the entire congregation brought him out of the camp; and the entire congregation stoned him with stones outside the camp, as the Lord commanded Moses.

37 And the Lord spoke to Moses, saying, 38 Speak to the sons of Israel, and thou shall tell them; and let them make for themselves fringes upon the borders of their garments throughout their generations; and ye shall put upon the fringes of the borders a lace of blue. 39 And it shall be on your fringes, and ye shall look on them, and ye shall remember all the commands of the Lord, and do them; and ye shall not turn back after your imaginations, and after *the sight of your* eyes in the things after which ye go a whoring; 40 that ye may remember and perform all My commands, and ye shall be holy unto your God. 41 I *am* the Lord your God that brought you out of the land of Egypt, to be your God; I *am* the Lord your God.

Chapter 16

And Kore the son of Isaar the son of Kaath the son of Levi, and Dathan and Abiron, sons of Eliab, and Aun the son of Phaleth the son of Ruben, spoke, 2 and rose up before Moses, and two hundred and fifty men of the sons of Israel, rulers of the assembly, chosen councilors, and men of renown. 3 They rose up against Moses and Aaron, and said, Let it be enough for you that the entire congregation *are* holy, and the Lord *is* among them; and why do ye set up yourselves against the congregation of the Lord? 4 And when Moses heard it, he fell on his face. 5 And he spoke to Kore and all his assembly, saying, God has visited and known those that are his and who are holy, and has brought them to himself; and whom he has chosen for himself, he has brought to himself. 6 This do ye; take to yourselves censers, Kore and all his company; 7 and put fire on them, and put incense on them before the Lord tomorrow; and it shall come to pass that the man whom the Lord has chosen, he shall be holy; let it be enough for you, ye sons of Levi. 8 And Moses said to Kore, Hearken to me, ye sons of Levi. 9 Is it a little thing for you that the God of Israel has separated you from the congregation of Israel, and brought you near to him to officiate in the liturgies of the tabernacle of the Lord, and to stand before the tabernacle to minister for them? 10 And he has brought thee near and all thy brethren the sons of Levi with thee, and do ye seek to be priests also?

Numbers 16

11 Thus *it is with* thee and thy entire congregation that is gathered together against God; and who is Aaron that ye murmur against him? 12 And Moses sent to call Dathan and Abiron sons of Eliab; and they said, We will not go up. 13 Is it a little thing that thou have brought us up * to a land flowing with milk and honey, to kill us in the wilderness, *and* that thou altogether governs over us? 14 And have thou brought us into a land flowing with milk and honey, and has thou given us an inheritance of land and vineyards? Would thou have cut out the eyes of those men? We will not go up.

15 And Moses was exceedingly indignant, and said to the Lord, Do thou take no heed to their sacrifice; I have not taken away the desire of any one of them, neither have I hurt any one of them. 16 And Moses said to Kore, Sanctify thy company, and be ready before the Lord, thou and Aaron and they, tomorrow. 17 And take each man his censer, and ye shall put incense upon them, and shall bring each one his censer before the Lord, two hundred and fifty censers, and thou and Aaron shall bring each his censer. 18 And each man took his censer, and they put in them fire, and laid incense on them; and Moses and Aaron stood by the doors of the tabernacle of witness. 19 And Kore arose against them *and* all his company by the door of the Tabernacle of Witness; and the glory of the Lord appeared to the entire congregation.

20 And the Lord spoke to Moses and Aaron, saying, 21 Separate yourselves from the midst of this congregation, and I will consume them at once. 22 And they fell on their faces, and said, O God, the God of spirits and of all flesh, if one man has sinned, the wrath of the Lord upon the whole congregation? 23 And the Lord spoke to Moses, saying, 24 Speak to the congregation, saying, Depart from the company of Kore around *him*.

25 And Moses rose up and went to Dathan and Abiron, and all the elders of Israel went with him. 26 And he spoke to the congregation, saying, Separate yourselves from the tents of these stubborn men, and touch nothing that belongs to them, lest ye be consumed with them in all their sin. 27 And they stood aloof from the tent of Kore around; and Dathan and Abiron went forth and stood by the doors of their tents, and their wives and their children and their store. 28 And Moses said, Hereby shall ye know that the Lord has sent me to perform all these works, that not of myself. 29 If these men shall die according to the death of all men, if also their visitation shall be according to the visitation of all men, then the Lord has not sent me. 30 However, if the Lord shall show by a vision, and the earth shall open her mouth and swallow them up, and their houses, and their tents, and all that belongs to them, and they shall go down alive into Hades, then ye shall know that these men have provoked the Lord.

31 When he ceased speaking all these words, the ground clave asunder beneath them. 32 And the ground opened, and swallowed them up, and their houses, and all the men that were with Kore, and their cattle.

Numbers 17

33 And they went down and all that they had, alive into Hades; and the ground covered them, and they perished from the midst of the congregation. 34 And all Israel around them fled from the sound of them, saying, Lest the earth swallow us up. 35 And fire went forth from the Lord, and devoured the two hundred and fifty men that offered incense.

* Alfred Rahlfs' *Septuaginta* supports the following reading of Chapter Sixteen verse thirteen, which is translated as follows: "...out of a land flowing with milk and honey..." Rahlfs' critical apparatus states that this reading is found in *Codex Venetus*.

Chapter 17

And the Lord said to Moses, 2 and to Eleazar the son of Aaron the priest, Take up the brazen censers out of the midst of the men that have been burned, and scatter the strange fire yonder, for they have sanctified the censers. 3 Of these sinners against their own souls, and do thou make them beaten plates a covering to the altar, because they were brought before the Lord and hallowed; and they became a sign to the sons of Israel. 4 And Eleazar the son of Aaron the priest took the brazen censers, which the men who had been burnt brought near, and they put them as a covering on the altar, 5 a memorial to the sons of Israel that no stranger might come near, who is not of the seed of Aaron, to offer incense before the Lord; so he shall not be as Kore and as they that conspired with him, as the Lord spoke to him by the hand of Moses. 6 And the sons of Israel murmured the next day against Moses and Aaron, saying, Ye have killed the people of the Lord. 7 And it came to pass when the assembly counseled against Moses and Aaron that they ran impetuously to the tabernacle of witness; and the cloud covered it, and the glory of the Lord appeared.

8 And Moses and Aaron entered in front of the Tabernacle of Witness. 9 And the Lord spoke to Moses and Aaron, saying, 10 Depart out of the midst of this assembly, and I will consume them at once; and they fell upon their faces. 11 And Moses said to Aaron, Take a censer, and put on it fire from the altar, and put incense on it, and carry it away quickly into the camp, and make atonement for them; for wrath is gone forth from the presence of the Lord, it has begun to destroy the people. 12 And Aaron took as Moses spoke to him, and ran among the congregation, for already the plague had begun among the people; and he put on incense, and made atonement for the people. 13 And he stood between the dead and the living, and the plague ceased. 14 And they that died in the plague were fourteen thousand and seven hundred, besides those that died on account of Kore. 15 And Aaron returned to Moses to the door of the Tabernacle of Witness, and the plague ceased. 16 And the Lord spoke to Moses, saying,

17 Speak to the sons of Israel, and take a rod of them, according to their fathers' houses, a rod from all their rulers, according to their fathers' houses, twelve rods, and write the name of each on his rod. 18 And the name of Aaron *shall be* written on the rod of Levi; for it is one rod, they shall give *them* according to the tribe of their fathers' houses. 19 And thou shall put them in the Tabernacle of Witness, before the testimony, where I will be made known to thee. 20 And it shall be, the man whom I shall choose, his rod shall blossom; and I will remove from Me the murmuring of the sons of Israel, which they murmur against you. 21 And Moses spoke to the sons of Israel, and all their rulers gave him a rod, for one ruler a rod, according to their fathers' houses, twelve rods; and the rod of Aaron *was* in the midst of the rods. 22 And Moses stored the rods before the Lord in the Tabernacle of Witness. 23 And it came to pass the next day, that Moses and Aaron went into the Tabernacle of Witness; and, behold, the rod of Aaron for the house of Levi blossomed, and put forth a bud, and bloomed blossoms and produced almonds. 24 And Moses brought forth all the rods from before the Lord to all the sons of Israel; and they looked, and each one took his rod. 25 And the Lord said to Moses, Lay up the rod of Aaron before the testimonies to be kept as a sign for the sons of the disobedient; and let their murmuring end from Me, and they shall not die. 26 And Moses and Aaron did as the Lord commanded Moses, so did they. 27 And the sons of Israel spoke to Moses, saying, Behold, we are cut off, we are destroyed, we are consumed. 28 Every one that touches the tabernacle of the Lord dies; shall we then completely die?

Chapter 18

And the Lord spoke to Aaron, saying, Thou and thy sons and thy father's house shall bear the sins of the holy things, and thou and thy sons shall bear the iniquity of your priesthood. 2 And take to thyself as thy brother the tribe of Levi, the family of thy father, and let them be joined to thee, and let them minister to thee; and thou and thy sons with thee before the Tabernacle of Witness. 3 And they shall keep thy charges and the charges of the tabernacle; only they shall not approach the holy items and the altar, so both they and you shall not die. 4 And they shall be joined to thee, and shall keep the charges of the Tabernacle of Witness, in all the liturgies of the tabernacle; and a stranger shall not approach to thee. 5 And ye shall keep the charges of the holy *things,* and the charges of the altar, and *so* there shall not be anger in the sons of Israel. 6 And I have taken your brothers the Levites out of the midst of the sons of Israel, a gift given to the Lord, to officiate in the liturgies of the Tabernacle of Witness.

Numbers 18

7 And thou and thy sons after thee shall keep up your priestly duties, according to the entire manner of the altar, and that which is within the veil; and ye shall officiate in the liturgies as the office of your priesthood; and the stranger that comes near shall die.

8 And the Lord said to Aaron, and, behold, I have given you the charge of the first fruits of all things consecrated to Me by the sons of Israel; and I have given them to thee as an honor, and to thy sons after thee as a perpetual law. 9 And let this be to you from all the holy *things* that are consecrated the burnt offerings, from all their gifts, and from all their sacrifices, and from every trespass offering of theirs, and from all their sin offerings, whatever things they give to Me of all their holy *things*, they shall be thine and thy sons'. 10 In the holy of holies shall ye eat them; every male shall eat them, you and thy sons; they shall be holy to thee. 11 And this shall be to you of the first fruits of their gifts, of all the wave offerings of the sons of Israel; to thee have I given them and to thy sons and thy daughters with thee, a perpetual law; every clean person in thy house shall eat them. 12 Every first offering of oil, and every first offering of wine, their first fruits of corn, whatever they may give to the Lord, to thee I have given them. 13 All the first fruits that are in their land, whatever they shall offer to the Lord, shall be thine; every clean person in thy house shall eat them. 14 Every devoted thing among the sons of Israel shall be thine. 15 And every thing that opens the womb of all flesh, whatever they bring to the Lord, whether man or beast, shall be thine; only the first born of men shall be surely redeemed, and thou shall redeem the first born of unclean cattle. 16 And the redemption of them *shall be* from a month old; their valuation of five shekels, according to the holy shekel, shall be twenty oboli. 17 But thou shall not redeem the first born among *the* calves and the first born of sheep and the first born of goats; they are holy; and thou shall pour their blood upon the altar, and thou shall offer the fat as a burnt offering for a sweet smelling savor unto the Lord. 18 And the flesh shall be thine, as also the breast of the wave offering and as the right shoulder, it shall be thine. 19 Every special offering of the holy *things*, whatever the sons of Israel shall specially offer to the Lord, I have given to thee and to thy sons and to thy daughters with thee, a perpetual law; it is a covenant of eternal salt before the Lord, for thee and thy seed after thee.

20 And the Lord said to Aaron, Thou shall have no inheritance in their land, neither shall thou have any portion among them, for I *am* thy portion and thine inheritance in the midst of the sons of Israel. 21 And, behold, I have given to the sons of Levi every tithe in Israel for an inheritance for their liturgies, wherever they officiate a liturgy in the Tabernacle of Witness. 22 And the sons of Israel shall never more draw near to the Tabernacle of Witness to sustain fatal guilt.

23 And the Levite himself shall officiate the liturgy of the Tabernacle of Witness; and they shall bear their iniquities, it is a perpetual law throughout their generations; and in the midst of the sons of Israel they shall not receive an inheritance. 24 Because I have given as a distinct portion to the Levites for an inheritance the tithes of the sons of Israel, whatever they shall offer to the Lord; therefore I said to them, In the midst of the sons of Israel they shall have no inheritance.

25 And the Lord spoke to Moses, saying, 26 And thou shall speak to the Levites, and shall say to them, If ye take the tithe from the sons of Israel, which I have given you from them for an inheritance, then shall ye separate from it a heave offering to the Lord, a tenth of the tenth. 27 And your heave offerings shall be reckoned to you as corn from the floor, and an offering from the wine press. 28 So shall ye also separate them from all the offerings of the Lord out of all your tithes, whatever ye shall receive from the sons of Israel; and ye shall give of them an offering to the Lord to Aaron the priest. 29 Of all your gifts ye shall offer an offering to the Lord and of every first fruit the consecrated part from it. 30 And thou shall say to them, When ye shall offer the first fruits from it, then shall it be reckoned to the Levites as produce from the threshing floor, and as produce from the wine press. 31 And ye shall eat it in any place, ye and your families; for this is your reward for your liturgies in the tabernacle of witness. 32 And ye shall not bear sin by reason of it, because ye shall have offered an offering of first fruits from it, and ye shall not profane the holy things of the sons of Israel, that ye not die.

Chapter 19

And the Lord spoke to Moses and Aaron, saying, 2 This is the distinction of the law, as the Lord has commanded, saying, Speak to the sons of Israel, and let them take for thee a red heifer without spot, which has no spot on her, and on which no yoke has been put. 3 And thou shall give her to Eleazar the priest; and they shall bring her out of the camp into a clean place, and shall kill her before his face. 4 And Eleazar shall take of her blood, and sprinkle of her blood seven times in front of the Tabernacle of Witness. 5 And they shall burn her to ashes before him; and her skin and her flesh and her blood, with her dung, shall be consumed. 6 And the priest shall take cedar wood and hyssop and red wool, and they shall throw them into the middle of the burning of the heifer. 7 And the priest shall wash his garments, and bathe his body in water, and afterwards he shall go into the camp, and the priest shall be unclean till evening. 8 And he that burns her shall wash his garments, and bathe his body, and shall be unclean till evening.

9 And a clean man shall gather up the ashes of the heifer, and lay them up in a clean place outside the camp; and they shall be for the congregation of the sons of Israel to keep; it is the water of sprinkling, it is a purification. 10 And he that gathers up the ashes of the heifer shall wash his garments, and shall be unclean until evening; and it shall be a perpetual law for the sons of Israel and for the strangers joined to them.

11 He that touches the *dead* soul of any man shall be unclean seven days. 12 He shall be purified on the third day and the seventh day, and shall be clean; but if he was not purged on the third day and the seventh day, he shall not be clean. 13 Every one that touches the *dead* soul of a man, if he should have died, and not have been purified, has defiled the tabernacle of the Lord; that soul shall be cut off from Israel, because the water of sprinkling has not been sprinkled upon him; he is unclean; his uncleanness is yet upon him.

14 And this *is* the law; if a man dies in a house, every one that goes into the house, and all things in the house, shall be unclean seven days. 15 And every open item that does not have a covering bound upon it shall be unclean. 16 And every one who, on the face of the plain, shall touch a man killed by violence, or a corpse, or a man's bone, or tomb, shall be unclean seven days. 17 And they shall take for the unclean of the burnt ashes of purification, and they shall pour upon them living water into a vessel. 18 And a clean man shall take hyssop, and dip it into the water, and sprinkle it upon the house, and the items, and all the souls that are therein, and upon him that touched the man's bone, or the *violently* killed man, or the corpse, or the tomb. 19 And the clean man shall sprinkle on the unclean on the third day and on the seventh day, and on the seventh day he shall purify himself; and shall wash his garments, and bathe himself in water, and shall be unclean until evening.

20 And whatever man shall be defiled and shall not purify himself, that soul shall be cut off from the midst of the congregation, because he has defiled the holy *things* of the Lord, because the water of sprinkling has not been sprinkled upon him; he is unclean. 21 And it shall be to you a perpetual law; and he that sprinkles the water of sprinkling shall wash his garments; and he that touches the water of sprinkling shall be unclean until evening. 22 And whatever the unclean man shall touch shall be unclean, and the soul that touches it shall be unclean till evening.

Chapter 20

And the sons of Israel, *even* the whole congregation, came into the wilderness of Sinai, in the first month, and the people stayed in Kades; and Mariam died there, and was buried there.

2 And there was no water for the congregation; and they gathered themselves together against Moses and Aaron. 3 And the people hated Moses, saying, Would we had died in the destruction of our brothers before the Lord! 4 And wherefore have ye brought up the congregation of the Lord into this wilderness, to kill our cattle and us? 5 And wherefore *is* this? Ye have brought us up out of Egypt, that we should come into this evil place; a place where there is no sowing, neither figs, nor vines, nor pomegranates, neither is there water to drink. 6 And Moses and Aaron went from before the face of the assembly to the door of the Tabernacle of Witness, and they fell upon their faces; and the glory of the Lord appeared to them.

7 And the Lord spoke to Moses, saying, 8 Take thy rod, and call the assembly, thou and Aaron thy brother, and speak ye to the rock before them, and it shall give forth its waters; and ye shall bring forth for them water out of the rock, and give drink to the congregation and their cattle. 9 And Moses took his rod which was before the Lord, as the Lord commanded.

10 And Moses and Aaron assembled the congregation before the rock, and said to them, Hear me, ye disobedient ones; must we bring you water out of this rock? 11 And Moses lifted up his hand and hit the rock with his rod twice; and much water came forth, and the congregation drank, and their cattle. 12 And the Lord said to Moses and Aaron, Because ye have not believed Me to sanctify Me before the sons of Israel, therefore ye shall not bring this congregation into the land which I have given them. 13 This is the Water of Strife, because the sons of Israel spoke insolently before the Lord, and He was sanctified in them.

14 And Moses sent messengers from Kades to the King of Edom, saying, Thus says thy brother Israel; Thou knows all the troubles that has found us. 15 And *how* our fathers went down into Egypt, and we traveled in Egypt many days, and the Egyptians afflicted our fathers and us. 16 And we cried to the Lord, and the Lord heard our voice, and sent an angel and brought us out of Egypt; and now we are in the city of Kades, at the edge of thy borders. 17 We will pass through thy land; we will not go through the fields, neither through the vineyards, nor will we drink water out of thy cistern; we will go by the king's highway; we will not turn aside to the right hand or to the left, until we have passed thy borders. 18 And Edom said to him, Thou shall not pass through me, and if otherwise, I will go forth to meet thee in war. 19 And the sons of Israel said to him, We will pass by the mountain; and if my cattle and I drink of thy water, I will pay thee; but it is no matter of importance, we will go by the mountain. 20 And he said, Thou should not pass through me; and Edom went forth to meet him with a heavy multitude, and a strong hand. 21 So Edom refused to allow Israel to pass through his borders, and Israel turned away from him.

Numbers 21

22 And they departed from Kades; and the sons of Israel, even the whole congregation, came to Mount Or. 23 And the Lord spoke to Moses and Aaron in Mount Or, on the borders of the land of Edom, saying, 24 Let Aaron be added to his people; for ye shall certainly not enter the land which I have given the sons of Israel, because ye provoked Me at the Water of Strife. 25 Take Aaron, and Eleazar his son, and bring them up to the Mountain *of* Or before the entire congregation, 26 and take Aaron's garments off of him, and put it on Eleazar his son; and let Aaron die there. 27 And Moses did as the Lord commanded him, and took him up to Mount Or, before the entire congregation. 28 And he took Aaron's garments off him, and put them on Eleazar his son, and Aaron died on the top of the mountain; and Moses and Eleazar came down from the mountain. 29 And the entire congregation saw that Aaron was dead, and they wept for Aaron thirty days, *even* the entire house of Israel.

Chapter 21

And the Canaanite King Arad, who lived by the wilderness, heard that Israel came by the way of Atharin; and he made war on Israel, and carried off a captivity of them as captives. 2 And Israel vowed a vow to the Lord, and said If thou will deliver this people into my power, I will devote it and its cities *to thee*. 3 And the Lord hearkened to the voice of Israel, and delivered the Canaanite into his power; and *Israel* devoted him and his cities, and they called the name of that place Anathema.

4 And having departed from Mount Or by the way to the Red Sea, they encompassed the land of Edom, and the people lost courage by the way. 5 And the people spoke against God and against Moses, saying, Why is this? Have thou brought us out of Egypt to kill us in the wilderness? For there is neither bread nor water and our soul loathes this light bread. 6 And the Lord sent among the people deadly serpents, and they bit the people, and much people of the sons of Israel died. 7 And the people came to Moses and said, We have sinned, for we have spoken against the Lord, and against thee; pray therefore to the Lord, and let him take away the serpent from us. 8 And Moses prayed to the Lord for the people; and the Lord said to Moses, Make thee a serpent, and put it on a signal; and it shall come to pass that whenever a serpent shall bite a man, every one bitten that looks upon it shall live. 9 And Moses made a serpent of brass, and put it upon a signal; and it came to pass that whenever a serpent bit a man, and he looked on the brazen serpent, he lived.

10 And the sons of Israel departed, and encamped in Oboth. 11 And having departed from Oboth, they encamped in Ahalgai, on the farther side in the wilderness, which is opposite Moab, toward the east.

Numbers 21

12 And thence they departed, and encamped in the valley of Zared. 13 And they departed thence and encamped on the other side of Arnon in the wilderness, which extends from the coasts of the Amorites; for Arnon is the border of Moab, between Moab and the Amorite. 14 Therefore it is said in a book, A war of the Lord has set on fire Zoob, and the brooks of Arnon. 15 And he has appointed brooks to cause Er to live *there*; and it lies near to the coasts of Moab.

16 And thence *they came to* the well; this the well of which the Lord said to Moses, Gather the people, and I will give them water to drink. 17 Then Israel sang this song at the well, Begin *to sing* of the well for it, 18 the rulers dug it, the kings of the gentiles in their kingdom, in their lordship sank it in the rock: and *they went* from the well to Manthanain, 19 and from Manthanain to Naaliel, and from Naaliel to Bamoth, and from Bamoth to Janen, which is in the plain of Moab *as seen* from the top of the quarried *rock* that looks toward the wilderness. 20 And Moses sent ambassadors to Seon King of the Amorites, with peaceable words, saying,

21 We will pass through thy land, we will go by the road; we will not turn aside to the field or to the vineyard. 22 We will not drink water out of thy well; we will go by the king's highway, until we have passed thy boundaries. 23 And Seon did not allow Israel to pass through his borders, and Seon gathered all his people, and went out to set the battle in array against Israel into the wilderness; and he came to Jassa, and set the battle in array against Israel. 24 And Israel killed him with the slaughter of the sword, and they became possessors of his land, from Arnon to Jabok, as far as the sons of Amman, for Jazer is the border of the sons of Amman. 25 And Israel took all their cities, and Israel lived in all the cities of the Amorite, in Esebon, and in all cities belonging to it. 26 For Esebon is the city of Seon king of the Amorites; and he before fought against the King of Moab, and they took all his land, from Aroer to Arnon.

27 Therefore say they who deal in dark speeches, Come to Esebon, that the city of Seon may be built and prepared. 28 For a fire have gone forth from Esebon, a flame from the city of Seon, and has consumed as far as Moab, and devoured the pillars of Arnon. 29 Woe to thee, Moab, thou art lost, thou people of Hamos; their sons are sold for preservation, and their daughters are captives to Seon King of the Amorite. 30 And their seed shall perish *from* Esebon to Daebon; and their women have yet farther kindled a fire against Moab.

31 And Israel lived in all the cities of the Amorite. 32 And Moses sent to spy out Jazer; and they took it, and its villages, and cast out the Amorite that lived there. 33 And having returned, they went up the road that leads to Basan; and Og the King of Basan went forth to meet them, and all his people to war to Edrain. 34 And the Lord said to Moses, Fear him not; for I have delivered him and all his people, and all his land, into thy hands; and thou shall do to him as thou did to Seon King of the Amorite, who lived in Esebon.

Numbers 22

35 And he killed him and his sons, and all his people, until he left none of his to be taken alive; and they inherited his land.

Chapter 22

And the sons of Israel departed, and encamped on the west of Moab by Jordan toward Jericho. 2 And when Balak son of Sepphor saw all that Israel did to the Amorite, 3 then Moab feared the people exceedingly because they were many; and Moab was grieved before the face of the sons of Israel. 4 And Moab said to the elders of Madiam, Now shall this assembly lick up all that are around us, as a calf would lick up the greens of the field; and Balak son of Sepphor was King of Moab at that time. 5 And he sent ambassadors to Balaam the son of Beor, to Phathura, which is on a river of the land of the sons of his people, to call him, saying, Behold, a people have come out of Egypt, and behold it has covered the appearance of the earth, and it has encamped close to me. 6 And now come, curse me this people, for it is stronger than we; if we may be able to kill some of them, and I will cast them out of the land; for I know that whomever thou does bless, they are blessed, and whomever thou does curse, they are cursed.

7 And the elders of Moab went, and the elders of Madiam, and their divining *instruments* in their hands; and they came to Balaam, and spoke to him the words of Balak. 8 And he said to them, Wait here the night, and I will answer you the things, which the Lord shall say to me; and the rulers of Moab stayed with Balaam. 9 And God came to Balaam, and said to him, Who are these men with thee? 10 And Balaam said to God, Balak son of Sepphor, King of Moab, sent them to me, saying, 11 Behold, a people has come forth out of Egypt, and has covered the appearance of the earth, and it has encamped near to me; and now come, curse it for me, if indeed I shall be able to kill it, and cast it out of the land. 12 And God said to Balaam, Thou should not go with them; neither shall thou curse the people; for they are blessed. 13 And Balaam arose in the morning, and said to the rulers of Balak, Depart quickly to your lord; God does not permit me to go with you. 14 And the rulers of Moab arose, and came to Balak, and said, Balaam will not come with us.

15 And Balak yet again sent more rulers and more honorable than they. 16 And they came to Balaam, and they said to him, Thus says Balak the son of Sepphor; I beseech thee, delay not to come to me. 17 For I will greatly honor thee, and will do for thee whatever thou shall say; come then, curse me this people. 18 And Balaam answered and said to the rulers of Balak, If Balak would give me his house full of silver and gold, I shall not be able to go beyond the word of the Lord God, to make it little or great in my mind. 19 And now you also wait here this night, and I shall know what the Lord will yet say to me.

20 And God came to Balaam by night, and said to him, If these men come to call thee, arise and follow them; nevertheless the word which I shall speak to thee, it shall thou do.

21 And Balaam arose in the morning, and saddled his mule, and went with the rulers of Moab. 22 And God was very angry because he went; and the angel of the Lord arose to withstand him. Now he had mounted his mule, and his two servants were with him. 23 And when the mule saw the angel of God standing opposite in the way, and his broadsword drawn in his hand, then the mule turned aside out of the path, and went into the field; and *Balaam* hit the mule with his staff to direct her in the path. 24 And the angel of the Lord stood in the avenues of the vines, a fence on this side and a fence on that. 25 And when the mule saw the angel of God, she thrust herself against the wall, and crushed Balaam's foot against the wall, and he hit her again. 26 And the angel of the Lord went farther, and came and stood in a narrow place where it was impossible to turn to the right or the left. 27 And when the mule saw the angel of God, she sat down under Balaam; and Balaam was angry, and struck the mule with his staff. 28 And God opened the mouth of the mule, and she said to Balaam, What have I done to thee, that thou have struck me this third time? 29 And Balaam said to the mule, Because thou has mocked me; and if I had a sword in my hand, I would now have killed thee. 30 And the mule says to Balaam, *Am* I not thy mule on which thou have ridden since thy youth till this day? Did I ever do thus to thee, utterly disregarding *thee*? And he said, No.

31 And God opened the eyes of Balaam, and he saw the angel of the Lord blocking *him* in the path, and his sword drawn in his hand, and he stooped down and worshipped on his face. 32 And the angel of God said to him, Why has thou struck thy mule this third time? And, behold, I came out to block thee, for thy path was not seemly before me; and when the mule saw me, she turned away from me this third time. 33 And if she had not turned out of the way, surely now, I should have killed thee, and should have saved her alive. 34 And Balaam said to the angel of the Lord, I have sinned, for I did not know that thou were standing opposite in the way to meet *me*; and now if it shall not be pleasing to thee *for me to proceed*, I will return. 35 And the angel of the Lord said to Balaam, Go with the men; nevertheless the word, which I shall speak to thee, that thou shall take heed to speak. And Balaam went with the rulers of Balak.

36 And when Balak heard that Balaam was coming, he went out to meet him, to a city of Moab, which is on the border of Arnon, which is on the *extreme* part of the border. 37 And Balak said to Balaam, Did I not send to thee to call thee? Why have thou not come to me? Shall I not indeed be able to honor thee? 38 And Balaam said to Balak, Behold, I am now come to thee; shall I be able to say anything? The word, which God shall put into my mouth, is what I shall speak.

Numbers 23

39 And Balaam went with Balak, and they came to the Cities of Villages. 40 And Balak offered sheep and calves, and sent to Balaam and to his rulers who were with him.

41 And it was morning; and Balak took Balaam, and brought him up to the Pillar of Baal, and showed him thence a part of the people.

Chapter 23

And Balaam said to Balak, Build me here seven altars, and prepare me here seven calves, and seven rams. 2 And Balak did as Balaam told him; and he offered up a calf and a ram on *every* altar. 3 And Balaam said to Balak, Stand by thy sacrifice, and I will go and see if God will appear to me in a meeting, and the word, which he shall show me, I will report to thee. And Balak stood by his sacrifice. 4 And Balaam went to enquire of God; and he went straight forward, and God appeared to Balaam; and Balaam said to him, I have prepared the seven altars, and have offered a calf and a ram on *every* altar. 5 And God put a word into the mouth of Balaam, and said, thou shall return to Balak, and thus shall thou speak. 6 And he returned to him, and moreover he stood over his whole burnt offerings, and all the rulers of Moab with him; and the Spirit of God came upon him.

7 And he took up his parable, and said, Balak king of Moab sent for me out of Mesopotamia, out of the mountains of the east, saying, Come, curse me Jacob, and Come, call for a curse for me upon Israel. 8 How can I curse whom the Lord curses not? Or how can I denounce whom God denounces not? 9 For from the top of the mountains I shall see him, and from the hills I shall observe him; behold, the people shall live alone, and shall not be reckoned among the gentiles. 10 Who has exactly calculated the seed of Jacob, and who shall number the families of Israel? Let my soul die with the souls of the righteous, and let my seed be as their seed.

11 And Balak said to Balaam, What have thou done to me? I called thee to curse my enemies, and behold thou has greatly blessed *them*. 12 And Balaam said to Balak, Whatever the Lord shall put into my mouth, should I not take heed to say this?

13 And Balak said to him, Come yet with me to another place where thou shall not see it, but only thou shall see a part of it, and shall not see them all; and curse it *for* me from there. 14 And he took him to a high place of the field to the top of the quarry, and he built there seven altars, and offered a calf and a ram on *every* altar. 15 And Balaam said to Balak, Stand by thy sacrifice, and I will go to enquire of God. 16 And God met Balaam, and put a word into his mouth, and said, return to Balak, and thus shall thou say.

17 And he returned to him; and he also was standing by his whole burnt sacrifice, and all the rulers of Moab with him; and Balak said to him, What has the Lord spoken?

18 And he took up his parable, and said, rise up, Balak, and hear, hearken as a witness, thou son of Sepphor. 19 God is not as man to waver, nor as the son of man to be threatened; shall he say and not perform? Shall he speak and not keep *to his word*? 20 Behold, I have received *a command* to bless; I will bless, and not turn back. 21 There shall not be trouble in Jacob, neither shall sorrow be seen in Israel; the Lord his God *is* with him, the glories of rulers *are* in him. 22 It was God who brought him out of Egypt as the glory of the only-horned *animal*. 23 For there is no divination against Jacob, nor enchantment in Israel; in season it shall be told to Jacob and Israel what God shall perform. 24 Behold, the people shall arise as a lion's cub, and shall exalt themselves as a lion; they shall not rest till they have eaten the prey, and drunk the blood of the violently wounded.

25 And Balak said to Balaam, Neither curse them at all for me, nor bless them at all. 26 And Balaam answered and said to Balak, did I not say to thee, saying, Whatever thing God shall speak to me, that will I do? 27 And Balak said to Balaam, Come, I will remove thee to another place, if it shall please God, and curse me them from there. 28 And Balak took Balaam to the top of Phogor, which extends to the wilderness. 29 And Balaam said to Balak, build me here seven altars, and prepare me here seven calves, and seven rams. 30 And Balak did as Balaam told him, and offered a calf and a ram on *every* altar.

Chapter 24

And when Balaam saw that it pleased God to bless Israel, he did not go according to his custom to meet the omens, but turned his face toward the wilderness. 2 And Balaam lifted up his eyes, and saw Israel encamped by their tribes; and the Spirit of God came upon him.

3 And he took up his parable and said, Balaam son of Beor, says the man who truly sees, 4 he says who hears the oracle of the Mighty One, who saw a vision of God in sleep; his eyes were opened: 5 How good *are* thy habitations, O Jacob, and thy tents, O Israel! 6 As shady groves, and as gardens by a river, and as tents, which God pitched, and as cedars by the waters. 7 There shall come a man out of his seed, and he shall rule over many nations; and the kingdom of Gog shall be exalted, and his kingdom shall be increased. 8 God led him out of Egypt; as the glory of only-horned *animal*; he shall consume the nations of his enemies, and he shall suck out the marrow of their fatness, and with his arrows he shall shoot through the enemy.

Numbers 25

9 He lay down; he rested as a lion, and as a young lion, who shall stir him up? They that bless thee are blessed, and they that curse thee are cursed.

10 And Balak was angry with Balaam, and clapped his hands together; and Balak said to Balaam, I called thee to curse my enemy, and behold thou has decidedly blessed *him* this third time. 11 Now therefore flee to thy place; I said, I will honor thee, but now the Lord has deprived thee of glory. 12 And Balaam said to Balak, Did I not speak to thy angels also whom thou sent to me, saying, 13 If Balak should give me his house full of silver and gold, I shall not be able to go beyond the word of the Lord to make it good or bad by myself; whatever things God shall say, them will I speak. 14 And now, behold, I return to my place; come, I will advise thee of what this people shall do to thy people in the last days.

15 And he took up his parable and said, Balaam the son of Beor, says the man who truly sees says, 16 hearing the oracles of God, knowing knowledge from the Most High, and having seen a vision of God in sleep his eyes were uncovered. 17 I will point to him, but not now; I bless him, but he draws not near; a star shall arise out of Jacob, a man shall spring out of Israel; and shall crush the rulers of Moab, and shall spoil all the sons of Seth. 18 And Edom shall be an inheritance, and Esau his enemy shall be an inheritance, and Israel wrought valiantly. 19 And *one* shall arise out of Jacob, and destroy him that escapes out of the city. 20 And having seen Amalek, he took up his parable and said, Amalek, the first of the gentiles; yet his seed shall perish.

21 And having seen the Kenite, he took up his parable and said, thy habitation *is* strong; yet though thou should put thy nest in a rock, 22 and though Beor should have a cunning nesting *place,* the Assyrians shall carry thee away captive.

23 And he looked upon Og, and took up his parable and said, Oh, oh, who shall live, when God shall put these things? 24 And one shall come forth from the hands of the Kitians, and shall afflict Assur, and shall afflict the Hebrews, and they shall perish together. 25 And Balaam rose up and departed and returned to his place, and Balak went to his own home.

Chapter 25

And Israel traveled in Sattin, and the people profaned themself by whoring after the daughters of Moab. 2 And they called them to the sacrifices of their idols; and the people ate of their sacrifices, and worshipped their idols. 3 And Israel consecrated themselves to Beelphegor; and the Lord was very angry at Israel. 4 And the Lord said to Moses, Take all the rulers of the people, and put them to shame before the Lord in the face of the sun and the anger of the Lord shall be turned away from Israel.

5 And Moses said to the tribes of Israel, Kill ye every one his friend that is consecrated to Beelphegor.

6 And, behold, a man of the sons of Israel came and brought his brother to a Madianite woman before Moses, and before the entire congregation of the sons of Israel; and they were weeping at the door of the Tabernacle of Witness. 7 And Phinees the son of Eleazar, the son of Aaron the priest, saw it, and arose out of the midst of the congregation, and took a dagger in his hand, 8 and went in after the Israelite man into the furnace, and pierced them both through, both the Israelite man, and the woman through her womb; and the plague was stayed from the sons of Israel. 9 And those that died in the plague were four and twenty thousand.

10 And the Lord spoke to Moses, saying, 11 Phinees the son of Eleazar the son of Aaron the priest has caused My wrath to cease from the sons of Israel, when I was exceedingly jealous with them, and I did not consume the sons of Israel in My jealousy. 12 Thus do thou say *to him*, Behold, I give him a covenant of peace; 13 and he and his seed after him shall have a perpetual covenant of priesthood, because he was zealous for his God, and made atonement for the sons of Israel.

14 Now the name of the killed Israelite man, who was killed with the Madianite woman, *was* Zambri son of Salmon, ruler of a house of the tribe of Simon. 15 And the name of the Madianite woman, who was killed, *was* Hasbi, daughter of Sur, a ruler of the nation of Ommoth: it is a chief house among the people of Madiam.

16 And the Lord spoke to Moses, saying, Speak to the sons of Israel, saying, 17 Harass the Madianites, and kill them, 18 for they harass and ensnare you by ensnaring you through Phogor, and through Hasbi their sister, daughter of a ruler of Madiam, who was killed in the day of the plague because of Phogor.

Chapter 26

And it came to pass after the plague, that the Lord spoke to Moses and Eleazar the priest, saying, 2 Take the sum of all the congregation of the sons of Israel, from twenty years old and upward, according to their fathers' houses, every one that goes forth to battle in Israel. 3 And Moses and Eleazar the priest spoke in Araboth of Moab at the Jordan by Jericho, saying, 4 from twenty years old and upward as the Lord commanded Moses. And the sons of Israel that came out of Egypt;

5 Ruben the firstborn of Israel; and the sons of Ruben, Enoch, and the people of Enoch, to Phallu belongs the people of the Phalluites. 6 To Asron, the people of Asroni; to Harmi, the people of Harmi.

Numbers 26

7 These *are* the peoples of Ruben; and their numbering was forty-three thousand and seven hundred and thirty. 8 And the sons of Phallu *were* Eliab. 9 And the sons of Eliab, Namuel, and Dathan, and Abiron; these renowned men of the congregation, these are they that arose against Moses and Aaron in the gathering of Kore, in the rebellion against the Lord. 10 And the earth opened her mouth, and swallowed them up and Kore, when their assembly perished, when the fire devoured the two hundred and fifty, and they were for a sign. 11 But the sons of Kore did not die.

12 And the sons of Simon; the people of the sons of Simon: to Namuel, the people of the Namuelites; to Jamin the people of the Jaminites; to Jahin the people of the Jahinites. 13 To Zara the people of the Zaraites; to Saul the people of the Saulites. 14 These *are* the peoples of Simon according to their numbering, two and twenty thousand and two hundred.

15 And the sons of Judah, Er and Aunan; and Er and Aunan died in the land of Canaan. 16 And these were the sons of Judah, according to their peoples; to Selom the people of the Selonites; to Phares, the people of the Pharesites; to Zara, the people of the Zaraites. 17 And the sons of Phares were, to Asron, the people of the Asronites; to Jamun, the people of the Jamunites. 18 These *are* the peoples of Judah according to their numbering, seventy-six thousand and five hundred.

19 And the sons of Issahar according to their peoples; to Thola, the people of the Tholaites; to Phua, the people of the Phuaites. 20 To Jasub, the people of the Jasubites; to Samram, the people of the Samramites. 21 These *are* the peoples of Issahar according to their numbering, sixty-four thousand and four hundred. 22 The sons of Zabulon according to their peoples: to Sared, the people of the Saredites; to Allon, the people of the Allonites; to Allel, the people of the Allelites.

23 These *are* the peoples of Zabulon according to their numbering, sixty thousand and five hundred. 24 The sons of Gad according to their peoples; to Saphon, the people of the Saphonites; to Angi, the people of the Angites; to Suni, the people of the Sunites; 25 to Azeni, the people of the Azenites; to Addi, the people of the Addites;

26 to Aroadi, the people of the Aroadites; to Ariel, the people of the Arielites. 27 These *are* the peoples of the sons of Gad according to their numbering, forty-four thousand and five hundred.

28 The sons of Aser according to their peoples; to Jamin, the people of the Jaminites; to Jesu, the people of the Jesusites; to Baria, the people of the Bariaites. 29 To Hober, the people of the Hoberites; to Melhiel, the people of the Melhielites. 30 And the name of the daughter of Aser, Sara. 31 These *are* the peoples of Aser according to their numbering, forty-three thousand and * four hundred.

32 The sons of Joseph according to their peoples, Manasse and Ephraim. 33 The sons of Manasse. To Mahir the people of the Mahirites; and Mahir begot Galaad; to Galaad, the people of the Galaadites. 34 And these *are* the sons of Galaad; to Ahiezer, the people of the Ahiezerites; to Heleg, the people of the Helegites.

35 To Esriel, the people of the Esrielites; to Sychem, the people of the Sychemites. 36 To Symer, the people of the Symerites; and to Opher, the people of the Opherites. 37 And to Salpaad the son of Opher there was no sons, but daughters; and these *were* the names of the daughters of Salpaad; Mala, and Nua, and Egla, and Melha, and Thersa.

38 These *are* the peoples of Manasse according to their numbering, * fifty-two thousand and seven hundred. 39 And these *are* the sons of Ephraim; to Suthala, the people of the Suthalanites; to Tanah, the people of the Tanahites. 40 These *are* the sons of Suthala; to Eden, the people of the Edenites. 41 These *are* the peoples of Ephraim according to their numbering, thirty-two thousand and five hundred: these *are* the people of the sons of Joseph according to their peoples.

42 The sons of Benjamin according to their peoples; to Bale, the people of the Balites; to Asyber, the people of the Asyberites; to Jahiran, the people of the Jahiranites. 43 To Sophan, the people of the Sophanites.

44 And the sons of Bale were Adar and Noeman; to Adar, the people of the Adarites; and to Noeman, the people of the Noemanites. 45 These *are* the sons of Benjamin by their peoples according to their numbering, thirty-five thousand and five hundred. 46 And the sons of Dan according to their peoples; to Same, the people of the Sameites; these *are* the peoples of Dan according to their peoples. 47 All the peoples of Samei according to their numbering, sixty-four thousand and * four hundred.

48 The sons of Nephthali according to their peoples; to Asiel, the people of the Asielites; to Gauni, the people of the Gaunites. 49 To Jeser, the people of the Jeserites; to Sellem, the people of the Sellemites. 50 These *are* the peoples of Nephthali, according to their numbering, forty thousand and three hundred.

51 This *is* the numbering of the sons of Israel, six hundred and one thousand and seven hundred and thirty.

52 And the Lord spoke to Moses, saying, 53 To these the land shall be divided, so that they may inherit according to the number of the names.

54 To the greater number thou shall give the greater inheritance, and to the less number thou shall give the lesser inheritance: to each one, as they have been numbered, shall their inheritance be given. 55 The land shall be divided to the names by lot; they shall inherit according to the tribes of their fathers. 56 Thou shall divide their inheritance by lot between the many and the few.

Numbers 27

57 And the sons of Levi according to their people; to Gedson, the people of the Gedsonites; to Kaath, the people of the Kaathites; to Merari, the people of the Merarites. 58 These *are* the peoples of the sons of Levi; the people of the Lobenites, the people of the Hebronites, the people of the Koreites, and the people of the Musites; and Kaath begot Amram. 59 And the name of his wife *was* Johabed, daughter of Levi, who bore these to Levi in Egypt, and she bore to Amram, Aaron and Moses, and Mariam their sister. 60 And to Aaron were born both Nadab and Abiud, and Eleazar, and Ithamar. 61 And Nadab and Abiud died when they offered strange fire before the Lord in the wilderness of Sinai. 62 And there were according to their numbering, twenty-three thousand, *and* every male from a month old and upward; for they were not numbered among the sons of Israel, because they have no inheritance in the midst of the sons of Israel.

63 And this *is* the numbering of Moses and Eleazar the priest, who numbered the sons of Israel in Araboth of Moab, at Jordan by Jericho. 64 And among these there was not a man numbered by Moses and Aaron, whom, *even* the sons of Israel, they numbered in the wilderness of Sinai. 65 For the Lord said to them, They shall die the death in the wilderness; and there was not left even one of them, except Kaleb the son of Jephonne, and Jesus the *son* of Naue.

* *Codex Alexandrinus* reads: "Six hundred".
* *Codex Alexandrinus* reads: "Sixty-two thousand and five hundred".
* *Codex Alexandrinus* reads: "Six hundred".

Chapter 27

And the daughters of Salpaad the son of Opher, the son of Galaad, the son of Mahir, of the tribe of Manasse, of the sons of Joseph, came near; (and these were their names, Maala, and Nua, and Egla, and Melha, and Thersa); 2 and they stood before Moses, and before Eleazar the priest, and before the rulers, and before all the congregation at the door of the Tabernacle of Witness, saying, 3 Our father died in the wilderness, and he was not in the midst of the congregation that rebelled against the Lord in the gathering of Kore; for he died for his own sin, and he had no sons. Let not the name of our father become blotted out of the midst of his people, because he has no son; give us an inheritance in the midst of our father's brothers. 4 And Moses brought their case before the Lord.

5 And the Lord spoke to Moses, saying, 6 The daughters of Salpaad have spoken rightly; thou shall surely give them a possession of inheritance in the midst of their father's brothers, and thou shall assign their father's inheritance to them. 7 And thou shall speak to the sons of Israel, saying, 8 If a man die, and have no son, ye shall assign his inheritance to his daughter.

9 And if he has no daughter, ye shall give his inheritance to his brother. 10 And if he has no brothers, ye shall give his inheritance to his father's brother. 11 And if there be no brothers of his father, ye shall give the inheritance to his nearest relation of his tribe, to inherit his possessions; and this shall be to the sons of Israel an ordinance of judgment, as the Lord commanded Moses.

12 And the Lord said to Moses, Go up to the mountain that is on the other side of Jordan (this Mount Nabau), and behold the land Canaan, which I give to the sons of Israel for a possession. 13 And thou shall see it, and thou also shall be added to thy people, as Aaron thy brother was added on Mount Or; 14 because ye transgressed My word in the wilderness of Sin, when the congregation resisted to sanctify Me; ye sanctified Me not at the water before them (This is the Water of Strife in Kades in the wilderness of Sin). 15 And Moses said to the Lord, 16 Let the Lord, the God of spirits and of all flesh look out for a man over this congregation, 17 who shall go out before the face of them, and who shall come in before the face of them, and who shall lead them out, and who shall bring them in; so the congregation of the Lord shall not be as sheep without a shepherd. 18 And the Lord spoke to Moses, saying, Take to thyself Jesus the son of Naue, a man who has the Spirit in him, and thou shall lay thy hands upon him. 19 And thou shall set him before Eleazar the priest, and thou shall give him a charge before the entire congregation, and thou shall give a charge concerning him before them. 20 And thou shall put thy glory upon him that the sons of Israel may hearken to him. 21 And he shall stand before Eleazar the priest, and they shall ask of him before the Lord the judgment of the Urim; they shall go out at his mouth, and at his mouth they shall come in, he and the sons of Israel with one accord, and the entire congregation. 22 And Moses did as the Lord commanded him; and he took Jesus, and set him before Eleazar the priest, and before the entire congregation. 23 And he laid his hands on him, and established him as the Lord ordered Moses.

Chapter 28

And the Lord spoke to Moses, saying, 2 Charge the sons of Israel, and thou shall speak to them, saying, Ye shall observe to offer to me in my feasts my gifts, my presents, my burnt offerings for a sweet smelling savor. 3 And thou shall say to them, These are the burnt offerings, all that ye shall bring to the Lord; two lambs a year old without blemish daily, for a whole burnt offering perpetually. 4 Thou shall offer one lamb in the morning, and thou shall offer the second lamb towards evening. 5 And thou shall offer the tenth part of an ephah of fine flour for a meat offering, mingled with oil, with the fourth part of a hin.

Numbers 28

6 A perpetual whole burnt offering, a sacrifice offered in the mount of Sinai for a sweet smelling savor to the Lord. 7 And its drink offering, the fourth part of a hin to each lamb; in the holy place shall thou pour strong drink as a drink offering to the Lord. 8 And the second lamb thou shall offer toward evening; thou shall offer it according to its meat offering and according to its drink offering for a sweet smelling savor unto the Lord.

9 And on the Sabbath day ye shall offer two lambs of a year old without blemish, and two tenth deals of fine flour mingled with oil for a meat offering, and a drink offering. 10 A whole burnt offering of the Sabbaths on the Sabbath days, besides the continued whole burnt offering, and its drink offering.

11 And at the new moons ye shall bring a whole burnt offering to the Lord, two calves of the herd, and one ram, seven lambs of a year old without blemish. 12 Three tenth deals of fine flour mingled with oil for one calf, and two tenth deals of fine flour mingled with oil for one ram. 13 A tenth deal of fine flour mingled with oil for each lamb, as a meat offering, a sweet smelling savor, a sacrifice to the Lord. 14 Their drink offering shall be the half of a hin for one calf; and the third of a hin for one ram; and the fourth part of a hin of wine for one lamb; this *is* the whole burnt offering monthly throughout the months of the year. 15 And one kid of the goats for a sin offering to the Lord; it shall be offered beside the continual whole burnt offering and its drink offering.

16 And in the first month, on the fourteenth day of the month, *is* the Passover to the Lord. 17 And on the fifteenth day of this month *is* a feast; seven days ye shall eat unleavened bread. 18 And the first day shall be to you a holy convocation; ye shall do no servile work. 19 And ye shall bring whole burnt offerings, a sacrifice to the Lord, two calves of the herd, one ram, seven lambs of a year old; they shall be to you without blemish. 20 And their meat offering shall be fine flour mingled with oil; three tenth deals for one calf, and two tenth deals for one ram. 21 Thou shall offer a tenth for each lamb, for the seven lambs. 22 And one kid of the goats for a sin offering, to make atonement for you. 23 Beside the perpetual whole burnt offering in the morning, which is a whole burnt sacrifice for a continuance, 24 these shall ye thus offer daily for * seven days, a gift, a sacrifice for a sweet smelling savor to the Lord; beside the continual whole burnt offering, thou shall offer its drink offering. 25 And the seventh day shall be to you a holy convocation; ye shall do no servile work in it.

26 And on the day of the new corn, when ye shall offer a new sacrifice *at the festival* of weeks to the Lord, there shall be to you a holy convocation; ye shall do no servile work, 27 and ye shall bring whole burnt offerings for a sweet smelling savor to the Lord, two calves of the herd, one ram, seven lambs without blemish. 28 Their meat offering *shall be* fine flour mingled with oil; there shall be three tenth deals for one calf, and two tenth deals for one ram. 29 A tenth for each lamb separately, for the seven lambs; and a kid of the goats,

30 for a sin offering, to make atonement for you; 31 beside the perpetual whole burnt offering, and ye shall offer to Me their meat offering. They shall be to you unblemished, and ye shall offer their drink offerings.

* *Codex Alexandrinus* reads: "Two days".

Chapter 29

And in the seventh month, on the first day of the month, there shall be to you a holy convocation; ye shall do no servile work; it shall be to you a day of *giving* signals. 2 And ye shall offer whole burnt offerings for a sweet savor to the Lord, one calf of the herd, one ram, *and* seven lambs of a year old without blemish. 3 Their meat offering shall be fine flour mingled with oil; three tenth deals for one calf, and two tenth deals for one ram, 4 a tenth deal for each several ram, for the seven lambs. 5 And one kid of the goats for a sin offering, to make atonement for you. 6 Beside the whole burnt offerings for the new moon, and their meat offerings, and their drink offerings, and their continual whole burnt offering; and their meat offerings and their drink offerings according to their ordinance for a sweet smelling savor to the Lord.

7 And on the tenth of this month there shall be to you a holy convocation; and ye shall afflict your souls, and ye shall do no work. 8 And ye shall bring near whole burnt offerings for a sweet smelling savor to the Lord; burnt sacrifices to the Lord, one calf of the herd, one ram, seven lambs of a year old; they shall be to you without blemish. 9 Their meat offering shall be fine flour mingled with oil; three tenth deals for one calf, and two tenth deals for one ram. 10 A tenth deal for each several lamb, for the seven lambs. 11 And one kid of the goats for a sin offering, to make atonement for you; beside the sin offering for atonement, and the continual whole burnt offering, its meat offering, and its drink offering according to its ordinance for a smell of sweet savor, a burnt sacrifice to the Lord.

12 And on the fifteenth day of this seventh month ye shall have a holy convocation; ye shall do no servile work; and ye shall keep it a feast to the Lord seven days. 13 And ye shall bring near whole burnt offerings, a sacrifice for a sweet smelling savor to the Lord, on the first day thirteen calves of the herd, two rams, fourteen lambs of a year old; they shall be without blemish. 14 their meat offerings *shall be* fine flour mingled with oil; there shall be three tenth deals for one calf, for the thirteen calves; and two tenth deals for one ram, for the two rams. 15 A tenth deal for every lamb, for the fourteen lambs. 16 And one kid of the goats for a sin offering; beside the continual whole burnt offering: there shall be their meat offerings and their drink offerings.

17 And on the second day twelve calves, two rams, fourteen lambs of a year old without blemish.

Numbers 29

18 Their meat offering and their drink offering shall be for the calves and the rams and the lambs according to their number, according to their ordinance. 19 And one kid of the goats for a sin offering; beside the continual whole burnt offering; their meat offerings and their drink offerings.

20 On the third day eleven calves, two rams, fourteen lambs of a year old without blemish. 21 Their meat offering and their drink offering shall be to the calves and to the rams and to the lambs according to their number, according to their ordinance. 22 And one kid of the goats for a sin offering; beside the continual whole burnt offering; *there shall be* their meat offerings and their drink offerings.

23 On the fourth day ten calves, two rams, fourteen lambs of a year old without blemish. 24 There shall be their meat offerings and their drink offerings to the calves and the rams and the lambs according to their number, according to their ordinance. 25 And one kid of the goats for a sin offering; beside the continual whole burnt offering *there shall be* their meat-offerings and their drink offerings.

26 On the fifth day nine calves, two rams, fourteen lambs of a year old without blemish. 27 Their meat offerings and their drink offerings to the calves and the rams and the lambs according to their number, according to their ordinance. 28 And one kid of the goats for a sin offering; beside the continual whole burnt offering; *there shall be* their meat offerings and their drink offerings.

29 On the sixth day eight calves, two rams, fourteen lambs of a year old without blemish. 30 There shall be their meat offerings and their drink offerings to the calves and rams and lambs according to their number, according to their ordinance. 31 And one kid of the goats for a sin offering; beside the continual whole burnt offering; *there shall be* their meat offerings and their drink offerings.

32 On the seventh day seven calves, two rams, fourteen lambs of a year old without blemish. 33 Their meat offerings and their drink offerings shall be to the calves and the rams and the lambs according to their number, according to their ordinance. 34 And one kid of the goats for a sin offering; beside the continual whole burnt offering; *there shall be* their meat offerings and their drink offerings.

35 And on the eighth day there shall be to you a solemn gathering: ye shall do no servile work in it. 36 And ye shall offer whole burnt offerings *as* sacrifices to the Lord, one calf, one ram, *and* seven lambs of a year old without blemish. 37 Their meat offerings and their drink offerings for the calf and the ram and the lambs according to their number, according to their ordinance. 38 And one kid of the goats for a sin offering; beside the continual whole burnt offering; *there shall be* their meat offerings and their drink offerings.

39 These shall ye offer to the Lord in your feasts, besides your vows; and your free will offerings and your whole burnt offerings, and your meat offerings and your drink offerings, and your salvation offerings.

Chapter 30

And Moses spoke to the sons of Israel according to all that the Lord commanded Moses. 2 And Moses spoke to the rulers of the tribes of the sons of Israel, saying, This *is* the thing which the Lord has commanded. 3 A man, *any* man who shall vow a vow to the Lord, or swear an oath, or bind himself with an obligation upon his soul, he shall not profane his word; all that shall come out of his mouth he shall do. 4 If a woman shall vow a vow to the Lord, or bind herself with an obligation in her youth in her father's house; and her father should hear her vows and her obligations, wherewith she has bound her soul, and her father should hold his peace at her, then all her vows shall stand, 5 and all the obligations with which she has bound her soul, shall remain with her.

6 However, if her father in any wise forbids *her* in the day in which he shall hear all her vows and her obligations, which she has contracted upon her soul, they shall not stand; and the Lord shall hold her guiltless, because her father forbade her. 7 But if she should be indeed married, and her vows be upon her according to the utterance of her lips, in respect of *the obligations* which she has contracted upon her soul; 8 and her husband should hear, and holds his peace at her in the day in which he should hear, then thus shall all her vows be binding, and her obligations, which she has contracted upon her soul shall stand.

9 However, if her husband in any wise forbids *her* in the day in which he should hear her, none of her vows or obligations, which she has contracted upon her soul, shall stand, because her husband has forbade her, and the Lord shall hold her guiltless. 10 And the vow of a widow and of her that is put away, whatever she shall vow upon her soul, shall stand to her. 11 And if her vow *be made* in the house of her husband, or the obligation upon her soul with an oath, 12 and her husband should hear, and hold his peace at her, and not forbade her, then all her vows shall stand, and all the obligations, which she contracted against her soul, shall stand against her. 13 However, if in canceling her husband should cancel the vow in the day in which he shall hear it, none of the things, which shall proceed out of her lips in her vows, and in the obligations upon her soul, shall stand to her; her husband has cancelled them, and the Lord shall hold her guiltless.

14 Every vow, and every binding oath to afflict her soul, her husband shall confirm it to her, or her husband shall cancel it.

Numbers 31

15 But if he be wholly silent at her from day to day, then shall he bind upon her all her vows; and he shall confirm on her the obligations upon herself, because he held his peace at her in the day in which he heard her. 16 If her husband should utterly cancel after the day in which he heard, then he shall bear his iniquity. 17 These *are* the ordinances which the Lord commanded Moses, between a man and his wife, and between a father and daughter in *her* youth in the house of *her* father.

Chapter 31

And the Lord spoke to Moses, saying, 2 Allow the sons of Israel to *take* revenge with vengeance on the Madianites, and *at* last thou shall be added to thy people. 3 And Moses spoke to the people, saying, Fully arm men from you, and set yourselves in array before the Lord against Madian, to inflict vengeance on Madian from the Lord. 4 Send a thousand of each tribe from all the tribes of the sons of Israel to set themselves in array. 5 And they numbered of the thousands of Israel a thousand of *each* tribe, twelve thousands; armed for war. 6 And Moses sent them away a thousand of every tribe with their forces, and Phinees the son of Eleazar the son of Aaron the priest; and the holy items, and the signal trumpets in their hands. 7 And they set themselves in array against Madian, as the Lord commanded Moses; and they killed every male. 8 And they killed the Kings of Madian together with their violently wounded; even Evi and Rocon, and Sur, and Ur, and Robok, five kings of Madian; and they killed with the broadsword Balaam the son of Beor with their violently wounded. 9 And they preyed on the women of Madian, and their store, and their cattle, and all their possessions; and they spoiled their forces. 10 And they burned with fire all their cities in the places of their habitation and they burned their villages with fire. 11 And they took all their plunder, and all their spoils, both man and beast. 12 And they brought to Moses and to Eleazar the priest, and to all the sons of Israel, the captives, and the spoils, and the plunder, to the camp to Araboth Moab, which is at Jordan by Jericho.

13 And Moses and Eleazar the priest and all the rulers of the synagogue went forth out of the encampment to meet them. 14 And Moses was angry with the overseers of the forces, the heads of thousands and the heads of hundreds who came from the battle array of the war. 15 And Moses said to them, Why have ye saved every female alive? 16 For they were to the sons of Israel by the word of Balaam of their revolting and despising the word of the Lord, because of Phogor; and there was a plague in the congregation of the Lord. 17 Now then kill every male in all the spoil, kill every woman, who has known the bed of *a* man.

18 And as for all the captivity of women, who have not known the bed of *a* man, save ye them alive. 19 And ye shall encamp outside the camp seven days; every one who has killed and who touches one being pierced, shall be purified on the third day, and ye and your captivity on the seventh day. 20 And ye shall purify every garment and every leather utensil, and all items of goatskin, and every wooden item.

21 And Eleazar the priest said to the men of the forces that came from the battle array of the war, This *is* the ordinance of the law which the Lord has commanded Moses. 22 Beside the gold, and the silver, and the brass, and the iron, and lead, and tin, 23 every thing that shall pass through the fire shall so be clean, nevertheless it shall be purified with the water of sanctification; and whatever will not pass through the fire shall pass through water. 24 And on the seventh day ye shall wash your garments, and be clean; and afterwards ye shall come into the camp.

25 And the Lord spoke to Moses, saying, 26 Take the sum of the spoils of the captivity both of man and beast, thou and Eleazar the priest, and the rulers of the fathers' *families* of the congregation. 27 And ye shall divide the spoils between the warriors that went out to battle, and the whole congregation. 28 And ye shall take a tribute for the Lord from the warriors that went out to battle; one soul out of five hundred, from the men, and from the cattle, even from the oxen, and from the sheep, and from the mules; and ye shall take from their half. 29 And thou shall give to Eleazar the priest *as* the first fruits of the Lord. 30 And from the half belonging to the sons of Israel thou shall take one of fifty from the men, and from the oxen, and from the sheep, and from the mules, and from all the cattle; and thou shall give them to the Levites that keep the commandments in the tabernacle of the Lord. 31 And Moses and Eleazar the priest did as the Lord commanded Moses.

32 And that which remained of the spoil which the warriors took, was of the sheep, six hundred and seventy-five thousand; 33 and oxen, seventy two thousand: 34 and mules, sixty one thousand. 35 And persons of women who had not known being in the bed of *a* man, all the souls, thirty two thousand. 36 And the half, the portion of them that went out to war, from the number of the sheep, was three hundred and thirty seven thousand and five hundred. 37 And the tribute to the Lord from the sheep was six hundred and seventy five. 38 And the oxen, six and thirty thousand, and the tribute to the Lord seventy-two. 39 And mules, thirty thousand and five hundred, and the tribute to the Lord, sixty one; 40 and the souls of men, sixteen thousand, and the tribute of them to the Lord, thirty two souls. 41 And Moses gave the tribute to the Lord, the heave offering of God, to Eleazar the priest, as the Lord commanded Moses, 42 from the half belonging to the sons of Israel, whom Moses separated from the men of war.

Numbers 32

43 And the half from the sheep, belonging to the congregation, was three hundred and thirty-seven thousand and five hundred. 44 And the oxen, thirty-six thousand; 45 mules, thirty thousand and five hundred; 46 and souls of men, sixteen thousand. 47 And Moses took of the half belonging to the sons of Israel the one out of the fifty, of men and of cattle, and he gave them to the Levites who keep the commandments of the tabernacle of the Lord, as the Lord commanded Moses.

48 And all those who were appointed to be officers of thousands of the host, rulers of thousands and rulers of hundreds, approached Moses, and said to Moses, 49 Thy servants have taken the sum of the men of war with us, and not one is missing. 50 And we have brought our gift to the Lord, *every* man who has found an item of gold, whether an armlet, or a chain, or a ring, or a bracelet, or a clasp for hair, to make atonement for us before the Lord. 51 And Moses and Eleazar the priest took the gold from them, even every wrought article. 52 And all the wrought gold, even the offering that they offered to the Lord, was sixteen thousand and seven hundred and fifty shekels from the rulers of thousands and the rulers of hundreds. 53 For the men of war took plunder every one for himself. 54 And Moses and Eleazar the priest took the gold from the rulers of thousands and rulers of hundreds, and brought them into the Tabernacle of Witness, a memorial of the sons of Israel before the Lord.

Chapter 32

And the sons of Ruben and the sons of Gad had cattle, a multitude, a great multitude; and they saw the country of Jazer, and the country of Galaad; and the place was a place for cattle; 2 and the sons of Ruben and the sons of Gad came, and spoke to Moses, and to Eleazar the priest, and to the rulers of the congregation, saying, 3 Ataroth, and Daebon, and Jazer, and Namra, and Esebon, and Eleale, and Sebama, and Nabau, and Baean, 4 the land that the Lord has delivered up before the sons of Israel, is pasture land, and thy servants have cattle. 5 And they said, If we have found grace in thy sight, let this land be given to thy servants for a possession, and do not cause us to pass over Jordan.

6 And Moses said to the sons of Gad and the sons of Ruben, Shall your brothers go to war, and shall ye sit here? 7 And why do ye corrupt the minds of the sons of Israel that they should not pass over into the land, which the Lord gives them? 8 Did not your fathers thus, when I sent them from Kades Barne to spy out the land? 9 And they went up to the Valley of the Cluster, and spied the land, and turned aside the heart of the sons of Israel that they should not go into the land, which the Lord gave them. 10 And the Lord was very angry in that day, and swore, saying,

11 Surely these men who came up out of Egypt from twenty years old and upward, who have knowledge of the good and the evil, shall not see the land which I swore to Abraham and Isaac and Jacob, for they have not closely followed after me; 12 save Kaleb the son of Jephonne, who was set apart, and Jesus the son of Naue, for they closely followed after the Lord. 13 And the Lord was angry with rage at Israel; and for forty years he caused them to wander in the wilderness, until the entire generation that did evil before the sight of the Lord was wholly consumed. 14 Behold, ye have arisen in the place of your fathers, a * fragmentation of sinful men, to increase yet farther the anger and rage of the Lord against Israel. 15 For ye will turn away from Him to desert Him yet once more in the wilderness, and ye will sin against this entire congregation.

16 And they came to him, and said, We will build here folds for our cattle, and cities for our possessions; 17 and we will arm ourselves and go as an advanced guard before the sons of Israel, until we shall have brought them into their place; and our possessions shall remain in walled cities because of the inhabitants of the land. 18 We will not return to our houses until the sons of Israel shall have been distributed, each to his own inheritance. 19 And we will no longer inherit with them from the other side of Jordan and onwards, because we have our full inheritance on the side beyond Jordan to the east. 20 And Moses said to them, If ye will do according to this word, if ye will arm yourselves before the Lord for battle, 21 and every one of you will pass over Jordan fully armed before the Lord, until His enemy be destroyed from before His face, 22 and the land shall be subdued before the Lord, then afterwards ye shall return, and be guiltless before the Lord, and as regards Israel; and this land shall be to you for a possession before the Lord. 23 But if ye will not do so, ye will sin against the Lord; and ye shall know your sin, when afflictions shall come upon you. 24 And ye shall build for yourselves cities for your store, and folds for your cattle; and ye shall do that which proceeds out of your mouth. 25 And the sons of Ruben and the sons of Gad spoke to Moses, saying, Thy servants will do as the Lord commands. 26 Our store, and our wives, and all our cattle shall be in the cities of Galaad. 27 But thy servants will go over all armed and set in order before the Lord to battle, as the Lord says.

28 And Moses appointed to them *judges*, Eleazar the priest, and Jesus the son of Naue, and the rulers of the fathers of the tribes of Israel. 29 And Moses said to them, If the sons of Ruben and the sons of Gad will pass over Jordan with you, every one armed for war before the Lord, and ye shall subdue the land before you, then ye shall give to them the land of Galaad for a possession. 30 But if they will not pass over armed with you to war before the Lord, then shall ye cause to pass over their possessions and their wives and their cattle before you into the land of Canaan, and they shall inherit with you in the land of Canaan.

Numbers 33

31 And the sons of Ruben and the sons of Gad answered, saying, Whatever the Lord says to his servants, that will we do. 32 We will go over armed before the Lord into the land of Canaan, and ye shall give us our inheritance beyond Jordan. 33 And Moses gave to them, even to the sons of Gad and the sons of Ruben, and to the half tribe of Manasse of the sons of Joseph, the kingdom of Seon King of the Amorites, and the kingdom of Og King of Basan, the land and the cities with its coasts, the cities of the land round about. 34 And the sons of Gad built Daebon, and Ataroth, and Aroer, 35 and Sophar, and Jazer, and they set them up, 36 and Namram, and Betharan, strong cities, and folds for sheep. 37 And the sons of Ruben built Esebon, and Eleale, and Kariatham, 38 and Beelmeon, surrounded, and Sebama; and they called the names of the cities, which they built, after their own names. 39 And a son of Mahir the son of Manasse went to Galaad, and took it, and destroyed the Amorite who lived in it. 40 And Moses gave Galaad to Mahir the son of Manasse, and he lived there. 41 And Jair the *son* of Manasse went and took their folds, and called them the folds of Jair. 42 And Nabau went and took Kaath and her villages, and called them Naboth after his name.

* Alfred Rahlfs' *Septuaginta* reads: "a band of sinful men".

Chapter 33

And these are the stations of the sons of Israel, as they went out from the land of Egypt with their forces by the hand of Moses and Aaron. 2 And Moses wrote their removals and their stages, by the word *of the* Lord, and these are the stages of their journeying. 3 They departed from Ramesses in the first month, on the fifteenth day of the first month; on the day after the Passover the sons of Israel went forth with a high hand before all the Egyptians. 4 And the Egyptians buried those that died of them, even all that the Lord killed every firstborn in the land of Egypt; also the Lord executed vengeance on their gods.

5 And the sons of Israel departed from Ramesses, and encamped in Sukkoth: 6 and they departed from Sukkoth and encamped in Buthan, which is a part of the wilderness. 7 And they departed from Buthan and encamped at the mouth of Iroth, which is opposite Beelsepphon, and encamped opposite Magdol. 8 And they departed from before Iroth, and crossed the middle of the sea into the wilderness; and they went a journey of three days through the wilderness, and encamped in * Pikriais. 9 And they departed from * Pikrion, and came to Aelim; and in Aelim *were* twelve fountains of water, and seventy palm trees, and they encamped there by the water. 10 And they departed from Aelim, and encamped by the Red Sea. 11 And they departed from the Red Sea, and encamped in the wilderness of Sin.

12 And they departed from the wilderness of Sin, and encamped in Raphaka. 13 And they departed from Raphaka, and encamped in Aelus. 14 And they departed from Aelus, and encamped in Raphidin; and there was no water there for the people to drink. 15 And they departed from Raphidin, and encamped in the wilderness of Sinai. 16 And they departed from the wilderness of Sinai, and encamped at the Graves of Lust. 17 And they departed from the Graves of Lust, and encamped in Aseroth. 18 And they departed from Aseroth, and encamped in Rathama. 19 And they departed from Rathama, and encamped in Remmon Phares. 20 And they departed from Remmon Phares, and encamped in Lebona. 21 And they departed from Lebona, and encamped in Ressan. 22 And they departed from Ressan, and encamped in Makellath. 23 And they departed from Makellath, and encamped in Saphar. 24 And they departed from Saphar, and encamped in Haradath. 25 And they departed from Haradath, and encamped in Makeloth. 26 And they departed from Makeloth, and encamped in Kataath. 27 And they departed from Kataath, and encamped in Tarath. 28 And they departed from Tarath, and encamped in Mathekka. 29 And they departed from Mathekka, and encamped in Selmona. 30 And they departed from Selmona, and encamped in Masuruth. 31 And they departed from Masuruth, and encamped in Banaea. 32 And they departed from Banaea, and encamped in the mountain Gadgad. 33 And they departed from the mountain Gadgad, and encamped in Etebatha. 34 And they departed from Etebatha, and encamped in Ebrona. 35 And they departed from Ebrona, and encamped in Gesion Gaber. 36 And they departed from Gesion Gaber, and encamped in the wilderness of Sin; and they departed from the wilderness of Sin, and encamped in the wilderness of Pharan; this is Kades. 37 And they departed from Kades, and encamped in Mount Or near the land of Edom.

38 And Aaron the priest went up by the command of the Lord, and died there in the fortieth year of the departure of the sons of Israel from the land of Egypt, in the fifth month, on the first of the month. 39 And Aaron was a hundred and twenty-three years old, when he died on Mount Or.

40 Arad the Canaanite King, and he too lived in the land of Canaan, having heard when the sons of Israel were entering 41 then they departed from Mount Or, and encamped in Selmona. 42 And they departed from Selmona, and encamped in Phino. 43 And they departed from Phino, and encamped in Oboth. 44 And they departed from Oboth, and encamped in Gai, on the other side on the borders of Moab. 45 And they departed from Gai, and encamped in Daebon Gad. 46 And they departed from Daebon Gad, and encamped in Gelmon Deblathaim. 47 And they departed from Gelmon Deblathaim, and encamped on the Mountains of Abarim, over against Nabau. 48 And they departed from the Mountains of Abarim, and encamped on the west of Moab, at Jordan by Jericho.

Numbers 34

49 And they encamped by Jordan between Aesimoth, as far as Belsa to the west of Moab.
50 And the Lord spoke to Moses at the west of Moab by Jordan at Jericho, saying, 51 Speak to the sons of Israel, and thou shall say to them, Ye are to pass over Jordan into the land of Canaan. 52 And ye shall destroy all that live in the land before your face, and ye shall destroy their watch towers, and all their molten idols ye shall destroy, and ye shall destroy all their pillars. 53 And ye shall destroy all the inhabitants of the land, and ye shall live in it, for I have given their land to you for an inheritance. 54 And ye shall inherit their land according to your tribes; to the greater number ye shall give the larger possession, and to the smaller ye shall give the less possession; to whatever *part* of his name shall go out, there shall be his; ye shall inherit according to your fathers' tribes. 55 But if ye will not destroy the inhabitants in the land from before your face, then it shall come to pass that whomever of them ye shall leave shall be thorns in your eyes, and arrows in your sides, and they shall be enemies to you on the land on which ye shall live; 56 and it shall come to pass that as I had determined to do to them, so I will do to you.

* In Greek this word is literally translated as "bitterness".

Chapter 34

And the Lord spoke to Moses, saying, 2 Command the sons of Israel, and thou shall say to them, Ye are entering into the land of Canaan; it shall be to you for an inheritance, the land of Canaan with its boundaries. 3 And your southern side shall be from the wilderness of Sin to the border of Edom, and your border to the south shall be on the side of the Salt Sea to the east. 4 And your border shall go around you to the south to the ascent of Akrabin, and shall proceed by Ennak, and the going out of it shall be to the south to Kades Barne, and it shall go forth to the village of Arad, and shall proceed by Asemona. 5 And the border shall go around from Asemona to the river of Egypt, and the sea shall be the end.

6 And ye shall have your border on the sea; the great sea shall be the boundary: this shall be to you the border on the west.

7 And this shall be your northern border; from the great sea ye shall measure to yourselves, from the mountain, *to* The Mountain. 8 And ye shall measure to yourselves the mountain from T*he* Mountain at the entering into Emath, and the end of it shall be the coast of Saradak. 9 And the border shall go out to Dephrona, and its end shall be at Arsenain; this shall be your border from the north.

10 And ye shall measure to yourselves the eastern border from Arsenain to Sepphamar.

11 And the border shall go down from Sepphamar to Bela to the east to the fountains, and the border shall go down from Bela behind the sea *of* Henereth to the east. 12 And the border shall go down to Jordan, and the termination shall be the Salt Sea; this shall be your land and its borders around.

13 And Moses commanded the sons of Israel, saying, This *is* the land which ye shall inherit by lot, even as the Lord commanded us to give it to the nine tribes and the half-tribe of Manasse. 14 For the tribe of the sons of Ruben, and the tribe of the sons of Gad have received according to their fathers' houses; and the half-tribe of Manasse has received their inheritances. 15 Two tribes and half a tribe have received their inheritance beyond Jordan by Jericho from the south to the east.

16 And the Lord spoke to Moses, saying, 17 These *are* the names of the men who shall inherit the land for you; Eleazar the priest and Jesus the *son* of Naue. 18 And ye shall take one ruler from *each* tribe to allot the land to you as a possession. 19 And these *are* the names of the men; of the tribe of Judah Kaleb the son of Jephonne. 20 Of the tribe of Simon, Salamiel the son of Semiud. 21 Of the tribe of Benjamin, Eldad the son of Haslon. 22 Of the tribe of Dan the ruler *was* Bakhir the son of Egli. 23 Of the sons of Joseph of the tribe of the sons of Manasse, the ruler was Aniel the son of Suphi. 24 Of the tribe of the sons of Ephraim, the ruler was Kamuel the son of Sabathan. 25 Of the tribe of Zabulon, the ruler was Elisaphan the son of Pharnak. 26 Of the tribe of the sons of Issahar, the ruler was Phaltiel the son of Oza. 27 Of the tribe of the sons of Aser, the ruler was Ahior the son of Selemi. 28 Of the tribe of Nephthali, the ruler was Phadael the son of Jamiud. 29 These did the Lord command to divide *the inheritance* to the sons of Israel in the land of Canaan.

Chapter 35

And the Lord spoke to Moses to the west of Moab by Jordan near Jericho, saying, 2 Give orders to the sons of Israel, and they shall give to the Levites cities to live in from the lots of their possession, and they shall give to the Levites the suburbs of the cities around them. 3 And the cities shall be for them to live in, and their areas set apart shall be for their cattle and all their beasts. 4 And the suburbs of the cities, which ye shall give to the Levites, shall be from the wall of the city and outwards two thousand cubits around. 5 And thou shall measure outside the city on the east side two thousand cubits, and on the south side two thousand cubits, and on the west side two thousand cubits, and on the north side two thousand cubits; and your city shall be in the midst of this, and the suburbs of the cities.

Numbers 35

6 And ye shall give the cities to the Levites, the six cities of refuge that ye shall give for the killer to flee thither, and in addition to these, forty-two cities. 7 Ye shall give to the Levites in all forty-eight cities, them and their suburbs. 8 And as for the cities, which ye shall give out of the possession of the sons of Israel, from those *that have* much *ye shall give* much, and from those that have less ye shall give less; they shall give of their cities to the Levites each one according to his inheritance that they shall inherit.

9 And the Lord spoke to Moses, saying, 10 Speak to the sons of Israel, and thou shall say to them, Ye are to cross over Jordan into the land of Canaan. 11 And ye shall appoint to yourselves cities; they shall be to you cities of refuge for the killer to flee to, every one who has struck a soul unintentionally. 12 And the cities shall be to you places of refuge from him that represents the next of kin for *avenging the* blood, and the killer shall not die until he stands before the congregation for judgment. 13 And the cities, which ye shall assign, *even* the six cities, shall be places of refuge for you. 14 Ye shall assign three cities on the other side of Jordan, and ye shall assign three cities in the land of Canaan. 15 It shall be a place of refuge for the sons of Israel, and for the stranger, and for him that travels among you; these cities shall be for a place of refuge, for every one to flee thither who has struck a soul unintentionally.

16 And if he should strike him with an iron instrument, and the man should die, he is a murderer; let the murderer by all means die the death. 17 And if he should strike him with a stone from his hand, whereby a man may die, and he *does* die, he is a murderer; let the murderer by all means die the death. 18 And if he should strike him with an item of wood from his hand, whereby he may die, and he *does* die, he is a murderer; let the murderer by all means die the death. 19 he who represents the next of kin for *avenging the* blood himself shall kill the murderer; whenever he shall meet him he shall kill him. 20 If he should thrust him through enmity, or cast any item upon him from an ambush, and the man should die, 21 or if he have struck him with his hand through anger, and the man should die, let the man that struck him die the death by all means, he is a murderer; let the murderer by all means die the death; the he who represents the next of kin for *avenging the* blood shall kill the murderer when he meets him.

22 But if he should thrust him suddenly, not through enmity, or cast any item upon him, not from an ambush, 23 or with any stone, whereby a man may die, not knowing, and it should fall upon him, and he should die, but he was not his enemy, nor sought to hurt him; 24 then the assembly shall judge between the one striking and he who represents the next of kin for *avenging the* blood, according to these judgments.

25 And the congregation shall rescue the murderer from him, who represents the next of kin for *avenging the* blood, and the congregation shall restore him to his city of refuge, whither he fled for refuge; and he shall live there until the death of the high priest, whom they anointed with the holy oil. 26 But if the murderer should in any wise go out beyond the borders of the city whither he fled for refuge, 27 and he who represents the next of kin for *avenging the* blood should find him outside the bounds of the city of his refuge, and he who represents the next of kin for *avenging the* blood should kill the murderer, he is not guilty. 28 For let him remain in the city of refuge until the high priest died, and after the death of the high priest the murderer shall return to the land of his possession.

29 And these things shall be to you for an ordinance of judgment throughout your generations in all your habitations. 30 Whoever strikes a soul, thou shall kill the murderer by *the testimony of* witnesses; and one witness shall not testify against a soul that he should die. 31 And ye shall not accept ransoms for a soul from a murderer who is worthy to be put to death by death. 32 Ye shall not accept a ransom *for* his fleeing to the city of refuge, so that he should again live in the land, until the death of the high priest. 33 So shall ye not pollute with murder the land in which ye live; for this blood pollutes the land, and the land shall not be purged from the blood shed upon it, but by the blood of him that shed it. 34 And ye shall not defile the land whereon ye live, on which I live in the midst of you; for I am the Lord having *My* tabernacle in the midst of the sons of Israel.

Chapter 36

And the rulers of the tribe of the sons of Galaad the son of Mahir the son of Manasse, of the tribe of the sons of Joseph, drew near, and spoke before Moses, and before Eleazar the priest, and before the rulers of the fathers' houses of the sons of Israel; 2 and they said, The Lord commanded our lord to render the land of inheritance by lot to the sons of Israel; and the Lord appointed our lord to give the inheritance of Salpaad our brother to his daughters. 3 And they will become wives in one of the tribes of the sons of Israel; so their inheritance shall be taken away from the possession of our fathers, and shall be added to the inheritance of the tribe into which the women shall marry, and shall be taken away from the portion of our inheritance. 4 And if there shall be a release of the sons of Israel, then shall their inheritance be added to the inheritance of the tribe into which the women marry, and their inheritance, shall be taken away from the inheritance of our father's tribe.

Numbers 36

5 And Moses commanded the sons of Israel by the commandment of the Lord, saying, Thus say the tribe of the sons of Joseph. 6 This *is* the thing that the Lord has appointed the daughters of Salpaad, saying, Let them be wives where they please, only let them marry of their father's tribe. 7 So shall not the inheritance of the sons of Israel go about from tribe to tribe, for the sons of Israel shall steadfastly continue each in the inheritance of his father's tribe. 8 And every daughter that is next of kin of an inheritance of the tribes of the sons of Israel, *these* women shall be married each to one of her father's tribe, that the sons of Israel may each receive the inheritance of his father's tribe. 9 And the inheritance shall not go about from one tribe to another, but the sons of Israel shall steadfastly continue each in his own inheritance.

10 As the Lord commanded Moses, so they did to the daughters of Salpaad. 11 So Thersa, and Egla, and Melha, and Nua, and Malaa, the daughters of Salpaad, married their cousins; 12 they were married of the tribe of Manasse of the sons of Joseph; and their inheritance was attached to the tribe of their father's people.

13 These *are* the commandments, and the ordinances, and the judgments, which the Lord commanded by the hand of Moses, to the west of Moab, at Jordan by Jericho.

The Book of
Deuteronomy

Chapter 1

These *are* the words that Moses spoke to all Israel on this side *of* Jordan in the desert towards the west near the Red Sea, between Pharan Tophol, and Lobon, and Aulon, and the gold works. 2 *It is* a journey of eleven days from Horeb to Mount Seir as far as Kades Barne. 3 And it came to pass in the fortieth year, in the eleventh month, on the first of the month, Moses spoke to all the sons of Israel, according to all things that the Lord commanded him for them: 4 after he had killed Seon king of the Amorites who lived in Esebon, and Og the king of Basan who lived in Astaroth and in Edrain;

5 beyond Jordan in the land of Moab, Moses began to declare this law, saying, 6 The Lord your God spoke to us in Horeb, saying, Let it suffice you to live in this mountain. 7 Turn ye and depart and enter into the mountain of the Amorites, and to all that live near about Araba, to the mountain and the plain and to the south, and the land of the Canaanites near the sea, and Antilibanus, as far as the great river, the river Euphrates. * 8 Behold, *God* has delivered the land before you; go in and inherit the land, which I swore to your fathers, Abraham, and Isaac, and Jacob, to give it to them and to their seed after them.

9 And I spoke to you at that time, saying, I will not be able by myself to bear you. 10 The Lord your God has multiplied you, and, behold, ye are this day as the stars of heaven a multitude. 11 The Lord God of your fathers increase you a thousand fold more than you are, and bless you as he has spoken to you. 12 How shall I alone be able to bear your labor, and your burden, and your gain sayings? 13 Give to yourselves wise and understanding and prudent men for your tribes, and I will set your rulers over you. 14 And ye answered me and said; The thing which thou have told us *is* good to do. * 15 So I took of you wise and understanding and prudent men, and I set them to govern over you as rulers of thousands, and rulers of hundreds, and rulers of fifties, and rulers of tens, and recorders for your judges. 16 And I charged your judges at that time, saying, Hear *grievances* between your brothers, and judge rightly between a man and *his* brother, and his stranger that is with him. 17 Thou shall not recognize a face in judgment, according to the small and the great thou shall judge equally; thou shall not shrink from before the person of a man, for the judgment is God's; and whatever matter shall be too hard for you, ye shall bring it to me, and I will hear it. 18 And I charged upon you at that time all the commands that ye shall perform.

Deuteronomy 1

19 And we departed from Horeb, and went through that entire great wilderness and terrible, which ye saw, by the way of the mountain of the Amorite, as the Lord our God charged us, and we came as far as Kades Barne. 20 And I said to you, Ye have come as far as the mountain of the Amorite, which the Lord our God gives to you. 21 Behold, the Lord your God has delivered to us the land before you; go up and inherit it as the Lord God of your fathers said to you; fear not, neither be afraid.

22 And ye all came to me, and said, Let us send men before us, and let them go up to the land for us; and let them bring back to us a report of the way by which we shall go up, and of the cities into which we shall enter. 23 And the saying pleased me, and I took of you twelve men, one man of each tribe. 24 And they turned and went up to the mountain, and they came as far as the Valley of the Cluster, and they spied it. 25 And they took in their hands of the fruit of the land, and brought it to you, and said, The land is good that the Lord our God gives us.

26 Yet ye would not go up, but rebelled against the words of the Lord our God. 27 And ye murmured in your tents, and said, Because the Lord hated us, he has brought us out of the land of Egypt to deliver us into the hands of the Amorites, to destroy us. 28 Where do we go up? And your brothers drew away your heart, saying, *It is a* great nation and populous, and mightier than we; and *there are* cities great and walled up to heaven: more so we saw there the sons of the giants. 29 And I said to you, Fear not, neither ye be afraid of them; 30 the Lord your God who goes before your face, he shall fight against them together with you effectually, according to all that he did for you in the land of Egypt; 31 and in this wilderness that ye saw, by the way of the mountain of the Amorite; how the Lord thy God will bear thee as a nursling, as if any man should nurse his son, through all the way which ye have gone until ye came to this place. 32 And in this matter ye believed not the Lord our God, 33 who goes before you in the way to choose you a place, guiding you in fire by night, showing you the way by which ye go, and a cloud by day.

34 And the Lord heard the voice of your words, and being greatly provoked he swore, saying, 35 If one of these men shall see this good land, which I swore to their fathers, 36 except Kaleb the son of Jephonne, he shall see it; and to him I will give the land on which he went up, and to his sons, because he followed closely after the Lord. 37 And the Lord was angry with me for your sake, saying, Neither shall thou by any means enter therein. 38 Jesus the son of Naue, who stands by thee, he shall enter in there; do thou strengthen him, for he shall cause Israel to inherit it. 39 And every new child who this day knows not good or evil, they shall enter therein, and to them I will give it, and they shall inherit it. 40 And ye turned and marched into the wilderness, by the way of the Red Sea.

41 And ye answered and said, We have sinned before the Lord our God; we will go up and fight according to all that the Lord our God has commanded us; and having taken every one his weapons of war, and being gathered together, ye went up to the mountain. 42 And the Lord said to me, Tell them, Ye shall not go up, neither shall ye fight, for I am not with you; thus shall ye not be destroyed before your enemies. 43 And I spoke to you, and ye did not hearken to me; and ye transgressed the commandment of the Lord; and ye forced your way and went up into the mountain. 44 And the Amorite who lives on that mountain came out to meet you, and pursued you as bees do, and wounded you from Seir to Herma. 45 And ye sat down and wept before the Lord our God, and the Lord hearkened not to your voice, neither did he take heed of you. 46 And ye stayed in Kades many days, as many days as ye stayed.

* The readings for vespers for July in the *Greek Menaion* and *Prophetologion* for Chapter One verses eight through eleven and verses fifteen through seventeen are slightly different than what is present in the texts as published by the *Apostoliki Diakonia* and *Zoe Brotherhood*. The passage reads as follows:

"Moses said to the sons of Israel, Behold, I have delivered the land before you; go in and inherit the land, which I swore to your fathers, Abraham, and Isaac, and Jacob, to give it to them and to their seed after them. And I spoke to you at that time, saying, I will not be able by myself to bear you. The Lord your God has multiplied you, and, behold, ye are this day as the stars of heaven a multitude. The Lord God of your fathers increase you a thousand fold more than you are, and bless you as he has spoken to you. So I took of you wise and understanding and prudent men, and I set them to govern over you as rulers of thousands, and rulers of hundreds, and rulers of fifties, and rulers of tens, and recorders for your judges. And I charged your judges at that time, saying, Hear *grievances* between your brothers, and judge rightly between a man and *his* brother, and his stranger that is with him. Thou shall not recognize a face in judgment, according to the small and the great thou shall judge equally; thou shall not shrink from before the person of a man, for the judgment is God's".

Chapter 2

And we turned and departed into the wilderness, by the way of the Red Sea, as the Lord spoke to me, and we circled mount Seir many days. 2 And the Lord said to me, 3 Let it suffice *for* you to encompass this mountain long enough; turn therefore toward the north. 4 And charge the people, saying, Ye are going through the borders of your brothers the sons of Esau, who live in Seir; and they shall fear you, and dread you greatly. 5 Do not engage in war against them, for I will not give you of their land even enough to set your foot upon, for I have given Mount Seir to the sons of Esau as an inheritance. 6 Buy food from them for money and eat, and ye shall receive water from them by measure for money, and drink.

Deuteronomy 2

7 For the Lord our God has blessed thee in every work of thy hands. Consider how thou went through that great and terrible wilderness; behold, the Lord thy God *was* with thee forty years; thou did not lack any thing. 8 And we passed by our brothers the sons of Esau, who live in Seir, by the way of Araba from Aelon and from Gesion Gaber; and we turned and passed by the way of the desert of Moab.

9 And the Lord said to me, Do not ye quarrel with the Moabites, and do not engage in war with them; for I will not give you of their land for an inheritance, for I have given Aroer to the sons of Lot to inherit. 10 Formerly the Ommin settled in it, a great nation and many and powerful, like the Enakim. 11 These also shall be accounted Raphain like the Enakim; and the Moabites call them Ommin. 12 And the Horrhite lived in Seir before, and the sons of Esau destroyed them, and utterly consumed them from before them; and they lived in their place, as Israel did to the land of his inheritance, which the Lord gave to them. 13 Now then, arise ye, and depart, and cross the valley of Zaret. 14 And the days, in which we traveled from Cades Barne till we crossed the valley of Zaret, *were* thirty and eight years, until the whole generation of the men of war failed, dying out of the camp, as the Lord God swore to them. 15 And the hand of the Lord was upon them to destroy them out of the midst of the camp, until they were consumed.

16 And it came to pass when all the men of war dying out of the midst of the people had fallen, 17 that the Lord spoke to me, saying, 18 Thou shall pass over this day the borders of Moab also *those of* Aroer; 19 and ye shall draw near to the sons of Amman: do not quarrel with them, nor wage war with them; for I will not give thee of the land of the sons of Amman for an inheritance, because I have given it to the sons of Lot for an inheritance. 20 It shall be accounted a land of Raphain, for the Raphain lived there before, and the Ammanites call them Zohommin. 21 A great nation and populous, and mightier than you, as also the Enakim: yet the Lord destroyed them from before them, and they inherited *their land*, and they lived *there* instead of them until this day. 22 As they did to the sons of Esau that live in Seir, even as they destroyed the Horrhite from before their face, and inherited them, and inhabited *therein* instead of them until this day. 23 And the Evites who live in Asedoth to Gaza, and the Cappadocians who came out of Cappadocia, destroyed them, and lived in their place. 24 Now then arise and depart, and pass over the Valley of Arnon; behold, I have delivered into thy hands Seon the king of Esebon the Amorite, and his land; begin to inherit, engage in war with him this day. 25 Begin to put thy terror and thy fear on the face of all the nations under heaven, who shall be troubled when they have heard thy name, and shall be in anguish for fear of thee. 26 And I sent emissaries from the wilderness of Kedamoth to Seon king of Esebon with peaceable words, saying,

27 I will pass through thy land, I will go by the road, I will not turn aside to the right hand or to the left. 28 Thou shall give me food for money, and I will eat; and thou shall give me water for money, and I will drink; I will only go through on my feet; 29 as the sons of Esau did to me, who lived in Seir, and the Moabites who lived in Aroer, until I shall have crossed Jordan into the land which the Lord our God gives us. 30 And Seon king of Esebon would not that we should pass by him, because the Lord our God hardened his spirit, and made his heart stubborn, that he might be delivered into thy hands, as on this day. 31 And the Lord said to me, Behold, I have begun to deliver before thee Seon the king of Esebon the Amorite, and his land, and do thou begin to inherit his land. 32 And Seon the king of Esebon came forth to meet us, all his people and him, to war at Jassa. 33 And the Lord our God delivered him before our face, and we killed him, and his sons, and all his people. 34 And we took possession of all his cities at that time, and we utterly destroyed every city in succession, and their wives, and their children; we left no living prey. 35 We only took the cattle captive, and took the spoils of the cities. 36 From Aroer, which is by the brink of the brook of Arnon, and the city, which is in the valley, and as far as the mount of Galaad; there was not a city which escaped us; the Lord our God delivered all of them into our hands. 37 We only did not go near to the sons of Amman, even all the parts bordering on the brook Jabok, and the cities in the mountain country, as the Lord our God charged us.

Chapter 3

And we turned and went by the way leading to Basan; and Og the king of Basan came out to meet us, he and all his people, to battle at Edraim. 2 And the Lord said to me, Fear him not, for I have delivered him, and all his people, and all his land, into thy hands; and thou shall do to him as thou did to Seon king of the Amorites who lived in Esebon. 3 And the Lord our God delivered him into our hands, even Og the king of Basan, and all his people; and we killed him until we left none of his seed. 4 And we controlled all his cities at that time; there was not a city that we took *that was* not from them; sixty cities, all the country round about Argob, belonging to king Og in Basan: 5 all strong cities, lofty walls, gates and bars; besides the very many cities of the Pherezites. 6 We utterly destroyed *them* as we dealt with Seon the king of Esebon, so we utterly destroyed every city in order, and the women and the children, 7 and all the cattle; and we took for a prey to ourselves the spoils of the cities. 8 And we took at that time the land out of the hands of the two kings of the Amorites, who were beyond Jordan, from the brook of Arnon even unto Aermon. 9 (The Phoenicians call Aermon Sanior, but the Amorite has called it Sanir),

Deuteronomy 3

10 All the cities of Misor, and all Galaad, and all Basan as far as Elcha and Edraim, cities of the kingdom of Og in Basan. 11 For only Og the king of Basan was left of the Raphain; behold, his bed *was* a bed of iron; behold, *it is* in the acropolis of the sons of Ammon; the length of it *is* nine cubits, and the breadth of it four cubits, according to the cubit of a man.

12 And we inherited that land at that time from Aroer, which is by the border of the torrent Arnon, and half the mount of Galaad; and I gave his cities to Ruben and to Gad. 13 And the rest of Galaad, and all Basan the kingdom of Og I gave to the half-tribe of Manasse, and all the country round about Argob, all that Basan; it shall be accounted the land of Raphain. 14 And Jair the son of Manasse took all the country around Argob as far as the borders of Gargasi and Mahathi: he called them by his name Basan Thavoth Jair until this day. 15 And to Mahir I gave Galaad. 16 And to Ruben and to Gad I gave *the land* under Galaad as far as the brook of Arnon, the border between the brook and as far as Jabok; the brook *is* the border to the sons Amman. 17 And Araba and Jordan *are* the boundary of Mahanareth, even to the sea of Araba, the Salt Sea under Asedoth Phasga eastward.

18 And I charged you at that time, saying, The Lord your God has given you this land by lot, arm yourselves, every one *that is* powerful, and go before your brothers the sons of Israel. 19 Only your wives and your young children and your cattle, I know that ye have much cattle, let them live in your cities that I have given you; 20 until the Lord your God give your brothers rest, as also he has given to you, and they also shall inherit the land, which the Lord our God gives them on the other side of Jordan; then ye shall return, each one to his inheritance which I have given you. 21 And I charged Jesus at that time, saying, Your eyes have seen all things that the Lord our God did to these two kings; so shall the Lord our God do to all the kingdoms against which thou crossest over thither. 22 Ye shall not be afraid of them, because the Lord our God himself shall fight for you.

23 And I sought the Lord at that time, saying, 24 Lord God, thou has begun to reveal to thy servant thy strength, and thy power, and thy mighty hand, and thy high arm; for what God is there in heaven or on the earth, who will do as thou has done, and according to thy might? 25 I will therefore go over and see this good land that is beyond Jordan, this good mountain and Antilibanus. 26 And the Lord because of you did not regard me, and hearkened not to me; and the Lord said to me, Let it suffice thee; speak not of this matter to Me any more. 27 Go up to the top of the quarried rock, and look with thine eyes to the west, and to the north, and to the south, and to the east, and behold with thine eyes, for thou shall not cross this Jordan. 28 And charge Jesus, and strengthen him, and encourage him; for he shall go before the face of this people, and he shall give them the inheritance of all the land, which thou have seen.

29 And we abode in the valley near the house of Phogor.

Chapter 4

And now, Israel, hear the ordinances and judgments, all that I teach you this day to do; that ye may live, and be multiplied, and that ye may go in and inherit the land, which the Lord God of your fathers gives you. 2 Ye shall not add to the word, which I command you, and ye shall not take from it; keep the commandments of the Lord our God, all that I command you this day. 3 Your eyes have seen all that the Lord our God did in *regards to* Beelphegor; for every man that went after Beelphegor, the Lord your God has utterly destroyed him from among you. 4 But ye that kept close to the Lord your God are all alive today. 5 Behold, I have shown you ordinances and judgments as the Lord commanded me, that ye should do so in the land into which ye go to inherit it. 6 And ye shall keep and do them; for this is your wisdom and understanding before all nations, as many as shall hear all these ordinances; and they shall say, Behold, this great nation *is* a wise and understanding people. 7 For what manner of nation *is* great, which has God so near to them as the Lord our God *is* in all things in whatever we may call upon him? 8 And what manner of nation *is* great, which has righteous ordinances and judgments according to all this law, which I set before you this day?

9 Take heed to thyself, and keep thy soul diligently; forget not any of the things, which thine eyes have seen, and let them not depart from thine heart all the days of thy life; and thou shall teach thy sons and thy sons' sons, 10 *In* the day in which ye stood before the Lord our God in Horeb in the day of the assembly; for the Lord said to me, Gather the people to me, and let them hear my words, that they may learn to fear me all the days that they live upon the earth, and they shall teach their sons. 11 And ye drew close and stood under the mountain; and the mountain burned with fire up to heaven; *there was* darkness, blackness, *and* tempest. 12 And the Lord spoke to you out of the midst of the fire a voice of words that ye heard, and ye saw no likeness, only *ye heard* a voice. 13 And he announced to you his covenant, which he commanded you to keep, even the Ten Words; and he wrote them on two tables of stone. 14 And the Lord commanded me at that time, to teach you ordinances and judgments, that ye should do them on the land, into which ye go to inherit it.

15 And guard well your souls, for ye saw no likeness in the day in which the Lord spoke to you in Horeb in the mountain out of the midst of the fire: 16 lest ye transgress, and make to yourselves a carved image, any kind of likeness, the likeness of male or female, 17 the likeness of any beast of those that are on the earth, the likeness of any winged bird which flies under heaven,

Deuteronomy 4

18 the likeness of any reptile which slithers on the earth, the likeness of any fish of those that are in the waters under the earth; 19 and lest having looked up to the sky, and having seen the sun and the moon and the stars, and all the order of sky, thou should go astray and worship them, and serve them, which the Lord thy God has distributed to all the nations under the sky. 20 But God took you, and led you forth out of the land of Egypt, out of the iron furnace, out of Egypt, to be to him a people of inheritance, as at this day. 21 And the Lord God was angry with me for the things said by you, and swore that I should not cross this Jordan, and that I should not enter into the land that the Lord thy God gives thee for an inheritance. 22 For I die in this land, and shall not cross this Jordan; but ye are to pass over, and shall inherit this good land. 23 Take heed to yourselves, lest ye forget the covenant of the Lord our God, which he made with you, and ye transgress, and make to yourselves a graven image of any of the things concerning that the Lord thy God commanded thee. 24 For the Lord thy God is a consuming fire, a jealous God.

25 And when thou shall have begotten sons, and shall have sons from sons, and ye shall have lived a long time on the land, and shall have transgressed, and made a graven image of any thing, and shall have done evil before the Lord your God to provoke him; 26 I call heaven and earth this day to witness against you, that ye shall surely perish from off the land, into which ye cross Jordan to inherit it there; ye shall not prolong your days upon it, but shall be utterly cut off. 27 And the Lord shall scatter you among all nations, and ye shall be left few in number among all the nations, among which the Lord shall bring you. 28 And ye shall there serve other gods, the works of the hands of men, wood and stones, which shall not see, or can they hear, or eat, or smell. 29 And there ye shall seek the Lord your God and ye shall find him whenever ye shall seek him with all thy heart and with all thy soul in thy affliction. 30 And all these words shall find thee in the last days, and thou shall turn to the Lord thy God, and shall hearken to his voice. 31 Because the Lord thy God *is* a God of pity; he will not forsake thee, nor destroy thee; he will not forget the covenant of thy fathers, which the Lord swore to them.

32 Ask of the former days that were before thee, from the day when God created man upon the earth, and at the *one* end of heaven to the other end of heaven, if there has happened any thing like unto this great event, if such a thing has been heard; 33 if a nation has heard the voice of the living God speaking out of the midst of the fire, as thou has heard and has lived; 34 if God has *ever* attempted to go and take to himself a nation out of the midst of *another* nation with trial, and with signs, and with wonders, and with war, and with a mighty hand, and with a high arm, and with great sights, according to all the things that the Lord our God did in Egypt before you *as you were* seeing. 35 So that thou should know that the Lord thy God he is God, and there is none beside him.

36 His voice was made audible from heaven to instruct thee, and he showed thee upon the earth his great fire, and thou heard his words out of the midst of the fire. 37 Because he loved thy fathers, he also chose you their seed after them, and he brought thee himself with his great strength out of Egypt, 38 to destroy nations greater and stronger than thou before thy face, to bring thee in, to give thee their land to inherit, as thou have it this day. 39 And thou shall know this day, and shall consider in thine heart, that the Lord thy God he *is* God in heaven above, and on the earth beneath, and there is none else but he. 40 And keep ye his commandments, and his ordinances, all that I command you this day; that it may be well with thee, and with thy sons after thee, that ye may live long upon the earth, which the Lord thy God gives thee forever.

41 Then Moses separated three cities beyond Jordan on the east, 42 that the killer might flee thither, who had killed his neighbor unintentionally, and have not hated him before yesterday and the third *day*, and he shall flee to one of these cities and live; 43 Bosor in the wilderness, in the plain country of Ruben, and Ramoth in Galaad *belonging to* Gaddi, and Gaulon in Basan *belonging to* Manasse.

44 This *is* the law that Moses set before the sons of Israel. 45 These *are* the testimonies, and the ordinances, and the judgments, which Moses spoke to the sons of Israel, when they came out of the land of Egypt: 46 on the other side of Jordan, in the valley near the house of Phogor, in the land of Seon king of the Amorites, who lived in Esebon, whom Moses and the sons of Israel defeated when they came out of the land of Egypt. 47 And they inherited his land, and the land of Og king of Basan, two kings of the Amorites, who were beyond Jordan to the east. 48 From Aroer, which is on the border of the brook Arnon, even to the Mount of Seon, which is Aermon. 49 All Araba beyond Jordan to the east under Asedoth: the quarried rock.

Chapter 5

And Moses called all *of* Israel, and said to them, Hear, Israel, the ordinances and judgments, all that I speak in your ears this day, and ye shall learn them, and observe to do them. 2 The Lord your God made a covenant with you in Horeb. 3 The Lord did not make this covenant with your fathers, but with you; ye are all here alive this day. 4 The Lord spoke to you face to face on the mountain out of the midst of the fire. 5 And I stood between the Lord and you at that time to report to you the words of the Lord, because ye were afraid before the fire, and ye did not go up to the mountain, saying,

6 I am the Lord thy God, who brought thee out of the land of Egypt, out of the house of slavery.

Deuteronomy 5

7 Thou shall have no other gods before my face. 8 Thou shall not make to thyself an image, nor likeness of any thing, whatever things *are* in the heaven above, and whatever *is* in the earth beneath, and whatever *is* in the waters under the earth. 9 Thou shall not bow down to them, nor shall thou serve them; for I am the Lord thy God, a jealous God, visiting the sins of the fathers upon the children to the third and fourth generation to them that hate me, 10 and doing mercifully to them that love Me to the *number of* thousands, and that keep my commandments.

11 Thou shall not take the name of the Lord thy God in vain, for the Lord thy God will certainly not acquit him that takes his name in vain.

12 Keep the Sabbath day to sanctify it, as the Lord thy God commanded thee. 13 Six days thou shall work, and thou shall do all thy works; 14 but on the seventh day *is* the Sabbath of the Lord thy God; thou shall do in it no work, thou, and thy son, and thy daughter, thy male slave, and thy female slave, thine ox, and thine mule, and all thy cattle, and the stranger that travels in the midst of thee; that thy male slave may rest, and thy female slave and thine ox, as well as thou. 15 And thou shall remember that thou were a slave in the land of Egypt, and the Lord thy God brought thee out thence with a mighty hand, and a high arm; therefore the Lord appointed thee to keep the Sabbath day and to sanctify it.

16 Honor thy father and thy mother, as the Lord thy God commanded thee; that it may be well with thee, and that thou may live long upon the land, which the Lord thy God gives thee.

17 Thou shall not commit murder.

18 Thou shall not commit adultery.

19 Thou shall not steal.

20 Thou shall not bear false witness against thy neighbor.

21 Thou shall not covet thy neighbor's wife; thou shall not covet thy neighbor's house, or his field, or his male slave, or his female slave, or his ox, or his mule, or any beast of his, nor any thing that is thy neighbor's.

22 These words the Lord spoke to the entire assembly of you on the mountain out of the midst of the fire *there was* darkness, blackness, storm, a loud voice and he added no more, and he wrote them on two tables of stone, and he gave them to me. 23 And it came to pass when ye heard the voice out of the midst of the fire, for the mountain burned with fire, that ye came to me, even all the heads of your tribes, and your elders; 24 and ye said, Behold, the Lord our God has showed us His glory, and we have heard His voice out of the midst of the fire; by this day we have seen that God shall speak to man, and he shall live. 25 And now let us not die, for this great fire will consume us, if we shall hear the voice of the Lord our God any more, and we shall die. 26 For what flesh that has heard the voice of the living God, speaking out of the midst of the fire, as we *have heard*, and shall live?

27 Do thou come near, and hear all that the Lord our God shall say, and thou shall speak to us all things whatever the Lord our God shall speak to thee, and we will hear, and do.

28 And the Lord heard the voice of your words as ye spoke to me; and the Lord said to me, I have heard the voice of the words of this people, even all things that they have said to thee. *They have* well *said* all that they have spoken. 29 Who will give that there should be such a heart, that they should fear Me and keep My commands always, that it might be well with them and with their sons forever. 30 Go, say to them, Return ye to your homes; 31 but stand thou here with Me, and I will tell thee all the commands, and the ordinances, and the judgments, which thou shall teach them, and let them do so in the land which I give them for an inheritance.

32 And ye shall take heed to do as the Lord thy God commanded thee; ye shall not turn aside to the right hand or to the left, 33 according to all the way, which the Lord thy God commanded thee to walk in it, that he may give thee rest; and that it may be well with thee, and ye may prolong your days on the land which ye shall inherit.

Chapter 6

And these *are* the commands, and the ordinances, and the judgments, as many as the Lord our God gave commandment to teach you to do so in the land on which ye enter to inherit it. 2 That ye may fear the Lord your God, keep ye all his ordinances, and his commandments, which I command thee today, thou, and thy sons, and thy sons' sons, all the days of thy life, that ye may live many days. 3 Hear, therefore, O Israel, and observe to do them, that it may be well with thee, and that ye may be greatly multiplied, as the Lord God of thy fathers said that he would give thee a land flowing with milk and honey; and these *are* the ordinances, and the judgments that the Lord commanded the sons of Israel in the wilderness, when they had gone forth from the land of Egypt.

4 Hear, O Israel, The Lord our God is one Lord. 5 And thou shall love the Lord thy God with thy entire mind, and with thy entire soul, and *with* thy entire strength. 6 And these words, all that I command thee this day, shall be in thy heart and in thy soul. 7 And thou shall teach them to thy sons, and thou shall speak of them sitting in the house, and walking by the way, and lying down, and rising up. 8 And thou shall fasten them for a sign upon thy hand, and it shall be immoveable before thine eyes. 9 And ye shall write them on the lintels of your houses and of your gates.

Deuteronomy 7

10 And it shall come to pass when the Lord thy God shall have brought thee into the land that he swore to thy fathers, to Abraham, and to Isaac, and to Jacob, to give thee great and beautiful cities, which thou did not build, 11 houses full of all good things which thou did not fill, pools dug in the rock which thou did not dig, vineyards and olive yards which thou did not plant, then having eaten and been filled, 12 beware lest thou forget the Lord thy God that brought thee forth out of the land of Egypt, out of the house of slavery. 13 The Lord thy God thou shall fear and him only shall thou serve; and thou shall cleave to him, and by his name thou shall swear. 14 Go ye not after other gods of the gods of the nations round about you; 15 for the Lord thy God *is* a jealous God, lest the Lord thy God be very angry with thee, and destroy thee from off the face of the earth.

16 Thou shall not tempt the Lord thy God, as ye tempted him in the temptation. 17 Thou shall by all means keep the commands of the Lord thy God, the testimonies, and the ordinances, which he commanded thee. 18 And thou shall do that which is pleasing and good before the Lord thy God, that it may be well with thee, and that thou may go in and inherit the good land, which the Lord swore to your fathers, 19 to chase all thine enemies from before thy face, as the Lord said.

20 And it shall come to pass when thy son shall ask thee tomorrow, saying, What are the testimonies, and the ordinances, and the judgments, which the Lord our God has commanded us? 21 Then shall thou say to thy son, We were slaves to Pharaoh in the land of Egypt, and the Lord brought us forth thence with a mighty hand, and with a high arm. 22 And the Lord gave signs and great and evil wonders in Egypt, on Pharaoh and on his house before us. 23 And he brought us out from there to give us this land, which he swore to give to our fathers. 24 And the Lord charged us to observe all these ordinances; to fear the Lord our God that it may be well with us forever that we may live, as even today. 25 And there shall be mercy to us, if we take heed to keep all these commands before the Lord our God, as he has commanded us.

Chapter 7

And when the Lord thy God shall bring thee into the land, into which thou goes to possess it, and shall remove great nations from before thy face, the Hettite, and Gergesite, and Amorite, and Canaanite, and Pherezite, and Evite, and Jebusite, seven nations *more* numerous and stronger than you, 2 and the Lord thy God shall deliver them into thy hands, then thou shall kill them; thou shall utterly destroy them: thou shall not make a covenant with them, neither shall ye pity them;

3 neither shall ye contract marriages with them; thou shall not give thy daughter to his son, and thou shall not take his daughter to thy son. 4 For he will draw away thy son from Me, and he will serve other gods; and the Lord will be very angry with you, and will soon utterly destroy thee. 5 But thus shall ye do to them; ye shall destroy their altars, and shall break down their pillars, and shall cut down their groves, and shall burn with fire the graven images of their gods.

6 For thou art a holy people to the Lord thy God; and the Lord thy God chose thee to be to Him a peculiar people beyond all nations that *are* upon the face of the earth. 7 It was not because ye are more numerous than all *other* nations that the Lord preferred you, and the Lord made choice of you: for ye are fewer in number than all *other* nations. 8 But because the Lord loved you, and as keeping the oath that he swore to your fathers, the Lord brought you out with a strong hand, and the Lord redeemed thee from the house of slavery, out of the hand of Pharaoh king of Egypt. 9 Thou shall know therefore, that the Lord thy God, he *is* God, a faithful God, who keeps covenant and mercy for them that love him, and for those that keep his commandments to a thousand generations, 10 and who recompenses them that hate him to their face, to destroy them utterly; and will not be slack with them that hate him; he will recompense them to their face. 11 Thou shall keep therefore the commands, and the ordinances, and these judgments, which I command thee this day to do.

12 And it shall come to pass when ye shall have heard these ordinances, and shall have kept and done them, that the Lord thy God shall keep for thee the covenant and the mercy, which he swore to your fathers. 13 And he will love thee, and bless thee, and multiply thee; and he will bless the offspring of thy belly, and the fruit of thy land, thy corn, and thy wine, and thine oil, the herds of thine oxen, and the flocks of thy sheep, on the land that the Lord swore to thy fathers to give to thee. 14 Thou shall be blessed beyond all nations; there shall not be among you an impotent or barren one, and among thy cattle. 15 And the Lord thy God shall remove from thee all sickness; and none of the evil diseases of Egypt, which thou has seen, and all that thou has known, will he lay upon thee; but he will lay them upon all that hate thee. 16 And thou shall eat all the spoils of the nations which the Lord thy God gives thee; thine eye shall not spare them, and thou shall not serve their gods; for this is an offence to thee.

17 But if thou should say in thine heart, This nation *is* more than I, how shall I be able to destroy them utterly? 18 thou shall not fear them; thou shall surely remember all that the Lord thy God did to Pharaoh and to all the Egyptians; 19 the great temptations which thine eyes have seen, those signs and great wonders, the strong hand, and the high arm; how the Lord thy God brought thee forth; so the Lord your God will do to all the nations, whom thou fear in their presence.

Deuteronomy 8

20 And the Lord thy God shall send against them the hornets, until they that are left and they that are hidden from thee are utterly destroyed. 21 Thou shall not be wounded before them, because the Lord thy God in the midst of thee *is* a great and powerful God. 22 And the Lord thy God shall consume these nations before thee little by little; thou shall not be able to consume them speedily, lest the land become desert and the wild beasts of the field be multiplied against thee. 23 And the Lord thy God shall deliver them into thy hands, and thou shall destroy them with a great destruction, until ye shall have utterly destroyed them. 24 And he shall deliver their kings into your hands, and ye shall destroy their name from that place; none shall stand up in opposition before thee, until thou shall have utterly destroyed them. 25 Ye shall burn with fire the graven images of their gods; thou shall not covet their silver, neither shall thou take to thyself gold from them, lest thou should offend thereby, because it is an abomination to the Lord thy God. 26 And thou shall not bring an abomination into thine house, so thou shall become an accursed thing like it; thou shall utterly hate it, and altogether abominate it, because it is an accursed thing.

Chapter 8

Ye shall observe to do all the commands which I charge you today, that ye may live and be multiplied, and enter in and inherit the land, which the Lord your God swore to your fathers. 2 And thou shall remember all the way which the Lord thy God led thee in the wilderness, that He might afflict thee, and try thee, and that the things in thine heart might be made manifest, whether thou would keep His commandments or not. 3 And He afflicted thee and straitened thee with hunger, and fed thee with manna that thy fathers knew not; that He might teach thee that man shall not live by bread alone, but by every word that proceeds out of the mouth of God shall man live. 4 Thy garments did not grow old from off thee, thy shoes were not worn from off thee, thy feet were not hardened, Behold! These forty years. 5 And thou shall know in thine heart, that as if any man should chasten his son, so the Lord thy God will chasten thee. 6 And thou shall keep the commands of the Lord thy God, to walk in His ways, and to fear him. 7 For the Lord thy God will bring thee into a good and extensive land, where there are torrents of waters, and fountains issuing from deep places through the plains and through the mountains; 8 a land of wheat and barley, vines, figs, pomegranates; a land of olive oil and honey; 9 a land on which thou shall not eat thy bread with poverty, and thou shall not want any thing upon it; a land whose stones are iron, and out of its mountains thou shall mine brass. 10 And thou shall eat and be filled, and shall bless the Lord thy God on the good land that He has given thee.

11 Take heed to thyself that thou forget not the Lord thy God, so as not to keep His commands, and His judgments, and ordinances, which I command thee this day; 12 lest when thou has eaten and are full, and have built goodly houses, and lived in them; 13 and thy oxen and thy sheep are multiplied to thee, and thy silver and thy gold are multiplied to thee, and all thy possessions are multiplied to thee, 14 thou should be exalted in heart, and forget the Lord thy God, who brought thee out of the land of Egypt, out of the house of slavery, 15 who brought thee through that great and terrible wilderness, where *is* the biting serpent, and scorpion, and drought, where there was no water; who brought thee a fountain of water out of the flinty rock: 16 who fed thee with manna in the wilderness, which thou knew not, and thy fathers knew not; that He might afflict thee, and thoroughly try thee, and do thee good in thy latter days. 17 Lest thou should say in thine heart, My strength, and the power of mine hand have brought me this great wealth. 18 But thou shall remember the Lord thy God that He gives thee strength to get wealth; even that He may establish His covenant, which the Lord swore to thy fathers, as today. 19 And it shall come to pass if thou do at all forget the Lord thy God, and should go after other gods, and serve them, and worship them, I call heaven and earth to witness against you today, that by destruction you shall be destroyed. 20 As also the other nations that the Lord God destroys before your face, so shall ye be destroyed, because ye hearkened not to the voice of the Lord your God.

Chapter 9

Hear, O Israel; Thou go today across Jordan to inherit nations greater and stronger than yourselves, cities great and walled up to heaven; 2 a people great and many and tall, the sons of Enak, whom thou knows, and concerning whom thou has heard, Who can stand before the sons of Enak? 3 And thou shall know today, that the Lord thy God He shall go before thy face; He is a consuming fire; he shall destroy them, and he shall turn them back before thy face, and shall destroy them quickly, as the Lord said to thee. 4 Speak not in thine heart, when the Lord thy God has destroyed these nations before thy face, saying, For my righteousness the Lord brought me in to inherit this good land. 5 Not for thy righteousness, nor for the holiness of thy heart, do thou go in to inherit their land, but because of the wickedness of these nations the Lord will destroy them from before thy face, and that he may establish the covenant that the Lord swore to our fathers, to Abraham, and to Isaac, and to Jacob.

6 And thou shall know today, that *it is* not for thy righteousness the Lord thy God gives thee this good land to inherit, for thou are a stiff necked people.

Deuteronomy 9

7 Remember, forget not, how much thou provoked the Lord thy God in the wilderness; from the day that ye came forth out of Egypt, even till ye came into this place, ye continued to be disobedient toward the Lord. 8 Also in Horeb ye provoked the Lord, and the Lord was angry with you to destroy you; 9 when I went up into the mountain to receive the tables of stone, the tables of the covenant that the Lord made with you, and I was in the mountain forty days and forty nights, I ate no bread and drank no water. 10 And the Lord gave me the two tables of stone written with the finger of God, and on them there had been written all the words which the Lord spoke to you in the mountain on the day of the assembly. 11 And it came to pass after forty days and forty nights, the Lord gave me the two tables of stone, the tables of the covenant. 12 And the Lord said to me, Arise, go down quickly from here, for thy people whom thou brought out of the land of Egypt have transgressed; they have gone aside quickly out of the way that I commanded them, and have made themselves a molten image.

13 And the Lord spoke to me, saying, I have spoken to thee once and again, saying, I have seen this people, and, behold, it is a stiff necked people. 14 And now suffer Me utterly to destroy them, and I will blot out their name from under heaven, and will make of thee a nation great and strong, and more numerous than this. 15 And I turned and went down from the mountain; and the mountain burned with fire to the sky; and the two tables of the testimonies *were* upon my two hands. 16 And when I saw that ye had sinned against the Lord your God, and had made to yourselves a molten image, and had gone astray out of the way, which the Lord commanded you to do; 17 then I took hold of the two tables, and cast them out of my two hands, and broke them before you. 18 And I made my petition before the Lord as also at the first forty days and forty nights; I ate no bread and drank no water, on account of all your sins that ye sinned in doing evil before the Lord God to provoke Him. 19 And I am greatly terrified because of the wrath and anger, because the Lord was provoked with you utterly to destroy you; yet the Lord hearkened to me at this time also. 20 And He was angry with Aaron to destroy him utterly, and I prayed for Aaron also at that time. 21 And your sin that ye had made, the calf, I took, and burned it with fire, and pounded it and ground it down till it became fine; and it became like dust, and I cast the dust into the brook that descended from the mountain.

22 Also in the Burning, and in the Temptation, and at the Graves of Lust, ye provoked the Lord thy God. 23 And when the Lord sent you forth from Kades Barne, saying, Go up and inherit the land that I give to you, then ye disobeyed the word of the Lord your God, and believed Him not, and hearkened not to His voice. 24 Ye were disobedient towards the Lord from the day in which you knew Him.

25 And I prayed before the Lord forty days and forty nights, the number that I prayed, for the Lord said that he would utterly destroy you.

26 And I prayed to God, and said, O Lord, King of gods, destroy not Thy people and Thy portion, whom Thou did redeem, whom Thou brought out of the land of Egypt with Thy great power, and with Thy strong hand, and with Thy high arm. 27 Remember Abraham, and Isaac, and Jacob Thy servants, to whom Thou swore by Thyself; look not upon the hardness of this people, and their impieties, and their sins. 28 Lest the inhabitants of the land whence thou brought us out speak, saying, Because the Lord could not bring them into the land of which He spoke to them, and because He hated them, has He brought them forth to kill them in the wilderness. 29 And these *are* Thy people and Thy portion, which Thou brought out of the land of Egypt with Thy great strength, and with Thy mighty hand, and with thy high arm.

Chapter 10

At that time the Lord said to me, Carve for thyself two stone tables as the first, and come up to me into the mountain, and thou shall make for thyself an ark of wood. 2 And thou shall write upon the tables the words that were on the first tables, which thou did break, and thou shall put them into the Ark. 3 And I made an ark of boards of incorruptible wood, and I hewed tables of stone like the first, and I went up to the mountain, and the two tables were in my hand. 4 And he wrote upon the tables according to the first writing *of* the Ten Commandments, which the Lord spoke to you on the mountain out of the midst of the fire, and the Lord gave them to me. 5 And I turned and came down from the mountain, and I put the tables into the ark that I had made; and there they were, as the Lord commanded me.

6 And the sons of Israel departed from Beeroth of the sons of Jakim *to* Misadai; there Aaron died, and there he was buried, and Eleazar his son was priest in his stead. 7 Thence they departed to Gadgad; and from Gadgad to Etebatha, a land *of* torrents of water. 8 At that time the Lord separated the tribe of Levi, to bear the Ark of the Covenant of the Lord, to stand near before the Lord, to minister and bless in his name to this day. 9 Therefore the Levites have no part or inheritance among their brothers, the Lord himself *is* their inheritance, as he said to them.

10 And I stayed on the mountain forty days and forty nights, and the Lord heard me at that time also, and the Lord would not destroy you. 11 And the Lord said to me, Go, set out before this people, and let them go in and inherit the land, which I swore to their fathers to give to them. 12 And now, Israel, what does the Lord thy God require of thee, but to fear the Lord thy God, and to walk in all his ways, and to love him, and to serve the Lord thy God with all thy heart, and with all thy soul,

Deuteronomy 11

13 to keep the commandments of the Lord thy God, and his ordinances, all that I charge thee this day, that it may be well with thee? * 14 Behold, the heaven and the heaven of heavens belong to the Lord thy God, the earth and all things that is in it. 15 Only the Lord chose your fathers to love them, and he chose out their seed after them, *even* you, beyond all nations, as at this day. 16 And ye shall circumcise the hardness of your heart, and ye shall not harden your neck. 17 For the Lord your God, He *is* God of gods, and the Lord of lords, the great, and strong, and terrible God, who does not wonder at a face, nor will He by any means accept a bribe; 18 executing judgment for the stranger and orphan and widow, and he loves the stranger to give him bread and raiment. 19 And ye shall love the stranger; for ye were strangers in the land of Egypt. 20 Thou shall fear the Lord thy God, and serve Him, and shall cling to Him, and shall swear by His name. 21 He *is* thy boast, and He *is* thy God, who has wrought in the midst of thee these great and glorious things, which thine eyes have seen. 22 With seventy souls your fathers went down into Egypt; but the Lord thy God has made thee as the stars of the sky in multitude.

* The phrase "Moses said to the sons of Israel" that is at the beginning of verse fourteen in the July reading for vespers in the *Greek Menaion* and *Prophetologion* is not present in either the Apostoliki Diakonia or Zoe Brotherhood texts. This phrase seems to be a liturgical interpolation.

Chapter 11

Therefore thou shall love the Lord thy God, and shall observe His appointments, and His ordinances, and His commandments, and His judgments, always. 2 And ye shall know today; for not to your children, who know not and have not seen the discipline of the Lord thy God, and His wonderful works, and his strong hand, and his high arm, 3 and his signs, and his wonders that he wrought in the midst of Egypt on Pharaoh king of Egypt, and all his land; 4 and what he did to the host of the Egyptians, and to their chariots, and their cavalry, and their host; how He made the water of the Red Sea to overwhelm the face of them as they pursued after you, and the Lord destroyed them until this day; 5 and all the things that He did to you in the wilderness until ye came into this place; 6 and all the things that He did to Dathan and Abiron the sons of Eliab the son of Ruben, whom the earth, opening her mouth, swallowed up, and their houses, and their tents, and all their substance that was with them, in the midst of all Israel; 7 for your eyes have seen all the mighty works of the Lord that He wrought among you this day. 8 And ye shall keep all His commandments, as many as I command thee this day, that ye may live, and be multiplied, and that ye may go in and inherit the land, into which ye go across Jordan to inherit it;

9 that ye may live long upon the land, which the Lord swore to your fathers to give to them, and to their seed after them, a land flowing with milk and honey. 10 For the land into which thou goes to inherit it, is not as the land of Egypt, whence ye came out, whenever they sow the seed, and water it with their feet, as a garden of herbs; 11 but the land into which thou goes to inherit it, is a land of mountains and plains; it shall drink water of the rain of the sky. 12 A land that the Lord thy God surveys continually, the eyes of the Lord thy God are upon it from the beginning of the year to the end of the year.

13 Now if ye will indeed hearken to all the commands which I charge thee this day, to love the Lord thy God, and to serve Him with all thy heart, and with all thy soul, 14 then He shall give to thy land the early and latter rain in its season, and thou shall bring in thy corn, and thy wine, and thine oil. 15 And He shall give food in thy fields to thy cattle; 16 and when thou has eaten and are full, take heed to thyself that thy heart be not broadened, and ye transgress, and serve other gods, and worship them; 17 and the Lord be angry with you, and restrain the sky; and there shall not be rain, and the earth shall not yield its fruit, and ye shall be destroyed quickly from off the good land that the Lord has given you.

18 And ye shall keep these words in your heart and in your soul, and ye shall bind them as a sign on your hand, and it shall be fixed before your eyes. 19 And ye shall teach them to your children, so as to speak about them when thou sit in the house, and when thou walk by the way, and when thou sleep, and when thou arise. 20 And ye shall write them on the thresholds of your houses, and on your gates; 21 that your days may be long, and the days of your sons, upon the land that the Lord swore to your fathers to give to them, as the days of heaven upon the earth. 22 And it shall come to pass that if ye will indeed hearken to all these commands, which I charge thee to observe this day, to love the Lord our God, and to walk in all his ways, and to cleave close to him; 23 then the Lord shall cast out all these nations before you, and ye shall inherit great nations and stronger than yourselves. 24 Every place whereon the sole of your foot shall tread shall be your; from the wilderness and Antilibanus, and from the great river, the river Euphrates, even as far as the west sea shall be your coasts. 25 No one shall stand before you; and the Lord your God will put the fear of you and the dread of you on the face of all the land, on which ye shall tread, as he told you.

26 Behold, I set before you this day the blessing and the curse; 27 the blessing, if ye hearken to the commands of the Lord your God, all that I command you this day; 28 and the curse, if ye do not hearken to the commands of the Lord our God, as many as I command you this day, and ye wander from the way that I have commanded you, having gone to serve other gods, which ye know not.

Deuteronomy 12

29 And it shall come to pass when the Lord thy God shall have brought thee into the land into which thou goes over to inherit it, then thou shall put blessing on mount Garizin, and the curse upon mount Gaebal. (30 Behold! Are not these beyond Jordan, behind, to the west in the land of Canaan that lies to the west near Golgol, by the high oak ;) 31 For ye are crossing Jordan, to go in and inherit the land that the Lord our God gives you to inherit always, and ye shall live in it. 32 And ye shall take heed to do all his ordinances, and these judgments, as many as I set before you this day.

Chapter 12

And these *are* the ordinances and the judgments that ye shall observe to do in the land, which the Lord God of your fathers gives you for an inheritance, all the days that ye live upon the land. 2 Ye shall utterly destroy all the places in which they served their gods, whose *land* ye inherit, on the high mountains and on the hills, and under the thick tree. 3 And ye shall destroy their altars, and break in pieces their pillars, and ye shall cut down their groves, and ye shall burn with fire the graven images of their gods, and ye shall abolish their name out of that place. 4 Ye shall not do so to the Lord your God. 5 But in the place that the Lord thy God shall choose in one of your cities to name his name there, and to be called upon, ye shall even seek out and go thither. 6 And ye shall carry thither your whole burnt offerings, and your sacrifices, and your first fruits, and your vows *as offerings*, and your freewill offerings, and your offerings of thanksgiving, the first born of your herds, and of your flocks. 7 And ye shall eat there before the Lord your God, and ye shall rejoice in all the things on which ye shall lay your hand, ye and your houses, as the Lord your God has blessed you. 8 Ye shall not do altogether as we do here this day, every man that which is pleasing in his own sight. 9 For hitherto ye have not arrived at the rest and the inheritance, that the Lord our God gives you. 10 And ye shall cross Jordan, and shall live in the land that the Lord our God takes as an inheritance for you; and He shall give you rest from all your enemies around, and ye shall live securely. 11 And there shall be a place which the Lord thy God shall choose for His name to be called there, thither shall ye bring all things that I order you this day; your whole burn offerings, and your sacrifices, and your tithes, and the first fruits of your hands, and every choice gift of yours, whatever ye shall vow to the Lord your God. 12 And ye shall rejoice before the Lord your God, ye and your sons, and your daughters, and your male slaves and your female slaves, and the Levite that is at your gates; because he has no portion or inheritance with you. 13 Take heed to thyself that thou offer not thy whole burnt offerings in any place that thou shall see;

14 save in the place that the Lord thy God shall choose, in one of thy tribes, there shall ye offer your whole burnt offerings, and there shall thou do all things whatever I charge thee this day.

15 But thou shall kill according to all thy desire, and shall eat flesh according to the blessing of the Lord thy God, which He has given thee in every city; the unclean that is within thee and the clean shall eat it on equal terms, as the doe or the stag. 16 Only ye shall not eat the blood; ye shall pour it out on the ground as water. 17 Thou shall not be able to eat in thy cities the tithe of thy corn, and of thy wine, and of thine oil, the firstborn of thine herd and of thy flock, and all *your* vows as many as ye shall have vowed, and your offerings of thanksgiving, and the first fruits of thine hands. 18 But before the Lord thy God thou shall eat it, in the place that the Lord thy God shall choose for himself, thou, and thy son, and thy daughter, thy male slave and thy female slave, and the stranger that is within thy gates; and thou shall rejoice before the Lord thy God, on whatever thou shall lay thine hand. 19 Take heed to thyself that thou do not desert the Levite all the time that thou live upon the earth.

20 And if the Lord thy God shall enlarge thy borders, as he said to thee, and thou shall say, I will eat meat; if thy soul should desire to eat meat, thou shall eat meat in all the desire of thy soul. 21 If the place were far from thee that the Lord thy God should choose for himself, that his name be called upon it, then thou shall kill of thy herd and of thy flock, which God shall have given thee, even as I commanded thee, and thou shall eat in thy cities according to the desire of thy soul. 22 As the doe and the stag are eaten, so shall thou eat it; the unclean in thee and the clean shall eat it in like manner. 23 Take diligent heed that thou eat no blood, for blood *is* the life of it; the life shall not be eaten with the meat. 24 Ye shall not eat *it*; ye shall pour it out on the ground as water. 25 Thou shall not eat it, that it may be well with thee and with thy sons after thee, if thou shall do that which is good and pleasing before the Lord thy God. 26 But thou shall take thy holy *things*, if thou has any, and thy vows *as offerings*, and come to the place that the Lord thy God shall choose to have His name upon it. 27 And thou shall sacrifice thy whole burnt offerings; thou shall offer the meat upon the altar of the Lord thy God; but the blood of thy sacrifices thou shall pour out at the foot of the altar of the Lord thy God, but the meat thou shall eat. 28 Beware and hearken, and thou shall do all the commands which I charge thee, that it may be well with thee and with thy sons forever, if thou shall do that which is pleasing and good before the Lord thy God.

29 And if the Lord thy God shall utterly destroy the nations, to whom thou goes in thither to inherit their land, from before thee, and thou shall inherit it, and live in their land, 30 take heed to thyself that thou seek not to follow them after they are destroyed before thee, saying, How do these nations act towards their gods? I will do likewise.

Deuteronomy 13

31 Thou shall not do so to thy God, for they have sacrificed among their gods the abominations of the Lord, which He hates, for they burn their sons and their daughters in fire to their gods.

Chapter 13

Every word that I command you this day, thou shall observe to do: thou shall not add to it, nor diminish from it. 2 And if there arise within thee a prophet, or one who dreams a dream, and he gives thee a sign or a wonder, 3 and the sign or the wonder come to pass that he spoke to thee, saying, Let us go and serve other gods that ye know not; 4 ye shall not hearken to the words of that prophet, or the dreamer of that dream, because the Lord thy God tries you, to know whether ye love your God with all your heart and with all your soul. 5 Ye shall follow the Lord your God, and fear Him, and ye shall hear His voice, and attach yourselves to Him.

6 And that prophet or that dreamer of a dream, shall die; for he has spoken to make thee *commit* error from the Lord thy God who brought thee out of the land of Egypt, who redeemed thee from slavery, to thrust thee out of the way which the Lord thy God commanded thee to walk in: so shall thou abolish the evil from among you. 7 And if thy brother by thy father or mother, or thy son, or daughter, or thy wife in thy bosom, or friend who is equal to thine own soul, entreat thee secretly, saying, Let us go and serve other gods, which neither thou nor thy fathers have known, 8 of the gods of the nations that are around you, who are near thee or at a distance from thee, from one end of the earth to the other; 9 thou shall not consent to him, neither shall thou hearken to him; and thine eye shall not spare him, thou shall feel no regret for him, neither shall thou at all protect him; 10 thou shall surely report concerning him, and thy hands shall be upon him among the first to kill him, and the hands of all the people at the last. 11 And they shall stone him with stones, and he shall die, because he sought to draw thee away from the Lord thy God who brought thee out of the land of Egypt, out of the house of slavery.

12 And all Israel shall hear, and fear, and shall not again do pursuant to this evil thing among you. 13 And if in one of thy cities that the Lord God gives thee to live therein, thou shall hear men saying, 14 Evil men have gone out from you, and have caused all the inhabitants of their land to fall away, saying, Let us go and worship other gods, whom ye knew not, 15 then thou shall enquire and ask, and search diligently, and behold, *if* the thing is clearly true, and this abomination has taken place among you, 16 thou shall utterly destroy all the inhabitants in that land with the edge of the sword; ye shall solemnly curse it, and all things in it.

17 And all its spoils thou shall gather into its public ways, and thou shall burn the city with fire, and all its spoils publicly before the Lord thy God; and it shall be uninhabited forever, it shall not be built again. 18 And there shall nothing of the cursed thing cleave to thy hand, that the Lord may turn from His fierce anger, and show thee mercy, and pity thee, and multiply thee, as He swore to thy fathers; 19 if thou will hear the voice of the Lord thy God, to keep His commandments, and all that I charge thee this day, to do that which is good and pleasing before the Lord thy God.

Chapter 14

Ye are the children of the Lord your God; ye shall not make any baldness between you eyes for the dead. 2 For thou art a holy people to the Lord thy God, and the Lord thy God has chosen thee to be a peculiar people to Him of all the nations on the face of the earth.

3 Ye shall not eat any abominable thing. 4 These *are* the beasts that ye shall eat; the calf of the herd, and lamb of the sheep, and kid of the goats; * 5 the stag, and doe, and white-tailed hart, and gazelle, and camelopard. 6 Every beast that divides the hoofs, and makes claws of two divisions, and that chews the cud among beasts, these ye shall eat. 7 And these ye shall not eat of them that chew the cud, and of those that divide the hoofs, and make distinct claws; the camel, and the hare, and the rabbit; because they chew the cud, and do not divide the hoof, these are unclean to you. 8 And as for the swine, because he divides the hoof, and makes claws of the hoof, yet he chews not the cud, he is unclean to you; ye shall not eat of their flesh, ye shall not touch their dead bodies.

9 And these ye shall eat of all that are in the water, ye shall eat all that have fins and scales. 10 And all that have not fins and scales ye shall not eat; they are unclean to you.

11 Ye shall eat every clean bird. 12 And these birds ye shall not eat; the eagle, and the ossifrage, and the osprey, 13 and the vulture, and the kite and the like to it, 14 and every raven and its kind, 15 and the sparrow, and the owl, and the sea-mew, 16 and the heron, and the swan, and the stork, 17 and the cormorant, and the hawk, and its kind, and the hoopoe, and the night-raven, 18 and the pelican, and the heron and its kind, and the flamingo and the bat. 19 All winged animals that creep are unclean to you; ye shall not eat of them. 20 Ye shall eat every clean bird.

21 Ye shall eat nothing that dies of itself; it shall be given to the traveler in thy cities and he shall eat it, or thou shall sell it to a stranger, because thou art a holy people to the Lord thy God. Thou shall not boil a lamb in his mother's milk.

Deuteronomy 15

22 Thou shall tithe a tenth of all the produce of thy seed, the fruit of thy field year by year. 23 And thou shall eat it in the place that the Lord thy God shall choose to have His name called there; ye shall bring the tithe of thy corn and of thy wine, and of thine oil, the firstborn of thy herd and of thy flock, that thou may learn to fear the Lord thy God always. 24 If the journey were too far for thee, and thou art not able to bring them, because the place *is* far from thee that the Lord thy God shall choose to have His name called there, because the Lord thy God will bless thee, 25 then thou shall sell them for money, and thou shall take the money in thy hands, and thou shall go to the place that the Lord thy God shall choose. 26 And thou shall give the money for whatever thy soul shall desire, for oxen or for sheep, or for wine, or on strong drink, or on whatever thy soul may desire, and thou shall eat there before the Lord thy God, and thou shall rejoice and thy house, 27 and the Levite, which is in thy cities, because he has not a portion or inheritance with thee. 28 After three years thou shall bring out all the tithes of thy fruits, in that year thou shall lay it up in thy cities. 29 And the Levite shall come, because he has no part or lot with thee, and the stranger, and the orphan, and the widow that is in thy cities; and they shall eat and be filled, that the Lord thy God may bless thee in all the works, which thou shall do.

* In Alfred Rahlfs' *Septuaginta* there is reference to a variant reading in verse five that makes mention of two additional animals after the "doe" and before the "white-tailed hart". The variant reads as follows:

"...the stag, and doe, *and roebuck, and antelope*, and white-tailed hart, and gazelle, and camelopard".

Chapter 15

Every seven years thou shall make a release. 2 And this *is* the ordinance of the release; thou shall remit every private debt that thy neighbor owes thee, and thou shall not ask payment of it from thy brother; for it has been called a release to the Lord thy God. 3 Of a stranger thou shall ask again whatever he has of thine, but to thy brother thou shall remit his debt to thee. 4 For there shall not be a poor person in the midst of thee, for the Lord thy God will surely bless thee in the land that the Lord thy God gives thee by inheritance, that thou should inherit it. 5 If ye shall indeed hearken to the voice of the Lord your God, to keep and do all these commandments, as many as I charge thee this day, 6 because the Lord thy God has blessed thee in the way of which He spoke to thee, then thou shall lend to many nations, but thou shall not borrow; and thou shall rule over many nations, but they shall not rule over thee.

Deuteronomy 15

7 If there shall be in the midst of thee a poor *man* of thy brothers in one of thy cities in the land, which the Lord thy God gives thee, thou shall not harden thine heart, neither shall thou by any means close up thine hand from thy brother who is in want. 8 Thou shall surely open thine hands to him, and shall lend to him as much as he wants according to his need. 9 Take heed to thyself that there be not a secret thing in thine heart, an iniquity, saying, The seventh year, the year of release, draws near; and thine eye shall be evil to thy brother that is in want, and thou shall not give to him, and he shall cry against thee to the Lord, and there shall be great sin in thee. 10 Thou shall surely give to him, and thou shall lend him as much as he wants, according as he is in need; and thou shall not grudge in thine heart as thou gives to him, because on this account the Lord thy God will bless thee in all thy works, and in all things on which thou shall lay thine hand. 11 For the poor shall not fall off thy land, therefore I charge thee to do this thing, saying, Thou shall surely open thine hands to thy poor brother, and to him that is distressed upon thy land.

12 If thy brother, a Hebrew man or a Hebrew woman, are sold to thee, he shall serve thee six years, and in the seventh year thou shall set him free from thee. 13 When thou shall set him free from thee, thou shall not send him out empty. 14 Thou shall give him provision for the way from thy flock, and from thy corn, and from thy wine; as the Lord thy God has blessed thee, thou shall give to him. 15 And thou shall remember that thou were a servant in the land of Egypt, and the Lord thy God redeemed thee from thence; therefore I charge thee to do this thing. 16 If he should say to thee, I will not go out from thee, because he continues to love thee and thy house, because he is well with thee, 17 then thou shall take an awl, and bore his ear through to the door, and he shall be thy slave forever; and in like manner shall thou do to thy female slave. 18 It shall not seem hard to thee when they are set free from thee, because *thy servant* has served thee six years according to the annual hire of a wage worker; so the Lord thy God shall bless thee in all things whatever thou may do.

19 Every firstborn that shall be born among thy kind and thy sheep, thou shall sanctify the males to the Lord thy God; thou shall not work with thy firstborn calf, and thou shall not shear the firstborn of thy sheep. 20 Thou shall eat it before the Lord year by year in the place that the Lord thy God shall choose, thou and thy house. 21 If there be on it a blemish, if it be lame or blind, an evil blemish, thou shall not sacrifice it to the Lord thy God. 22 Thou shall eat it in thy cities; the unclean in thee and the clean shall eat it in like manner, as the doe or the stag. 23 Only ye shall not eat the blood; thou shall pour it out on the earth as water.

Chapter 16

Observe the month of the new *corn*, and thou shall sacrifice the Passover to the Lord thy God; because in the month of new corn thou came out of Egypt by night. 2 And thou shall sacrifice the Passover to the Lord thy God, sheep and oxen in the place that the Lord thy God shall choose to have His name called upon it. 3 Thou shall not eat leaven with it; seven days shall thou eat unleavened *bread* with it, bread of affliction, because ye came forth out of Egypt in haste; that ye may remember the day of your coming forth out of the land of Egypt all the days of your life. 4 Leaven shall not be seen with thee in all thy borders for seven days, and there shall be no meat left that thou shall sacrifice at evening on the first day until the morning. 5 thou shall not have power to sacrifice the Passover in any of the cities, which the Lord thy God gives thee. 6 But in the place that the Lord thy God shall choose to have his name called there, thou shall sacrifice the Passover at evening at the setting of the sun, at the time when thou came out of Egypt. 7 And thou shall boil and roast and eat it in the place that the Lord thy God shall choose; and thou shall return in the morning, and go to thy houses. 8 Six days shall thou eat unleavened bread, and on the seventh day is a holiday, a feast to the Lord thy God; thou shall not do on it any work, save what shall be done by a soul.

9 Seven weeks shall thou number to thyself; when thou have begun *to put* the sickle to the corn, thou shall begin to number seven weeks. 10 And thou shall keep the feast of weeks to the Lord thy God; accordingly as thy hand has power in as many things as the Lord thy God shall give thee. 11 And thou shall rejoice before the Lord thy God, thou and thy son, and thy daughter, thy male slave and thy female slave, and the Levite, and the stranger, and the orphan, and the widow that lives among you, in whatever place the Lord thy God shall choose that His name should be called there. 12 And thou shall remember that thou were a slave in the land of Egypt, and thou shall observe and do these commands.

13 Thou shall keep for thyself the Feast of Tabernacles seven days, when thou gather in from thy corn floor and thy wine press. 14 And thou shall rejoice in thy feast, thou, and thy son, and thy daughter, thy male slave, and thy female slave, and the Levite, and the stranger, and the orphan, and the widow that is in thy cities. 15 Seven days shall thou keep a feast to the Lord thy God in the place that the Lord thy God shall choose for Himself; and if the Lord thy God shall bless thee in all thy fruits, and in every work of thy hands, then thou shall rejoice.

16 Three times in the year shall all thy males appear before the Lord thy God in the place that the Lord shall choose in the Feast of Unleavened Bread, and in the Feast of Weeks, and in the Feast of Tabernacles; thou shall not appear empty before the Lord thy God. 17 Each one according to your ability, according to the blessing of the Lord thy God which he has given thee.

18 Thou shall make for thyself judges and officers in thy cities, that the Lord thy God gives thee in *thy* tribes, and they shall judge the people with righteous judgment; 19 they shall not wrest judgment, nor *grant* favor *before certain* faces, nor receive a gift; for gifts blind the eyes of the wise, and pervert the words of the righteous. 20 Thou shall justly pursue justice, that ye may live, and go in and inherit the land which the Lord thy God gives thee.

21 Thou shall not plant for thyself a grove; thou shall not make for thyself any tree near the altar of thy God. 22 Thou shall not set up for thyself a pillar, which the Lord thy God hates.

Chapter 17

Thou shall not sacrifice to the Lord thy God a calf or a sheep, in which there is a blemish, *or* any evil thing; for it is an abomination to the Lord thy God.

2 If there should be found in any one of thy cities, which the Lord thy God gives thee, a man or a woman who shall do that which is evil before the Lord thy God, so as to transgress his covenant, 3 and they should go and serve other gods, and worship them, the sun, or the moon, or any of the host of heaven, that He commanded thee not to do, 4 and it be told thee, and thou shall have enquired diligently, and, behold, the thing actually took place, this abomination has been done in Israel; 5 then shall thou bring out that man, or that woman, and ye shall stone them with stones, and they shall die. 6 He shall die on the testimony of two or three witnesses; a man who dies shall not die for one witness. 7 And the hand of the witnesses shall be upon him among the first to put him to death, and the hand of the people at the last; so shall thou remove the evil one from among yourselves.

8 If a matter shall be too hard for thee in judgment, *as in the case of* between blood and blood, and between cause and cause, and between stroke and stroke, and between contradiction and contradiction, matters of judgment in your cities; then thou shall arise and go up to the place which the Lord thy God shall choose, 9 and thou shall come to the priests the Levites, and to the judge who shall be in those days, and they shall search out and report the judgment to thee. 10 And thou shall act according to the thing that they shall report to thee out of the place that the Lord thy God shall choose and thou shall observe to do all whatever shall have been by law appointed to thee.

Deuteronomy 18

11 Thou shall do according to the law and to the judgment that they shall declare to thee: thou shall not swerve to the right hand or to the left from any sentence, which they shall report to thee. 12 And the man whoever shall act in haughtiness, so as not to hearken to the priest who stands to minister in the name of the Lord thy God, or the judge who shall preside in those days, that man shall die, and thou shall remove the evil one out of Israel. 13 And all the people shall hear and fear, and shall no more commit impiety.

14 When thou shall enter into the land which the Lord thy God gives thee, and shall inherit it and live in it, and shall say, I will set a ruler over me, as also the other nations around me; 15 thou shall surely set over thee the ruler whom the Lord God shall choose; of thy brothers thou shall set over thee a ruler; thou shall not have power to set over thee a stranger, because he is not thy brother. 16 For he shall not multiply to himself horses, and he shall by no means turn the people back to Egypt, lest he should multiply to himself horses; for the Lord said, Ye shall not any more turn back by that way. 17 And he shall not multiply to himself wives, lest his heart change; and he shall not greatly multiply to himself silver and gold.

18 And when he shall be established in his government, then shall he write for himself this second law into a book by the hands of the priests the Levites; 19 and it shall be with him, and he shall read in it all the days of his life, that he may learn to fear the Lord thy God, and to keep all these commandments, and to observe these ordinances: 20 that his heart be not lifted up from his brothers, that he depart not from the commandments on the right *hand* or on the left *hand*; that he and his sons may reign long in his government among the sons of Israel.

Chapter 18

The priests, the Levites, even the whole tribe of Levi, shall have no part or inheritance with Israel; the burnt offerings of the Lord *are* their inheritance, they shall eat them. 2 And they shall have no inheritance among their brothers; the Lord himself *is* his portion, as he said to him.

3 And this *is* the due of the priests in the things coming from the people from those who offer sacrifices, whether it is a calf or a sheep; and thou shall give the shoulder to the priest, and the cheeks, and the great intestine: 4 and the first fruits of thy corn, and of thy wine, and of thine oil; and thou shall give to him the first fruits of the fleeces of thy sheep; 5 because the Lord has chosen him out of all thy tribes, to stand before the Lord thy God, to minister and bless in His name, himself and his sons among the sons of Israel.

6 If a Levite comes from one of the cities of all the sons of Israel, where he himself lives, accordingly as his mind desires, to the place, which He shall have chosen, 7 he shall minister to the name of the Lord his God, as all his brothers the Levites, who stand there present before the Lord thy God. 8 He shall eat an allotted portion, besides the sale of his hereditary property.

9 When thou shall have entered into the land that the Lord thy God gives thee, thou shall not learn to do according to the abominations of those nations. 10 There shall not be found in thee one who purges his son or his daughter with fire, one who divines, who deals with omens, and augury, 11 a sorcerer employing incantation, one who has in him a divining spirit, and observer of signs, questioning the dead. 12 For every one that does these things is an abomination to the Lord thy God; for because of these abominations the Lord will destroy them from before thy face. 13 Thou shall be perfect before the Lord thy God. 14 For all these nations whose *land* thou shall inherit, they will listen to omens and divinations; but the Lord thy God has not permitted thee so.

15 The Lord thy God shall raise up to thee a prophet from thy brothers, like Me; Him shall ye hear; 16 according to all things which thou did desire of the Lord thy God in Horeb in the day of the assembly, saying, We will not again hear the voice of the Lord thy God, and we will not any more see this great fire, and we shall not die. 17 And the Lord said to me, They have spoken correctly all that they have said to thee. 18 I will raise up to them a prophet from their brothers, like thee; and I will put My words in His mouth, and He shall speak to them, as I shall command Him. 19 And whatever man shall not hearken to whatever words that prophet shall speak in My name; I will take vengeance on him. 20 However, the prophet whoever shall impiously speak in My name a word, which I have not commanded him to speak, and whoever shall speak in the name of other gods, that prophet shall die. 21 If thou shall say in thine heart, How shall we know the word which the Lord has not spoken? 22 Whatever words that prophet shall speak in the name of the Lord, and they do not come true, and not come to pass, this *is* the thing which the Lord has not spoken; that prophet has spoken wickedly; ye shall not spare him.

Chapter 19

When the Lord thy God shall have destroyed the nations, which God gives thee, *even* the land, and ye shall inherit them, and live in their cities, and in their houses, 2 thou shall separate for thyself three cities in the midst of thy land that the Lord thy God gives thee. 3 Take a survey of thy way, and thou shall divide the coasts of thy land, which the Lord thy God apportions to thee, into three parts, and there shall be there a refuge for every man killer.

Deuteronomy 19

4 This shall be the ordinance of the man killer, who shall flee thither, and shall live, whoever shall have killed his neighbor ignorantly, whereas he hated him not before yesterday and three days *ago*. 5 And whoever shall enter with his neighbor into the thicket, to gather wood, if the hand of him that cuts wood with the axe should be violently shaken, and the axe head falling off from the handle should fall on his neighbor, and he should die, he shall flee to one of these cities, and live. 6 Lest the avenger of blood pursue after the murderer, because his heart is hot, and overtake him, if the way be too long, and he strike his life, though there is to this man no sentence of death, because he hated him not in time past. 7 Therefore I charge thee, saying, Thou shall separate for thyself three cities. 8 If the Lord shall enlarge thy borders, as He swore to thy fathers, and the Lord shall give to thee all the land that he said he would give to thy fathers; 9 If thou shall hearken to do all these commands, which I charge thee this day, to love the Lord thy God, to walk in all his ways continually; thou shall add for thyself yet three cities to these three. 10 So innocent blood shall not be spilt in the land that the Lord thy God gives thee to inherit, and there shall not be in thee one guilty of blood.

11 But if there should be in thee a man hating his neighbor, and he should lay wait for him, and arise against him, and strike his life, that he die, and he should flee to one of these cities, 12 then shall the elders of his city send, and take him thence, and they shall deliver him into the hands of the avengers of blood, and he shall die. 13 Thine eye shall not spare him; so shall thou clean innocent blood from Israel, and it shall be well with thee.

14 Thou shall not move the landmarks of thy neighbor, which thy fathers set in the inheritance, in which thou has obtained a share in the land that the Lord thy God gives thee to inherit.

15 One witness shall not remain to testify against a man for any iniquity, or for any fault, or for any sin that he may commit; by the mouth of two witnesses, or by the mouth of three witnesses, shall every thing be established. 16 If an unjust witness rises up against a man, alleging iniquity against him, 17 then shall the two men between whom the controversy is, stand before the Lord, and before the priests, and before the judges, who may be in those days. 18 And the judges shall make diligent inquiry, and, behold, *if* an unjust witness has borne unjust testimony; *and* has stood up against his brother; 19 then shall ye do to him as he wickedly devised to do against his brother, and thou shall remove the evil from yourselves.

20 And the rest shall hear and fear, and do no more according to this evil thing in the midst of you. 21 Thine eye shall not spare him; *thou shall exact* life for life, eye for eye, tooth for tooth, hand for hand, *and* foot for foot.

Chapter 20

And if thou should go forth to war against thine enemies, and should see horse, and rider, and a people more numerous than thyself; thou shall not be afraid of them, for the Lord thy God *is* with thee, who brought thee up out of the land of Egypt. 2 And it shall come to pass whenever thou shall come near to battle, that the priest shall come near and speak to the people, and shall say to them, 3 Hear, O Israel; ye are going this day to battle against your enemies; let not your heart faint, fear not, neither be confounded, neither turn aside from their face. 4 For *it is* the Lord your God who advances with you, to fight with you against your enemies, *and* to save you. 5 And the scribes shall speak to the people, saying, What man *is* he that has constructed a new house, and has not dedicated it? Let him go and return to his house, lest he dies in the war, and another man dedicates it. 6 And what man *is* he that has planted a vineyard, and not been made happy with it? Let him go and return to his house, lest he dies in the war, and another man be made happy with it. 7 And what man *is* he that has betrothed a wife, and has not taken her? Let him go and return to his house, lest he dies in the war, and another man takes her. 8 And the scribes shall speak further to the people, and say, What man *is* he that fears and is cowardly in his heart? Let him go and return to his house, lest he make the heart of his brother fail, as his own. 9 And it shall come to pass when the scribes shall have ceased speaking to the people, that they shall appoint generals of the army to be leaders of the people.

10 If thou shall come near to a city to overcome them by war, then call them out peaceably. 11 If then they should answer peaceably to thee, and open to thee, it shall be that all the people found in it shall be tributary and subject to thee. 12 But if they will not hearken to thee, but wage war against thee, thou shall invest it; 13 until the Lord thy God shall deliver it into thy hands, and thou shall strike every male of it with the slaughter of the sword, 14 except the women and the belongings, and all the cattle, and whatever shall be in the city, and all the plunder thou shall take as spoil for thyself, and shall eat all the plunder of thine enemies whom the Lord thy God gives thee. 15 Thus shall thou do to all the cities that are very far off from thee, not of the cities of these nations that the Lord thy God gives thee to inherit their land. 16 Behold, of the cities of these people, which the Lord thy God does give thee *for* an inheritance ye shall not suffer any thing to live that breaths; 17 However, ye shall surely curse them, the Hittite, and the Amorite, and the Canaanite, and the Pherezite, and the Evite, and the Jebusite, and the Gergesite; as the Lord thy God commanded thee; 18 that they may not teach you to do all their abominations, which they did to their gods, and *so* ye should sin before the Lord your God.

Deuteronomy 21

19 If thou should besiege one city many days to prevail against it by war to take it, thou shall not destroy its trees, by applying iron to them, but thou shall eat of it, and shall not cut it down; Is the tree that is in the field a man, to enter against thee into the trench of the siege? 20 However, the tree that thou knows to be not fruit bearing, this thou shall destroy and cut down; and thou shall construct a mound against the city, which makes war against thee, until it be delivered up.

Chapter 21

If one were found traumatized with the sword in the land that the Lord thy God gives thee to inherit, having fallen in the field, and they do not know who has killed *him*, 2 thine elders and thy judges shall come forth, and shall measure the distances of the cities round about the traumatized *man*: 3 and it shall be that the city which is nearest to the traumatized *man* the elders of that city shall take a heifer of the herd, which has not labored, and which has not drawn a yoke. 4 And the elders of that city shall bring down the heifer into a rough valley, which has not been tilled and is not sown, and they shall cut the sinews of the heifer in the valley. 5 And the priests the Levites shall come, because the Lord God has chosen them to stand by him, and to bless His name, and from their mouth shall every controversy and every stroke be *decided*. 6 And all the elders of that city who drew near to the killed man shall wash their hands over the head of the heifer, which was killed in the valley; 7 and they shall answer and say, Our hands have not shed this blood, and our eyes have not seen *it*. 8 Be merciful to thy people Israel, whom thou has redeemed, O Lord, that innocent blood may not be in thy people Israel; and the blood shall be atoned for to them. 9 Thou shall take away innocent blood from among you, if thou should do that which is good and pleasing before the Lord thy God.

10 If when thou goes out to war against thine enemies, the Lord thy God should deliver them into thine hands, and thou should take their spoil, 11 and should see among the spoil a woman beautiful in countenance, and should ponder upon her, and take her to thyself for a wife, 12 and should bring her within thine house; then shall thou shave her head, and pare her nails; 13 and shall take away her garments of captivity from off her, and she shall abide in thine house, and shall bewail her father and mother the days of a month; and afterwards thou shall go in to her and live with her, and she shall be thy wife. 14 And it shall be if thou do not delight in her, thou shall send her out free; and she shall not by any means be sold for money, thou shall not treat her contemptuously, because thou have humbled her.

15 And if a man has two wives, the one loved and one of them hated, and both the loved and the hated should have born him *children*, and the son of the hated should be first-born; 16 And it shall be that whenever he shall divide by inheritance his goods to his sons, he shall not be able to give the right of the firstborn to the son of the loved one, having overlooked the son of the hated, which is the firstborn. 17 But he shall acknowledge the firstborn of the hated one to give to him double of all things, which shall be found by him, because he is the first of his children, and to him belongs the birthright.

18 If any man has a disobedient and contentious son, who hearkens not to the voice of his father and the voice of his mother, and they should correct him, and he should not hearken to them; 19 then shall his father and his mother take hold of him, and bring him forth to the elders of his city, and to the gate of the place; 20 and they shall say to the men of their city, This our son is disobedient and contentious, he hearkens not to our voice, he is a reveler and a drunkard. 21 And the men of his city shall stone him with stones, and he shall die; and thou shall remove the evil one from yourselves, and the rest shall hear and fear.

22 If there be sin in any one, the judgment of death *shall be upon him*, and he *shall* be put to death, and ye *shall* hang him on a tree; 23 his body shall not remain all night upon the tree, but ye shall by all means bury it in that day; for every one that is hanged on a tree is cursed of God; and ye shall by no means defile the land, which the Lord thy God gives thee for an inheritance.

Chapter 22

When thou see the calf of thy brother or his sheep wandering in the way, thou shall not overlook them; thou shall by all means turn them back to thy brother, and thou shall restore them to him. 2 If thy brother does not come near thee, and thou dose not know him, thou shall bring it into thy house within; and it shall be with thee until thy brother shall seek them, and thou shall restore them to him. 3 Thus shall thou do to his donkey, and thus shall thou do to his garment, and thus shall thou do to every thing that thy brother has lost; whatever shall have been lost by him, and thou shall have found, thou shall not have power to overlook. 4 Thou shall not see the donkey of thy brother, or his calf, fallen in the way: thou shall not overlook them; thou shall surely help him to raise them up.

5 The clothing of a man shall not be on a woman, neither shall a man put on a dress of a woman; for every one that does these things is an abomination to the Lord thy God. 6 And if thou should come upon a brood of birds before thy face in the way or upon any tree, or upon the earth, young or eggs, and the mother is brooding on the young or the eggs, thou shall not take the dam with the young ones.

Deuteronomy 22

7 Thou shall by all means let the mother go, but thou shall take the young to thyself; that it may be well with thee, and that thou may live long.

8 If thou should build a new house, then shall thou make a parapet to thy house; so thou shall not bring blood guiltiness upon thy house, if one should in any wise fall from it.

9 Thou shall not sow thy vineyard with diverse seed, lest the fruit be devoted, and whatever seed thou may sow, with the fruit of thy vineyard.

10 Thou shall not plough with an ox and a donkey together.

11 Thou shall not wear an adulterated *garment*, woolen and linen together.

12 Thou shall make fringes on the four borders of thy garments, with which thou may be clothed.

13 If any one should take a wife, and live with her, and hate her, 14 and attach to her reproachful words, and bring against her an evil name, and say, I took this woman, and when I came to her I found not her tokens of virginity; 15 then the father and the mother of the damsel shall take and bring out the damsel's tokens of virginity to the elders of the city to the gate. 16 And the father of the damsel shall say to the elders, I gave this my daughter to this man for a wife; 17 and now he has hated her, and attaches reproachful words to her, saying, I have not found tokens of virginity with thy daughter; and these *are* the tokens of my daughter's virginity. And they shall unfold the garment before the elders of the city. 18 And the elders of that city shall take that man, and shall chastise him, 19 and shall fine him a hundred shekels, and shall give to the father of the damsel, because he has brought forth an evil name against a virgin of Israel; and she shall be his wife: he shall never be able to put her away. 20 However, if this report be true, and the tokens of virginity be not found for the damsel; 21 then shall they bring out the damsel to the doors of her father's house, and shall stone her with stones, and she shall die; because she has wrought folly among the sons of Israel, to defile the house of her father by whoring; so thou shall remove the evil one from among you.

22 If a man be found lying with a woman married to a man, ye shall kill them both, the man that lay with the woman, and the woman; so shall thou remove the wicked one out of Israel.

23 If there be a young damsel espoused to a man, and a man should have found her in the city and have lain with her; 24 ye shall bring them both out to the gate of their city, and they shall be stoned with stones, and they shall die; the damsel, because she cried not in the city; and the man, because he humbled his neighbor's spouse; so shall thou remove the evil one from among you.

25 However, if a man find in the field a damsel that is betrothed, and he should force her and lie with her, ye shall kill the man only that laid with her. 26 And the damsel has not *committed* a sin worthy of death; as if a man should arise against his neighbor, and slaughter his life, so *is* this thing;

27 because he found her in the field; the betrothed damsel cried, and there was none to help her.

28 If any one should find a young virgin who has not been betrothed, and should force *her* and lie with her, and be found, 29 the man who lay with her shall give to the father of the damsel fifty silver didrachms, and she shall be his wife, because he has humbled her; he shall never be able to put her away.

Chapter 23

A man shall not take his father's wife, and shall not uncover his father's skirt. 2 He that is fractured or mutilated in his private parts shall not enter into the assembly of the Lord. 3 *One born* of a harlot shall not enter into the assembly of the Lord. 4 The Ammanite and Moabite shall not enter into the assembly of the Lord, even until the tenth generation he shall not enter into the assembly of the Lord, forever: 5 because they met you not with bread and water by the way, when ye went out of Egypt; and because they hired against thee Balaam the son of Beor of Mesopotamia to curse thee. 6 But the Lord thy God would not hearken to Balaam; and the Lord thy God changed the curses into blessings, because the Lord thy God loved thee.

7 Thou shall not speak peaceably or profitably to them all thy days forever. 8 Thou shall not abhor an Edomite, because he is thy brother; thou shall not abhor an Egyptian, because thou were a stranger in his land.

9 If sons are born to them, in the third generation they shall enter into the assembly of the Lord. 10 If thou should go forth to engage with thine enemies, then thou shall keep thee from every wicked thing. 11 If there should be in thee a man who is not clean by reason of his issue by night, then he shall go forth out of the camp, and he shall not enter into the camp.

12 And it shall come to pass toward evening he shall wash his body with water, and when the sun has gone down, he shall go into the camp. 13 And thou shall have a place outside of the camp, and thou shall go out there, 14 and thou shall have a trowel on thy belt; and it shall come to pass when thou would relieve thyself abroad, that thou shall dig with it, and shall bring back the earth and cover thy nuisance.

15 Because the Lord thy God walks in thy camp to deliver thee, and to give up thine enemy before thy face; and thy camp shall be holy, and there shall not appear in thee a disgraceful thing, and *so* he shall turn away from thee. 16 Thou shall not deliver a slave to his master, who *coming* from his master attaches himself to thee. 17 He shall live with thee, he shall live among you where he shall please; thou shall not afflict him.

Deuteronomy 24

18 There shall not be a harlot of the daughters of Israel, and there shall not be a fornicator of the sons of Israel; there shall not be one who completes auguries of the daughters of Israel, and there shall not be an initiated person *into mystical pagan rites* of the sons of Israel. 19 Thou shall not bring the hire of a harlot, nor the price of a dog into the house of the Lord thy God, for any vow; because both are an abomination to the Lord thy God.

20 Thou shall not lend to thy brother on usury of silver, or usury of meat, or usury of any thing which thou may lend out. 21 Thou may lend on usury to a stranger, but to thy brother thou shall not lend on usury; that the Lord thy God may bless thee in all thy works upon the land, into which thou art entering to inherit it.

22 If thou will vow a vow to the Lord thy God, thou shall not delay to pay it; for the Lord thy God will surely require it of thee, *otherwise* it shall be sin in thee. 23 However, if thou should be unwilling to vow, it is not sin in thee. 24 Thou shall observe the words that proceed from between thy lips; and as thou have vowed a gift to the Lord God, *so* shall thou do that which thou have spoken with thy mouth.

25 If thou should go into the cornfield of thy neighbor, then thou may gather the ears with thy hands; but thou shall not put the sickle to thy neighbor's corn. 26 If thou should go into the vineyard of thy neighbor, thou shall eat grapes sufficient to satisfy thy desire; but thou may not put them into a vessel.

Chapter 24

If any one should take a wife, and should live with her, then it shall come to pass if she should not have found favor before him, because he has found some unbecoming thing in her, that he shall write for her a bill of divorce, and give it into her hands, and he shall send her away out of his house. 2 And *if* she should go away and be married to another man; 3 and the last man should hate her, and write for her a bill of divorce; and should give it into her hands, and send her away out of his house, and the last man should die, who took her to himself for a wife, 4 the former man who sent her away shall not be able to return and take her to himself for a wife, after she has been defiled; because it is an abomination before the Lord thy God, and ye shall not defile the land that the Lord thy God gives thee to inherit.

5 If any one should have recently taken a wife, he shall not go out to war, neither shall any thing be laid upon him; he shall be guiltless in his house; for one year he shall cheer his wife whom he has taken. 6 Thou shall not take for a pledge the under millstone, nor the upper millstone; for this man *that* does so takes a soul for a pledge.

7 If a man should be caught stealing the life of his brothers of the sons of Israel, and having overcome him he should sell him, that thief shall die; so shall thou remove that evil one from among you.

8 Take heed to thyself in *regard to* the plague of leprosy; thou shall take great heed to do according to all the law, which the priests the Levites shall report to you; take heed to do, as I have charged you. 9 Remember all that the Lord thy God did to Mariam in the way, when ye were going out of Egypt.

10 If thy neighbor owes thee a debt, any debt whatever, thou shall not go into his house to take his pledge; 11 thou shall stand without, and the man who is in thy debt shall bring the pledge out to thee. 12 If the man is poor, thou shall not sleep with his pledge. 13 Thou shall surely restore his pledge at sunset, and he shall sleep in his garment, and he shall bless thee; and it shall be mercy to thee before the Lord thy God.

14 Thou shall not unjustly withhold the wages of the poor and needy of thy brothers, or of the strangers who are in thy cities. 15 Thou shall pay him his wages the same day, the sun shall not go down upon it, because he is poor and he trusts in it; and he shall cry against thee to the Lord, and it shall be sin in thee.

16 The fathers shall not be put to death for the children, and the sons shall not be put to death for the fathers; every one shall die in his own sin.

17 Thou shall not rest the judgment of the stranger and the orphan, and widow; thou shall not take the widow's garment for a pledge. 18 And thou shall remember that thou were a bondman in the land of Egypt, and the Lord thy God redeemed thee from thence; therefore I charge thee to do this thing.

19 If thou shall have reaped corn in thy field, and shall have forgotten a sheaf in thy field, thou shall not return to take it; it shall be for the stranger, and the orphan, and the widow, that the Lord thy God may bless thee in all the works of thy hands. 20 If thou should gather thine olives, thou shall not return to collect the remainder; it shall be for the stranger, and the orphan, and the widow, and thou shall remember that thou were a bondman in the land of Egypt; therefore I command thee to do this thing. 21 And whenever thou shall gather the grapes of thy vineyard, thou shall not glean what thou have left; it shall be for the stranger, and the orphan, and the widow; 22 and thou shall remember that thou were a slave in the land of Egypt; therefore I command thee to do this thing.

Chapter 25

And if there should be a dispute between men, and they should come forward to judgment, and *the judges* judge, and justify the righteous, and condemn the wicked;

Deuteronomy 25

2 then it shall come to pass, if the unrighteous should be worthy of stripes, thou shall lay him down before the judges, and they shall scourge him before them according to his iniquity. 3 They shall scourge him with forty stripes in number, they shall not inflict more, for if thou should scourge him more stripes beyond these stripes, thy brother will be disgraced before thee.

4 Thou shall not muzzle the ox that treads out the corn.

5 If brothers should live together, and one of them should die, and should not have seed, the wife of the deceased shall not marry out to a man not related; her husband's brother shall go in to her, and shall take her to himself for a wife, and shall live with her. 6 And it shall come to pass that the child, whom she shall bear, shall be constituted by the name of the deceased, and his name shall not be blotted out of Israel. 7 If the man should not be willing to take his brother's wife, then shall the woman go up to the gate to the elders, and she shall say, My husband's brother will not raise up the name of his brother in Israel, my husband's brother has been unwilling. 8 And the elders of his city shall call him, and speak to him; and if he stand and say, I will not take her; 9 then his brother's wife shall come forward before the elders, and shall loose one shoe from off his foot, and shall spit in his face, and shall answer and say, Thus shall they do to the man who will not build his brother's house in Israel. 10 And his name shall be called in Israel, The house of him that has had his shoe loosed.

11 If men should strive together, a man with his brother, and the wife of one of them should advance to rescue her husband out of the hand of him that strikes him, and she should stretch forth her hand, and take hold of his private parts; 12 thou shall cut off her hand; thine eye shall not spare her.

13 Thou shall not have in thy bag divers weights, a great or a small. 14 Thou shall not have in thine house divers measures, a great or a small. 15 Thou shall have a true and just weight, and a true and just measure that thou may live long upon the land that the Lord thy God gives thee for an inheritance. 16 For every one that does this *is* an abomination to the Lord thy God, even every one that does injustice.

17 Remember what things Amalek did to thee by the way, when thou went forth out of the land of Egypt; 18 how he withstood thee in the way, and harassed thy rear, *even* those that were weary behind thee, and thou did hunger and were weary; and he did not fear God. 19 And it shall come to pass whenever the Lord thy God shall have given thee rest from all thine enemies round about thee, in the land which the Lord thy God gives thee to inherit, thou shall blot out the name of Amalek from under heaven, and shall not forget.

Chapter 26

And it shall be when thou shall have entered into the land, which the Lord thy God gives thee to inherit it, and thou shall have inherited it, and thou shall have lived upon it, 2 that thou shall take of the first of the fruits of thy land, which the Lord thy God gives thee, and thou shall put them into a basket, and thou shall go to the place that the Lord thy God shall choose to have his name called there. 3 And thou shall come to the priest who shall be in those days, and thou shall say to him, I testify this day to the Lord my God, that I am come into the land that the Lord swore to our fathers to give to us. 4 And the priest shall take the basket out of thine hands, and shall set it before the altar of the Lord thy God,

5 and he shall answer and say before the Lord thy God, My father abandoned Syria, and went down into Egypt, and traveled there with a small number, and became there a mighty nation and a great multitude. 6 And the Egyptians afflicted us, and humbled us, and imposed hard tasks on us: 7 and we cried to the Lord our God, and the Lord heard our voice, and saw our humiliation, and our labor, and our affliction. 8 And the Lord brought us out of Egypt himself with his great strength, and his mighty hand, and his high arm, and with great visions, and with signs, and with wonders. 9 And he brought us into this place, and gave us this land, a land flowing with milk and honey. 10 And now, behold, I have brought the first of the fruits of the land, which thou gave me, O Lord, a land flowing with milk and honey; and thou shall leave it before the Lord thy God, and thou shall worship before the Lord thy God; 11 and thou shall rejoice in all the good that the Lord thy God has given thee, and thy family, and the Levite, and the stranger that is within thee.

12 If thou shall have completed all the tithings of thy fruits in the third year, thou shall give the second tenth to the Levite, and stranger, and fatherless, and widow; and they shall eat it in thy cities, and be merry. 13 And thou shall say before the Lord thy God, I have fully collected the holy things out of my house, and I have given them to the Levite, and the stranger, and the orphan, and the widow, according to all commands which thou did command me; I did not transgress thy command, and I did not forget it. 14 And in my distress I did not eat them, I have not gathered them for an unclean person, I have not given them to the dead; I have hearkened to the voice of the Lord our God, I have done as thou has commanded me. 15 Look down from thy holy house, from heaven, and bless thy people Israel, and the land which thou have given them, as thou did swear to our fathers, to give to us a land flowing with milk and honey.

Deuteronomy 27

16 On this day the Lord thy God charged thee to keep all the ordinances and judgments; and ye shall observe and do them, with all your heart, and with all your soul. 17 Thou have chosen God this day to be thy God, and to walk in all his ways, and to observe his ordinances and judgments, and to hearken to his voice. 18 And the Lord has chosen thee this day that thou should be to him a peculiar people, as he said, to keep his commands; 19 and that thou should be above all nations, as he has made thee renowned, and a boast, and glorious, that thou should be a holy people to the Lord thy God, as he has spoken.

Chapter 27

And Moses and the elders of Israel commanded, saying, Safeguard all these commands, all that I command you this day. 2 And it shall come to pass in the day when ye shall cross Jordan into the land that the Lord thy God gives thee, that thou shall set up for thyself great stones, and shall plaster them with plaster. 3 And thou shall write on these stones all the words of this law, as soon as ye have passed Jordan, when ye are entered into the land, which the Lord God of thy fathers gives thee, a land flowing with milk and honey, according as the Lord God of thy fathers said to thee. 4 And it shall be as soon as ye pass over Jordan, ye shall set up these stones, which I command thee this day, on Mount Gaebal, and thou shall plaster them with plaster. 5 And thou shall build there an altar to the Lord thy God, an altar of stones; thou shall not lift up iron upon it. 6 Of whole stones shall thou build an altar to the Lord thy God, and thou shall offer upon it whole burnt offerings to the Lord thy God. 7 And thou shall there offer a peace offering; and thou shall eat and be filled, and rejoice before the Lord thy God. 8 And thou shall write upon the stones all this law very plainly.

9 And Moses and the priests the Levites spoke to all Israel, saying, Be silent and hear, O Israel; this day thou art become a people to the Lord thy God. 10 And thou shall hearken to the voice of the Lord thy God, and shall do all his commands, and his ordinances, as many as I command thee this day.

11 And Moses charged the people on that day, saying, 12 These shall stand to bless the people on mount Garizin having passed over Jordan; Simon, Levi, Judas, Issahar, Joseph, and Benjamin. 13 And these shall stand for cursing on mount Gaebal; Ruben, Gad, and Asher, Zabulon, Dan, and Nephthali. 14 And the Levites shall answer and say to all Israel with a great voice,

15 Cursed *is* the man whoever shall make a graven or molten image, an abomination to the Lord, the work of the hands of craftsmen, and shall put it in a secret place: and all the people shall answer and say, So be it.

16 Cursed is the man that dishonors his father or his mother: and all the people shall say, So be it.

17 Cursed is he that removes his neighbor's landmarks; and all the people shall say, So be it.

18 Cursed is he that makes the blind to wander in the way, and all the people shall say, So be it.

19 Cursed is every one that shall pervert the judgment of the stranger, and orphan, and widow: and all the people shall say, So be it.

20 Cursed is he that lies with his father's wife, because he has uncovered his father's skirt; and all the people shall say, So be it.

21 Cursed is he that lies with any beast: and all the people shall say, So be it.

22 Cursed is he that lies with his sister by his father or his mother: and all the people shall say, So be it.

23 Cursed is he that lies with his daughter-in-law: and all the people shall say, So be it. Cursed is he that lies with his wife's sister: and all the people shall say, So be it.

24 Cursed is he that kills his neighbor secretly; and all the people shall say, So be it.

25 Cursed is he whoever shall have taken a bribe to strike the life of innocent blood, and all the people shall say, So be it.

26 Cursed is every man that continues not in all the words of this law to do them: and all the people shall say, So be it.

Chapter 28

And it shall come to pass, if thou will indeed hear the voice of the Lord thy God, to observe and do all these commands, which I charge thee this day, that the Lord thy God shall set thee on high above all the nations of the earth; 2 and all these blessings shall come upon thee, and shall find thee. If thou will indeed hear the voice of the Lord thy God,

3 blessed *shall* thou *be* in the city, and blessed shall thou be in the field. 4 Blessed shall be the offspring of thy belly, and the fruits of thy land, and the herds of thy oxen, and the flocks of thy sheep. 5 Blessed shall be thy barns, and thy stores. 6 Blessed shall thou be in thy coming in, and blessed shall thou be in thy going out.

7 The Lord delivers thine enemies that withstand thee utterly broken before thy face; they shall come out against thee one way, and they shall flee seven ways from before thee.

Deuteronomy 28

8 The Lord send upon thee His blessing in thy barns, and on all on which thou shall put thine hand, in the land that the Lord thy God gives thee.
9 The Lord raise thee up for himself a holy people, as He swore to thy fathers; if thou will hear the voice of the Lord thy God, and walk in all his ways. 10 And all the nations of the earth shall see thee that the name of the Lord is called upon thee, and they shall stand in fear of thee. 11 And the Lord thy God shall multiply thee for good in the offspring of thy belly, and in the offspring of thy cattle, and in the fruits of thy land, on thy land, which the Lord swore to thy fathers to give to thee. 12 May the Lord open to thee his good treasure, the heaven, to give rain to thy land in season; may he bless all the works of thy hands; so shall thou lend to many nations, but thou shall not borrow; and thou shall rule over many nations, but they shall not rule over thee. 13 The Lord thy God make thee the head, and not the tail; and thou shall then be above and thou shall not be below, if thou will hearken to the voice of the Lord thy God, in all things that I charge thee this day to observe. 14 Thou shall not turn aside from any of the commandments, which I charge thee this day, to the right or to the left, to go after other gods to serve them.
15 But it shall come to pass, if thou will not hearken to the voice of the Lord thy God, to observe all His commandments, as many as I charge thee this day, then all these curses shall come on thee, and overtake thee.
16 Cursed *shall* thou *be* in the city, and cursed shall thou be in the field. 17 Cursed shall be thy barns and thy stores. 18 Cursed shall be the offspring of thy body, and the fruits of thy land, the herds of thine oxen, and the flocks of thy sheep. 19 Cursed shall thou be in thy coming in, and cursed shall thou be in thy going out.
20 The Lord send upon thee want, and famine, and consumption of all things on which thou shall put thy hand, until He shall have utterly destroyed thee, and until He shall have consumed thee quickly because of thine evil devices, because thou has forsaken me. 21 May the Lord causes the pestilence to cleave to thee, until He shall have consumed thee off the land into which thou go to inherit it. 22 The Lord strikes thee with distress, and fever, and cold, and inflammation, and blighting, and paleness, and they shall pursue thee until they have destroyed thee. 23 And thou shall have over thine head a sky of brass, and the earth under thee shall be iron. 24 The Lord thy God make the rain of thy land dust; and dust shall come down from heaven, until it shall have destroyed thee, and until it shall have quickly consumed thee.
25 The Lord give thee up for slaughter before thine enemies; thou shall go out against them one way, and flee from their face seven ways; and thou shall be a dispersion in all the kingdoms of the earth. 26 And your dead men shall be food to the birds of the sky and to the beasts of the earth; and there shall be none to scare them away.

27 The Lord strikes thee with the botch of Egypt in the seat, and with a malignant scab, and itch, so that thou cannot be healed. 28 The Lord strikes thee with insanity, and blindness, and astonishment of mind. 29 And thou shall grope at midday, as a blind man would grope in the darkness, and thou shall not prosper in thy ways; and then thou shall be unjustly treated and plundered continually, and there shall be no helper.

30 Thou shall take a wife, and another man shall have her; thou shall build a house, and thou shall not live in it; thou shall plant a vineyard, and shall not gather the grapes of it. 31 Thy calf *shall be* killed before thee, and thou shall not eat of it; thine donkey shall be violently taken away from thee, and shall not be restored to thee; thy sheep shall be given to thine enemies, and thou shall have no helper. 32 Thy sons and thy daughters shall be given to another nation, and thine eyes wasting away shall look for them; thine hand shall have no strength. 33 The produce of thy land and all thy labors shall be eaten by a nation, which thou shall not know; and thou shall be injured and crushed always. 34 And thou shall be distracted, because of the sights of thine eyes that thou shall see. 35 The Lord strike thee with an evil sore, on the knees and the legs, so that thou shall not be able to be healed from the sole of thy foot to the crown of thy head.

36 The Lord carry thee away and thy rulers, whom thou shall set over thee, to a nation which neither thou nor thy fathers know; and thou shall there serve other gods, *of* wood and stone. 37 An thou shall be there for a wonder, and a parable, and a tale, among all the nations, to which the Lord thy God shall carry thee away.

38 Thou shall carry forth much seed into the field, and thou shall bring in little, because the locust shall devour it. 39 Thou shall plant a vineyard, and dress it, and shall not drink the wine; neither shall thou delight thyself with it, because the worm shall devour them. 40 Thou shall have olive trees in all thy borders, and thou shall not anoint thee with oil, because thine olive shall *be* utterly shed *away*. 41 Thou shall beget sons and daughters, and they shall not be *thine*, for they shall depart into captivity. 42 All thy trees and the fruits of thy land shall the blight consume. 43 The stranger that is among thee shall get up very high, and thou shall come down very low. 44 He shall lend to thee, and thou shall not lend to him; he shall be the head, and thou shall be the tail. 45 And all these curses shall come upon thee, and shall pursue thee, and shall overtake thee, until he shall have consumed thee, and until he shall have destroyed thee, because thou did not hearken to the voice of the Lord thy God, to safeguard His commands, and His ordinances that He has commanded thee. 46 And *these things* shall be signs in thee, and wonders among thy seed forever.

47 And thou did not serve the Lord thy God with gladness and a good heart because of the abundance of all things.

Deuteronomy 28

48 And thou shall serve thine enemies, which the Lord will send forth against thee, in hunger, and in thirst, and in nakedness, and in the want of all things; and thou shall wear upon thy neck a yoke of iron until he shall have destroyed thee. 49 The Lord shall bring upon thee a nation from the ends of the earth, like the swift flying of an eagle, a nation whose voice thou shall not hear, 50 a nation bold in countenance that shall not wonder at the elder and shall not pity the young. 51 And it shall eat up the young of thy cattle, and the fruits of thy land, so as not to leave thee corn, wine, oil, the herds of thine oxen, and the flocks of thy sheep, until it shall have destroyed thee; 52 and have thee utterly crushed in thy cities, until the high and strong walls be destroyed, in which thou trust, in all thy land; and it shall afflict thee in thy cities, which He has given to thee. 53 And thou shall eat the fruit of thy belly, the flesh of thy sons and of thy daughters, all that he has given thee, in thy straightness and thy affliction, with which thine enemy shall afflict thee. 54 He that is tender and very delicate within thee shall look with an evil eye upon his brother, and the wife in his bosom, and the children that are left, which may have been left to him; 55 so as *not* to give to one of them of the flesh of his young, whom he shall eat, because of his having nothing left him in thy straightness, and in thy affliction, with which thine enemies shall afflict thee in all thy cities. 56 And she that is tender and delicate among you, whose foot has not assayed to go upon the earth for delicacy and tenderness, shall look with an evil eye on her husband in her bosom, and her son and her daughter, 57 and her offspring that come out between her feet, and the child which she shall bear; for she shall eat them because of the want of all things, secretly in thy straightness, and in thy affliction, with which thine enemy shall afflict thee in thy cities.

58 If thou will not hearken to do all the words of this law that have been written in this book, to fear this glorious and wonderful name, the Lord thy God, 59 then the Lord shall magnify thy plagues, and the plagues of thy seed, great and wonderful plagues, and evil and abiding diseases. 60 And he shall bring upon thee all the evil pain of Egypt, which thou did fear before their face, and they shall cleave to thee. 61 And the Lord shall bring upon thee every sickness, and every plague that is not written, and every one that is written in the book of this law, until he shall have destroyed thee. 62 And ye shall be left few in number, whereas ye were as the stars of the sky in multitude, because thou did not hearken to the voice of the Lord thy God.

63 And it shall come to pass that as the Lord rejoiced over you to do you good and to multiply you, so the Lord will rejoice over you to destroy you; and ye shall be quickly removed from the land, into which ye go to inherit it. 64 And the Lord thy God shall scatter thee among all nations, from one end of the earth to the other; and thou shall there serve other gods, *of* wood and stone, which thou have not known, nor thy fathers.

65 However, among those nations he will not give thee quiet, neither by any means shall the sole of thy foot have rest; and the Lord shall give thee there another and a misgiving heart, and failing eyes, and a diminishing soul. 66 And thy life shall be in suspense before thine eyes; and thou shall be afraid by day and by night, and thou shall have no assurance of thy life. 67 In the morning thou shall say, Would it were evening; and in the evening thou shall say, Would it were morning; for the fear of thine heart with which thou shall fear, and for the sights of thine eyes which thou shall see. 68 And the Lord shall bring thee back to Egypt in ships, by the way of which I said, Thou shall not see it again; and ye shall be sold there to your enemies as male slaves and female slaves, and none shall buy you. 69 These *are* the words of the covenant, which the Lord commanded Moses to make with the sons of Israel in the land of Moab, besides the covenant that He made with them in Horeb.

Chapter 29

And Moses called all the sons of Israel and said to them, Ye have seen all things that the Lord did in the land of Egypt before you to Pharaoh and his slaves, and all his land,
2 the great temptations which thine eyes have seen, the signs, and those great wonders. 3 Yet the Lord God has not given you a heart to know, and eyes to see, and ears to hear, until this day. 4 And He led you forty years in the wilderness; your garments did not grow old, and your sandals were not worn away off your feet. 5 Ye did not eat bread, ye did not drink wine or strong drink, that ye might know that I *am* the Lord your God. 6 And ye came as far as this place; and there came forth Seon king of Esebon, and Og king of Basan, to meet us in war, and we deposed them 7 and took their land, and I gave it for an inheritance to Ruben and Gad, and to the half-tribe of Manasse. 8 And ye shall take heed to do all the words of this covenant that ye may understand all things that ye shall do. 9 Ye all stand this day before the Lord your God, your tribal rulers, and your elders, and your judges, and your officers, every man of Israel,
10 your wives, and your children, and the stranger who is in the midst of your camp, from your hewer of wood even to your drawer of water, 11 that thou should enter into the covenant of the Lord thy God and into his oaths, as many as the Lord thy God appoints thee this day, 12 that He may appoint thee to Himself for a people, and He shall be thy God, as He said to thee, and as He swore to thy fathers, Abraham, and Isaac, and Jacob. 13 And I do not appoint to you alone this covenant and this oath,
14 but to those also who are here with you this day before the Lord your God, and to those who are not here with you this day.

Deuteronomy 30

15 For ye know how we lived in the land of Egypt, how we came through the midst of the nations through whom ye came. 16 And ye beheld their abominations, and their idols, wood and stone, silver and gold, which are among them. 17 Lest there be among you man, or woman, or family, or tribe, whose heart has turned aside from the Lord your God, having gone to serve the gods of these nations; lest there be in you a root springing up with gall and bitterness. 18 And it shall be if one shall hear the words of this curse, and shall flatter himself in his heart, saying, May holy things happen to me, for I will walk in the error of my heart, lest the sinner destroy the innocent. 19 God shall by no means be willing to pardon him, but then the wrath of the Lord and his jealousy shall flame out against that man; and all the curses of this covenant shall attach themselves to him, which are written in this book, and the Lord shall blot out his name from under heaven.

20 And the Lord shall separate that man for evil of all the sons of Israel, according to all the curses of the covenant that are written in the book of this law. 21 And another generation shall say even your sons who shall arise after you, and the stranger who shall come from a land afar off, and shall see the plagues of that land and their diseases, which the Lord has sent upon it, 22 brimstone and burning salt, the whole land shall not be sown, neither shall any green thing spring, nor arise upon it, as Sodom and Gomorrah were overthrown, Adama and Seboim, which the Lord overthrew in his wrath and anger, 23 and all the nations shall say, Why has the Lord done thus to this land? What *is* this great fierceness of anger? 24 And shall say, Because they forsook the covenant of the Lord God of their fathers, the things which He appointed to their fathers, when He brought them out of the land of Egypt, 25 and they went and served other gods, which they knew not, neither did He assign to them. 26 And the Lord was exceedingly angry at that land to bring upon it according to all the curses, which are written, in the book of this law, 27 and the Lord removed them from their land in anger, and wrath, and very great indignation, and cast them out into another land as at present. 28 The secret things *belong* to the Lord our God, but the things that are revealed *belong* to us and to our children forever, to do all the words of this law.

Chapter 30

And it shall come to pass when all these things shall have come upon thee, the blessing and the curse, which I have set before thy face, and thou shall receive them into thine heart among all the nations, wherein the Lord shall have scattered thee, 2 and shall return to the Lord thy God, and shall hearken to his voice, according to all things which I charge thee this day, with all thy heart, and with all thy soul,

Deuteronomy 30

3 then the Lord shall heal thine iniquities, and shall pity thee, and shall again gather thee out from all the nations, among which the Lord has scattered thee. 4 If thy dispersion were from one end of heaven to the other, thence will the Lord thy God gather thee, and thence will the Lord thy God take thee. 5 And the Lord thy God shall bring thee in from thence into the land, which thy fathers have inherited, and thou shall inherit it; and he will do thee good, and multiply thee above thy fathers. 6 And the Lord shall purge thy heart, and the heart of thy seed, to love the Lord thy God with all thy heart, and with all thy soul, that thou may live. 7 And the Lord thy God will put these curses upon thine enemies, and upon those that hate thee, who have persecuted thee. 8 And thou shall return and hearken to the voice of the Lord thy God, and shall keep his commands, all that I charge thee this day. 9 And the Lord thy God shall bless thee in every work of thine hands, in the offspring of thy belly, and in the offspring of thy cattle, and in the fruits of thy land, because the Lord thy God will again rejoice over thee for good, as he rejoiced over thy fathers, 10 if thou will hearken to the voice of the Lord thy God, to keep His commandments, and His ordinances, and His judgments written in the book of this law, if thou turn to the Lord thy God with all thine heart, and with all thy soul.

11 For this command, which I give thee this day, is not grievous, neither is it far from thee. 12 It is not in heaven above, saying, Who shall go up for us into heaven, and shall take it for us, and we will hear and do it? 13 Neither is it beyond the sea, saying, Who will go over for us to the other side of the sea, and take it for us, and make it audible to us, and we will do it? 14 The word is very near thee, in thy mouth, and in thine heart, and in thine hands to do it.

15 Behold, I have set before thee this day life and death, good and evil. 16 If thou will hearken to the commands of the Lord thy God, which I command thee this day, to love the Lord thy God, to walk in all his ways, and to keep his ordinances, and his judgments; then ye shall live, and shall be many in number, and the Lord thy God shall bless thee in all the land into which thou goes to inherit it. 17 And if thy heart change, and thou will not hearken, and thou shall go astray and worship other gods, and serve them, 18 I declare to you this day, that ye shall utterly perish, and ye shall by no means live long upon the land, into which ye *shall* cross Jordan to inherit it.

19 I call both heaven and earth to witness this day against you, I have set before you life and death, the blessing and the curse; choose thou life, that thou and thy seed may live, 20 to love the Lord thy God, to hearken to his voice, and cleave to him; for this *is* thy life, and the length of thy days, that thou should live upon the land, which the Lord swore to thy fathers, Abraham, and Isaac, and Jacob, to give to them.

Chapter 31

And Moses finished speaking all these words to all the sons of Israel, 2 and said to them, I am this day a hundred and twenty years; I shall not be able any longer to come in or go out; and the Lord said to me, Thou shall not cross the Jordan. 3 The Lord thy God who goes before thee, he shall destroy these nations before thee, and thou shall inherit them; and Joshua *shall* go before thy face, as the Lord has spoken. 4 And the Lord thy God shall do to them as he did to Seon and Og the two kings of the Amorites, who were beyond Jordan, and to their land, as he destroyed them. 5 And the Lord has delivered them to you; and ye shall do to them, as I charged you. 6 Be courageous and strong, fear not, neither be cowardly neither be afraid before them; for the Lord your God advances with you in the midst of you, neither will he by any means forsake thee, nor desert thee.

7 And Moses called Jesus, and said to him before all Israel, Be courageous and strong; for thou shall go in before this people into the land which the Lord swore to your fathers to give to them, and thou shall give it to them for an inheritance. 8 And the Lord that goes with thee shall not forsake thee nor abandon thee; fear not, nor be afraid.

9 And Moses wrote the words of this law in a book, and gave it to the priests the sons of Levi who bear the Ark of the Covenant of the Lord, and to the elders of the sons of Israel. 10 And Moses charged them in that day, saying, After seven years, in the time of the year of release, in the Feast of Tabernacles, 11 when all Israel comes together to appear before the Lord your God, in the place which the Lord shall choose, ye shall read this law before all Israel in their ears, 12 assembling the people, the men, and the women, and the children, and the stranger that is in your cities, that they may hear, and that they may learn to fear the Lord your God; and they shall hearken to do all the words of this law. 13 And their sons who have not known shall hear, and shall learn to fear the Lord thy God all the days that they live upon the land, into which ye cross Jordan to inherit it.

14 And the Lord said to Moses, Behold, the days of thy death are at hand; call Jesus, and stand ye by the doors of the Tabernacle of Testimony, and I will give him a charge. And Moses and Jesus went to the Tabernacle of Testimony, and stood by the doors of the Tabernacle of Testimony. 15 And the Lord descended in a cloud, and stood by the doors of the Tabernacle of Testimony; and the pillar of the cloud stood by the doors of the Tabernacle of Testimony.

16 And the Lord said to Moses, Behold, thou shall sleep with thy fathers, and this people will arise and go a whoring after the foreign gods of the land, into which they are entering, and they will forsake me, and break my covenant, which I made with them. 17 And I will be very angry with them in that day, and I will leave them and turn my face away from them, and they shall be devoured; and many evils and afflictions shall come upon them; and they shall say in that day, Because the Lord my God is not with me, these evils have come upon me. 18 And I will surely turn away my face from them in that day, because of all their evil doings that they have done, because they turned aside after foreign gods. 19 And now write the words of this song, and teach it to the sons of Israel, and ye shall put it into their mouth, that this song may witness for me among the sons of Israel to their face. 20 For I will bring them into the good land, which I swore to their fathers, to give to them a land flowing with milk and honey; and they shall eat and be filled and be satisfied; then will they turn aside after foreign gods, and serve them, and they will provoke me, and break my covenant. 21 And this song shall stand as a witness against them; for they shall not forget it out of their mouth, or out of the mouth of their seed; for I know their wickedness, what they are doing here this day, before I have brought them into the good land, which I swore to their fathers. 22 And Moses wrote this song on that day, and taught it to the sons of Israel. 23 And he charged Jesus, and said, Be courageous and strong, for thou shall bring the sons of Israel into the land that the Lord swore to them, and He shall be with thee.

24 And when Moses finished writing all the words of this law in a book to the *very* end, 25 then he charged the Levites who bear the Ark of the Covenant of the Lord, saying, 26 Take the book of this law, and ye shall put it inside of the Ark of the Covenant of the Lord your God; and it shall be there within thee for a testimony. 27 For I know thy provocation, and thy stiff neck, for yet during my life with you at this day, ye have been provoking in your conduct toward God, how shall ye not also be so after my death? 28 Gather together to me the rulers of your tribes, and your elders, and your judges, and your officers, that I may speak in their ears all these words; and I call both heaven and earth to witness against them. 29 For I know that after my death ye will utterly transgress, and turn aside out of the way that I have commanded you; and evils shall come upon you at the end of the days, because ye will do evil before the Lord, to provoke Him to anger by the works of your hands.

30 And Moses spoke all the words of this song to the *very* end, in the ears of the whole assembly.

Chapter 32

Attend, O heaven, and I will speak; and let the earth hear the words out of my mouth. 2 Let my speech be looked for as the rain, and my words come down as dew, as the shower upon the herbage, and as snow upon the grass. 3 For I have called on the name of the Lord, assign ye greatness to our God.

4 God's works are true, and all his ways *are* judgments; God *is* faithful, and there is no unrighteousness *in him,* just and holy *is* the Lord. 5 They have sinned, not *pleasing* him; spotted children, a forward and perverse generation.

6 Do ye thus recompense the Lord? *Are the* people thus foolish and unwise? Did not he himself thy father purchase thee, and make thee, and form thee? 7 Remember the days of old, consider the years in *the* ages of ages; ask thy father, and he shall relate to thee, thine elders, and they shall tell thee. 8 When the Most High divided the nations, when He separated the sons of Adam, He set the bounds of the nations according to the number of the angels of God. 9 And his people Jacob became the portion of the Lord; Israel was the line of his inheritance.

10 He maintained him in the wilderness, in burning thirst and a dry land; He led him about and instructed him, and kept him as the apple of His eye. 11 As an eagle would watch over his brood, and yearns over his young, receive them having spread his wings, and takes them up on his back. 12 The Lord alone led them; there was no foreign god with them. 13 He brought them up on the strength of the land; he fed them with the fruits of the fields; they sucked honey out of the rock, and oil out of the solid rock. 14 Butter of cows, and milk of sheep, with the fat of lambs and rams, of calves and kids, with fat of kidneys of wheat; and he drank wine, the blood of the grape.

15 So Jacob ate and was filled, and the beloved one kicked; he grew fat, he became thick and broad; then he forsook the God that made him, and departed from God his Savior. 16 They provoked Me to anger with foreign gods; with their abominations they bitterly angered Me. 17 They sacrificed to demons, and not to God; to gods whom they knew not; new and fresh came in, whom their fathers knew not. 18 Thou has forsaken God that begot thee, and forgotten God who feeds thee.

19 And the Lord saw, and was jealous; and was provoked by the anger of His sons and daughters, 20 and said, I will turn away My face from them, and will show what shall happen to them in the last days; for it is a perverse generation, sons in whom *there* is no faith. 21 They have provoked Me to jealousy with *that which is* not God, they have exasperated Me with their idols; and I will provoke them to jealousy with them that are no nation, I will anger them with a nation void of understanding.

22 For a fire has been kindled by My wrath, it shall burn to Hades below; it shall devour the land, and the fruits of it; it shall set on fire the foundations of the mountains.

23 I will gather evils upon them, and will cause My weapons to war together against them. 24 *They shall be* consumed with hunger and the devouring of birds, and there shall be *an* irremediable falling away; I will send forth against them the teeth of wild beasts, with the rage of *serpents* creeping on the ground. 25 Without, the sword shall bereave them of children, and terror out of the secret chambers; the young man shall perish with the virgin, the suckling with him who has grown old. 26 I said, I will scatter them, and I will cause their memorial to cease from among men. 27 Were it not for the wrath of the enemy, lest they should live long, lest their enemies should combine against them; lest they should say, Our own high arm, and not the Lord, has done all these things.

28 It is a nation that has lost counsel; neither is there in them understanding. 29 They had not sense to understand; let them reserve these things against the time to come. 30 How shall one pursue a thousand and two rout tens of thousands, if God had not sold them, and the Lord delivered them up? 31 For their gods are not as our God, but our enemies *are* void of understanding. 32 For their vine *is* of the vine of Sodom, and their branch of Gomorrah, their grape *is* a grape of gall; their cluster *is* one of bitterness. 33 Their wine *is* the rage of serpents, and the incurable rage of asps.

34 Behold, are not these things stored up by me, and sealed among my treasures? 35 In the day of vengeance I will recompense, whenever their foot shall be tripped up; for the day of their destruction *is* near to them, and the judgments at hand are close upon you.

36 For the Lord shall judge his people, and shall be comforted over his servants; for he saw that they were paralyzed, and failed in the hostile invasion, and were become feeble. 37 And the Lord said, Where are their gods on whom they trusted? 38 The fat of whose sacrifices ye ate, and ye drank the wine of their drink offerings? Let them arise and help you, and be your protectors.

39 Behold, behold that I am, and there is no god beside me; I kill, and I will make to live; I will strike, and I will heal; and there is none who shall deliver out of my hands. 40 For I will lift up my hand to heaven, and swear by my right hand, and I will say, I live forever. 41 For I will sharpen like lightning my sword, and shall take hold of judgment with my hand; and I will render judgment to my enemies, and will recompense them that hate me. 42 I will make my weapons drunk with blood, and my sword shall devour flesh with the blood of the wounded, and from the captivity of the * heads of *their* enemies that rule over them.

Deuteronomy 33

* 43 Rejoice, ye heavens, with Him, and let all the angels of God worship Him; rejoice ye Gentiles, with His people, and let all the sons of God strengthen themselves in Him; for He will avenge the blood of His sons, and He will render vengeance, and recompense justice to His enemies, and will recompense them that hate Him; and the Lord shall purge the land of His people.

44 And Moses wrote this song in that day, and taught it to the sons of Israel; and Moses went in and spoke all the words of this law in the ears of the people, he and Jesus the *son* of Naue. 45 And Moses finished speaking to all Israel. 46 And he said to them, Take heed with your heart to all these words, which I testify to you this day, which ye shall command your sons, to observe and do all the words of this law. 47 For this *is* no vain word to you; for it *is* your life, and because of this word ye shall live long upon the land, into which ye cross Jordan to inherit it.

48 And the Lord spoke to Moses in this day, saying, 49 Go up to the mount Abarim, this mountain Nabau that is in the land of Moab over against Jericho, and behold the land of Canaan, which I give to the sons of Israel, as a possession, 50 and die on the mount whither thou goes up, and be added to thy people; as Aaron thy brother died on mount Or, and was added to his people. 51 Because ye disobeyed my word among the sons of Israel, at the waters of strife of Kades in the wilderness of Sin; because ye sanctified me not among the sons of Israel. 52 Thou shall see the land before *thee*, but thou shall not enter into it.

* *Codex Alexandrius* reads: "Gentiles".

* The Zoe Brotherhood text lists an alternative reading for verse forty-three, without citation as to where the alternative reading is found, and reads as follows:

"Rejoice, ye heavens, with Him, and let all the sons of God *commence in* worship; rejoice ye Gentiles, with his people, and let all the angels of God strengthen themselves; for He will avenge the blood of His sons, and He will render vengeance, and recompense justice to His enemies, and will recompense them that hate Him; and the Lord shall purge the land of His people."

Chapter 33

And this *is* the blessing with which Moses the man of God blessed the sons of Israel before his death. 2 And he said, The Lord is come from Sinai, and has appeared from Seir to us, and has rushed out of the mount of Pharan, with the ten thousands of Kades; on his right hand his angels with him. 3 And he spared his people, and all his sanctified ones *are* under thy hands; and they are under thee; and he received of his words 4 the law that Moses charged us, an inheritance to the assemblies of Jacob.

5 And he shall be *a* ruler with the beloved one, when the rulers of the people are gathered together with the tribes of Israel.

6 Let Ruben live, and not die; and let him be many in number.

7 And of Judah; Hear, Lord, the voice of Judah, and do thou visit his people; his hands shall contend for him, and thou shall be a help from his enemies.

8 And to Levi he said, Give to Levi his manifestations, and his truth to the holy man, whom they tempted in the temptation; they reviled him at the water of strife. 9 Who says to his father and mother, I have not seen thee; and he knew not his brothers, and he refused to know his sons; he kept thine oracles, and observed thy covenant. 10 They shall declare thine ordinances to Jacob, and thy law to Israel; they shall place incense in *the time of* thy wrath continually upon thine altar. 11 Bless, Lord, his strength, and accept the works of his hands; break the loins of his enemies that have risen up against him, and let them not that hate him rise up.

12 And to Benjamin he said, The beloved of the Lord shall live in confidence, and God overshadows him always, and he rested between his shoulders.

13 And to Joseph he said, His land *is* of the blessing of the Lord, of the seasons of sky and dew, and of the deeps of wells below, 14 and of the fruits of the changes of the sun in season, and of the produce of the months, 15 from the top of the ancient mountains, and from the top of the everlasting hills, 16 and of the fullness of the land in season, and let the things pleasing to him that live in the bush come on the head of Joseph, and on the crown glorified above his brothers. 17 His beauty *is as* the firstling of his bull, his horns *are* the horns of the only horned *animal*; with them he shall thrust the nations at once, even from the end of the earth; these *are* the ten thousands of Ephraim, and these *are* the thousands of Manasse.

18 And to Zabulon he said, Rejoice, Zabulon, in thy going out, and Issahar in his tents. 19 They shall utterly destroy the nations, and ye shall call *men* there, and there offer the sacrifice of righteousness; for the wealth of the sea shall suckle thee, and so shall the marts of them that live by the sea coast.

20 And to Gad he said, Blessed *be* he that enlarges Gad; as a lion he rested, having broken the arm and the ruler. 21 And he saw his first fruits, that there the land of the rulers gathered with the rulers of the people was divided; the Lord wrought righteousness, and His judgment with Israel.

22 And to Dan he said, Dan *is* a lion's whelp, and shall leap out of Basan.

23 And to Nephthali he said, Nephthali *has* the fullness of good things; and let him be filled with blessing from the Lord; he shall inherit the Sea and the south. 24 And to Asher he said, Asher *is* blessed with children; and he shall be acceptable to his brothers; he shall dip his foot in oil.

25 His sandal shall be iron and brass; as thy days, so *shall be* thy strength.

26 There are none as the God of the beloved; He who rides upon the heaven *is* thy helper, and the Great One of the firmament. 27 And the rule of God shall protect thee, and under the strength of the everlasting arms; and he shall cast forth the enemy from before thy face, saying, Perish. 28 And Israel shall alone possess in confidence the land of Jacob, with corn and wine; and the sky *shall be* misty with dew upon thee.

29 Blessed *art* thou, O Israel; who *is* like unto thee, O people saved by the Lord? Thy helper shall hold his shield over thee, and *his* sword *is* thy boast; and thine enemies shall speak falsely to thee, and thou shall tread upon their neck.

Chapter 34

And Moses went up from Araboth Moab to the mount of Nabau, to the top of Phasga, which is before Jericho; and the Lord showed him all the mount of Galaad to Dan, and all the land of Nephthali, 2 and all the land of Ephraim and Manasse, and all the land of Judah to the farthest sea; 3 and the wilderness, and the country round about Jericho, the city of palm trees, to Segor. 4 And the Lord said to Moses, This *is* the land of which I swore to Abraham, and Isaac, and Jacob, saying, To your seed will I give it, and I have showed it to thine eyes, but thou shall not go in thither.

5 So Moses the servant of the Lord died in the land of Moab by the word of the Lord. 6 And they buried him in Gai near the house of Phogor; and no one has seen his sepulcher to this day. 7 And Moses was a hundred and twenty years old at his death; his eyes were not dimmed, nor were his natural powers destroyed. 8 And the sons of Israel wept for Moses in Araboth of Moab at Jordan near Jericho thirty days; and the days of the sad mourning for Moses were completed.

9 And Jesus the son of Naue was filled with the spirit of knowledge, for Moses had laid his hands upon him; and the sons of Israel hearkened to him; and they did as the Lord commanded Moses.

10 And there never arose a prophet in Israel like Moses, whom the Lord knew face to face, 11 in all the signs and wonders, which the Lord sent him to work in Egypt on Pharaoh, and his servants, and all his land; 12 the great wonders, and the mighty hand which Moses displayed before all Israel.

www.ingramcontent.com/pod-product-compliance
Lightning Source LLC
Chambersburg PA
CBHW021834220426
43663CB00005B/240